WORKING OUT EGYPT

Wilson Chacko Jacob

WORKING OUT EGYPT

EFFENDI MASCULINITY AND SUBJECT FORMATION IN COLONIAL MODERNITY, 1870–1940

DUKE UNIVERSITY PRESS / DURHAM & LONDON / 2011

© 2011 DUKE UNIVERSITY PRESS
All rights reserved
Printed in the United States of America
on acid-free paper ∞
Designed by C. H. Westmoreland
Typeset in Monotype Fournier
by Tseng Information Systems, Inc.

Frontispiece photograph:
Hajj Shimmi and his brother illustrate the power
of the effendi modern with youthful exuberance against
the backdrop of the archetypal monuments of Egyptian
identity, ca. 1950s. *Gift to the author from Hajj Shimmi's*
private collection, Cairo.

Library of Congress Cataloging-in-Publication Data
appear on the last printed page of this book.

TO MY PARENTS,
Kochuputhen Eapen Jacob
Aleyamma Jacob

AND IN MEMORY OF
Manu

CONTENTS

NOTE ON TRANSLITERATION

I have used a simplified version of the system of transliteration of Arabic words followed by the *International Journal of Middle East Studies*. Diacritical marks are given only to indicate the Arabic letters *'ayn* (') and *hamza* ('). A hamza appearing at the beginning of a word is normally dropped, as is the *ta marbuta* at the end of a word, including in those cases when it should be vocalized as part of an elision with the following word. The Arabic letter *jim* has been rendered as *j*, except when the Egyptian pronunciation (*gim*) is more common, as in *gallabiya*, or when transcribing colloquial phrases. In the transliteration of colloquial words, a hamza is used to denote the letter *qaf* when it is not vocalized. All Arabic names are transliterated following the *IJMES* system, except in cases where a more commonly accepted version exists or when the person named has provided a transliteration.

ACKNOWLEDGMENTS

It is hard to fathom now but this book has been twelve years in the making and perhaps even longer in the dreaming. The dreaming cannot be acknowledged here properly, so I will focus on the tangible work and those who made it possible. I say twelve years because the very first seminar paper I wrote for Zachary Lockman at New York University was the seed from which all else has grown; indeed much of chapter 1 and some of chapter 2 are based on the research I conducted for that original essay. It is a testament to Professor Lockman's enormous capacity for creative guidance that he did not put an end to the marathon journey before it started; his wise counsel has been and remains important to me. My teachers and mentors at NYU — Michael Gilsenan, Molly Nolan, Khaled Fahmy, Timothy Mitchell, and Lisa Duggan — have not only contributed in significant ways to what appears between these covers but have also made a huge impression on the type of scholar I am today. If there are weaknesses or faults in the book, as there are sure to be, I am solely responsible for these. From an earlier period, there are other teachers whose imprint remains an indelible factor in my thinking about the Middle East, about history, and about the postcolonial: the late Hana Batatu, John Ruedy, Judith Tucker, the late Hisham Sharabi, and Lalitha Gopalan at Georgetown University. If I had to single out my most influential teacher, it would be Martina Rieker, who taught me at the American University in Cairo (AUC); she showed me that there are other intellectual and personal horizons to explore and opened the door to worlds previously unimagined or thought impossible.

Studying and researching in Egypt have been among the greatest joys of my life. Of course there were the normal and, on occasion, extraordinary hassles of bureaucratic oversight, but the luxury of swimming in someone else's historical sea and of thinking through someone else's cultural past have afforded me far greater pleasure than pain, and the experience has also transformed my own historical subjectivity. For that invaluable gift I can only offer Egypt and Egyptians these humble words of gratitude. I hope that what is written here will not be a disappointment.

The individuals I've met in Egypt who have in one way or another shaped me and this project include some of the most memorable personalities I have met, so I regret recognizing them in this most impersonal format: James Conlon (who left this earth long before his time), Tamer Mustafa, the late Ra'uf Abbas, Nabila al-Assiouty, Emad Abu Ghazi, Zaynab Taha, Husayn Amin, Maurice Pomerantz, Jimmy Bishara, John Willis, Garay Menicucci, Ahmad Abd al-Fattah, Adel Lashin, Kamal Fahmi, Anthony Shadid, Hossam Bahgat, Lisa Pollard, Amr Emran, Waleed Asfour, Fergus Hann, Garret Dorer, Shahnaz Rouse, Kamran Rastegar, Kambiz GhaneaBassiri and family, Elizabeth Smith, Betsy Bishop, Nadine Naber, Mario Ruiz, Shaun Lopez, Hanan Kholoussy, Asef Bayat, and Linda Herrera. I wish to thank separately the librarians, archivists, and others in Egypt who facilitated my access to materials without which this book would never have been realized: the staffs at the AUC, ARCE, Dar al-Kutub, and Dar al-Watha'iq, especially the director, Dr. Saber Arab, who went above and beyond the call of duty by helping me secure digital copies of images at the critical final stage; Mahmud Fahmy, the administrative staffs of Al-Nadi al-Ahli and of the Egyptian Olympic Committee, and head coach Kamal Mahjub of the Egyptian Weightlifting Association; Mustafa and Muhammad al-Sadiq; the late Cynthia Nelson as dean of the School of Humanities and Social Sciences at AUC, then again as the director of the Institute of Gender and Women's Studies, for making sure I had the necessary affiliations, providing the first public forum in which to share my research, and welcoming me into her home; and finally, Hajj Shimmi for sharing with me his memories of athletic exploits during his youth: I learned much from these reminiscences as well as from the photographs he gave me. Outside Egypt, I would like to acknowledge the helpful assistance of the staffs at the Public Record Office, the International Olympic Committee Museum, Bobst Library at NYU, the British Library, the Bodleian Library at Oxford University, and the Rare Books and Special Collections Division of McGill University Library.

No project of this nature can begin or end without financial support, so for their generous assistance at various stages I thank the Social Science Research Council's Joint Committee on the Near and Middle East; the American Research Center in Egypt; New York University for multiple grants and fellowships to research and study in Cairo, London, and Paris;

and the Provost's Academic Diversity Postdoctoral Fellowship at Cornell University, which allowed for the necessary transition time between dissertation and book. During the revision stage, my current institution, Concordia University, has provided the necessary funds for me to make additional visits to archives in Cairo, London, and Lausanne in order to track down some of the missing pieces of the puzzle. A generous grant from the Fonds québécois de recherche sur la société et la culture also contributed to the completion of this book.

The difficult road from graduate school to the real world has been navigated jointly by a cohort of stupendous human beings and intellects with whom I have shared more than this work or Egypt. To Laura Bier and Samera Esmeir I owe so much that it no longer suffices to reduce to words what I hope they know and feel. Michael Gasper has provided comic relief when necessary, a challenge at all times, and friendship that has somewhat surprisingly endured. Arang Keshavarzian heard me out and offered valuable insight on a subject and a method quite foreign to political science. Zehra Gulbahar stayed a friend despite long distances and great personal challenges; she is also now a valuable collaborator on my new project. She and her husband, Julien Cuniellera, have opened their home to me in Paris on numerous occasions, for which hospitality I hope to repay them one day in Montreal. Others from the New York years who have not already been mentioned who gave support and inspiration are Rabab abd al-Hadi, Dennis Bland, Sherene Seikaly, Sinan Antoon, Sabri Ates, Josh Schreier, Ozlem Altan, Koray Caliskan, Dahna Abourahme, Wael Qattan, Munir Fakhr al-Din, Shiva Balaghi, Bill Carrick, Barbara Pryce, Nicolas Johnson, Corey Capers, Sandra Green, and John Corso.

The people who have read and commented on the manuscript or parts of it are too many to name. I have presented various chapters in numerous writing groups, conferences, workshops, and as job talks over the years and have received valuable feedback from scholars in Egypt, the United States, Italy, Britain, and Canada. The following have offered comments and posed questions that have affected the work and its direction in significant ways at different points, and I am grateful to all of them: my dissertation committee; the participants at the Oxford Workshop on Egyptian National Culture organized by Walter Armbrust, Lucie Ryzova, and Ron Nettler; my discussant at the Yale "Urban Charisma" Conference, Saba Mahmood; Elizabeth Frierson and Sükrü Hanioglu for inviting me to present a chapter at the Princeton Ertegun Lecture Series, which forced me to move along on revisions faster than I would have otherwise; the students and historians at the Berkshire seminar "Colonialism, Sexuality, and

Body" organized by Antoinette Burton; Mary Renda, who after the seminar, provided necessary encouragement and advice on the act of writing; the members of the "Sports in Africa and Asia" workshop at the ZMO in Berlin organized by Katrin Bromber and Birgit Krawietz; and last, but by no means least, the two anonymous readers of Duke University Press.

Some of the most insightful readings, criticisms, and even epiphanies have come from more intimate settings, sometimes a spontaneous conversation over a beer or during a walk. Here again I must thank Laura Bier and Samera Esmeir for generously sharing their ideas and always keeping an eye out lest the larger picture be lost. On two visits to London, extended conversations I had with Ella Simpson proved illuminating. The scene in my new city of work and life, Montreal, has been both intellectually stimulating and productive and emotionally uplifting. Those who have read and commented on parts of my manuscript here have been vital to pushing it through the final stage, but perhaps more important they have made me feel at home through their generosity and kindness. Andrew Ivaska, Setrag Manoukian, Michelle Hartman, Najat Rahman, and Laila Parsons have all been perspicacious interlocutors. The spirit of Concordia has meant that some of my most challenging moments since finishing the dissertation have come from the brilliant students who are uninhibited enough to ask the tough questions and curious enough to think along with me about what makes the questions tough in the first place and why they're worth asking. Others contributed in a myriad of ways to making life in the True North a warmer prospect: Rachel Berger, Fred Bode, Graham Carr, Nitika Dosaj, Meredith Evans, Claudia Fabbricatore, John Gagne, Anthony Hilton, Homa Hoodfar, Norman Ingram, Delphine Mauger, Ted McCormick, Shannon McSheffrey, Omri Moses, Nicola Nixon, Elena Razlogova, Eric Reiter, Janice Simpkins, Jim Taylor, Elizabeth Van Every, and Rob Wisnovsky. Lara Braithstein, Shahin Parhami, Gavin Taylor, and Anya Zilberstein have showered me with care and gracious hospitality that I did not always deserve. For our Monday chat nights, I owe a special thanks to Khalid Medani. It is a rare and welcome twist of fate that Andy Ivaska and I have once again found ourselves in the same city and at the same university after shadowing each other across different ages and four continents; we are no longer the somewhat green youngsters who volunteered in Appalachia, defended God, and shared revelations, but I hope we are still the same in other ways; in any case, I am very thankful for this most unusual of coincidences.

Mere weeks before submitting the final draft of the manuscript, I met an Egyptophile in a most unsuspecting place—a village in Bretagne—who has made a valuable contribution to the book by providing some crucial illustrations. I wish to thank Max Karkegi for sharing his personal memories of Egypt (he left the country in 1963) and for granting me access to and then guiding me through his enormous collection of photographs, postcards, documents, and books.

Parts of chapters six, seven, and eight have had prior incarnations as: "The Turban, the Tarbush, and the Top Hat: Masculinity, Modernity, and National Identity in Interwar Egypt," in *Al-Ra'ida* [magazine of the Institute for Women's Studies in the Arab World at the Lebanese American University] (Winter/Spring 2004), 23–37; "Overcoming 'Simply Being': Straight Sex, Masculinity and Physical Culture in Modern Egypt" in *Gender and History* Special Issue on "Historicizing Gender and Sexuality," ed. Jennifer M. Spear and Kevin P. Murphy (November 2010); "Eventful Transformations: *Al-Futuwwa* between History and the Everyday," in *Comparative Studies in Society and History* 49/3 (July 2007), 689–712.

Bringing this book to print could not have been easier, and I suspect it is mostly due to the light touch with which Ken Wissoker runs his ship at Duke University Press. I thank Ken, Courtney Berger, Leigh Barnwell, Mark Mastromarino, and the hawk-eyed copyeditor for making the publication process veritably painless.

Finally, to my parents: this book is dedicated to you because just as Egypt transformed me you have formed me. And those traces of a formation run throughout this book even as they show signs of change and might vanish at points. A way of being in the world is never simply taught, and despite their occasional loss of patience they have always shown what is true and powerful about our special kinship, *aasnehathina inglishilo malayamilo vak illa*. For this and for your many other selfless gifts I will remain always in awe and in your debt. And for my brother, the bookworm misses you.

INTRODUCTION

Subject Formation and History in
the Performances of Effendi Masculinity

When the most basic concepts — the concepts, as it is said, from
which we begin — are suddenly seen to be not concepts but problems, not analytic problems either but historical movements that
are still unresolved, there is no sense in listening to their sonorous summons or their resounding clashes. We have only, if
we can, to recover the substance from which their forms were
cast. — RAYMOND WILLIAMS, *Marxism and Literature*

The early Egyptian nationalist and social reformer, the young firebrand
Mustafa Kamil, was in Europe during the summer of 1894. In July and
August, he visited two world exhibitions held in Belgium and France. He
was highly perturbed at one and disconcerted by the other because of
what he saw in the "Arab-style" (*'arabiyyat al-shakl*) pavilions. He was
a discerning critic, and he compared the Antwerp Exhibition less favorably to the Lyons International and Colonial Exhibition. The exhibition at
Lyons was sophisticated and presented a unique and "solid study of conditions in the East, its industries, and trade"; at Antwerp the exhibition
managed to cause great offense through its inept model of an "Egyptian
Street.".2 At Lyons, Kamil was able to maintain somewhat of a distance
since the displays presented scenes and settings from elsewhere in North
Africa and the Arabian Peninsula. He reported on the pavilions of Algeri-
ans, Tunisians, and Arabians as if they were alien, or Other, to the Egyptian. Politically and personally, however, the two exhibitions were similarly provocative.

Kamil described the colonial installation of the Lyons International and Colonial Exhibition as a scene that would certainly bring pride to French visitors and reaffirm their patriotism. But for the Easterner, Kamil wrote, it cannot but elicit tears for his country and people, who had lost their land to strangers: "While the sons of France are gladdened at the sight [of the exhibit] and sons of the East saddened, it is not strange that philosophers share with the sons of the East their sadness and grief. For they consistently view conquests as an inexcusable crime and colonialism as an offense whether it lasts hours or days."[3] In what was a criticism of the ongoing British occupation of Egypt, the young anticolonial nationalist who was in France seeking moral and political support in the struggle to attain his nation's freedom had necessarily to emphasize the critical spirit of French enlightenment and revolution and to downplay France's own imperialism.[4]

Aside from the stark politico-economic and technological divergences between the International and the Colonial at the Lyons Exhibition, the reason for the colonized to feel distressed upon viewing the colonial exhibits also resided in their presentation as particular kinds of spectacle. Kamil did not reject the accuracy of these depictions of Eastern life; in fact, he reported on the fine workmanship and genius of Arab building that were on display. Kamil's response demonstrates and departs from Timothy Mitchell's characterization of how non-Europeans experienced world exhibitions as illustrations of "the strange character of the West, a place where one was continually pressed into service as a spectator by a world ordered so as to represent."[5] Although the "effect of reality" produced by the exhibitions was not lost on Kamil, it was the contrasting representations of reality in "the East" and "the West" that made the biggest impression on him.[6] For it was in that display of difference that the powerful norm of modern civilization, which judged one culture superior to the other, was enacted. Under those hierarchical conditions, differing kinds of sentiments were elicited: celebration by those who possessed civilization, and mourning by those who had fallen behind.

In his description of the Algerian pavilion at Lyons, the irony of Kamil's partial defense of France by way of its philosophers was amplified. Kamil's encounter there is remarkable. He was forced to see himself and his image of a future Egypt in a mirror that refused to flatter his mastery of civilizational symbols and for a moment left him speechless. (It was also probably what distracted him from reflecting on Algeria's colonial situation.) At the door to the pavilion, he had a conversation in Arabic with the Algerian guards: "The first thing they asked me about was our imitation of the

Europeans in [our] dress. I gave them an answer that was honestly unconvincing and left them."[7] He did not reveal to the reader what he had told
the guards. Perhaps more important, it is not clear to whom the response
was unconvincing—to the guards or to himself.[8]

The colonial section of the Lyons Exhibition provided Kamil with a
dense simulacrum of the world of nonwhites, of the conquered and dominated. He virtually traveled through Algeria, Sudan, Congo, Guinea,
Guadeloupe, Tunisia, the Arabian Peninsula, Vietnam, Cambodia, Da-
homey, and Senegal. While on the one hand he could read the colonizer's
panoramic vision of the East as a staged spectacle, on the other he was
willing to accept their representation as reality, that is, as long as it did not
impinge on or contradict his own ideas of a national home and a national
subject.[9]

This is what the Belgians did and why it earned them his ire.[10] The
Egyptian Street at Antwerp was a cause of embarrassment for Kamil. He
felt it presented visitors with a picture of Egypt as lacking and of Egyptians as content in their backwardness. He believed the real aim of the exhibit was mockery. The reason for this belief and his indignation had much
to do with *which* Egypt was put on display. The street scene was from the
old Cairo and depicted traditional vendors, hashish-smoking donkey cart
drivers, and a belly-dance café. All Egyptians were implicated in these
base characters.[11] Most of his anger, though, was directed at the representation of the East as a feminized and sexualized body. He was especially upset after coming across yet another belly-dancing exhibit. After
describing it, he pointedly remarked, "As if the East was famous only for
dancing."[12] He ended his letter from Antwerp with a reiteration of the difference between the portrayals of Europe and of the East: "The reader of
this fourth letter sees that Europe is represented in this important Exhibition by the greatest of deeds and the finest of noble characteristics—the
clearest indicator of the human condition [*maqam al-insan*]. Whereas the
East (regretfully and with utmost shame) is not represented but by belly-
dance cafés gathering within it the dregs of mankind and the lowliest of
creation."[13]

Europe is active and virile, the East degenerate and feminine. The style
and content of Kamil's politics would be profoundly affected by this sexu-
alization, feminization, and temporalization of the East as Other. The
recursive public performances that showcased sensual female dancers
and indolent medieval male characters as signs of the Egyptian present
seemed to fix the entire non-European world in a past beyond which the
inhabitants showed no desire or will to advance. This depiction of the

East, which underwrote and facilitated a paternalistic colonial politics,[14] cast a long shadow from which Kamil's class of Egyptian men (the *effendiyya*) struggled to escape.[15] In this book I explore how attempts to free a distinctively modern and Egyptian self from the colonial gaze were manifested explicitly in discourses of gender and sexuality during the British colonial period (1882–1936),[16] and I demonstrate that the product of these efforts, which entailed a complex set of pedagogic and performative acts, was the ambivalent subject of what I call effendi masculinity.

The term "effendi" (plural "effendiyya") was initially restricted to members of the clerical corps of the Ottoman bureaucracy, but in the Egyptian context of the late nineteenth century it came to designate groups of men who approximated a cultural bourgeoisie, to the extent that they could not be considered peasants, workers, or aristocrats. However, this subject position could not easily be pinned down to one location in a socio-economic structure either; occupations of the nationalist effendiyya were largely bureaucratic and professional in the late nineteenth century and early twentieth, but by the interwar period the effendi was a far more capacious category, including sons of small merchants, students, unemployed graduates, and essentially anyone who was able to affect the proper look.[17] The effendiyya might still be fruitfully analyzed as a class, in the Weberian or Marxist sense, but its full range of meaning and praxes would be elided, as those discussions necessarily focus on formal political movements and iterations of capitalism.[18] Effendi masculinity is conceived here as a performance or, more accurately, a set of performances that spans history and the everyday and that makes legible otherwise overlooked discursive formations that were both important objects of struggle and means by which power was normalized.[19] Consequently, the subject of effendi masculinity presents with a tremendous consciousness of time, one whose inaugural condition of possibility was making a spatial distinction between the colonial and the national.[20] In the interwar years that opposition, although not undone, was increasingly relegated to the normalized and delimited spheres of politics and history; with nominal independence and the expansion of capitalist development, the spatial and temporal relationship of effendi masculinity binding its subject to a national future was spliced by other trajectories specific to the performances through which the subject was formed and reproduced.

Nonetheless, at the turn of the twentieth century, when Kamil and others like him pondered the prospect of a future for themselves, it was nearly impossible not to consider simultaneously the future of Egypt. This moment, encapsulated in the poignant encounter between Kamil and the Algerian guards in Lyons, may mark the beginning of what Amitav Ghosh eloquently termed the "irreversible triumph of the language that has usurped all the others in which people once discussed their differences."[21] In other words, Egypt could reemerge as modern only by traveling through the West first,[22] and to be Egyptian required a revised grammar and style of presentation.[23] Although or precisely because Kamil's life was a testament to this suggestion of an imbricated history of the colonial and the national, he was unwilling to allow the models of the East—no matter how accurate he found them—to dictate his, and by extension Egypt's, future possibilities. Indeed, his public expression of preference for the French over the Belgian displays of the colonial was in part strategically motivated. He viewed himself as the voice of Egypt and was hopeful that the French would hear him as such and support his cause of uprooting the British occupation of his country.[24] Kamil's response to the world-as-exhibition illustrates that the choice of which reality to model mattered, and further suggests that although the modern logic of enframing outlined by Mitchell was indeed powerfully constitutive of the real, it was differentially constitutive of the observing subject across the colonial divide. This is a book about that subject's formation on the nonmetropolitan side yet between and betwixt the West and the East, emerging into history as questionably Egyptian and less certainly modern and debatably masculine.[25]

At least three interconnected arguments are pursued here through the performances of effendi masculinity. First, the national subject was a distinctly nineteenth-century solution to emerging social, political, and cultural problems; that subject had simultaneously local and global roots whose geographical and genealogical linkages might be retraced through the mutually constitutive histories of empire, gender, and sexuality. Second, modernity as a repeated and variable performance, or staging, of civilizational progress was colonial in nature, in a doubled sense that justifies speaking in terms of *colonial modernity*.[26] In the first sense, modernity references a new relationship to time growing out of Europe's colonial encounters with peoples who were deemed at once to be on an earlier rung of development and to be incapable of moving forward. With the expansion of capitalism and the attendant colonial conquests between the late eighteenth century and the late nineteenth this particular relation to time would be universalized and enshrined in history, which would encompass the world but with its "centre and end" firmly in Europe.[27] In another sense, the pedagogical impulses inherent in modernity almost always assumed a colonial relationship to its objects, whether that object was self or other, in metropole or colony, or somewhere in between.[28] Third, it is argued that the temporal structure of the modern performance—if one assumes its intelligibility is contingent on iterability as a given in the nature of the sign—always poses the risk of communicative and pedagogical failure with each performative repetition and consequently opens the possibility for a subject's resignification.[29] Thus, effendi masculinity as a historically constructed nexus of power relations and site of subject formation must be regarded as a moving vehicle; that is, sometimes the driver and destination were apparent, but at other times the vehicle appeared driverless, pursuing unanticipated directions with an uncertain destination. This mobile conception of effendi masculinity has determined in large part a methodology that follows certain threads of an event, a life, or a practice only so far and not to any obvious end before moving on to another line of subject formation.

The arguments about the national subject, colonial modernity, and gender performativity are threaded through a historical frame composed of four moving planes. While all four are to some extent present in each chapter of the book, they will not always be explicit; moreover, each plane is multidimensional, which makes their points of intersection difficult but not impossible to locate in a single space.[30] The first plane is a map of the late nineteenth-century British discourse on masculinity and empire, which is the focus of chapter 1 but forms a silent and sometimes not-so-silent counterpoint in other chapters. On the second plane emerges an explicitly nationalist discourse on Egyptian masculinity that is tracked in chapters 2 and 3. The third plane, situated in chapters 4 through 7, features the variegated performances of effendi masculinity that proliferated in the interwar period, from scouting and competitive sports to sex talk and fashion; it also marks the slippages from pedagogical objectives and illuminates the international as the emergent scene of the modern. The final plane, located in chapter 8, might be visualized as cutting through the others in that its main character, *al-futuwwa*,[31] struggles to maintain intelligibility as a subject within or over and against the biopower of colonial modernity and British or effendi nationalist iterations of sovereignty.[32] In sum, the book shows the formation of effendi masculinity in a fluid, multidimensional space within and across which a national subject, colonial modernity, and gender and sexuality were normalized over time, but always as partial, unfinished, and contested performances.

Effendi Masculinity

If one were to imagine the unreported words exchanged between Kamil and the Algerian guards about Egyptians' sartorial mimicry of Europeans, what might they be? What sentiments would they express? Did Kamil feel ashamed in the face of his Arabic-speaking compatriots' challenge to his decision to don the frock coat instead of the *gallabiya*?[33] Or was he proud of his ability to master the symbols of colonial modernity? Might he have had mixed feelings, ambivalence toward his position as an anticolonial "mimic man"? Why did Kamil censor the account of this speech: for its harmfulness or insignificance? How does one capture the occasion of this feeling of shame, sense of pride and superiority, or perhaps confusion as a historically significant event?

Historical accounts of this period have overlooked this exchange, perhaps considering it insignificant and thereby sharing in Kamil's putative evaluation of the situation. However, since we do not actually know the reason for his elision of this speech act, it bears further reflection. In Ghosh's admittedly somewhat romantic rendering of the passing of an Islamic order, its usurpation by colonialism, and the subsequent distorted development of the colonized as the "irreversible triumph of the language that has usurped all the others," one nonetheless glimpses a possible suppressed history of Egypt and a key to reading Kamil's encounter with difference. The language to which Ghosh attributes so much effectivity is the particularistic yet universalizing discourse of modernization, which took within its reformist purview matters of science and technology, warfare, economy and government, and the cultivation of the self. This totalizing language was from its inception structured around racialized differences, and in order to engage the other matters — as Kamil and those like him around the globe sought to do — one would also be implicated, at some level, in the use of its hierarchical grammar.[34] Between grammar and usage there was a space of slippage.[35] Although Kamil wrote hundreds of pages and delivered countless speeches on the question of Egypt's future, it is the absence in the written record, the moment of silence around an Arabic conversation between an Egyptian and an Algerian, that promises to be far more telling of the affective dimensions of a subject in formation in colonial modernity.

This unspoken tale might tangentially index what Eve Powell has described as assuming the stance of the "colonized colonizer," based on

Egypt's political and metaphorical relationship to Britain and Sudan.[36] Indeed, Kamil was a vocal advocate of maintaining Egyptian sovereignty over the vast expanse of the Nile Valley added nominally to Ottoman domains during the reigns of Mehmed Ali Pasha (1805–48) and Khedive Ismail (1863–79). Commenting on the British designs in Egypt and Sudan, he wrote in an article published the same year he visited Lyons and Antwerp, "Sudan as a land is to Egypt as the soul is to the body."[37] Despite this metaphysical incorporation of Sudan to Egypt, as Powell argues, the nationalist justification for such an inclusion was more often dependent on a discourse of racialized difference in which the Sudanese figured unchangingly as "oversexed, underclothed, and beyond the structures of either British or Egyptian morality."[38] Powell's calculus of the colonized colonizer, while adding another axis to Egyptian nationalism and complicating the vectors of colonialism, cannot capture the full range, in particular the affective domain, of effendi masculinity.[39] Moreover, an analytics of the political mobilization of culture confined within the nation-state falters when confronted with the kind of silence through which Kamil marked his feelings about appearing modern in his bodily self.[40]

The central work by Israel Gershoni and James Jankowski on a cultural aspect of the effendiyya has focused on the intellectual currents circulating among them as a changing social and political class and in their relation to an emerging Egyptian national identity.[41] Gershoni's and Jankowski's thorough two-part study of the rise of various strands of nationalism in Egypt between 1900 and the end of the Second World War shows how the Ottoman legacy, Islam, Arabism, "Pharaonicism," and forms of "Supra-Egyptianism" were all competing, contradictory, and sometimes overlapping poles of identification, political mobilization, and intellectualization.[42] Before the end of the First World War it was still possible to struggle, as Kamil did, for Egyptian independence from the British while feeling loyalty to the Ottoman sultan, especially in his capacity as the caliph of Islam.[43] One way to categorize who thought what and why was to distinguish between generations of effendiyya. Gershoni and Jankowski attribute to the earlier nationalist generation (born between 1880 and 1900) a deeper grasp of Western culture and subsequently more modern worldviews and secularist politics.[44] The opening of the gates, so to speak, in the 1920s following Egypt's nominal independence, which came with relatively increased Egyptian control of domestic affairs, resulted in an expansion of education and the subsequent outpouring of unemployed and underemployed graduates into the economically harsh era of the 1930s. Their larger numbers, lesser training, and disaffection toward

the previous generation for its limited political and economic achievements led Gershoni and Jankowski to characterize the worldview of the
new effendiyya as traditional and their politics as more supra-Egyptianist
(Arab and Islamic). This becomes an intelligible distinction between generations based on a series of other oppositions the two works leave in place
(East and West, Islam and secularism, Arab and European), again, perhaps in an act of fidelity to the sources. Moreover, their conception of the
political as an exclusive field of contestation around the state renders history (of people and ideas) legible only within a narrow band; in this framing, effendi culture is relevant to the extent that it impacts on nation-state
formation.[45]

The authors' implicit reliance on a conceptualization of culture as a
superstructural formation is the limit to the range of effendi discourses
that could be deemed historically significant.[46] Accordingly, affective
matters and body cultures that effect styles of modernity or tradition fall
off the radar as trajectories in the story of nationalism, and subject formation consequently remains firmly a question of ideology.[47] Furthermore,
the intellectual dispositions and political divisions among the effendiyya
were contemporaneously indexed and debated; hence, analytically the authors fall short of explaining how a subject could be formed as modern
rather than traditional or vice versa.

The kinds of issues that subtended Kamil's public silence about his response to the critique of Egyptian mimicry, much less the question itself,
do not fall into place neatly within a framework of "imagined communities" and as a result are normally elided.[48] This is in part because such
a framework relies on a diffusionist model of modernity, which renders
non-Western nationalisms as derivative discourses.[49] More important,
historicized ideology critiques often presume a subject prior to its formation in discourse, which is again related to history's modern location
almost exclusively in the nation-state.[50] In other words, the name Mustafa
Kamil, which exists for readers only as a product of discourse, nevertheless appears only as its producer in most historical narratives, in which he
is intelligible to the extent that he was a founder of Egyptian nationalism.

If this is true, the question is not how to get beyond appearances but
how to explain the relationship between the two sides of production.
Louis Althusser's elaboration of the ideological interpellation of the subject as a key moment in the reproduction of the capitalist social formation
is apposite here to a certain extent.[51] His "Ideological State Apparatus"
delimits a sphere (education, religion, family, politics, and so forth) outside the typical sites of capitalist production and beyond its repressive

state agents but which nonetheless facilitates the reproduction of the relations of production. The ideological state apparatuses—the dominant
one being education—through which the willing subject of a capitalist
society (worker, manager, intellectual, and so forth) is recursively formed
are at once determinations of the economic base and potential sites of
class struggle but meaningful only insofar as a subject is formed. The subject of ideology might be said to belong to a concrete reality (in particular) and to exceed it simultaneously (in general): "The category of the subject is constitutive of all ideology, but at the same time and immediately
I add that *the category of the subject is only constitutive of all ideology insofar as all ideology has the function (which defines it) of 'constituting' concrete
individuals as subjects.* In the interaction of this double constitution exists
the functioning of all ideology, ideology being nothing but its functioning in the material forms of existence of that functioning."[52] Interpellation, the hailing into being of a subject by an ideology to which it remains attached, dislocates the place of agency from within an exclusively
agonistic or revolutionary framework. Thus the paradox of subjection—
making and being made—conceived in terms of interpellation pushes beyond the base-superstructure metaphor to show the materiality of ideological work, which takes place in discrete yet interconnected domains of
everyday life and is equally critical to the reproduction of a social order.[53]

The condition of possibility of effendi masculinity at the close of the
nineteenth century was the changed relations of production resulting
from the previous decades of global social and political transformations,
which brought Egypt fully into the capitalist world system and put in
place a "(Repressive) State Apparatus" characterized by the institution
of new legal and military bodies.[54] The Ottoman governor Mehmed Ali
Pasha's strategy for wresting greater autonomy from the sultan through
a modernized fighting force involved the establishment of factories, hospitals, schools, and the commoditization of cotton; he also reformed and
expanded the bureaucracy to manage all of these new institutions.[55] The
new apparatus was staffed predominantly by Arabic-speaking subjects,
many of whom were trained in Europe, sent there as part of numerous
state-funded educational missions.[56] The new policy of universally con-
scripting the peasantry as soldiers and as labor, the order to exclusively
plant cotton coupled with the formation of large estates, and the training
and recruitment of Arabic speakers for the administrative cadre produced
a radical rupture in the historical reality of the inhabitants of the Egyptian
province.[57]

On the one hand, that nineteenth-century rupture could be narrated as the story of an increasingly interventionist state:

> The Pasha's army was above all crucial for the rise of the modern nation-state of Egypt by introducing practices that together changed the nature of the Egyptian state and its relationship to its "citizens" and completely transformed the very fabric of Egyptian society. By catching its deserters, punishing its criminals, educating its youth, vaccinating its children, silencing its women, interning its insane, and by doing all this in a subtle, "humane" and "rational" manner . . . this is how the Egyptian nation came into being in modern times. It was by a process of violence, silence and exclusion that Egyptians were taught the essential truths of the nation.[58]

On the other hand, from the 1870s the reverse of this violent process of state formation was the emerging society of the newly disciplined subjects, interpellated as such by the not-always-intended productions of the process, namely, politics, religion, education, and gender.[59] As a result, although the changed condition of possibility for the constitution of concrete individuals as subjects in the nineteenth century was the emergence of a repressive state imbricated in a capitalist world economy, the reproduction of the subject and the reproduction of the new relations of production, while linked through the Ideological State Apparatus, were not of the same power. In other words, the power and knowledge proper to the subject of politics, religion, education, and gender, which may facilitate the reproduction of the same dominant relations of production, do not necessarily always reproduce the same subject. This is not a claim that depends on the existence of "eternal psychic facts." "Interpellation is 'barred' from success not by a structurally permanent form of prohibition (or foreclosure), but by its inability to determine the constitutive field of the human."[60] Hence, effendi masculinity might be a complex discursive formation made possible by the emergence of a modern state and a new condition of production, but in tracking the reproduction of its subject beyond the law one witnesses unanticipated consequences that are also moments of resignification. This is possible only if the subject of power and power are not entirely identical.[61]

Perhaps this critical recognition encouraged Michel Foucault to radically revise his research agenda toward the end of his life in order to investigate the subject's formation, not through modes of subjection (power and knowledge), as he had previously done in his studies of madness, incarceration, and the disciplines, but as "subjectivation" (practices of the self). He explored the subject's activation through techniques of the self as possibly irreducible to the biopolitical technologies of regulatory apparatuses.[62] His famously incomplete elaboration of a history of sexuality veered away from the modern to the ancient, from "a genealogy of systems" to "a problematization of the subject" and took within its purview "forms of the relation to the self."[63] While the ancient history of these forms is beyond the scope of this book, for my purposes it is important to note "the culture of the self" that Foucault found emerging during Hellenistic times and flourishing in the Roman Empire, for it is a pivotal moment in the history of bodies and their relationship to the truth.[64] According to Foucault, the dominant philosophical injunction to know oneself was deeply informed and shaped, for a long time and in different ways and before the modern era, by the complementary principle of "care of the self."[65] Self-caring entailed elaborate and sustained exercises for the body and soul (physical and spiritual as well as mental training), which together constituted an "art of living," whose sole objective was a final relationship of self to self that was true and free — "the crown, realization, and reward of a life lived as test."[66]

Among the techniques of self that formed the art of living was one that will both recall the question of Kamil's silence and move beyond it: "the expression, transmission, and acquisition of true discourse."[67] Foucault spent a substantial amount of time in his lectures of 1982 on the principles of *parrhesia*, "speaking freely." Such speech seemed most advanced in a master-disciple or councilor-patron relationship, in which the repeated act formed a program of caring for the self through acquiring true discourse. He contrasted speaking freely to flattery, which was to be resisted and overcome, and to rhetoric, a rule one must strive to release oneself from but cannot avoid entirely.[68] Kamil, a councilor and an orator who saw himself as a teacher with pupils, encountered a moment in which his ability to speak freely — and by extension, his mastery of true discourse — was called into question.[69] If flattery is translated as colonial paternalism and rhetoric as the language of colonial modernity, then Kamil was a fierce opponent of the former and a creative wordsmith within the latter. The location of the self within this matrix was a fraught one. According to Foucault, the positive definition of speaking freely involved the authorization of the speaker through a line of prior authorities: "He can and will speak the truth, which is precisely the truth of the master from whom he derives indirectly."[70] In the face of the Algerian challenge, the relationship of master and pupil and hence the true discourse were all brought into crisis. By whom was Kamil authorized to speak the truth and what was the truth?

The anticolonial nationalist speech acts through which Kamil strove for freedom and truth for himself and for others were temporarily rendered ineffective and were in this instance inscribed as an absence. The moment of recognition (among Arabic speakers) was also a moment that threatened to undo, for Kamil, the painstakingly achieved self in relation to itself. It was a moment in which the subject's ethical formation was called into question through the seemingly insignificant matter of dress, on which the truth of being Egyptian *and* Mustafa Kamil seemed to ride. Meanwhile, precisely because of such an ethical and aesthetic formation the political valence of this national subject of Egypt in the final years of the nineteenth century, entangled as it was in the present imperial ambitions of Britain and the past of the Ottomans, tended toward a regular suppression of the Other.[71]

It may seem to be a vast overstatement to hinge a phenomenology, much less a history, of effendi masculinity on this one quiet encounter, but the remainder of this book shows that the intelligibility of the gendered modern Egyptian subject—the said and the unsaid, the true and untrue—was profoundly conditioned by principles of caring for the self. While Foucault explicitly dismissed the late twentieth-century injunctions of "getting back to oneself, freeing oneself, being oneself, being authentic, etcetera" as meaningless mantras, he did pause at the nineteenth-century attempts "to reconstitute an ethics and aesthetics of the self," but only to say, "There is a question here, a series of problems, which could be raised."[72] The discourses of effendi masculinity certainly show he was right to suspect that in the nineteenth century a momentary convergence of ethics and politics, which, I would submit, was the product of empire and its opposition, had the promise of recovering a way of being that was at once a way of acting on the self and in the world.[73] As the rest of his career attests, Kamil's silence, rather than merely representing a disabling moment or ambivalence, reaffirms that the cultivation of feelings and bodies proper to a modern national subject was no less an important site of self-knowing than the acquisition of the new sciences of man and nature; to grasp the full historical significance of those feelings and bodies, their subject must be traced beyond the games of truth and across the tightening borders of nation-states.

Caring for the Self
GENDER, SEX, AND NATION

The reconfiguration of *riyadat al-nafs* (caring for the soul) was central to the Egyptian project of fashioning a modern self.[74] One might date from as early as the 1870s the beginning of this process of translating emerging techniques of the self in terms of the classical Islamic tradition of caring for the soul. The discourse, tied as it was to effendi masculinity, proliferated dramatically in the wake of the British occupation, especially by the 1890s with the deepening Egyptian perception that colonial domination was open-ended. The translation[75] of the ancient formula for salvation by tending to the soul took interesting turns in the context of anticolonial nationalism and within circuits of colonial modernity.[76]

The care of the self would be integral to the process of forming a new national subject, but in turn it would also constitute new, universal knowledge about the body, gender, and sex. Work by feminist scholars on women and gender in Egyptian history has been one of the most productive arenas in which the rethinking of older binary frames, in particular the divisions between modernity and tradition and public and private, has taken place.[77] Within that scholarship some of the first treatments of the question of modern self-cultivation are to be found. Lisa Pollard's study of the constitutive aspects of gender in the formation of modern Egypt highlights the specific modalities by which men, women, and children were reimagined and remade as national subjects through what she terms "family politics."[78] She notes that a crucial site of family politics from the nineteenth century on was the ever-increasing production of knowledge about the world, initially orchestrated through a massive translation effort: "Translation established a relationship among the politics of socioeconomic reform, the knowledge through which reform was undertaken, and the intimate activities of the people who would be subjected to it. Official knowledge about the 'modern' world created clear connections among the men who worked in the state's employ, the 'national character' that resulted from their behavior, and their place in the universal system of nations."[79] People's "intimate activities" ultimately came to involve some form of relationship to "official knowledge." As Pollard shows, the pedagogic efforts of the nation could expand only if the subject's relationship to self was also a relationship to others (at home and everywhere); in other words, nationalist pedagogy became crucial at the point that the salvation of individuals was conceived as the sine qua non of a nation's

progress toward modernity and inclusion in the "universal system of nations." The primary entry point for the techniques of salvation was the
family. Good mothers and wives became the indispensable first line of
national advancement since they had the responsibility for rearing healthy
sons and nurturing happy, productive men.[80]

The pedagogical aspect would grow in importance through the interwar
period as public education gradually became accessible to greater numbers and as reformist discourses proliferated in the expanding press, the
new social sciences, and the nascent state and civil society programs targeting the population.[81] Following the trail of effendi masculinity through
the notion of *al-riyada* (cultivating, caring) eventually leads to arenas in
which techniques of the self were involved, but the nation formed a less
evident horizon. At this point the question of effendi masculinity reaches
an impasse when considered within the available Egyptian social and cultural history frameworks. The limits of the national subject become evident as crypto-Scouts, libidinal bodies, "fashionistas," and gangsters are
thrown up from the folds of effendi masculinity. Accordingly, the formation of the modern subject analyzed in terms of nationalist discourses cannot account for these troubling and unanticipated presences—which are
the very products of the preceding pedagogic strategies—without repeating their prior reduction to the status of supposed bad subjects. And, paradoxically, the profoundly *national* discursive formation of effendi masculinity can be apprehended in its totality, in its contradictions and fissures,
only by situating the practices of subjection and subjectivation on a transnational grid.

Colonial Modernity
HISTORY AND PERFORMANCE

The transnational grid is both presupposed in colonial modernity and
persistently foreclosed by it. In the historians' craft this foreclosure has
long been related to the archive's primary organization within nation-
state projects.[82] Despite the fact that empire was the condition for increased human interactions and the pursuit of modern historical knowledge, the objects of such interaction and knowledge always appeared to
radiate from a center outward.[83] History as the herald of modernity could
not resolve its contradiction as the promise of an ever-expanding category of the human and as the erasure of human difference.[84] The power
of the centripetal forces generated by the nation was most apparent dur-

ing the interwar period, when, just as the world seemed to shrink in un-precedented ways, it also witnessed the rise of the most virulent forms of nationalism. Perhaps ironically that shrinking was characterized by a massive acceleration of networks of knowledge and practice predicated on a highly self-conscious cosmopolitanism and explicit internationalism. Especially in the arenas of physical culture and sports there was a simulta-neously nationalist and internationalist claim on the form and significance of their activities, a claim which momentarily put the colonial in question and foreshadowed its demise.[85] Chapters 4 and 5, which present Egyptian histories of the Boy Scouts and the Olympic Games, respectively, illumi-nate the tensions involved in the adoption of those international practices at the levels of nationalist discourse and the subject; also, these chapters examine the narration of the practices as a historiographical problem. The location of the subject of modernity in history, as a question of transcend-ing place, becomes legible in these conjunctural spaces and between ar-chives as a complex set of negotiations with no clear or final resolution, despite strong claims to the contrary.

Departing from Edward Said's classic depiction of the production of the Orient as a sexualized and feminized place and from more recent ac-counts, such as Joseph Massad's, which have characterized modern Arab engagements with sexuality as simply adopting Western terms, my book argues for a more historically nuanced and conceptually interconnected understanding of the modern subject as a product and productive of global discourses of power, such as gender and sexuality.[86] It would be hard to limn from Said's *Orientalism*, for example, that the European cir-culation of images of the feminized Orient as a place of unbridled and aberrant sexuality was actually familiar to the inhabitants of this so-called Orient and that they managed to marshal quite sophisticated responses.[87] That said, this is not a call for giving agency back to the natives, for a his-tory from below, or for a subaltern perspective.[88] Rather, I retrace here the possibility of history in colonial modernity as a question: How can an authentic narrative of Egypt be written when its terms always appear to be produced elsewhere?[89] As Antoinette Burton, Catherine Hall, Ann Stoler, and others have demonstrated, attempts to apprehend and to nar-rativize modern history through narrowly bounded geographical frames, such as the nation or the West, falter at the historical threshold of colonial-ism, the sine qua non of which was its global reach and the proliferation of new categories of racial difference, gender, and sexuality.[90] Moreover, any treatment that abstracts exclusively from a circulation of metaphors these domains of biopolitical power is bound to miss the historically variable political and cultural work they perform, not to mention the ambiguity, incompleteness, and ordinariness of human performances that disrupt those regulatory and disciplinary efforts and that momentarily reveal the fissures, gaps, and ambivalences of such power.[91] Indeed, the virtue of a genuine historical method is its vigilant attention to the specificity of time and place and its inescapable logic of difference, and it is with the determination of eventfulness that history is ineluctably and continuously brought into the present.[92]

The discovery and deployment of knowledge about racial difference in the various colonial projects of European states had long and violent histories that were from the very beginning linked to sex and gender; but they also constituted events that could occasion surprise and generate varying and unpredictable outcomes at different moments.[93] By the latter part of the nineteenth century, when this book begins, an elaborate discourse of racial hierarchies was firmly in place, and it was underpinned by increasingly rigid and diligently policed sexual boundaries.[94] Unlike other colonial contexts, however, in the Middle East it was the very inaccessibility of indigenous women that fueled the fantastic and libidinal imaginations of European travelers, writers, painters, and photographers, who penetrated virtually the intimate domains otherwise prohibited to them.[95] Did this make the Middle East an exception in colonial histories of race, gender, and sexuality? Yes and no. The other side of the exoticization and eroticization of the Orient was the moralizing rhetoric of European feminists and colonial administrators, whose scope was truly global in reach but in Muslim lands tended to fixate on "Muhammedan laws and customs" as the root of all social ills, particularly gender inequalities.[96] In turn, Middle Eastern responses to these rhetorical and material assaults generally took the reform of Islam and the reform of gender to be mutually constitutive.[97] In the Egyptian context, British occupation of formally Ottoman territory in 1882 generated a political nationalism that was profoundly gendered in its rhetorical and material plans for liberating the nation.[98] The place of men and women in society had been a subject of prior reformist discourses, unwittingly initiated by the state-building projects of the ambitious Mehmed Ali and proliferated further during the reign of his grandson Khedive Ismail.[99] However, by century's end, the growing identity of the colonial and the West with the modern ostensibly rendered all of these other pasts unusable in the massive and simultaneous creative efforts of nation building and subject formation.[100]

Then again, when performance—conceived as a recursive act of communicating a truth through varied forms of representation—is deployed as a critical lens through which to view the past, more complex relationships to time and place become visible. In some instances this requires a rewriting of the subjects of empire, nation, gender, and sexuality. For the formation of a subject through performative acts implies a temporality specific to the terms of the performance, which may range from the novel and (auto)biography to bodybuilding and scouting. If the subject's emergence into history occurs through multiple performative acts, then any historical individual, between life and death, will have inhabited multiple temporalities.[101] By extension, the nation-state as the birth and burial place of a new subject called the citizen cannot exist in a singular time and space. The modern nation form was from its inception a plural enactment distinguishable from, but contingent on, other discursive and material formations such as empire, gender, and sexuality. Moreover, the nation and its subject must be continuously reborn in order to persist in the world. The repetition of the conditions of reproduction ensures the stability of Egypt and the Egyptian.[102] However, in the same way that Mustafa Kamil reiterated the truth of the exhibition with a colonial difference, the national does not reappear in the exact same terms in different times and spaces.[103] A performative theory of subject formation thus enables a *historical* account of the paradox of the nation and its subject in colonial modernity as simultaneously the same and different.

Times of Change
THE SUBJECT, SOVEREIGNTY, AND SELF-GOVERNMENT

Definitions of the nation and the inauguration of national identity, going back to Johann Gottfried von Herder and Johann Gottlieb Fichte, make explicit reference to the feelings, spirit, or sensibilities that are either prerequisites for or products of their formation; love, pride, and belonging are perhaps the most basic.[104] This "structure of feeling" has been extensively examined from various perspectives,[105] but in the context of anticolonial nationalism it has usually received a negative or overly psychological treatment.[106] The history of the formation of a national subject in Egypt reveals a thoroughly material process that certainly implicated the psyche but not any more than it did the physical and social body; also, it was a global process in which the colonial divide was at once a site of the proliferation and disavowal of difference.[107] Effendi masculinity tethered its claims of identity with modernity to an explicitly nationalist vehicle just as the gendered articulations of empire in Britain and France became crucial to those national projects and depended in part on constructing civilizational hierarchies and feminizing the colonized.[108] Although race as a peculiarly modern scientific category may have been central to establishing colonial (and national) difference, it was not the sole axis along which Egyptians came to feel their identity. The nation as a site of affect was overdetermined by the multisited formation of its subject. Contrary to early theories of nationalism and some of its historical accounts, the national subject can be shown to have emerged paradoxically as a product and productive of a new structure of feeling that was spatially and temporally one and many.[109] Moreover, this domain of public sentiment, associated with the advancement and expansion of technologies of communication and discipline, could not have achieved its objective through a negative strategy alone.[110]

Historians of early modern Europe have shown in recent studies of print culture that the chronology normally given for the making of the modern public must be adjusted. Its conventional dating from the eighteenth century is based on an overly narrow definition, notably in Jürgen Habermas's influential theory of the public sphere as a domain of rational debate specific to a conjuncture of new market relations, print forms, and bourgeois sociability.[111] Rather than being merely addressees of public authority, the revisionists show that early modern communities of print formed active and often oppositional publics. However much Habermas may idealize the eighteenth-century formation of the bourgeois public sphere, his account of its disintegration in the last quarter of the nineteenth century is highly instructive for my purposes.

Habermas writes, "The *principle* of the public sphere, that is, critical publicity, seemed to lose its strength in the measure that it expanded as a *sphere* and even undermined the private realm."[112] Habermas gives 1873, the year perhaps of the first worldwide depression, as the beginning of the end of the "liberal era," a notable marker of which was a movement toward protectionism in trade and increased state interventions in society. His argument here, perhaps overly simplified, is that the larger role of the neomercantilist state combined with the political inclusion of other social classes and actors—the expansion of the public sphere—came at a cost, which was the erosion of the conditions for autonomous political action, or, "[private] people's public use of their reason."[113] The historical merits of Habermas's theory aside, the notion of an expanding public as a kind of disintegration is interesting because it repeats to some extent the prevailing view in the last quarter of the nineteenth century of national and even civilizational degeneration.

The properly historical question here is, what exactly was lost in this age of high imperialism or the highest stage of capitalism and for whom was it a loss? In Habermas, the fiction of the private bourgeois individual was a historical reality, a condensation of economic, social, and political transformations, that was further transformed out of existence (and out of its usefulness for the formulation of liberal political theory?).[114] Thinking the loss of this constituting, or sovereign, subject in the face of the formative state historically is also generative theoretically.

Habermas's location of such a loss in the last quarter of the nineteenth century is peculiar, for precisely at that time there was a global upsurge of discourses about self-fashioning. During this period, there was a proliferation of state and civil society projects — rhetorical and material — for the physical and spiritual reformation of the masses into suitably modern, national subjects.[115] This is the sort of expansion of the public sphere Habermas is problematizing, one wherein culture moves from being a site of debate to a site of consumption, and the individual moves from significantly shaping his social reality to being significantly shaped; however, if the subject is understood as never prior to culture, then the time of loss in Habermas's theory of the bourgeois public sphere becomes in fact a moment of plenitude. From North America to Japan, self-making was the business of making the public modern and the national public.

If one brings this discussion back to Egypt, it becomes clear why identifying the fictional nature of the bourgeois individual and his public sphere matters to history and theory. The discourse of the civilizing mission underwriting European imperial ventures between the Napoleonic conquest of Egypt and the British occupation was predicated on maintaining a slippage between universal theories and particular histories. Otherwise, it was impossible to hold the universalist position required for a politics of emancipation, which was the promise of enlightened imperialism and nationalism. I am not saying anything new: the contradictions of bourgeois politics animated an entire tradition of Western philosophical critique. However, as Dipesh Chakrabarty and Gayatri Chakravorty Spivak, among others, have demonstrated, in liberal, Marxist, or poststructuralist framings of this theoretical and epistemological tension, history's subject always remains the sovereign, self-constituting individual of bourgeois modernity.[116] Or, as Spivak puts it, "Although the history of Europe as Subject is narrativized by the law, political economy, and ideology of the West, this concealed Subject pretends it has no geo-political determinations."[117] The concept of the bourgeois individual as a bearer of uni-

versal rights has had tremendous political purchase in Europe and elsewhere, but it was only ever as successful as its contingent formation could
be elided in theory and temporalized in practice (the not yet of colonial
modernity).[118] Perhaps a historical irony, Kamil was desirous of this very
same subjectivity—not only for himself but for the Egyptian as well.[119]

The ambivalences of this relationship to a desirable self are in part what
my book tracks, but it also pauses to ask whether decentering, or provincializing, the Western subject of history is the absolute limit of a genuine
historical critique, if the latter is understood as more than the sum of its
disciplinary formation. In other words, the modern and national public
that is mapped by the self-making of effendi masculinity may appear as the
only intelligible site of Egypt and the Egyptian in history, but given other
relations to time, do not Others emerge? How might they be narrated?

Before ending with the question of narrating historical otherness, I must
delve somewhat deeper into the sovereign subject of colonial modernity
as a peculiar arrangement of empire, nation, gender, and sexuality. In this
book, effendi masculinity is a loose designation for that arrangement, a
mobile category that serves as a receptacle for, and a lens into, the work
of purification through which a universal subject was materialized in the
name of Egypt.[120] The openings, closures, and ambivalences of this process are what a performative approach to subject formation helps make
visible.[121] But what are the larger historiographical and theoretical advantages of posing the question of the sovereign subject of colonial modernity in this way?

In recent years scholars of the non-Western world have applied, tested,
expanded, and critiqued Foucault's method of tracking the emergence of
a new form of power between the seventeenth century and the twentieth. Indeed, his conception of nonsovereign power, wherein there was no
single location or owner of power, was tremendously useful in opening
new vistas of colonial history and identifying a host of thorny problems
previously ignored, in particular the relationship between disciplinary
knowledge and domination.[122] Traditionally, critics of this approach have
floundered because they have aimed their attacks at the wrong target. It is
rather simple—albeit entailing laborious historical research—to apprehend the contextual difference between places in the world experiencing
massive social and political transformation sparked by the scientific and
industrial revolutions and places undergoing asymmetrical incorporation
into the world system cobbled together by those revolutionary states and
their agents.[123] Indeed, within this historical frame, coercive power ap-

pears merely to have been transferred from metropoles to colonies.[124] It is argued that even if one were to grant Foucault's genealogy of the disciplines and biopolitical technologies as sites of modern power such a situation did not exist or existed only in truncated form outside of Europe and could not have been a means of subjecting millions. What is left out here, in large part because power and politics are still viewed in the exclusive terms of domination and resistance and as historically and geographically discontinuous, is that colonialism, regardless of its repressive or adaptive character, insinuated a shape of things to come into the languages and historical trajectories of places the world over.[125] That future possibility, or possibility of a future — variously imagined in political, economic, social, and technological terms — was compelling precisely because it was not theoretically rooted in time and place or in a specific politics or culture.[126] The language of society, the terms of its formation and transformation, although colonial in genealogy, was also modern and consequently desirable for its promise of progress in the world.[127] The shape of things to come could then theoretically ride on desires and expectations as well as on techniques of governance and subject formation, however partial and projected.

The problem with using Foucault to read the colonial archives therefore lies elsewhere. Between a history (liberal or left) of the rights-bearing individual and a genealogy of the biopolitical subject, as historians themselves have shown, is a sea of difference. Whether it was the question of internal others (women, religious, ethnic and sexual minorities, peasants, tribes, and so on) or external foes and deciding the boundaries between and among them, division and multiplication — a proliferation of subjects and subjectivities — was the story of the long nineteenth century. This story of difference can be read productively through either lens, as it has been. Neither model, however, can claim to exhaust the historical diversity of human life and ways of living in the world, which were not always legible, for example, through categories of rights, labor, or discipline, but at issue here is not simply a matter of inadequate scope. The difference, in the in-between of these two approaches to the past, implicates the troubling subject of time itself.

The time of the modern subject in Whiggish, Marxist, and Foucaultian historical narratives presupposes a spatial singularity, the interpretation of which may diverge at several points but converges nonetheless around a constitution or a question of sovereignty. Whether constituted or constituting, the modern subject, it has been argued, is contingent on being in a specific relation to the biological, social, and political body:

It is not possible to understand the "national" and biopolitical development and vocation of the modern state in the nineteenth and twentieth
centuries if one forgets that what lies at its basis is not man as a free and
conscious political subject but, above all, man's bare life, the simple birth
that as such is, in the passage from subject to citizen, invested with the
principle of sovereignty. The fiction implicit here is that *birth* immediately
becomes *nation* such that there can be no interval of separation (*scarto*)
between the two terms. Rights are attributed to man (or originate in him)
solely to the extent that man is the immediately vanishing ground (who
must never come to light as such) of the citizen.[128]

Through bare life, a later incarnation of *homo sacer* (a figure of Roman
law), Giorgio Agamben shows the constitutive exclusions that were foundational to modern politics in its right or left trajectories, which produced
the paradox of the human as simultaneously sacred and extinguishable.
To live *and* to have rights became a cause of universalistic revolutionary
undertakings that just as immediately became a question of which lives
were worthy of rights, and when and where. As groundbreaking as this
intervention in modern politics and the subject of human rights may be,
it remains a formulation that conceals Europe as the subject; the particular movement of history, in which bare life that forms the ground of the
citizen was suppressed at birth only to return in the figure of the refugee
or camp prisoner, is compelling yet strangely incomplete.[129] As Stoler has
shown in relation to Foucault's work, the political, juridical, and technological boundaries of subjection appear chronologically and geographically other when regarded through the lens of colonialism, urging a reconfiguration of the modern subject's genealogy.[130] Such a reconfigured
subject is paradoxical in the terms Agamben outlines, but the formation of
the modern state, sovereignty, and the new biopolitical body of humanity,
which supposedly had their twentieth-century apogee in national socialism and fascism, might be seen otherwise from its colonial margins.

As Samera Esmeir argues in her study of modern law and colonialism
in Egypt, critical theories of sovereignty and sovereign power that have
emphasized the exception and, by extension, violence as constitutive of
the norm are nonetheless "trapped . . . by the liberal political category
of state agents and institutions."[131] The history of the colonial state, for
which the birthing of a nation was not an explicit objective and was in
fact at cross purposes, makes visible "multiple zones of sovereignty." In
Esmeir's work, modern colonial law was productive of what she terms
"spectral legalities," which were located in the expanding domains of pri-

vate property in land dotting the countryside. The political settlement after the British occupation entailed abandoning these large estates and the souls inhabiting them to their ostensibly traditional forms of administration, even as the colonial rule of law established its claim to produce the human and protect its humanity over and against that very same precolonial despotism.[132] In this accounting, sovereign power was always already plural and subject to history, yet the colonial rule of law performed its singularity by effecting a pure and universal "juridical humanity," which in turn was not without its effects. The very production of the human was at stake in law's temporal and spatial constitution.

The subject of effendi masculinity was a partial effect of this formation of modern law in Egypt. Indeed, Mustafa Kamil, like many early nationalist leaders, was a lawyer and staunch advocate of applying the liberal principles of sovereignty to his national community. I show in chapters 2 and 8 that the claim of anticolonial nationalists to represent the people by virtue of their mastery of the terms of being modern involved the articulation of a counterdiscourse of protection and legitimacy. That discourse was repeated with a difference that illuminates the location of Egypt in colonial modernity that was at the same time universal. Speaking for peasants with the promise of ameliorating their condition, reducing their suffering, and thereby enhancing humanity in general was a justification for the colonial rule of law that would be reiterated in nationalist discourse but only through the supplementary performance of its authenticity and modernity.

As chapters 3 through 7 demonstrate, that performance was far more varied than political and social histories of Egypt normally allow, implicated — and was constituted by — gender in very specific ways, and entailed unexpected consequences. Claims of alleviating pain and suffering had necessarily to address the causes of and solutions to the people's ailments. Initially, in the late nineteenth century (and continuing to some extent into the interwar period) the locus of this address within nationalist discourse was the care of a generic male body that suffered from deficiencies, against which the traditional concept of al-riyada was reworked and redeployed (as sports) in order to produce a genuinely modern, national subject. Later in the interwar period, a host of social scientific discourses in a nationalist mode matured and came to specifically target women and peasants with the aim of improving their social welfare and obtaining a "healthy, productive, and efficient population";[133] meanwhile, the discourses and practices related to al-riyada continued to proliferate beyond its nationalist framings, carving out new spaces of desire and self-fashioning. It is on these two moments in the history of effendi masculinity as a site of subject formation that my book focuses: between nationalist claims to modernity, which exhibited a complex yet somewhat predictable relationship to the body and sovereignty, and the less predictable outcomes accompanying the repetition of the new practices of self in the times and spaces of the everyday, which opens a window onto al-futuwwa and its vanishing order of masculinity.

The unexpected excavation of al-futuwwa (an internal Other), while in search of effendi masculinity through discourses of al-riyada, produced a tear in the fabric of historical time that is critically examined in chapter 8. Shifting gears to consider debates about the modernity of al-futuwwa, chapter 8 also examines the stakes of writing postcolonial history. While chapter 2 considers the purchase of the past and its narration for effendi masculinity within the terms of colonial modernity, chapter 8 queries whether those same terms, which enable a critical and connected history of empire, nation, and subjectivity, might in their repetition obscure other experiences of time and place. Sovereignty was an immanent concept for the tradition of al-futuwwa, which made it problematic within the time-space of the nation-state.

The colonial state and modern public sphere of the effendiyya were made national through a variety of legal and political maneuvers that have been extensively documented by scholars; although less well studied, the ways in which the national was made public through gendered cultural practices have also increasingly been a focus of historical research in recent years.[134] Nevertheless, subject formation as a historical question remains virtually untouched by historians except to disavow the Orientalizing claims of mimicry and to demonstrate the pedagogic functions of the modern state or biopower or both. This neglect has produced a blind spot in the way the Egyptian past is regarded.

The appearance of al-futuwwa as gangster and outlaw in the interwar period was coeval with the expansion of the effendiyya through the 1920s and 1930s, which was characterized by a broader base, more publicity, and greater political legitimacy as national actors; moreover, as I have argued above, beyond modern law and the government of others was a related but distinct domain of sovereignty manifested in the care of the self, its object being self-government conceived as an ethical and aesthetic formation. It is tempting to argue in this context that al-futuwwa became either the abject or excluded of Egypt's colonial modernity, a nonhuman.[135] That move, however, reproduces al-futuwwa in the present as merely an object of the same disciplinary discourses through which the effendi emerged as subject and exclusive site of self-government. Accordingly, the temporality of history, which belongs to that nexus of modern power and knowledge, is allowed to usurp other possible relations to time.

Treating subject formation as a historical question, however, releases al-futuwwa from the exclusive terms of effendi masculinity and of history. As I elaborate in the following chapters, the practices of self that marked the modern subject—and that had as their explicit objects self-government and the government of others—indexed multiple temporalities that were contingent on the terms of performance. In that regard, the dynamic of social inclusion and exclusion appears far more diffuse in the constitution of the subject, and the subject's intelligibility becomes contingent on historical perspective. Tracing the phenomenon of self-government beyond the dominant practices and spatial formations (national and international) of effendi masculinity, chapter 8 points to a complex field of embodied power inhabited by al-futuwwa; this space of sovereignty overlapped with but was irreducible to the global bourgeois projects of nation building and self-fashioning that assiduously distinguished between good and bad subjects. Thereby, in a postcolonial reframing of the Egyptian past as plural spatially and temporally, the modern subject and its location historically reappear as unresolved problems rather than as history. While this does not fully recuperate al-futuwwa as subject it does demand of history a more explicit accounting of its own particularity, which begins with the refusal of modernity's "sonorous summons" and "resounding clashes."

1

IMAGINATION

———

Projecting British Masculinity

> Rarely has public opinion in England been so deeply moved as when the news arrived of the fall of Khartoum. The daily movements of the relief expeditions had been watched by anxious multitudes of General Gordon's countrymen, yearning for news of one who seemed to embody in his own person the peculiar form of heroism which is perhaps most of all calculated to move the Anglo-Saxon race. When General Gordon's fate was known a wail of sorrow and disappointment was heard throughout the land. —EVELYN BARING, Earl of Cromer, *Modern Egypt*

The imperialism of the last third of the nineteenth century, which ignited the scramble for Africa, heightened the Great Game, and incited anticolonial nationalisms, was a highly complex phenomenon involving multiple actors and events, and even today occasions debate among historians. Some are revisiting old arguments—in favor of empire—that it seemed had been put to rest by the culmination of anticolonial movements around the world half a century ago.[1] These arguments will not be rehearsed here.[2] The concern of this chapter is an image central to the justificatory claims of imperialism in the period of high colonialism in the late nineteenth century that has reemerged in the current post–cold war twenty-first century: the masculine Western subject as heroic savior.[3]

The narrative of salvation, which had a somewhat longer genealogy, became an increasingly normal aspect of English and French colonial projects during the Victorian age, even though it had detractors from the very beginning and was critiqued as largely disingenuous by those who

were ostensibly to be saved.[4] Nonetheless, it came to serve as a powerful ideological tool in the service of justifying empire at home to metropolitan populations that were beginning to identify as national subjects
and were becoming increasingly active in the domain of politics carved
out by liberalism.[5] In the multilayered iconography of imperialism being
produced from the second half of the nineteenth century within an expanded liberal political framework, the heroic Englishman was a privileged figure.[6] The appearance of this icon was every bit as material as
imperial architecture, for example, and just as effective in representing an
official image of empire.[7]

The Englishman was densely fashioned, an ornament, "hierarchy made
visible, immanent and actual," in David Cannadine's language.[8] He was
not being sold to the British public only: the secret of his success was investigated and the results disseminated in France, Egypt, and elsewhere.[9]
The constitution of his manly character—physical and moral—was
hailed as the model for individual and national progress.

The Sudan campaigns of the 1880s and 1890s popularized as household
names, in Britain as well as in Egypt, two exemplars of this ideal: General
Charles Gordon (1833–85) and General Herbert Kitchener (1850–1916).[10]
As the epigraph vividly suggests, the intersections of Gordon's life in particular with Britain's imperial adventures tell a fascinating story of how
masculinity was shaped and might in turn shape policy and play a crucial
role in the composition of a national drama.[11]

By the 1880s, Gordon had achieved a certain level of popularity through
his participation in the Crimean War and later in suppressing the Taiping
Rebellion, which earned him the nickname Chinese Gordon. He was the
product of an age in which the "muscular Christian" model of masculinity became popular.[12] The possession of a Christian morality defined
by charity, self-sacrifice, and purity combined with physical fortitude was
supposed to create a new man who would be successful in all of his domains—family, nation, and empire.[13] The rapid expansion from around
midcentury of sports, physical culture activities, and youth groups such
as the Boy Brigades evinced the impact of this model.[14]

By the end of the century, an important perspective emerged that regarded the empire as being in a state of decline. The evidence had been
building from the Indian rebellions of 1857 to the Afghan Wars, the successes of the Mahdi's army in Sudan, and the Boer War. These signs of imperial weakness, ironically coming to a head at the time of Britain's greatest expansion, served to consolidate a sense of national degeneration and

to reaffirm the need for programs of masculine regeneration on an ever larger scale.[15]

Within this context, images of proper masculinity—sometimes represented by an earlier generation of sturdy men like Gordon and other times by a new breed reared on scientific principles, or a mix of the two—were being circulated by the popular press through newspapers, magazines, and novels. Often-cited examples are Thomas Hughes's *Tom Brown's School Days* (1856), the adventure stories of H. Rider Haggard and G. A. Henty, and boys' magazines like *The Boy's Own Paper* and *Chums*. By the end of the century, eyewitness accounts from the scene of imperial battles became a highly popular journalistic genre.[16] The young Winston Churchill contributed reports to British papers from Cuba, India, South Africa, and Sudan. His dispatches on the reconquest of Sudan were collected and published as *The River War* in 1899.[17] The heroic Englishman was a globe-trotter if nothing else.

The number of published materials issued during and after the Sudan campaigns is astonishing. A quick search of works in English of varying genres, including travel narratives, official reports, speeches, opinions, histories, ethnologies, biographies, memoirs, novels, poetry, illustrations, and sheet music number well into the hundreds for the 1880s and 1890s. And as Cromer noted, the British public, "the Anglo-Saxon race," was hooked on these narratives (prosaic, poetic, and musical apparently) of spectacular heroism. The proliferation of new images of masculinity in the last third of the nineteenth century was the product of a number of social and technological transformations occurring on a global scale.[18] For those in power in London and Paris, the political and economic changes at home and in the colonies meant contending with new voices in the public sphere and the subsequent challenges to the bourgeois and aristocratic monopoly on power. One of the strategies for containing the emergence of new interests onto the political playing field was through the resignification of empire and nation as a shared family enterprise.[19] The rearticulation of hegemonic masculinity was essential to this process, as Robert Nye suggests in the case of France:

> The sense of danger and decline in fin de siècle France so permeated the cultural atmosphere that courage became the obligation of all citizens. Paul Gerbod has written of the extraordinary explosion of a literature of heroism between 1870 and 1914 that was deployed in the form of a "pedagogical strategy" and applied in a variety of public domains. Mili-

tary heroism was chronicled in statues to the heroes of the 1870 war, in a yearly *Almanach du Drapeau* listing the heroic exploits of soldiers and policemen, and in the revival of the cult of Joan of Arc, which celebrated the tradition of sacrifice to the fatherland. Civic heroism became an aim of religious teaching, of the numerous patriotic and veterans' organizations of the period, the colonial movement, and even the nascent sporting movement. As though it were the most natural thing in the world, both civic and military heroism were incorporated into the official pedagogy of the Third Republic and served up to the students in lectures and textbooks.[20]

Although Nye refers to the colonial movement here in passing, France's participation in the imperial contests at the close of the nineteenth century is noticeably absent from his discussion of the contexts in which a redefinition of masculinity took place. Nye's focus is perhaps narrowed by the looming importance in the historiography of this period of France's crushing defeat at the hands of the recently formed North German Federation in 1870.

Interestingly, the colonial official was more mindful of the material and psychic implications of empire for his compatriots. Cromer's analysis of the forces driving London's decision to reconquer Sudan, ostensibly for Egypt, illustrates the centrality of imperialism's virile self-image in the formation of policy and identity. He described the public desire to avenge Gordon's killing in Sudan and to (re)dress this injury to national honor as a force that was impossible to stop:

> It might have been possible to have postponed decisive action. It would probably have been impossible to have altogether prevented it. The national honour was not to be indefinitely baulked of the salve for which it yearned. An argument of this sort, albeit it is based on sentiment, is of intrinsic importance. *In the execution of the Imperialist policy, to which England is pledged almost as a necessity of her existence, it is not at all desirable to eliminate entirely those considerations which appeal to the imaginative, to the exclusion of the material side of the national character.* Moreover, whatever may be thought of the undesirability of admitting any emotional lines of thought as guides to practical action in politics, it may be regarded as certain that the politician who endeavours to run absolutely counter to the impulse of the national imagination instead of seeking to guide it will find that he is attempting an impossible task (emphasis added).[21]

He added that one could explain the decision to reconquer Sudan otherwise; for example, controlling the headwaters of the Nile was critical to Egyptian security. But this explanation apparently only mattered much for a "man on the spot" like himself, less so for the British public and politicians in London.

Anticipating Benedict Anderson by nearly a century, Cromer, who was no fan of popular political participation, articulated what was perhaps one of his most astute observations of empire and nation.[22] Although he did not explicitly examine the role of print capitalism in the formation of a British national identity, it was very much implicit in his connection of the "imaginative" and the affective. Unlike many contemporary historians of Britain (and France), Cromer sensed the significance of and connection between the diverse cultural renderings of empire and the material requirements of nation building. Cromer's recollection of a popular affective investment in empire was an interested reading of a situation that had gone awry and an attempt to deflect direct moral and political responsibility for the death of Gordon. As Roger Owen has noted, "The hasty and ill-considered decision to send General Charles Gordon back to Sudan . . . was to haunt Gladstone, the members of his Cabinet, and Evelyn Baring for the rest of their lives."[23] Whatever his motivation, Cromer's reflection provides a rare contemporary glimpse of how an empire man through and through envisioned the national as a dependency of the imperial and vice versa. How much the empire actually mattered to the British public at large is perhaps an impossible question to answer, but what is certain is that the cultural conception of that public as a national body became intertwined with the idea of empire during the later Victorian Age.[24] This identification was true even if it occurred in an oppositional mode.[25]

In what follows I examine the idealization of English masculinity in one example of the cultural dissemination of "the Sudan" for consumption by and for the production of "the national imagination" in Britain. Since most of the British accounts published by participants in the actual campaigns were of interest to a limited reading public, I will examine a popular fictionalized account that takes the general and mainly young male reader through the events leading to the loss of Sudan in the 1880s and to its reconquest in the 1890s.

Imperial Fiction
SUDAN, EGYPT, AND MASCULINITY

In the following reading of Henty's *With Kitchener in the Soudan*, I focus on the importance of class and race—specifically the configuration of race within a new colonial space—to the rearticulation of British masculinity at a time of perceived internal and external threats.[26] This novel, written in the metropole, makes extensive use of reports from the field filed by newspaper correspondents, a recent phenomenon in itself, to construct an increasingly realistic adventure narrative. *With Kitchener in the Soudan* is one example of a significant genre of juvenile fiction popular during the Victorian age, a genre that became an important vehicle for sustaining enthusiasm for Britain's imperial project.[27] Henty himself was the author of over ninety such novels aimed mostly at young boys and quite often set in an imperial context in which the conqueror's position was always under threat by a less civilized or savage force.[28]

The hero of Henty's stories was usually a young man who is supposed to embody all the qualities of a properly raised English boy. The standard of masculinity to which he must conform was that of a reformed, revitalized, and robust public school and Oxbridge model.[29] This template of the ideal masculine will be elaborated further in the following discussion of the main character in the novel, the boy-hero Gregory. Suffice to say here that the Victorian ideal of masculinity shaped and was shaped in part through this genre of juvenile fiction, for which the imperial social formation was the raison d'être. Conversely, and *pace* Cromer, the empire as a moral project was materialized for millions across the colonial divide precisely through such imaginative fictions.[30]

With Kitchener in the Soudan begins with an evocation of Victorian society's strict class boundaries, but as the condition of possibility for a romantic transgression. The father of the novel's young hero, Gregory Hilliard Hartley, a member of a landed aristocratic family, falls in love with and marries a woman who works as a governess. He does so in defiance of his father's wishes and is forced to make a way in the world for himself and his new wife without the assistance of his family. After living together in one room in London on the verge of destitution, he manages to find a job as a minor clerk with a trading firm in Alexandria, Egypt, a year before the British occupation. In order to save enough money to return to England, Hartley looks for a better-paying position with the new colonial administration and finds work as a translator for the Hicks expedition to Sudan.[31] He does not return from this mission—the actual force was annihilated by the Mahdi's army in October 1883—but for the sake of the novel's plot he is not declared dead.[32] It is now up to the mother to raise the child born shortly before Hartley's departure for the Sudan. She cannot leave Egypt because her husband had given her explicit instructions not to turn to his family for assistance and not to let the boy know his father's family name until she felt it was absolutely impossible to continue to leave him in ignorance. The boy also must make his own way in the world.

As any resourceful Victorian woman would when left with instructions from her husband, Annie Hilliard sets about her tasks with vigor and industry. She works as a private tutor and dedicates herself to providing her son, Gregory, with a proper upbringing.[33] The following passage illustrates the spirit of fin-de-siècle notions of education as a form of gendered enculturation; specifically, it articulates a program for raising a boy to become an English gentleman:

> While she was occupied in the afternoon with her pupils the boy had liberty to go about as he pleased, and indeed she encouraged him to take long walks, to swim, and to join in all the games and exercises. "English boys at home," she said, "have many games, and it is owing to these that they grow up so strong and active. They have more opportunities than you, but you must make the most of those that you have. We may go back to England some day, and I should not at all like you to be less strong than others." As however, such opportunities were very small, she had an apparatus of poles, horizontal bars, and ropes set up, such as those she had seen in England in use by the boys of the families where she had taught before her marriage, and insisted upon Gregory's exercising himself upon it for an hour every morning, soon after sunrise. As she had heard her husband say that fencing was a splendid exercise, not only for developing the figure, but for giving a good carriage as well as activity and alertness, she arranged with a Frenchman who had served in the army, and had gained a prize as a swordsman in the regiment, to give the boy lessons two mornings in the week. Thus, at fifteen Gregory was well grown and athletic, and had much of the bearing and appearance of an English public school boy. His mother had been very particular in seeing that his manners were those of an Englishman.[34]

Although physical strength is the quality underscored in this portrayal of cultivated English masculinity, the last line hints at other properties that will determine whether the boy was properly raised. The unspecified

"manners" would include chivalry, wit, compassion, and charity, the last
two also being vital ingredients of Britain's paternalistic colonial logic.[35]
Nevertheless, increasingly essential to the cultivation of a proper masculine subject in late Victorian bourgeois culture, as is reflected clearly
above, was the primacy of the disciplined body.[36] The centering of the
body signaled a small opening for the negotiation of class difference, however narrow. Gregory would have "much of the bearing and appearance of
an English public school boy," but not all. This partial presence, to misuse
a phrase from Bhabha, was resolved differently when the subject was the
white boy-hero of metropolitan fiction rather than the colonized.[37] It is
the possibility of becoming whole, that is, a card-carrying bourgeois male
citizen, that Henty inscribed onto his character's heroic body. Although
a confusion of liberalism's fiction and autobiography often passes as historical truth, Henty's representation of Gregory's physical and personal
cultivation as a precursor to social legibility and political agency was not
a reflection of everyman's reality as much as a moment in the expansion
of representational fictions.[38] It has been argued persuasively that the offer
of inclusion, which forms the cornerstone of liberal political theory, was
in need of constant reiteration precisely because exclusionary strategies
were constitutive of liberal politics.[39] This was true just as much in Britain
as it was in Egypt, although fictions of representation would have more
enduring value in the political and imaginary domains of Britain.

In Henty's rendering, the manners and measure of an Englishman were
made contingent on the site of enactment. For example, although Gregory
was raised to be like a proper English gentleman he could not be considered a genuine article, as he was not the product of the public school
education that normally signified an upper-class standing and conferred
status. Nevertheless, since the locus of Gregory's entry into manhood is
Egypt, or out in the empire, the rigidity of this class-based definition of
a gentleman is attenuated or deferred in the face of racial difference and
ruling anxieties.

In this way Gregory is able to gain honorary membership in the league
of proper colonial gentlemen.[40] The following conversation between Captain Ewart, whom Gregory has just met in order to discuss joining General
Kitchener's expedition to reclaim the Sudan, and Mr. Murray, the bank
manager, highlights the exception empire makes for the performance of
proper masculinity: "'He seems to be a fine young fellow,' he said, 'well-
grown and active, not at all what one would expect from a product of
Cairo.' 'No, indeed; of course you have not seen him to advantage in that
black suit, but in his ordinary clothes I should certainly take him, if I had

"HIS KEEN GLANCE SEEMED TO GREGORY TO TAKE HIM IN FROM HEAD TO FOOT"

1. "A Fine Young Fellow." G. A. Henty, *With Kitchener in the Soudan: A Story of Atbara and Omdurman* (London: Blackie and Sons, Ltd., 1903). Credit: Rare Books and Special Collections, McGill University Library.

not seen him before, to be a young lieutenant freshly come out to join.'"[41] The sartorial marker that brands his difference in class does not foreclose on Gregory's ambitions because of his striking physical features and his respectable comportment. The poorly tailored, ill-fitting suit is a cause for some hesitancy, but it cannot efface Gregory's physical superiority. In the background of the illustration of this "fine young fellow" is a map of the future site of conquest. Here, an active manhood is literally imposed onto a visual representation of colonial space.

Henty's fictionalized depiction of colonial Cairo society, although alluding to the differences that obtained between metropolitan whites and the local product, for the most part glosses over a highly stratified system in which upward social mobility was actively blocked. Mabel Caillard, who lived in Egypt for several decades between the 1870s and 1930s, observed, "In the seventies the British colony, already considerable, stood for sober worth and respectability among the adventurers of all nations who flocked to the Egyptian Tom Tiddler's ground 'picking up gold and silver.' . . . Now and then a shady character would crop up in its very midst; but a withering intolerance declared his fault and his ostracism in a breath and he quietly faded away."[42] After the occupation, British society grew in numbers, and correspondingly the policing of class boundaries became more obnoxious. Dangers of being polluted by association with the lower ranks led to extreme measures and creative compromises:

> The Ladies' Club had, indeed, to close its doors owing to the fact that they could not be kept open without the support of the lower ranks of the community. . . . It was a solecism to mix the "sets," even inadvertently, at a luncheon or a dinner-party; and at the big receptions it was everybody's object to climb into a more rarefied atmosphere than that to which he was accustomed, so that one of the parties to a conversation was always discontented. This, perhaps, was why the hotel dances became so popular—the risk of being obliged to speak to the wrong people was reduced to a minimum: there were no standards of hospitality to be observed and you could be as frankly rude as you pleased. It cannot be denied that the Cairenes were terribly snobbish.[43]

There is no indication Caillard considered haughtiness a negative virtue since she herself seemed to hover in "rarefied" climes, that is, until she fell from the heights when her father died, leaving her virtually penniless.[44]

The expanding imperial geography became a laboratory, quite literally, for a reconfiguration of elite English masculinity that was being forced to come to terms with struggles emanating from class and sex differences

war

at home and an increasing feeling of weakness and vulnerability abroad, fueled by the Indian Mutiny, the Crimean War, and especially the Boer War (1899–1902). A more egalitarian cultural fiction of *the* Englishman was a highly partial resolution to some of these crises of the social and political domains in the late nineteenth century, yet one with staying power. In the introduction to one of the earliest treatments of imperialism and popular culture, MacKenzie notes other important performative sites: "The new traditions of Christian militarism, militarist athleticism in the public schools, and a recreated and perverted 'medieval' chivalry contributed readily to the national rituals and political progresses which were part of the British imperial cult." [45] The young hero of *With Kitchener in the Soudan* is able to refashion himself from "product of Cairo" to the equivalent of a metropolitan gentleman through the process of serving his queen and country. This experience, or at least its imagined possibility, was relevant to ever greater numbers of men as the army again became "a central element in national life," and a man's mettle was measured by the experience he gained abroad. [46] Henty illustrates this point in the following:

war

soldier

> The contrast between the newly-arrived brigade and the hardy veterans who had fought at the Atbara was striking. Bronzed and hearty, inured to heat and fatigue, the latter looked fit to go anywhere and do anything, and there was hardly a sick man in the four regiments. On the other hand, the new-comers looked white and exhausted with the heat. Numbers had already broken down, and the doctors at the hospital had their hands full of fever patients. They had scarcely marched a mile since they landed in Egypt, and were so palpably unfit for hard work that they were, if possible, to proceed the whole way in boats to be in fighting condition when the hour of battle arrived. [47]

The new man had to be whipped into shape to be "fit to go anywhere and do anything." One of his fellow officers explained it to Gregory: "If it wasn't for wars like this [in the Sudan], and our little wars in India, where men do learn to think and take responsibility, I don't know where our general officers would get their training." [48] Maintaining the balance between managing an empire and reconstructing masculinity without unraveling the prevailing social and political hierarchies was accomplished through a geographical projection that was simultaneously a prediction of perpetual war. [49]

Compounding the prevalent sense of masculine degeneration was the ubiquitous threat of native rebellion, made to seem especially ominous after 1857. [50] Fictional representations of rebellion, such as Henty's *With*

Kitchener in the Soudan, offered a compensatory scheme for ruling anxieties as they deployed the taxonomies of colonial anthropology to familiarize and domesticate the natives. Native groups were quite often differentiated according to levels of strength and martial abilities. In fiction, at least, that capacity was almost always attenuated by juxtaposing it to the Englishman's preponderantly superior physical and, perhaps most important, moral force. The possession of moral fortitude was indispensable in the discourse of masculinity and militarism because without it there was little separating the English use of brute force from, in this case, that of the rebellious Mahdi.

Henty wrote the Egyptian *fallah* [peasant] into the role of the strong and sturdy representative of Egyptian males. The fallah, however, prefers working the land to fighting, unlike the black Sudanese, described as "splendid fellows—they love fighting for fighting's sake. It is in their opinion the only worthy occupation for a man, and they have shown themselves worthy to fight for the side of our men."[51] Although this description suggests a kind of parity between the Sudanese black and the English soldier, the rigid hierarchy is quickly restored in the following sentence: "They have a perfect confidence in us, and would, I believe, go anywhere we led them. They say themselves, 'We are never afraid—just like the English.'"[52] Or: "They seemed to Gregory as full of fun and life as a party of school-boys—laughing, joking, and playing practical tricks on each other. The physique of some of the regiments was splendid, the men averaging over six feet in height, and being splendidly built."[53] Any resemblance to or desire for the Other is immediately qualified and disavowed by infantilizing the black man and requiring the proper (read: English) leadership and disciplining in order to maximize his utility.[54]

 The comparison of Egyptian fallah masculinity to black masculinity is repeated in the next passage, in which Gregory gives a pep talk to the Egyptian regiment he is about to lead into a town where they anticipate engaging the Khalifa's forces led by his son Mahmud: "I hope that two hundred will have been left there; it will add to our glory to have won a battle as well as taken the town! Your children will talk of it in their tents, your women will be proud of you, and the men of the black regiments will say that we have shown ourselves to be as proud as they are."[55] The hierarchy of the brave and courageous is clearly delineated. The black tribes and the Dervishes (the Mahdist forces) are closely tied. The Dervishes' zealous belief in the Mahdi's cause made them fearless of death and thus brave warriors. The Egyptian fallah, once trained and commanded by Englishmen, were not far behind.[56] The Englishman, owing to his civilizational advancement and moral force, was too superior to be ranked on the same scale, the criteria for which were one-dimensional and suited for man at a more primitive stage of development.

Henty the novelist did not merely invent these distinctions made among the fighting abilities of the different races.[57] He was simply citing from an abundance of expert opinion on the matter that was widely available at the time. Alfred Milner's authoritative assessment in 1892 of the need for continued occupation of Egypt laid the foundations for this typology that was repeatedly cited as fact well into the twentieth century.[58] A chapter of Milner's *England in Egypt* entitled "The Fellah as Soldier" is introduced with two contradictory dispatches on the quality of Egyptian soldiers. The first from Sudan in 1884 refers to them as cowards who turned tail and ran when the Mahdi's forces attacked; the second tells exactly the opposite story of a battle in the same vicinity but in 1891. Milner's point was that the British reorganization of the army and retraining of fallah soldiers were eventually successful.

These typologies became fixed in the imperial imagination in spite of contradictory voices from within. For example, the following is a passage from a dispatch submitted to the British government's special commissioner Henry Drummond Wolff, who was charged with negotiating the Egyptian question with the Ottomans. In this report on the Egyptian army assembled by the War Office in Cairo, Lieutenant-Colonel Parr wrote, "There has been an effort on the part of a portion of the English press to account for the good behaviour of our men by stating that those who so distinguished themselves are black troops. This is, however, a misconception; at Magraket no blacks were engaged, and at Guinniss, out of the whole force of the Egyptian troops engaged, only 150 men were blacks."[59] Parr goes on to question the typical argument about the improvement of Egyptian troop performance being the result of the general reorganization of the army and the leadership of English officers by suggesting rather that it was the cultivation of "native officers" that made the difference. In fact, he notes, "there have been many instances of personal gallantry."[60] Although Parr's memo was presented to Parliament, the nuances he offered were ultimately too self-defeating to publicize widely.[61] Caillard, in her reminiscences of Egypt published in 1935, could reproduce the same image of cowardly Egyptian soldiers while describing the death of an acquaintance who had fought in Sudan: "[Major] Jim Morice had died a gallant death, fighting a forlorn hope with native troops who had failed him, against savage hordes who had no ruth even for the fallen."[62]

A sustained belief in English moral superiority could persist only through repetition of stereotypic images of cowardly, savage Others.[63] Furthermore, that belief assumed a distinctly gendered form in the high imperial age. It was England's virile and virtuous masculinity that made possible its imperial victories and guaranteed its future. The following passages from the novel further reflect the specificity of the moral force ostensibly internalized by a properly raised Englishman and lacking in his other. After just barely getting out of a bind and on the run, Gregory attempts to explain to his servant, Zaki, why he did not finish off one of their assailants: "'I know that I ought to have paused a moment and given him another stab, but I could not bring myself to do it. It is one thing to stab a man trying to take one's life, but it is another when he has fallen and is helpless.' Zaki had made no reply. He could scarcely understand his master's repugnance to making matters safe when another blow would have done so, but it was not for him to blame."[64] Even at the expense of risking his own life and that of his servant, Gregory does not go against his gentlemanly creed in the process of escaping from a difficult situation. Zaki's failure to understand his master's actions is due to his race's not having evolved yet to the level of English civility. This particular enactment of Gregory's superior morality becomes a general characteristic of all Englishmen in the unfolding of the next predicament.

Here another aspect of chivalrous behavior is highlighted. In this scene, after jumping off of his gunboat and saving a drowning woman, Gregory and Zaki, who jumped in after his master while imploring him to let the woman go so they could swim away from enemy territory, are captured by the Khalifa's son, Mahmud. He turns out to be the rescued woman's husband. In response to Mahmud's surprise that Gregory would risk his life to save a foreign woman, Gregory says, "What I did, Emir, I believe any white officer who was a good swimmer would have done. No Englishman would see a woman drowning without making an effort to save her, if he had it in his power. As to the fact that she was not of the same race or religion, he would never give it a thought. It would be quite enough for him that she was a woman."[65] Henty's inelegant reenactment of what MacKenzie refers to as a "perverted 'medieval' chivalry" is staged here on a coveted colonial terrain, which further necessitates underscoring the ultimately moral vision of the imperial project in gendered terms.

Perversion here references only the symbolic dimension of the peculiar authority that imperial masculinity claimed over the feminine, which, since Said, is casually read as a metaphor for colony.[66] However, as Ann Stoler has shown, sexual control was not merely a function of or metaphor for social hierarchies and racial boundaries but a constitutive element of colonial power.[67] Despite Stoler's sobering injunction that more careful attention be paid to the constitutive role of gender and sexuality in the formation of colonial society in specific times and places, I argue in the following chapters that it was precisely the claims of colonizers rather than the complexity of their lives that informed Egyptian nationalists' articulation of the properly masculine during the British occupation. The notion of a civilizing mission with its heroic masculine agent was deployed unevenly within imperial political strategies and rhetoric, but its terms would have unanticipated consequences for the formation of national subjects in the colonies. The impulse to differentiate and delineate a moral and physical hierarchy of subjects formed a logic of rule that exceeded the bounds of formal colonialism and found itself rearticulated in nation-building projects everywhere. This does not, however, mean that these hierarchies were unproblematically maintained as social reality anywhere.

Henty's predictable resolution of Gregory's quest returns him to the metropole to reclaim his rightful place as heir to the Hartley fortune after discovering his father's fate and securing the empire against the wild dervish hordes.[68] He also brings back his loyal manservant, Zaki, who finds everything wonderful, declaiming, "We poor Arabs could not dream of such things."[69] In response to Zaki's enthusiasm for his new metropolitan home, Gregory offers to support him for the remainder of his life and allow him to be his "own master," which he refuses, saying, "I should be a fool to wish to be my own master . . . after having such a good one at present."[70] This fictional ending to the Sudan adventure, which reaffirms the class, racial, and gender hierarchy of colonial discourse, was also a projection of continued British rule as a moral and benevolent project desired by its conquered subjects.

Conclusion

The hegemonic masculinity of British imperialism I have outlined in this chapter will seem to many historians a far cry from the actual lives of men and women in the British Empire. One response may be that this is not a social history but a discursive analysis of a particular ideal. Such a reply would grant as a given the initial division made between the real and the imagined, which leaves the materiality of masculinity unexamined or, at best, understood as a determination of a priori social and economic structures. It would indeed be arrogant to presume that hegemonic masculinity captures the diversity of life that was surely present in fin-de-siècle Britain, but it would be wrong to presume that actual lives in the past can be accessed without mapping the representational schemes in which they were enmeshed.

As Lord Cromer perceived at the start of the twentieth century, a persuasive connection prevailed among gender, nation, and empire. Although not interested in exploring their mutually constitutive history, he was acutely aware that the image of imperial masculinity mattered to consumers of a new public culture back in Britain, and, correspondingly, he was invested in shaping and projecting a manly face of empire in Egypt. In this enterprise the arsenal of imperial iconography that had taken shape over the preceding years was a useful aid. What Cromer missed, and what most imperial historians of this period continue to ignore, was that the images of masculinity proliferating throughout the empire were not solely products of a propaganda machine.

Rather, masculinity and femininity in Britain underwent a series of transformations from the eighteenth century to the late Victorian age as shown by the social and cultural histories written in the past twenty years or so, and empire was both a cauldron for and a cause of these changing conceptions of gender. Gender, as the regulatory apparatus it became in this period, was not only a means of distinguishing male and female roles, which, contrary to the modernization paradigm, had not dramatically changed.[71] Gender was also an entirely new disciplinary formation productive of the modern subject. Supporting this technology surely were the apparatus of scientific knowledge and institutions of modern power Foucault has outlined, yet the new representational techniques in print and politics were also fundamental to the operations of gender.

Henty's novel and Cromer's anxious allusion to a politics of public opinion are only two examples in the discursive formation of a new gendered political subject. This subject was hailed to live as normally as possible the paradoxes of late nineteenth-century British liberalism and imperialism and was sustained by the proliferation of a dense network of representational practices. The images of hegemonic masculinity and the masculinities of individual persons were not mutually exclusive but mutually constitutive and equally material.

Finally, as I have noted in the chapter, the political positioning—right or left—of the individual was beside the point; rather, when viewed across the imperial social formation, it becomes possible to detect the lineaments of a subject whose legibility was contingent on a geographical projection, a naturalization of West and East as ontologically different spaces. This is not to say that politics was irrelevant; on the contrary, the expansion of political franchise and participation might have been a raison d'être of this turn-of-the-century concatenation of masculinity and empire. Conjuring the "national imagination," for adults and children, through the exploits of a moral militarist imperialism was not part of an evil master plan; nonetheless, it had the effect of sustaining a paternalist attitude even in moments when there was clear and overwhelming evidence of greed, self-interest, and gratuitous violence.

2

GENEALOGY

Mustafa Kamil and Effendi Masculinity

Nations require subjects, and in a liberal polity they are citizen subjects. The history of that form of political being appears different when viewed through the prism of empire. Despite its persistence in scholarly and popular understanding, it is becoming increasingly clear that the emergence of a juridical, rights-bearing subject was not simply the story of a gradually expanding field of representative politics. The history of the nineteenth-century evolution of liberalism has undergone a radical revisioning since the appearance of Michel Foucault's groundbreaking study *Discipline and Punish* over three decades ago.[1] Indeed, Foucault's recasting of modern power as the management of populations through new disciplinary technologies and discourses, which also furnished the docile subjects of modern politics, has dislocated history from its traditional place as custodian, or critical narrator, of the past. For in its disciplinary form, history, like sociology, anthropology, psychology, and so on, is not simply an inert force but an active site in the production of subjects.

Ironically, despite Foucault's critical insights into history and power, it is precisely in historical terms that his genealogies of the modern subject fall short. In her engagement with one of Foucault's later and better-known works, volume 1 of *The History of Sexuality*, Ann Stoler demonstrates how imperial history and geography were crucial circuits in the emergence of race and sexuality as interrelated discourses of power that contributed to the constitution of a seemingly fixed European "bourgeois order":[2] "If race already makes up a part of that 'grid of intelligibility' through which the bourgeoisie came to define themselves, then we need to locate its coordinates in a grid carved through the geographic distributions of 'unfreedoms' that imperial labor systems enforced. These were colonial regimes prior to and coterminous with Europe's liberal bourgeois order. . . . The colonies have provided the allegorical and practical terrain against which European notions of liberty and its conceits about equality were forged."[3] Through her careful attention to the ways in which the category of the colonizer fractured along class and racial lines as sexual boundaries shifted and hardened with the transformations in the political economy of colonialism in the nineteenth century, Stoler provides an alternative, more expansive genealogy for the bourgeois subject of European modernity. But the "geographic distributions of 'unfreedoms'" that were a condition of possibility for more or less liberal politics in European history would haunt the subject of Egyptian modernity in ways that were and still are significantly different.

The growing scholarship in colonial studies and the new imperial history that has urged scholars to rethink the relationship between metropoles and peripheries as taking shape within one analytical field has done much to destabilize many received notions about the past trajectories of social categories and theoretical concepts.[4] Whether it is class, race, gender, and nation or state, liberalism, and governmentality, we now have in something like Sinha's "imperial social formation" or Barlow's "colonial modernity" modes of apprehending those histories as multiply interconnected, local, and global. In this chapter and the next, I examine early efforts to locate Egypt within this expanded geography of subject formation as a nation at once distinct from and the same as other nations. Correspondingly, I develop a basis for thinking about the particular and universal masculine subjectivity that became a norm of Egyptian nationalist discourse and of Egyptian modernity. I map one of the routes by which the figure of the effendi was inscribed within the emerging politics of representation as the exemplary national subject.

The category of the effendi in the precolonial period designated a social rank within the Ottoman administration or, more generally, distinguished the religious-scribal class from military officialdom.[5] In this system of lords, the effendi was at the bottom of the hierarchy that included the royals, the pashas, and the beys. Despite Ottoman efforts to fix the title of effendi to specific positions in government or military service, by the latter part of the nineteenth century, the term's popular use expanded and overlapped with the English equivalent of gentleman. Within a social and political landscape broadly divided among the *'amma* (commoners at this point, although the term would come to acquire some of the modern connotations of public in the second half of the twentieth century) and the *khassa* (the elite), to be an effendi was in a sense to rise above historical obscurity and the faceless mass of ordinary subjects.

In the last quarter of the nineteenth century, the effendiyya (as noted, the plural of effendi) as a social group came to include men who occupied positions in the modern professions and upper-level students.[6] It is a problematic synonym for "middle class," but it did connote a kind of bourgeois identity.[7] "Effendiyya," as Lucie Ryzova has noted recently, also conjures an ideal type.[8] During the early twentieth century "effendiyya" signified, in a sense, the imagined and material embodiment of Egyptian modernity and the building blocks of Egypt itself. Throughout the book I attempt to show how this category was invested with varying, competing, and sometimes contradictory definitions of masculinity based on new sets of cultural translations that included in their purview physical culture, dress, and sexuality.

The Modern Effendi under the Colonial Gaze

> Anybody who knows the social life of modern Egypt is well acquainted with the Effendi class. Their familiar characteristics, the obsequious manner, the slouching gait, the shortsightedness which is often so extreme as to amount almost to blindness, the worn official frock-coat buttoned up to the chin, the general air of dinginess and servility—all these are calculated to make the most unfavourable impression upon the typical Briton.—ALFRED MILNER, *England in Egypt*

Lord Milner's familiarization of the effendi in Egypt echoes a prior engagement with the babu in India.[9] The problem with this depiction is not that it fails to be accurate or that it does not account for the rise of a class of educated effendis who were increasingly unwilling to be servile. In fact, Milner acknowledges this possibility after cataloguing, in a fashion similar to his account of Egyptian soldiers that we saw in the previous chapter, the treatment they received under prior regimes:

> They were ordered about like slaves, ordered often to do what they knew themselves to be wrong, yet they durst not for their lives breathe an objection to the commands of their superiors. . . . Discipline under these

circumstances was no doubt perfect, but it was discipline of a wrong sort. It degraded the subordinate, and made a tyrant of the chief. . . . Here, as elsewhere, a change of system was the first condition of a change of character. Treat the Effendi like a man; let him understand that you expect from him obedience, but not servility, that a reasonable objection properly urged will not be resented, and that, if he does his duty, his rights are secure — and you will be able to get plenty of good work out of him.[10]

As Britain's occupation of Egypt began to look more permanent, re-forming effendis into properly obedient individuals was deemed desirable and possible, through the institution of something resembling Foucaultian discipline. Evoking Hegel's master–slave dialectic, Milner also reiterated the ethical mission of colonial liberalism as the transformation of sociopolitical conditions such that a new self-consciousness could eventually emerge.[11] The colonial nature of this power to re-form made the paradox of subjection briefly legible to contemporaries like Milner.[12] In other words, the subject that he predicated as an agential being here was to evolve through a change of system, and as such the new effendi would be produced, but he would also produce himself through a new relationship to power—obedient but not servile. Perhaps what Milner missed and Foucault certainly intimated was that disciplinary power could indeed form subjects, but the performances of the subjects might not always conform to script. Indeed, less than three decades after he wrote these words on the future of the effendi, Milner personally witnessed some of the unanticipated consequences of this process in the spectacular events of the revolution of 1919.[13]

History played a vital role in the reconstruction of effendi masculinity. By bypassing the lived and consequently messy realities of Egyptians who performed government service during the precolonial period with the graft of an abstract disciplined civil servant, it became possible to speak about the failures of a despotic, nonrationalized system in equally abstract terms.[14] For colonial officials, Egypt's history as a burden to the realization of an emancipated masculine subject simultaneously substituted for the burden of history, which would have required an engagement with the particular and the empirical, and served as a justification for the continuation of colonial guidance.[15]

The ultimate aims of colonial liberalism, at least theoretically, were to bring better government, progress, and a better life to Egyptians. Better government entailed creating men who were properly disciplined and properly men. Only such men could be entrusted with real responsibility.

The colonial rhetoric of building good and responsible government was implicitly and sometimes explicitly concerned with the problem of subject formation.[16]

The refashioning of Egyptian men to suit the needs of modern government, in Milner's mind, would entail recruiting from the "Sheikh class," a "class of native society which fills the interspace between the small body of dissatisfied aristocrats at the top, and the vast mass of toiling peasants at the bottom." It would also require changing the educational system so as not to continue producing the old effendi type.[17] This way it would be possible to maintain the good qualities of the Sheikh, such as "physique, shrewdness, energy" and some principles and erase the bad ones like "selfishness, avarice, narrow-mindedness" and the "Oriental combination of servility to those above, and arrogance to those beneath them," and cultivate a new "manly spirit."[18]

Lord Edward Cecil described a similar split in Egyptian masculinity between shaykh types and effendi types, but along a more explicit rural–urban divide.[19] His assessment was made in reference to the members of a standing committee at the Ministry of Finance, of which he was undersecretary in 1905. The members were meeting one night to discuss allocations of government concessions to private businesses. The target of his humor was someone he terms "the Minister of Arts and Crafts," who was also the president of the committee. After going through the corrupt ways in which this Egyptian, a certain Muhammad Pasha Ahmad of the landowning class, rose to this fine position, he went on to credit him for his rural virtues: "the rough, rather jolly way of the peasant." His description of peasantness also mentions an egalitarian attitude in dealings with people, "irrespective of race or creed."[20] Cecil attributed a cultural verisimilitude to the shaykh type that was confirmed by their resemblance in character and appearance to the bearers of Egyptian authenticity: peasants.

The contrapuntal figure to the paragon of rural masculinity was the urban intellectual or effendi; "the oily, snake-like manner of the town-bred Egyptian" was inscribed in opposition to the rough and jovial. The discursive process of devaluing the urban professional male has implicit political connotations. The rural gentleman was privileged in this context precisely because the machinations he engaged in to get ahead did not seem to preclude active participation in colonial enterprises and cooperation with colonial authorities; in other words, he had no qualms about being a collaborator. It is safe to say that the nationalist politics of the "oily, snake-like" effendi was the real target of Cecil's mockery and the motivation behind Milner's desire to reform Egyptian masculinity.[21]

Mehta's comments on the implications of the logic behind a similar descriptive and reformist impulse in India are apposite here:

> This agenda—namely, the proper education of Indians—became almost the central preoccupation of imperial reform in the nineteenth century. In the empire, the epistemological commitments of liberalism to rationality and the progress that it was deemed to imply constantly trumped its commitments to democracy, consensual government, limitations on the legitimate power of the state, and even toleration. Moreover, it is the epistemological commitments that are symptomatic of a narrowness in which the challenge of understanding an unfamiliar world, with multiple singularities, forms of living and experiencing life, is most starkly betrayed by liberals.[22]

In Egypt, although colonial policy aimed to limit educational possibilities (as a result of having learned the lesson of the Indian experiment),[23] the "epistemological commitments" of colonial liberalism were quite similar in their deployment of the discursive strategies Mehta refers to as "inscrutability" and "civilizational infantilism."[24] The centrality and force of the liberal discourse of progress in ordering the ideas and practices of empire as a moral project were evidenced in part by the fact that Egyptian nationalist effendis saw no choice but to do battle on the very same terrain.

Mustafa Kamil (1874–1908), with whom this book opened and the founder of one of Egypt's first political parties, was, in a sense, the new effendi imagined by Milner, but not the one he had wished for. The representative of colonial liberalism might take credit for the conditions that could produce and sustain an educated political subject in the abstract. Kamil, however, was, in terms of the exigencies of rule, a perfect example of why the educational system needed to be reorganized further.[25] In the monumental biography assembled by his brother Ali Fahmi Kamil, the life of Mustafa Kamil appears as a form of resistance to the colonial attempts to familiarize and domesticate his type.[26]

Mustafa Kamil was the exemplar of a new, confident, young Egypt. By the turn of the century, he had attained considerable fame at home and abroad as a fiery orator and patriotic nationalist leader. His story was quite unlike that of the preceding generation of effendis in many ways. That he received a modern education, including advanced training in law from the University of Toulouse, distinguished him from the majority of Egyptians, but not necessarily from past effendis. Rather, the difference was that Kamil came of age under the occupation and was formed as a subject from a consciousness freighted with a sense of loss. The determination to recover that lost object would shape the political and ethical horizons of his and ensuing generations in completely new ways while inscribing the limits of a gendered, modern Egypt.

Egypt, for Kamil and his cohort, was not so much a question as it was an answer. The problem of Egypt, which both animated European diplomatic debates and military rivalries and preoccupied Ottoman provincial rulers since Muhammad Ali for much of the nineteenth century, had been treated by the emergent bureaucratic and technical elite (the effendiyya) as a question of modernization. Despite the importance accorded the brief French occupation of Egypt from 1798 to 1801 in later nationalist narratives as the famous moment of modern awakening,[27] the effendis' identity as Arabic-speaking Ottomans was never really at stake—if anything it was accentuated—as a new state was built and society was reorganized.[28] The true challenge for these earlier generations of the effendiyya lay in overcoming the fears of a new state that was interventionist on an unprecedented scale.[29] If ever that was accomplished, the mastery of new knowledge and new techniques was coded as a means of achieving material progress at the individual and kinship levels, with national progress yet to be constituted fully as an object of political or historical discourse. The borrowing of foreign ideas, styles, and methods, although open to contestation, was not a cause for shame as it was not yet a reminder of loss.[30] Once Egypt became the vital site of political longings and organization, a decade or so into the British occupation, the construction of effendi identity had necessarily to pass through the multifaceted gauntlets of tradition battling modernity: authenticity versus imitation, resistance versus collaboration, and, later, religion versus secularism. In all of these negotiations, through which the new effendi was formed as subject, the question of masculinity was always front and center with the repossession of Egypt as an answer.[31]

Mustafa Kamil's biography was an instance of such negotiation with an uncertain present. Compiled, as noted, by his brother and published the year of Mustafa's premature death in 1908, *Mustafa Kamil Pasha in 34 Springs* was a textual and temporal seam that joined a rearticulated past with a new vision of the future. A rhetorical nationalist strategy making a claim on the emerging and contested public sphere, the text was also a telling moment in the genealogy of the effendi. The nationalism has been suitably addressed in numerous volumes.[32] I do not seek new truths of Egyptian history in this biography; rather I explore the kinds of problems encountered and the questions posed by a young effendi at the close of the nineteenth century—and the ways in which these were framed after his death—to illuminate the world of a nascent gendered political subjectivity.

The Effendi as Great Man and Kin
AN EGYPTIAN GENEALOGY

Mustafa Kamil's biography was carefully arranged by his brother to achieve a certain effect of continuity. It exhibits a profound awareness of colonial representations of Egypt and Egyptians. The foreword was written by Muhammad Farid, who succeeded Kamil as the leader of the National Party, established in October 1907, just a few months before Kamil's death. The next section features a brief but highly significant biography of their father, Ali Effendi Muhammad. The remainder of the three volumes is a combination of biographical notes and reprints of previously published material spanning a period of three years (1893–96). One possible reading of Kamil's biography is as an attempt to represent and normalize a novel relationship, the subject in political modernity, through the articulation of an embedded Egyptian masculinity. In other words, the claim to political identity that was being made in a nationalist register required a universal subject that was also particularly Egyptian and specifically gendered. This paradox will be elaborated throughout the book, but in this instance I examine how Kamil's life was performatively incorporated into the life of the nation as an iconic figure of politics and masculinity.

In his foreword Farid treated the general question of what makes a "great man" (al-rajul al-azim), then proceeded to match Kamil with the results.[33] The general grid on which greatness was plotted was national, and it was measured on a scale of talent, education, and patriotism. Women were excluded from the start. But, as we shall see, so were the vast majority of men.

Farid defined a great man as a nationalist who inspires others to become nationalists. He was not a conqueror or one who freed his nation with the sword. Dependence on the pen and the tongue affirmed God's privileging of knowledge and eloquence and was the way to "enchant hearts" and "form a nation."[34] The ability to win hearts and minds over to the nationalist cause made for a great man. Although there is a strong contemporary resonance to this position that might lead one to pass over it quickly, its articulation at the time reflected a radical shift in the fundamental order of things.[35]

The negative aspect of the definition of the great man created a distance not only from the British conquerors and the failed 'Urabists,[36] but also from the ideal masculinity of the warrior-hero inaugurated within Islamic history by the Prophet and his successors, of whom 'Ali ibn Abi Talib, the fourth caliph, had assumed an exemplary status.[37] Apparently conscious of this genealogical estrangement, Farid then reappropriated another figure of ideal masculinity also associated with the Prophet in his person and his sayings: the knowledgeable and eloquent orator.[38] At stake here was what Mitchell has described as a transformation of "political authority in the use of words."[39] Heralding the new "mechanical process of communication," nationalist reformers and activists like the Kamils and Farid reconfigured Arabic terms such as *jihad* ("to struggle," "to strive") to fit within the modern machinery of the properly political and properly masculine.[40] This was the ground on which Kamil and Farid claimed a future role for the effendi.[41]

Farid's definition of the great man involves a revaluation of the one who speaks and writes for someone else.[42] Here the recuperation of the effendi as nationalist hero required addressing two audiences: the British and the Egyptian people. On the one hand it was necessary to respond to British criticisms disparaging effendi masculinity and suitability to participate in government; on the other hand, the case had to be made to other "original Egyptians" that these effendis were really their brothers and that they were the rightful heads of the household. And it was precisely in family metaphors, as we shall see, that Kamil's biographers sought to naturalize the nation and its representation.[43]

The following is a catalogue of virtues a great man must exhibit: a powerful will (*quwwat al-irada*), self-reliance (*al-i'timad ala al-nafs*), sincerity, courage, fidelity, striving for good, exceptionally active, quickness of mind (*sur'at al-khatir*), proper knowledge, power of oration, complete honesty, and a clear and effective use of language.[44] Farid went on to elaborate on each of these at length. He described the power of oration as "the capital [*ra's mal*] of a leader of feelings."[45] The braiding together of knowledge and sentiment through the vehicle of discourse was viewed as essential to making claims on the new national space in which unrelated bodies were increasingly bound together in their shared activity as readers and, even more, as listeners. But who gets to speak?

Farid suggested a great man was made of the same clay as the rest of mankind but his spirit was exceptional. Mustafa Kamil was then introduced as an extraordinary, great Egyptian man. The loudness and clarity of his voice were key elements of his greatness. His voice was raised loud when some men were settling into the occupation and others were waiting for salvation from God. Farid was careful to contextualize the loud voice as being employed in a public space and in particular places, Egypt *and* Europe. Other aspects of his comportment were also made explicit. His head was always raised proudly, and he taught others to follow his example. He was not cowed by the display of unprecedented military might, by the spectacles accompanying "the army of occupation going and coming, reinforced by mighty fleets and soldiers assembled on the shores of Great Britain."[46] Kamil was a powerful phoenix rising from the ashes of a once majestic culture to reclaim for it its lost glory, honor, and freedom.

The aim of the eulogy was not to examine why only certain men get heard in certain arenas. How a particular kind of education (Western-style) and particular skills, whether legal, journalistic, or oratorical, pre-figured the new model of the great man or why greatness and masculinity could be aligned only on a bourgeois nationalist axis were not queried. Such questions were beyond the scope of Farid's account. In effect, the nation's representative, who was also the representative national subject, appears to be both a part of and apart from the Egyptian family. The repetition and normalization of this paradox would require addressing some parts of the preceding questions, even if unwittingly and inadequately. This was left for the next section, the biography of Ali Effendi Muhammad written by Mustafa Kamil's brother, Ali.[47]

It was through the notion of *wakil* (proxy or trustee; literally, one who is deputed or entrusted) and through the familiarity of kinship that Ali Kamil attempted to materialize the abstract authority that had been claimed by his brother, the fallen national hero, and was now being claimed in his stead by the Watani Party. The biography of the two men's father was presented in order to provide a genealogy for and thereby authorize Mustafa and his type as representative(s) of the nation.

Ali Effendi Muhammad was born near the Nile Delta town of Tanta in 1231 AH (1816 CE), during the reign of Muhammad Ali. He came from a family of prosperous grain merchants. The family wealth was accumulated in the mid-eighteenth century by the great-grandfather al-Sayyid Ali. The grandfather, al-Sayyid Muhammad, had three sons, of whom only Ali survived. Ali was educated at first in the traditional manner by a *faqih* in reading, writing, and memorizing the Quran. Showing intellectual promise in his studies, he caught the eye of the local authorities and at the age of ten was entered into Muhammad Ali's recently established military school at Tura along with other children of merchants. One of his classmates, Isma'il Muhammad, later became president of the Legislative Council (*majlis shura al-qawanin*).[48]

The biographer provides some details about his father's admission to the Tura school that convey the ambivalence, if not fear, that was associated with government schooling in its early days. For one, his mother went with him and stayed in a house his father had purchased nearby. Ostensibly, the proximity of his mother would ensure that his link to the family was not severed. Second, a special written dispensation was obtained from the governor of Gharbiyya Province, Ali Bey, and given to the principal, Salim Agha, to "permit his son to leave the school whenever he wanted" in order to visit his mother.[49] Attendance at a government school during the first phase of the experiment in public education caused quite a bit of trepidation, to say the least. However, the author's aim was not to highlight the coercive aspects of Muhammad Ali's education policy.

Through perseverance and personal striving Ali Muhammad flourished intellectually; moreover, he developed traits of piety and propriety (al-taqwa wa al-salah) that he exhibited throughout his life. After five years at Tura, he was transferred to the Khankah School on the island of Rawda near Cairo, where he studied for another four years. At nineteen, he earned the rank of al-mulazim al-thani ("second lieutenant") as an artillery engineer (muhandis tubji) and was appointed as a tutor at his school. Soon he was transferred to the Bridge and Barracks unit of the engineering corps, rising to the rank of al-mulazim al-awal ("lieutenant"). All of these accomplishments took place during the reign of Muhammad Ali. He continued to rise through the ranks but more slowly under the successors Abbas and Said. Under Abbas he earned the rank of al-yuzbashi al-thani and under Said al-yuzbashi al-awal ("captain"), with an appointment to the general staff.[50] He also served for awhile under Khedive Isma'il in the Department of Public Works, until he was finally placed in retirement in 1298 AH (1880/81).

Because of Ali Effendi Muhammad's induction into the state apparatus that Muhammad Ali began to build, Mustafa and Ali Kamil's family became intimately tied to the modernization of Egypt. Their father's first wife was the daughter of Muhammad Hijazi, whose eldest son, Ahmad Effendi Hijazi, was the head secretary (ra'is kitab) of the Office of Irrigation in the Department of Public Works. Ali Muhammad's first son, whom he had with his first wife when he was forty-two, became a pharmacist and died in 1320 AH (1902), at the age of forty-eight; the second son studied law, held a position in the Mixed Courts, and died in 1305 (1888) at twenty-nine; the third son, Husayn Bey Wasif, was an irrigation inspector in Fayum and became Ali's and Mustafa's guardian when their father died.

After Ali Muhammad's first wife died, he married again in 1280 (1863), this time the daughter of Abd al-Rahman Effendi Khalil, an engineer. Their firstborn died at twenty-six after graduating from the School of Medicine and just as he was beginning a promising career as a doctor. In 1286 (1869) he married a third time, taking as his wife Mustafa Kamil's mother, the daughter of Captain Muhammad Effendi Fahmi.[51] The maternal grandfather's grave in the village of Ibnas in Minufiyya became a site on the annual *mawlid* circuit because of his descent from the Prophet.[52] Ali was born in 1287 (1870) and Mustafa in 1291 (1874).

The author underscored the point that his father "served the government for 48 years" and delineated the ways in which he helped, literally at times, to build and to defend Egypt. He cited the construction of new barracks and railroad stations, the inspection and renovation of fortresses on the Red Sea coast. He noted his father's devotion to the education of all his male children as another act in the making of Egypt. Furthermore, he apparently assumed responsibility for numerous others as the wakil for families of relatives and friends who had lost their head of household; at one point, he was the wakil of thirty-two families. Highlighted also was the fact that he kept meticulous records so each of his children knew not only their date of birth, which was a rarity, but also the hour and minute they were born.[53] Ali Effendi Muhammad died in 1303 (1886) at the age of seventy-two and left behind a substantial estate.

The narration of their father's life was perhaps of more central importance to the nine-volume biography than any of Mustafa Kamil's political speeches and articles. At times the details of Ali Muhammad's biography might appear quite irrelevant to the larger story, which was intended to portray a life quite distinct from Kamil's. Nevertheless, I think it was precisely in order to minimize the starkness of that difference that the two stories are braided together. In the person of the young effendi Mustafa Kamil there was on exhibit a world of change for which very little in the popular imaginings of place and identity in the early twentieth century provided adequate templates for a sensible translation. A rehabilitation of the violence of Muhammad Ali Pasha's state-building practices into a narrative of modernization and Egyptianization through the figure of a familiar paterfamilias was essential to the larger story.[54]

The figure of the father was also crucial to naturalizing the new notion of representation that nationalist politics presupposed. The "nature of the new politics," as Mitchell has demonstrated, was already changing in the 1860s, and the institution of a new education policy was the harbinger of and vehicle for that change: "The placing of the schools at the centre of the city can mark the moment when a new politics of the modern state appeared. From this centre was to extend the surface of a field that had no previous existence. Education was to be set up as an autonomous practice, spread over 'the entire surface of society,' with a distinct purpose. The new schooling introduced earlier in the century under Muhammad Ali had been intended to produce an army and the particular technicians associated with it; schooling was now to produce the individual citizen."[55] Father and son inhabited two moments in a history of intersections between the expansion of modern state power and education. In the father figure, a loyal effendi of an old order (which had itself only recently been new) was materialized. In the son, a citizen effendi of the new national order was struggling to emerge.[56] Mustafa Kamil's right to make claims on the state was authorized by indexing his father's service to the precolonial Egyptian state, but his right to do so on behalf of all Egyptians was made meaningful through the concept of wakil. That concept would have been intelligible to the majority of Egyptians since it was both a name of God — the ultimate guardian and provider — and, as the biography reveals, it was part of common legal practice.[57]

The defense, sustenance, and advocacy of the weak and the voiceless presumed in the definition of wakil also presumed a conception of masculinity. Adulthood and masculinity are normatively located in the male person at the moment he begins to demonstrate an ability to protect and provide for others. This was also a moment of authorization, which Cromer sought to deny Egyptians in his taxonomy of races in Egypt:

> But with all this [a whole host of flaws], the Turco-Egyptian has some redeeming qualities. The glamour of a *dominant race* still hovers as an aureole, albeit a very dimmed aureole, round his head. He is certainly not more corrupt than the Egyptian; he is more *manly*, and the greater the quantity of Turkish blood running in his veins, the more will his manly qualities appear. He is sometimes truthful and outspoken after his own fashion. He has a rude standard of *honour*. Go where you will in Egypt, if any bit of administrative work requiring a certain amount of energy has been well done by a native official, it will generally be found that the official in question is a Circassian or a Turco-Egyptian, who is probably more Turk than Egyptian. The Turco-Egyptian can, in fact, still to a certain extent *command*, and that is why, with all his defects, and in spite of the fact that the class to which he belongs is generally Anglophobe — although there are some notable exceptions — it will often be found that the individual Englishman will get on well with the individual Turk, and better with the Turco-Egyptian than with the pure Egyptian, the Syrian or the

PUNCH, OR THE LONDON CHARIVARI.—November 21, 1891.

THE "EGYPTIAN PET."

Professor of the Noble Art of Self-Defence. "NOT UP TO IT YET, YOUNG 'UN."

"We desire that Egypt should be strong enough of herself to repel all external attack, and to put down all internal disturbance."
Lord Salisbury's Speech at the Guildhall, November 9th.

2. Not Fit to Rule. *Punch*, November 21, 1891. Credit: Rare Books and Special Collections, McGill University Library. Reproduced also in Mansfield, *The British in Egypt*.

Armenian. The northerner and the Oriental meet on the common ground that the Englishman is masterful, and that the Turco-Egyptian, though less masterful than the pure Turk, is more so than the pure Egyptian. The Englishman belongs to an imperial race, and the Turco-Egyptian to a race which but yesterday was imperial. The English, Nubar Pasha once said to me, "are the Turks of the West."[58]

Cromer made the "pure" Egyptian male's ability to rule himself and others contingent on possessing a proper masculinity, epitomized by the Englishman and followed by other imperial races. There was a very clear calculus behind this derivation of dominant masculinity, in which race and empire were fundamental factors, and all three were considered mutually constitutive.

Mustafa and Ali Fahmi Kamil's intervention by way of providing a self-consciously alternative and oppositional history interwove a distinctively Egyptian masculinity with the story of national rejuvenation. In the speech Mustafa Kamil made in Alexandria marking the centenary (according to the lunar calendar) of "the choice made by the people of the great Muhammad Ali as governor of Egypt," national history and national manhood met on the field of battle:

The Mamluks had barely been crushed [as] Muhammad Ali turned his attention to these people [*ce peuple*] in order to see what they were capable of. He saw, that even after such calamities and perils, they could still accomplish great things. He divined a latent force that slept within them that could overturn mountains. With his subjects, he shaped the soldiers of his army, and what soldiers? Conquerors who carried the flag of victory, men whom no people could see without surrendering, heroes who held high the prestige of their commander and made the name of Egypt synonymous with glory and strength. Muhammad Ali made these fellahs [*sic*], for so long mistreated by events, indomitable [soldiers] who made the earth quake and with whom no army dare measure themselves. This man created energy from lethargy, willpower from quietness, and above all he was victorious. From where did this extraordinary force come that completely changed the Egyptian to such a degree that the wounded refused to leave the battlefield and that even the child became enamored of war? *From where did this upheaval rise that has stupefied the universe and how did this people oppressed until late and without willpower suddenly become a warrior people, conquering and dominating?* The secret of this change and upheaval resides in Muhammad Ali's comprehension that

there was in Egypt buried treasures of courage and intelligence, treasures
that he knew how to find, exploit and make admired by the entire world.[59]

Although from the current historiographical perspective it is possible to
dismiss Kamil's account of Muhammad Ali's transformative accomplishments as a romanticized picture of an enormously violent, painful (especially for the newly heroic *fallah*), and complex period of Egyptian history, at the same time one should be careful not to elide the contestatory
nature of the cultural politics of the colonial period. It was against the
backdrop of a highly charged matrix of negative racialized and gendered
signifiers that Kamil attempted to normalize this narrative of national
manhood and national becoming.

Another intervention by a prominent Egyptian figure from this period
illustrates the intensity with which this new field of cultural politics was
suffused. A characterization of Egyptian masculinity similar to Cromer's
prompted Qasim Amin, usually heralded as the father of Egyptian feminism,[60] to write an impassioned defense of his people's manhood against
the racist claims made by a French traveler.[61] Charles François Marie's
offensive book *L'Égypte et Les Égyptiens* was published in 1893.[62] In this
book, Le Duc d'Harcourt (as the title page identifies him) devoted an entire chapter to the topic of Egyptian masculinity in the form of martial
spirit or, more precisely, the lack thereof.[63] The basic argument, surprisingly, given the anti-British position of the French at the time, supports
continued British tutelage on the grounds that the Egyptians were infants
just barely crawling out of their "state of barbarism." He invoked history
to demonstrate Egyptians' lack of national feeling, which he understood
as a collective willingness to die bravely in war. He maintained that it
was a passivity born out of centuries of submission to foreign conquerors,
such that, "The idea of open resistance and struggle seemed incompatible
with their nature."[64]

Perhaps aware of the nationalist appropriation of Muhammad Ali as
a founding father and rueful of the French mishandling of the Egyptian
Question, Marie attacked the myth of the founder's great citizen army.
Comparing the present (at the end of the nineteenth century) to the 1820s
and 1830s, the author conceded that Muhammad Ali's period might have
seemed different. Even a French spy had reported on the well-trained
force at the Pasha's disposal — one that would have required fifty thousand
French troops to defeat. However, he continued, as the French regretfully
discovered in 1840 and again in 1882 (when the British took action and the
French idly stood by), appearances could be misleading.[65] The Egyptian

troops lacked valor and courage because they lacked the proper spirit; in other words, they were not patriotic: "Can one believe that military training alone—learning to handle arms according to theory or the precise application of military rules—has the ability to transform men? Can one, by using this method, turn a subject, miserable, and cowardly people into brilliant (robust) and courageous troops?"[66] He answered himself a few pages later: "No military education, I believe, can transform the present Egyptians into good soldiers as long as the officers—the ones who are indigenous—are made of the same stuff; that is, under the uniform all one finds is a fellah."[67] By the end he has elaborated a racialized masculinity with a base, cruel, and indolent core that the British, even if they were inclined to, could not fundamentally change.[68] What he termed the "abaissement de la race égyptienne" and the consequent "persistance . . . de certains traits peu à l'honneur de la race" were attributed to moral (and climactic) conditions that could take centuries to undo.

Qasim Amin's response, published in 1894 in book form under the title *Les Égyptiens*, was a "summary refutation" of d'Harcourt's thesis on Egypt.[69] His essential strategy was to reverse the claims of his opponent. One point of near convergence was Amin's claim that, although Egyptians were clearly not cowardly, a people with a nation to defend fought more ferociously and were more willing to die than a people ruled by foreigners. The evidence of this was to be found in Egypt itself during the reign of Muhammad Ali. This not-so-subtle critique implicitly places the blame for any deficit in contemporary Egyptian masculinity squarely on the shoulders of the British occupiers.

Amin's very first words conjured the peasant body as an image of strength and endurance: "The contemporary fellah, Muslim or Copt, is in height generally tall, strong, and well-built, he possesses a rare physical energy. He is simply dressed, very poorly nourished and even more poorly housed. He completes the most grueling work, under a burning sun, without murmuring and almost content with his lot."[70] He then argued through the interpellated peasant form that Egyptian men are indeed courageous, and had d'Harcourt bothered to meet any real Egyptians he would have seen that; he would have also seen the passion for education and the respect among Egyptians for those who had acquired education.[71] Amin's location of the educated effendi and the physically strong fallah in one orbit was necessary to recuperate an embattled Egyptian masculinity.

Performing an early Saidian deconstruction of Orientalism, Amin wrote:

But I understand M. le duc d'Harcourt perfectly. He presented himself during several winters a trip not lacking in charm. He consulted some travel novels, taking care to choose those that said the worst of Islam which he detests with his entire soul. He saw, from the veranda of the New Hotel and from the carriage that transported him, a poor population, having a simple exterior, and voilà, he's got his book. Let us, however, apply a little reason. If, on my arrival in France, I had met a cripple, would I have written in my notebook: France is peopled by cripples? Would I have told the truth about the French nation?[72]

Key to Amin's refutation of d'Harcourt's opinion of Egyptian backwardness was the place of history in a nation's progress. First, he faulted the Frenchman for failing to cite any examples from the present (Egypt in the 1890s). He argued, somewhat contradictorily, that d'Harcourt deliberately drew all of his evidence from the time of Muhammad Ali, Said, and Ismail: "He did not note, or did not want to note, the transformation—I would say revolution—that has occurred in the lives of the fellah today."[73] Amin then went on to list the same accomplishments cited by Cromer and others to justify British rule in Egypt: the peasant was now safe in his person, taxes were fixed and regular, the rule of law was applied, etc. Most important, he argued, was a change in peasant consciousness that was manifested in their increasing sense of being legal persons, citizens with rights and expectations of good government: "il commence à s'occuper des affaires publiques et à émettre des opinions sur les actes de son gouvernement."[74]

This statement represents an instance of producing the rupture in historical time necessary for the emergence of modern Egypt, to the extent that its prior histories, including a long tradition of peasant petitioners, were obscured or erased, while its national manhood was simultaneously rooted in an authentic, indigenous precolonial past.[75] Amin inscribed the rupture in evolutionary terms, arguing that a "real government" was established during Muhammad Ali's reign, which placed Egypt on the path of progress and civilization.[76] Ironically, it was in his colonial present that the reality of self-government based on the rule of law, the marker of modernity, was closer to becoming a reality. In other words, it was that imminent realization of a new order that he had to historicize and explain. Throughout the book and up to the very end he strategically elided the fact of the British colonial presence. He alluded to his reason for doing so in the conclusion, where he rejected d'Harcourt's assertion that the reforms Egypt had experienced were all the result of English administration.[77]

Amin mapped the birth of a nation-state with new temporal and episte-mological bases across the improving bodies of the *fallahin* and into the receding spaces of nonrational government ("le dernier asile de l'esprit de l'ancien régime"), all mediated and made possible by the new educated effendi. He charts the barbaric feudal stage through which the French themselves had to pass before becoming "a great and beautiful nation." He expresses his bewilderment at d'Harcourt's refusal to grant Egyptians even the possibility of becoming modern, at his insistence "that our past will forever be an obstacle to our reawakening." [78] By performatively insti-tuting a rupture in historical time, glossing over the colonial, and making a claim on progress, Amin was able to distance himself from a past, which he admits was in part shameful, and insist on a present reality that contra-dicted the need for continued British rule.

Conclusion

Amin, like Kamil, was forced to take up a position in relation to time — signaled in part by appropriating a narrative of material and ideologi-cal transformations in the lives of Egyptian peasants — in order to view the recent past and present as essentially different. This move marked the arrival of national time. A novel epistemology and ontology of Egyp-tian identity were being articulated in these texts, in which difference, of race, class, and gender, and its persistent erasure constituted the modern nationalist claim on what were diverse and contested political and cul-tural fields.

The subjectivity of the authors was strategically muted or amplified de-pending on the point of entry within these fields. In the insistence on a nationalist history, the authors assumed a position of objective authority so that they might freely imagine a shared, unfragmented culture. In the articulation of a nationalist politics both viewed authorization in this do-main to be contingent on the habitus of a new masculine subject. [79] In a letter to Muhammad Farid, Kamil expressed as much. He was writing to decline a prize that Farid had arranged to be awarded to Kamil in recog-nition of his political work in Europe on behalf of Egypt: "Thank you all very much. However, I am unable to accept a commendation I do not de-serve and an honor I did nothing to win. I also cannot accept that patriotic sentiment [*al-shu'ur al-watani*] is something a man should be rewarded for having, since he would not be a man without it." [80] In Kamil's formulation, nationalism became a prerequisite for manhood and vice versa. Although nationalism was accorded a certain level of historicity, as we have seen, masculinity was perceived as being always present, merely waiting for someone "to exploit and make admired by the entire world." However, masculinity is not an empty signifier, naturally occurring and common-sensical or outside history. It is an effect of gender that, in this instance, was being produced as resistance to colonialism and as a necessary condition of national identity.

That resistance did not always take the shape of an organized nationalist movement or explicit denunciations of imperialism, as in the case of Mustafa Kamil. There were other responses to the colonial attempts to define Egyptian masculinity as aberrant or deficient. These did not aim to deny the claims but rather incorporated them into proposals for the regeneration of Egyptian men. Even for Kamil, the claim that Egyptian men could be real men only through expressions of patriotism presupposed certain ideas of masculinity and the body that were current at the time.

First and foremost was ubiquitous talk of character formation, in which self-discipline was a grounding principle. Kamil was a model subject, as illustrated by his daily routine after becoming a lawyer:

6 AM – 7 AM: wake, pray, breakfast, walk to the Qasr al-Nil Bridge
    for exercise
7 AM – 12 PM: reading, writing, legal business
12 PM – 3 PM: lunch, nap
3 PM – 5 PM: reading
5 PM – 7 PM: visits to friends and relatives
7 PM – 9 PM: reading
9 PM – 12 AM: dinner, socializing

This information was not restricted to private papers and forgotten but was published and circulated with an explicitly didactic intention.[81] The character of the next generation was to be formed through modern education at school and proper upbringing at home, and upbringing would enable success at school.

Ali Kamil stressed that the relationship between Mustafa and his father was especially close. In a long section that follows a scene illustrating Kamil's achievements as a student, the author explored the influence of their father on the development of his son's personality and emphasized how he transmitted his strength of character to him.[82] He then generalized about the importance of father-son relationships, asserting that teaching by example has a much deeper effect on the student than teaching through books. It was the same difference as that between "ingrained excellence" (*al-husn al-matbu'*), which was ever-present, and "manufactured excellence" (*al-husn al-masnu'*), which was fickle. Ali appealed to Egyptian fathers to give their sons both kinds of education since they would complement one another and produce in the boy a virtuous character and bring him closer to perfection.[83] He reiterates the importance of fathers and ancestors by arguing that if the reader were to look at any of the great heroes from history they always had an example to follow from among their own genealogical line.[84]

The institution of a pedagogical relationship between fathers and sons enabled an interesting expansion of the notion of kinship. The author pushed the paternalistic analogy by associating the father's role as the wakil of thirty-two families with his brother's stewardship of "hundreds of thousands of families" as a "father of the oppressed" (*abi al-mazlumin*), "author of a new generation" (*munshi' al-jil al-jadid*), and "creator of Young Egypt" (*mukawwin misr al-fatat*). He was all of these things because of his representation of the people's collective demand "for their rights that the occupation had taken away."[85] But perhaps more important, Mustafa Kamil was an exemplar of the respectable masculinity that was a necessary condition of the modern politics of nationalism.

By forcefully locating the source of his brother's genius, the strength of his character, and his will to represent the deprived in their paternal line, Ali Fahmi Kamil ensured that the modern effendi as a new kind of gendered subject — translatable across geographies — would nonetheless have local roots. Moreover, the move from his father's custodial duties involving a specific set of people connected to him by kinship (or similarly close) ties toward his brother's responsibility for "hundreds of thousands of families" connected to him only by their ostensibly common demand for the return of what was stolen from all of them was accomplished by making that object of loss simultaneously particular and universal, historical and eternal. The nation had to be figured, paradoxically, as a family with an identifiable local genealogy that was necessarily variable in time and space and at the same time as the manifestation of an abstract set of rights and responsibilities that were invariable over time and similar across space.[86] As we will see in the following chapters, making Egypt appear timeless and in time with other nations continued to require the repeated reworking of masculinity through diverse forms of embodied and discursive practices.

3

INSTITUTION

Physical Culture and Self-Government

As the nation's paternity was being settled, effendi masculinity cast its attention on a project of reproduction. The generation of new bodies, imagined in national terms, emerged as a primary facet of the discourse. This explains in part why at the beginning of the twentieth century education was a hotly contested issue in the politics of the modern state. Education was at once constrained by colonial policies and championed by nationalists as the key to Egypt's future as a renascent nation. However, despite the critical battles over curricula and budgets resulting from these conflicting objectives, education in this period assumed a far more expansive definition than schooling.[1] Relating character development to masculinity, the nationalist pedagogy of the effendiyya incorporated a growing interest in physical culture, the care of the body. As figure 2 in chapter 2 illustrates, the colonizer deemed the body of the Egyptian male unfit for national service. While that illustration, like many of the other colonial examples we have seen, singled out the Egyptian soldier, the Arabic discourse on physical culture that emerged in Egypt at the end of the nineteenth century positioned the effendi as the target of reform.

In the broader colonial discourse on subject races and their capacity for self-government, the effendi-type, as we saw with Cecil and Milner, was generically deficient. Caught in the colonizer's gaze, the typical Egyptian male body was weaker, less disciplined, and insufficiently masculine. Yet that difference instituted at the metaphoric level could not in the practice of colonial rule be sustained as the final truth of the native. It was the likelihood of reforming the indolent and corrupted offspring of the precolonial body that provided justification for a continued colonial presence.

In the right hands and with rigorous discipline, proper training, and efficient administration it was possible to produce balanced budgets, but ultimately this was not sufficient reason to continue the occupation. Rather, it was colonialism's ethical mission—to re-form Egyptians in order to reproduce a solid race of men constituted on a principle of government of the self and eventually capable of self-government—that finessed the right of conquest.[2]

In this regard, there was no need to establish explicit time frames or for policy to conform to ideals, since the project of self-constitution could always be considered incomplete because of native inadequacies. Humphrey Bowman's commentary on the condition of sports education in the Egyptian schools—in which he was a government inspector, appointed in 1906—reiterates this colonial view of Egyptian bodies and their capacity for change decades later. In his memoirs Bowman wrote of a football match between two primary schools that he refereed (one of his duties as schools inspector):

> On one occasion the score was love-all at the end of the stipulated hour. This was due not so much to the equality of the sides as to the indifferent standard of the play. I decided (as the rule was) to let them play another ten minutes each way, in order if possible to obtain a result. Immediately the Egyptian teacher in charge of one of the two schools came up to protest. "Sir," he said, "my boys are very tired, sir, and," he added, "one of my boys has broken his leg." This I learnt referred to no more than a slight graze on the shin, and I was firm. "Well," I said, "that's my decision as referee, and if you will not let the boys play, I shall have to give the game to the other side." This had its effect. The protester's school, making a prodigious effort, scored a goal just before time. He came up again, this time all "nods and becks and wreathed smiles." "Thank you, sir, so much for letting them play longer. I knew they would win if they only had this chance."[3]

The condescending tone that leaps from Bowman's text was typical of colonial officials' racist attitudes toward members of the effendiyya. The class from which the potential caretakers of the nation would come was especially denigrated by colonial discourse. Such treatment did not go unnoticed by Egyptian men, like the teacher in this passage, who lived under this infantilizing and feminizing regime. The retired official did accord the natives—here, the children of the middle classes—a modicum of approbation. It could be said he was obliged to do so if his career as a missionary of civilization was to have meant anything. Bowman observes in the next paragraph: "But the British influence in games and sports was certainly all to the good, and fair play has been instilled as an axiom. To-day the Egyptians excel in football, swimming, and other sports, and an Egyptian has represented Cambridge University at 'soccer.'"[4] This type of praise was part and parcel of the broader discourse of colonial liberalism. The rest of Bowman's text belies this positive rendering of Egyptian athleticism as it expresses a general feeling that Egyptians were still in need of proper molding to become fully formed and suitably civilized—that is, the colonial project must continue.[5]

The magnitude of the change in the way Egyptian male bodies were portrayed by the end of the nineteenth century is conveyed in the following description written by Edward Lane in the first half of the century: "In general, the Muslim Egyptians attain the height of about five feet eight or five feet nine inches. Most of the children under nine or ten years of age have spare limbs and a distended abdomen; but as they grow up their forms rapidly improve. In mature age most of them are remarkably well-proportioned—the men, muscular and robust; the women, very beautifully formed and plump; and neither sex is too fat."[6] According to Lane, the most famous and perhaps most perceptive of English observers of Egyptian life in the nineteenth century, the average Egyptian body seemed to measure up quite well to the ideal physical form of that period. If he had still been around in the early twentieth century, Lane might have been at least puzzled by the likes of Bowman, but he certainly would have been amused by the Egyptians who began to articulate a discourse of sports and fitness that seemed to be based on a profound sense of physical inferiority. As much as its appearance may have been based on misplaced anxiety and an inaccurate perception of Egypt's corporeal reality, this discourse and the numerous practices related to it came to play a critical role in the Egyptian nationalist project and the constitution of effendi masculinity.

Print Culture and Modern Subjects

It is instructive to review the history of print in Egypt since the main sources for this chapter are magazines that began publication in the latter years of the nineteenth century and, more broadly, since the epistemological and linguistic transformations accompanying this new mode of cultural production had significant bearing on the history of subject formation.[7]

Much had changed in the fortunes of Egypt in the half century since Lane's writing of *Manners and Customs of the Modern Egyptians*. With the signing of the Anglo-Ottoman Treaty of Balta Liman (1838), a commercial agreement enforced by the London Convention (1840), Egypt had been firmly inserted into the world economy as a dependent monocultural producer of cotton. The resulting formation of large estates impoverished a large segment of the country's peasant majority, conceivably leaving them in much poorer health. At the same time, an upper and middling Arabic-speaking elite began to take shape. The Egyptian intellectual and cultural scene underwent tremendous growth, supported by the economic boom resulting from the high price of cotton in the international market in the 1860s, largely affected by the civil war being fought in the United States. Under Khedive Isma'il (r. 1863–79) a number of reform projects were newly undertaken or renewed. The educational system was expanded on the primary and secondary levels, and the student missions abroad that had been suspended since the end of Muhammad Ali's rule were restored. One historian has referred to it as a period of "great intellectual flourishing."[8]

During this period new technologies of communication were born — print journalism, wire services, and more rapid forms of transportation. Juan Cole argues that this phenomenon was responsible for the growth of a shared political consciousness among a broad spectrum of the Egyptian social formation and that it was a major factor in the 'Urabi revolution.[9] In this regard, print journalism was perhaps the most significant of the new forms of communication.

Muhammad Ali had established the first printing press at Bulaq around 1820 for the publication of military instruction manuals and other materials related to the administration of state.[10] From 1826 school textbooks were printed for such subjects as composition and grammar, arithmetic, logic, religion, poetry, and literature.[11] An official broadsheet, *al-Waqa'i' al-Misriyya* (Egyptian Gazette), was published starting in 1828. Eventually this press, the Bulaq Press, became a major source of the dissemination of translations of historical, literary, and scientific texts from European languages.[12] Other presses were established in the years after in Cairo and Alexandria.

The 1870s witnessed a vigorous expansion of the press and publications. The first Arabic daily newspaper, *Kawkab al-Sharq* (Star of the East), was established initially as a weekly in Alexandria in 1873. The first issue of Rifa'a Rafi' al-Tahtawi's educational magazine *Rawdat al-Madaris* (Garden of Schools) came out in April 1870. In 1875, the Taqla brothers, Salim and Bashara, began publication of a newspaper that has survived into the present as Egypt's leading daily: *al-Ahram* (The pyramids). Literary, scientific, and women's magazines were also established during the last quarter of the century.[13] Two prestigious journals, *al-Muqtataf* (The collection) and *al-Hilal* (The crescent), which is still in print, were founded, respectively, in 1876 and 1892. *Al-Muqtataf* had its first run in Beirut but was moved to Cairo in 1885 and ceased publication in 1952, a few months after the Nasserist revolution.

As we will see below, these two journals were major promoters of physical culture as an exemplary modern practice having a national value for Egypt. The preoccupation with sports and fitness, or physical culture, was not limited to these two sources. During the British occupation there was a gradual proliferation of discourse about physical culture both in established journals and in new journals devoted solely to the subject, not to mention the publication of books and instruction manuals. There were also attempts to institutionalize sports and physical education, the early developments of which are sketched at the end of this chapter.

My readings of *al-Muqtataf* and *al-Hilal* are positioned against this broad historical canvas of new material and symbolic investments in Arabic cultural production. For some historians this may seem to be a poor way of situating these journals, pointing to their founders' Syrian Christian origins as already problematizing the story I wish to tell of Egyptian self-fashioning. While this kind of nuance is important on one level, a radical recontextualization of the texts appearing in these journals is necessary to illuminate the nature of the work that seemingly scientific tales of sports and fitness were made to perform at the end of the nineteenth century. In other words, the cultural field created by the textual practices of magazines such as *al-Muqtataf* and *al-Hilal* must be mapped on the discursive level for what they did as much as on the social historical for what they were or intended to be. Lauren Berlant has described this kind of interventionist scholarship as "writing [that] does not aspire merely to comment on or contextualize its object; it brings new objects into being via the textual performance."[14] The religious, ethnic, and political identities of the magazines' owners are important for answering certain questions. For my inquiry, which seeks to materialize effendi masculinity as a historical object, it is more important to regard these sources as sites of cultural production, which leaves open the possibility of their intended meanings being made over in the process of their dissemination and reception.[15] Moreover, it could be argued that "bring[ing] new objects into being" was a fundamental aim of the historical culture producers.[16]

Al-Muqtataf and *al-Hilal* were two of the first and most popular cultural and scientific journals to appear in the Arab East in the nineteenth century. They are regarded as hallmarks of a literary and cultural renaissance that started in the mid-nineteenth century and became known as the Arab *nahda*.[17] The historiography of Egyptian modernity, whether in its conventional or revisionist mode, tends to mine these sources for evidence of continuity or change. They are read here as constituting spaces in which an Egyptian modern was being enacted, rather than as products of a sudden modern reawakening serving the cause of disseminating Western ideas to a somnolent Arab mind. Accordingly, the pasts of these magazines and their audiences could just as well be situated in a history of state and society reform initiated in the Ottoman Empire in the eighteenth century as in a history of European economic and political expansion in the region in the nineteenth.[18] Holding the local and the global in the same line of vision makes the form and content of the effendi's engagement with modernity appear as accented variations of similar engagements elsewhere.[19]

The magazines and the texts they disseminated not only evince the emergence of a self-conscious modern subject, but also constitute a performative cultural space in which the making and potential unmaking of subjects was accorded an iterative structure, one guaranteed by the apparent fixity and irreversibility of the new print capitalism. The masculine subject that was produced through the pages of these magazines assumed a temporality by virtue of being repeatable. In the ensuing chapters, I will show how this performative character of the modern subject enabled its proliferation as well as its resignification, within the limits of an asymmetrical colonial modernity and nationalist politics.

One could locate the historical shift represented by the body politics of these journals and their discourse of physical culture by contrasting it to the state discourse of public health and hygiene that arose in the 1870s. In *Colonising Egypt* Timothy Mitchell presents the concern for the population exhibited by such discourse as one example of the complicated ways in which techniques of governmentality inaugurated a new form of power in Egypt.[20] For Mitchell, the drive to create clean, healthy spaces and bodies was a sign of modern power at work, regulating the population while simultaneously individualizing its subjects. Although the overall argument of *Colonising Egypt* — that governmentality conditioned and perhaps narrowed the grounds for agency — conforms to the historical evidence, I aim here to show how the ends of this power were also beginnings by tracing the specific contours of the political subject emerging through an allied, gendered discourse of the healthy body. The injunction in this discourse of caring for the self was related to governmentality but not reducible to it.

Regenerating Men's Bodies, Redeeming the Nation: Games and Exercise

Most of the games of the Egyptians are of kinds which suit their sedate dispositions. They take great pleasure in chess . . . , draughts . . . , and trictrac or backgammon. — EDWARD LANE, *Manners and Customs of the Modern Egyptians*

Gymnastic games, or such diversions as require much bodily exertion, are very uncommon among the Egyptians. Sometimes two peasants contend with each other, for mere amusement, or for a trifling wager or reward, with "nebboots," which are thick staves, five or six feet long: the object of each is to strike his adversary on the head. . . . Wrestling matches are also sometimes witnessed in Egypt: the combatants (who are called "musare'een," in the singular "musare") strip themselves of all their clothing except their drawers, and generally oil their bodies; but their exercises are not remarkable, and are seldom performed but for remuneration, on the occasion of festivals, processions, etc. On such occasions, too, mock combats between two men, usually clad only in their drawers, and each armed with a sabre and a small shield, are not unfrequently witnessed. Neither attempts to wound his adversary: every blow is received on the shield. — EDWARD LANE, *Manners and Customs of the Modern Egyptians*

Edward Lane, our keen observer of Egyptian life during the first half of the nineteenth century, recorded these notes about the games Egyptians played sometime between 1833 and 1835. In the next half century, Egypt underwent massive transformations, including the reconfiguration of the centuries-old political rationality of Ottoman governance. That reshaping was already en route, so to speak, when the British assumed control of Egyptian affairs in 1882. Nonetheless, or precisely as a result, the act of occupation by a foreign colonial power deploying its self-proclaimed superior epistemological and moral armory alongside its military arsenal resulted in the formulation of some novel responses from the new subject race. One of these responses was to theorize the nature of that subjugation in terms of a deficient masculine corporeality.

By the period of nominal independence in the 1920s, physical culture formed a critical element in the discourse of national progress. For example, it would become quite natural to deliver in the same breath an apocryphal quote from the Duke of Wellington—who supposedly attributed his victory over Napoleon to his men's physical preparation, which they had gained from the games they played in school—and an exhortation to Egypt's youth to rise to the challenges of a new era.[21] The *national* framing of the discourse of health and hygiene gained traction in the 1880s and became a matter of common sense to elite and middle-class Egyptians by the 1920s, constituting the bases for the proliferation of physical culture.

The precolonial prescription of exercise for individuals played an insignificant role in the general targeting of the population as a site of reform. Recently, historians of Egypt, drawing on Foucault and building on Mitchell, have begun to explore in detail how the interventionist state through its juridico-medical practices ordered and disciplined society in new ways.[22] The various technologies incorporated in establishing more numerous and denser relationships between state and society also produced a new kind of political subject. In Egypt as elsewhere, the national sentiments and nationalist politics of that subject remained inchoate until the end of the nineteenth century. Whereas the production of national subjects in the metropole involved distinct yet often-obscured imperial horizons, in Egypt the comparable subjects appeared most legibly in the anticolonial register of the nationalist movement.

Before elaborating this point, I want to consider a question of translation: "physical culture" into *al-riyada al-badaniyya*. The term in English, though present in the late eighteenth century, did not gain popularity until the emergence of a physical culture movement in the second half of the nineteenth century. Focusing on building the body through various forms of exercise, including weightlifting, physical culture emerged in places like Britain[23] and the United States[24] as a response to prevailing cultural anxieties about degeneration resulting from factors specific to the respective sociopolitical context: imperial overextension, rebellions, labor unrest, abolition of slavery, immigration, urbanization, etc.

In *al-riyada al-badaniyya*, the second term, a modifier derived from *badan* (body), is rather easily rendered as "physical." The first term, *al-riyada*, is less easily assimilated. It is conceptually complex, having had a long and often virtuous history in the Arab-Islamic tradition. Derived from the root r-w-d, the word was initially used to refer to the domestication, training, and care of animals.[25] When combined with *al-nafs*, the self or the mortal soul, as *riyada* was in early Muslim ethical writings, the expression denotes a process of self-disciplining with the goal of attaining a higher spiritual state.[26] The modern reinscription of *al-riyada* as physical culture was accomplished to some extent through the combination of these two dimensions: the profane and the sacred.

Although the concept continued to have multiple meanings in the twentieth century, standing alone, *al-riyada* came to signify almost exclusively sports or physical exercise in general. Despite this semantic fixity, which firmly externalizes the acts of discipline and signification on the body's surface, the concept always retained a close connection, however reconfigured, to the tradition of spiritual and ethical self-formation. Physical culture, or al-riyada al-badaniyya, that peculiar phenomenon which began to gain global popularity in the late nineteenth century as a character-building practice, was viewed as an essential bridge between the soul and the body in a time of massive material and spiritual displacement. The initial reconceptualization of al-riyada, undertaken in the new cultural field featuring, and significantly shaped by, *al-Muqtataf* and *al-Hilal*, illuminates a crucial performative moment in the construction of the modern subject hailed by Egyptian nationalist politics.

An oft-cited text of Egyptian modernity in nationalist and revisionist discourses is Tahtawi's *al-Murshid al-amin lil-banat wa al-banin* (The trusted guide for girls and boys), published in 1872.[27] Tahtawi (1801–73), although older, was roughly a contemporary of Ali Effendi Muhammad, Mustafa Kamil's father. He was born in the Upper Egyptian village of Tahta to a wealthy family soon to be impoverished by Muhammad Ali's new land policy, which resulted in the confiscation of *iltizam*s (tax farms). He studied at Al-Azhar under the guidance of Shaykh Muhammad al-Attar.[28] Tahtawi served as the imam and chaperone for the students sent on the first Egyptian study mission to France from 1826 to 1831. While there he also studied French and translation and had already begun his long career as a translator of military, legal, scientific, and literary texts. Muhammad Ali's successor, Abbas I, exiled Tahtawi to Sudan. He returned under Said and held various posts in translation and education. Tahtawi became a member of the Diwan al-Madaris (Department of schools) that was re-established under Ismail, and it was this body, according to his introduction to the book, which commissioned him to write *al-Murshid al-Amin*.

In this guidebook on the proper course of education (*tarbiyya*), Tah-

tawi's scope ranged from definitions of civilization and patriotism to treatises on love and marriage. He made some intriguing observations about
the body and sexuality, which I reference in chapter 5. His recommendations for nurturing and growing (al-riyada) the body were nested within
discussions of education and marriage.

Tahtawi first uses al-riyada in its classical sense of nurturing, caring for,
and cultivating character (*al-akhlaq*).[29] It is then deployed to signify organized games in a discussion of forms of sociability in the development of
an urban Islamic culture. A clue that there was a common perception of
games as being childish or even sinful during Tahtawi's time is given by
his emphasis on the fact that they were not proscribed: "Games including
exercises that cause fatigue were not forbidden."[30] The stress on the ac-
ceptability of strenuous exercises is noteworthy.

Tahtawi joined his discussion of al-riyada to an interesting analogy of
the body and the city-state.[31] Reversing the common political metaphor of
the body, Tahtawi references an ancient Sufi proverb which says that when
God wanted a model for the creation of man he looked to the city and its
built geography. The center, containing the ruler's palace, was like a heart
from which life and all circulation emanated. His aim was to establish the
divinely ordained natural inclination of men for community and sociality;
in other words, civilization and urbanity were immanent to humanity. To
thrive, however, the body required tending, al-riyada.

When the idea of riyada as *la'b* (play) appeared again in the *Murshid* it
was in an explicitly pedagogical framework, and it was recommended as
a break from rigorous instruction, a chance for rest and recuperation.[32] In
this case the games were not to be too taxing (*la'b jamil ghayr mut'ib*).[33]
Tahtawi ended the book with a discussion of the importance of caring for
one's health. Exercise, riyada, was prescribed as a cure for laziness and
indolence and as a prophylactic against common ailments that result from
a lack of physical activity. He illustrated its significance by relating the
story of an Arab king whose only son was struck with an illness no doctor could diagnose or treat. He sent for a famous doctor who lived outside
the city. The medicines the healer prescribed were a ball and a polo stick
(*suwlajan*). The first round of treatment included exercises for the arms,
which the boy could perform inside the palace — presumably he was practicing his swing. Then he was to go outside the city walls and exercise by
throwing the ball at the stick to try to knock it down. The boy followed
the doctor's advice and soon his taste for food and sleep returned, and by
the end of the month he was fully restored to health.[34]

Another example of the precolonial-era discussions of physical exercise comes from *al-Muqtataf* when it was still based in Beirut. In 1879, the magazine ran two articles in the same issue under the title *"Al-riyada al-jasadiyya"* (physical exercise).[35] This is the earliest text I have found in the new journalistic press presenting a scientific argument why the body required exercise. The first article spelled out the physiological benefits of exercise and proper breathing to the circulation of blood, the prevention of illness, the strengthening of organs, increasing energy, etc.[36] The second broke down the types of exercises that should be performed and their advantages by age group and class.[37]

The first age group discussed in the article was children from the ages of one to six. Rich or poor, boy or girl, exercise was recommended as a guarantee for a healthier future. Imperative to this process was having the proper space; every family and community, whether rural or urban, was enjoined to organize places in their homes, villages, and towns where children could play unimpeded.

The next group addressed was schoolboys from the ages of six to twenty-one. The obvious benefit of exercise to this group was the strong link between a healthy body and a healthy mind. A cautionary note here expressed the difference between play and organized games. It was argued that in cases where boys were left to play games without proper supervision more harm than good may be caused. It was likely that the leader of the pack, who was usually the strongest and fittest of the bunch, could rally the students around him and eventually defy the teacher's authority off the field. Games played without rules and supervision ended up being pointless and in fact counterproductive to the goal of establishing the disciplinary order sought by the institution of modern education.

The last section of the article addressed two groups of adults: those who worked with their minds and those who worked with their bodies. The author differentiated among classes in order to determine the proper type of exercise to be performed. Because of their general inactivity, the people who worked with their minds (that is, the professional-bureaucratic middle and upper classes) had a greater need for exercise, as it would enhance their mental work and productivity. This also applied to their women. The poor of both sexes, whether urban or rural, were not encouraged to engage in formal exercises because the amount of their bodily movement during the course of a normal week was more than enough to build strong physiques. They were encouraged to take strolls in places with clean air. The article contended that it was the responsibility of the state to provide those spaces for the workers, who were its "source of wealth and pillar of strength." It was recommended that the state build public parks and pay entertainers to perform in them in order to attract the maximum number of people, most of whom would otherwise be whiling away their time and money in cafés and other places of ill repute, breathing dirty air and mixing with bad elements.[38]

Only as European colonial penetration of the Mashriq became a reality did these journals start to consider explicitly the relationship between national success (or decline) and physical culture. *Al-Muqtataf* addressed this link as early as 1882, and *al-Hilal* published its first article on the topic in 1899. The *al-Muqtataf* article, "*Riyadat al-Kuhul*" (Disciplining adults)[39] made the argument that devotion to sports and exercise was a cause of a nation's greatness, while its neglect was a sign and a cause of its decline.[40] The examples of Greece and Rome were given to demonstrate this rule—at the height of their glory, the commitment to playing games and building the body was also at its height. But their fall from greatness had much to do with diminished enthusiasm and support for the physical games. More currently, it was suggested, this axiom was easily proven by observing the Gezira area on a Friday: "One might see the locals riding about in their carriages as if they were sick or ailing. Or one may see young and old Englishmen and their girls and ladies playing croquet, cheeks reddening, and sweat pouring."[41] The class and gender of the sporting English were underscored. The people playing games on Fridays, the article noted, ranged from the experienced politician and the brave leader to the rich merchant and the busy scholar, from young ladies to distinguished women. This anecdote was figured as an explicit critique of the aspiring native elite and the once-ruling class, who saw exercise or any form of physical exertion as something from which their servants were supposed to spare them. The loss of Egypt's freedom was blamed on this idle class. The recovery of freedom would require a regeneration of the native body.

At the time this article was written, Egypt was still officially an autonomous province of the Ottoman Empire, even though its finances had been under the supervision of the Caisse de la Dette Publique (also known as the Dual Control, reflecting the primacy of British and French interests) since 1876. Freedom here was not thought of in terms of political sovereignty alone, but also as a gradually acquired product of personal physical discipline leading to a transformation of or rupture from the old order. To the extent that this free self was constituted as a national subject was taken as a given in the article.[42] Finally, that that subject was imagined as emerging along secular lines was evident from the last sentence, which located religion in relation to the English experience of cultivating bodies:

"The science of bodies did not take precedence over religious knowledge except to instill in souls the duty to uphold its truth."[43] This sentence was added at the end to blunt the explicitly secular argument developed throughout the article, wherein riyada was effectively made to serve the worldly goal of constructing a new social body.[44]

The same article told another story of the rise and fall of civilizations, one which also carefully sidestepped the issue of religion. This time, the two nations compared were the Arabs and the Anglo-Saxons: "The first is a remnant of two peoples [perhaps Arabs and Turks], who, in their conquests, reached India in the east, Spain in the west, Circassia in the north, and Ethiopia in the south. Now she resides in a hut simply hoping to be left alone. Whereas the other nation is a branch of a people who grew to the point that their emigrants filled the lands of America, Australia, and New Zealand. These people now rule vast lands and prevail over three hundred million people."[45] That the critique was of Islamic (masquerading as Arabo-Turkic) civilization's failure to keep up with the West was not very muted. Whether the author of this article was aware at the time of writing that he was foretelling Egypt's own fate is unknown. Only a month or so after his article appeared, the Anglo-Saxon nation was bombarding Alexandria and preparing to occupy Cairo, adding Egyptians to its millions of subjects.[46]

The authors of these articles, who were often Francophone or Anglophone or both, could not have been completely unaware of the internal crises of European societies at the end of the nineteenth century.[47] But their objectives and positioning were such that the reinterpretation of the causes of Western (read at the time as French and British) superiority elided what was obviously problematic about the social realities of those nations and almost exclusively focused on them as offering modalities of success.[48]

It was not only in articles and journals specifically addressing the issue of physical fitness that anxiety over the achievement of the proper masculine form was expressed. A much talked about text among Egyptian reformers at the time was the Frenchman Edmond Demolins's *À Quoi tient la supériorité des Anglo-Saxons?* (To what is the superiority of Anglo-Saxons owed?) which was translated into Arabic in 1899 by Ahmad Fathi Zaghlul under the title *Sirr taqaddum al-inkliz al-saksuniyyin* (The secret of Anglo-Saxon progress).[49] This putatively scientific work established that the secret of Anglo-Saxons' advancement lay in their unique system of education, which placed equal emphasis on the development of the pupil's mind and character (moral and physical). The relationship of the sound body to the sound mind, which had long ago been elaborated within various Islamic traditions, was revisited in the wake of the circulation of Demolins's text and in the context of the redressing of national humiliation by two very prominent figures of the fin-de-siècle period.

In *Hadir al-Misriyyin aw sirr ta'akhkhurihim* (The present state of Egyptians, or the reason for their backwardness), published in 1902, Muhammad 'Umar pondered the needs of a new generation:

> At the center of the umma are numerous young men who are educated and cultured. They need societies which do not reduce their potential, do not do harm to their honor, and do not extinguish the fire of energy and ambition burning in their souls. They are in need of training for their bodies, fitness exercises, breathing clean air in places far from the city. This is necessary to provide because, as we have mentioned, these are educated, cultured youth who know that physical training is the reason for the rise and success of the European peoples — especially the English — who have achieved such obvious mastery through the strengthening of their muscles and the training of their bodies and their various parts. They would not have been so successful if they had not brought gymnastics back into their schools. These people grew up knowing the benefits of exercise.[50]

In *Ghunyat al-mu'addibin fi al-turuq al-haditha li al-tarbiyya wa al-ta'lim* (The essential guide for teachers to modern approaches in education and schooling), published a year after 'Umar's book, 'Abd al-'Aziz Jawish, an inspector of schools for the Ministry of Public Instruction, echoed a similar theme of national rejuvenation achieved through the physical improvement of young men.[51] In a section titled "Influence of the Physical State on the Mind," Jawish considered the difference between weak and strong bodies in their impact on men's character: "The weak one's character and nature change over time. He might become ill-tempered when he used to be mild-tempered, impatient when he used to be patient. The earth cannot bear his cry nor the sky his resentment and anger. This is why it should be obligatory to train bodies and protect them from weakness and sickness. This way the mind would be in a state that would allow it to be instructed and taught."[52] Perhaps not surprisingly, this process of uplifting the body and mind was applicable specifically to the male subject. A few pages later Jawish recommended that to complete the process, it was necessary to avoid the company of the foolish, the profligate, women, and the depraved.[53] Both 'Umar and Jawish were also speaking about and to a classed subject, specifically of the middle and upper classes.

Others had stumbled upon the idea that a successful civilization must have physically fit women as well. In the issue of *al-Muqtataf* for February 1891 a new section was added to the magazine under the heading "Household Management." The "mission statement" which the editors presented to readers as a preface to this section and which was repeated in other issues read as follows: "This section was added to the magazine in order to incorporate in it all that might interest households [*ahl al-bayt*] in terms of knowledge on raising children, organizing food, clothes, drink, as well as the home and décor—things which should be useful to all families."[54] It was in this vein that advice was usually given to women about exercise; that is, it was their responsibility to stay fit in order to take care of their children and home and be attractive to their husbands or, if they were single, in order to obtain a husband and bear children.[55] Women's exercise was in fact the central concern of this inaugural section. The article admonished new wives to exercise vigorously every day by walking outdoors for at least an hour. This activity was to help ensure that when the woman had a baby, he or she would be born healthy and strong. In addition, since it was the natural desire and greatest dream of every woman to have a child, she would want to take these necessary precautions in order to realize that desire and dream. The great majority of articles in both magazines when they talked about strenuous physical exercise, were addressing boys and men; when women and girls were addressed, only light exercise was prescribed, usually under the rubric of cultivating eligible brides and fertile wives.[56]

The ultimate celebration of an idealized male physical form in the modern period was represented in the sport of bodybuilding. At the end of the nineteenth century in Egypt weightlifting as a technique of building bodies captured the imaginations of those who exercised and those who wrote about fitness. To a reader of *al-Muqtataf* who wrote in to the "Issues" section asking about the easiest exercise to do at home, the editor responded with an enthusiastic endorsement of working with weights.[57] *Al-Hilal* ran a series of articles starting in 1899 in which detailed sketches were provided demonstrating the proper use of weights; one article depicts even the type of weightlifting ostensibly practiced among the Pharaohs of ancient Egypt.[58] Older forms of bodybuilding are treated as an ancient phenomenon, never as existing coevally with the modern practice. Other sketches show the various kinds of equipment that could be used in the sport of bodybuilding. Weightlifting and bodybuilding assumed great importance especially in the landscape of Egyptian sports in the decades following the revolution of 1919.[59]

3. "The Ancients and Exercise." *Al-Hilal*, March 1, 1902, 404–5.

The muscular male form was celebrated as a model for emulation. In 1901, *al-Hilal* ran an article reporting on the completion of the body cast made of the famous turn-of-the-century bodybuilder Eugen Sandow.[60] The author exhorted readers to regard the picture of Sandow's statue and marvel at the development of his body. As a boy, the author continued, Sandow was skinny and weak, but he dedicated himself to training his body and learning the proper techniques for physical exercises as well as the physiological principles behind them. As a result, he was now the strongest and most popular of English wrestlers.[61] Although the Arabic noun *musariʿ* is used in the article to identify Sandow and is typically translated as "wrestler"—as I have rendered it here—this was not in fact Sandow's profession.[62] He was a strongman performer who cleverly capitalized on the prevailing sense of British imperial weakness at the start of the twentieth century and developed his own health and fitness industry. The company even published its own trade magazine bearing the founder's name: *Sandow's Magazine*. Sandow also made an effort to go global, as one would say today, by touring South and Southeast Asia attempting to market the special Sandow technique for physical development.[63]

The globalization of the model male physique is evidenced in traces that remained of an "Egyptian Sandow" who traveled the country exhibiting his body and demonstrating his strength at regional saint's fairs and specially organized events in Alexandria and Cairo. His name was Abd al-Halim al-Misri, and he was said to have inspired a generation of wrestlers and weightlifters.[64] He seems also to have been a man of letters and a proselytizer of sorts who contributed articles to nationalist journals about the importance of physical fitness to national progress. In 1911, Abd al-Halim al-Misri wrote an article titled "Cultivate Your Bodies before Your Minds" for the newspaper *al-Huriyya* (Freedom): "The nation's happiness rests on its youth. The men of tomorrow must care for their bodies properly. . . . Physical education will alter their cowardliness and indolence by raising within them a courageous and indefatigable spirit and by teaching them to love freedom and independence."[65] The moral lessons surrounding the care of the body, which accompanied the growing commodification of figures like Misri, were couched in a language of national value. He naturally represented himself as a model of virtuous living and a good son of Egypt over and against his economic and practical role as a circus performer. I discuss both of these themes, the commodification of the body and national value, further in chapter 4.

In the early period of the physical culture discourse the use-value of the body was theorized along largely idealistic lines. *Al-Hilal* took much more interest in this field than *al-Muqtataf*. The journal assiduously reiterated the link between the physically fit individual body and the strong body politic. As I mentioned above, the subject targeted by and developing through these exhortations to exercise belonged to the upper and middle classes. *Al-Hilal* ran a series of articles starting in 1899 under the heading "Exercise and Society" (*al-riyada al-jasadiyya wa al-hay'a al-ijtima'iyya*) in which the explicit aim was to demonstrate the connection between historically great nations and their commitment to encouraging sport.[66] All of these articles reflected the influence of Demolins's popular work *À Quoi tient la supériorité des Anglo-Saxons?* and were in a sense authorized by it.

Demolins, as we have seen, located the origins of the English people's success in their educational and social traditions. Unlike the French and the Germans, the English, Demolins argued, strived to cultivate men who were well rounded and embodied the principle of "self help":[67] "Young men raised, as I have just said, strong of body, accustomed to the real world [*les choses réelles*], having contact with material affairs, always treated as men, accustomed to depending on themselves, envisaging life as a struggle (which is eminently Christian), confront the difficulties of life with a youthfulness superabundant in power [*force*]; they love these [difficulties], they need them, they triumph over them."[68] The figure of the youthful masculine hero, readapted for Egypt's specific sociohistorical circumstances, was constantly reproduced in Egyptian nationalist discourse, especially as the struggle for independence intensified after the First World War.

The first article in *al-Hilal*'s "Exercise and Society" series explicitly cited Demolins in order to underscore the importance of physical education in schools. The article stated that Demolins's study had shown that the English pupil devoted eight hours to sports and non-book learning. This followed the general claim that "scholars who study the character of civilizations have decided that the English have gained their vigor, courage, and equanimity as a product of physical training."[69]

What was wrong with Egyptians that they appeared deficient? In diagnosing the causes of Egyptian weakness, an article from 1899 that served as a preface to the series "Exercise and Society" argued that the fundamental obstacle to a nation's progress was the backwardness of its women.[70] The anonymous author of "Hidden Agents in Society" maintained that whereas government corruption, the ignorance of the population, and fallow land were obvious explanations for the decline of a nation, they did not reveal the fundamental factors underlying the existence of corruption, ignorance, and indolence. And although the author identifies four hidden factors — women, general morals, domestic life, and religiosity — that affect the health and wealth of a society, in the end he boils them all down to the status of women. To the extent that women are at the heart of managing the household and instilling values in children, they hold the most powerful key to a nation's progress. The author concludes with a call for "the instruction, training, and cultivation of women."

What about those other factors? Who were the agents of decline there? They were men: men who visit prostitutes and gamble; who eat, drink, and stay out in excess; who reject religion in the name of science and secular authority. Yet in the final analysis men's public inadequacies were the result of women's private failures as mothers and wives. It was an all-too-easy patriarchal response to colonial occupation: men were weak and that is why it happened, but they were weak because of their women. In chapter 6 I demonstrate, to the contrary, that this gendering of national decline was in no way a simple resolution. A hint of what was truly at stake in the way blame was assigned for national decline was given in a later article appearing in the "Exercise and Society" series. According to this author, also anonymous, "Hidden Agents in Society" had omitted one of the "strongest factors" in making a nation great: physical culture.[71]

The series in general diagnosed the individual upper- and middle-class Egyptian male body as weak from indolence and excess. It argued that the rich used the debilitating heat of the Egyptian environment as an excuse for moving the body as little as possible:

> They order food and eat it while seated. After finishing their meal the servant comes bearing water and a basin so they can wash their faces; then, they dry their faces and have coffee. They remain sitting the rest of the day engaged in listless and rambling conversation. Even when they feel like going out for a stroll, the servant arrives carrying shoes and puts them on their feet and perhaps helps them change their clothes; while another servant hurries to prepare the carriage. As they get in, they complain about the trouble of moving from their original position to the seats in the carriage. . . . This is how they are with everything else in their lives, and gradually their bodies grow fatter and . . . [weaker].[72]

It was from this premise — that elite bodies were not fit for modern life — that *al-Hilal* exhorted its readers to start exercising. They offered scientific evidence of how the body's muscles, bones, and cells were all dependent on exercise for nourishment and growth.[73] The scientific explanation of al-riyada's benefits to the individual and the social body signaled a turn from the spiritual coding that had defined its function as a bettering of the soul. The turn to the body did not mean a turn away from the soul. The shift that was taking place in the concept of al-riyada was one in which the religious, ethical, and political intersected in new ways. Herein, the willing submission of the subject to a regime of corporeal discipline was viewed as essential to building a modern social and political order in Egypt. The remolding of character and morals was identified equally as a major advantage gained from the reconfiguration, or expansion, of al-riyada. Within the cultural field resulting from this extension of al-riyada's ethical parameters to encompass the national subject, the religious self registered ambiguously or as only one part of the modern political subjectivity of effendi masculinity.

Texts relating physical culture and nationalism continued to proliferate through the ensuing decades, spilling beyond the pages of *al-Hilal* and *al-Muqtataf* and becoming gradually recontextualized within a field of sports and fitness with its own specialized rules of practice.[74] In the fin-de-siècle period I examine here the discourse of al-riyada focused broadly on questioning the traditional conceptions of ruling-class culture, on interrogating older models of masculinity, and on centering the effendi body as a site of reform aligned increasingly with a youthful and intensely self-conscious nationalist politics.

The Practice of Physical Culture

One might object that thus far I have demonstrated only that the reform of the indolent and weak male body was a popular topic for a small, educated elite and that the effendiyya could be regarded as targets of a few loquacious, profit-seeking individuals who wished to sell magazines to the same small audience. It would not be outside the realm of possibility, either, that these texts genuinely reflected an existing set of gender anxieties and obliquely expressed new political aspirations. But could they be said to have produced an entirely new subject? Indeed, effendi masculinity was not confined to rhetorical musings, which I have argued were in themselves much more than a new narcissistic exercise. The rhetoric of effendi masculinity was continued and sustained as discourse through its institutionalization beyond the press. The birth and reproduction of Egypt as modern and free could not be accomplished otherwise.

The extent to which the early nationalists were convinced of the need to reform Egyptian masculinity was revealed in some of the institutional locations—for example, schools, clubs, sporting teams, and youth groups—in which new practices of the body were explicitly mandated and enacted. The institutionalization of al-riyada was a contested process, one that addressed questions of national and gender identity in interesting and complex ways, and although formal politics played a role in its shaping, by being a site for the working out of new knowledge about masculinity and youth it would shape the political in turn.

There was a relationship between everyday performances and political modernity. Yet while political strategies—nationalist, monarchical, and colonial—played a critical role in delimiting a particular domain of action they do not fully explain the formation of the political subject that could, or could not, inhabit this new space.[75] Such an explanation requires not only turning to other archives for new evidence—as I do here—but also demands asking another set of questions altogether. What was this political modernity that Egypt inherited from the West, according to some accounts, or crafted for itself, according to others, or creatively adapted, according to still others? Is it sufficient to reevaluate the formal political playing field by including new actors and new events in order to understand the nature of this modernity? Or must one move beyond the agonistic terrain of colonial and nationalist politics, "interrupting the teleologies of Romance,"[76] and explore the question of modernity in terms of the kinds of subjection it required and from which escape, liberation, was a prescripted (im)possibility?

Institutionalizing al-Riyada: Effendi Masculinity and Youth

Demolins's pronouncement that "these young men are the hope of the country"[77] referred to English boys educated in the public school method, which ostensibly prepared them for "triumphing over life itself." Mustafa Kamil was most likely familiar with Demolins's work. Since his return from France with a law degree, he busily engaged in the mobilization of an anticolonial political consciousness among students and young professionals. In a speech he gave on February 19, 1904, at the annual awards ceremony of the primary school he had founded in 1898, Kamil echoed Demolins's assessment of the importance of schools in shaping future men and leaders: "Schools shape the men who become powerful arms for the nation [la patrie]. By showing more interest in these schools, you are giving to the nation more power and more energy, and you are preparing for her better days."[78] Through his speeches, articles (in French and Arabic), and organizing efforts, one of Kamil's major objectives was to build a sense of solidarity among the young effendi class. It is not an exaggeration to say that Kamil instituted and later represented the figure of the heroic masculine youth as a political subjectivity within the emergent Egyptian nationalist discourse. This figure was not only a rhetorical device. It was to be made real through a process one might call the institutionalization of youthful energy.[79]

On April 8, 1907, A. Mitchell Innes, an Englishman, and several Egyptian notables, including Idris Bey Ragheb, Isma'il Pasha Sirry, Umar Bey Lutfi, and Abd al-Khaliq Tharwat Bey, met to discuss the formation of an Egyptian sporting club.[80] They decided to establish the club on the southeastern side of the Gezira (the present-day chic neighborhood of Al-Zamalak) and to issue a thousand shares in the endeavor at five Egyptian pounds per share. Innes, the British adviser to the Ministry of Finance, was selected as president, probably in order to facilitate acquisition of the land for the club from the government. The group met again on April 24 at Innes's residence, Amin Sami Pasha taking the place of Tharwat Bey and Muhammad Effendi Sharif serving as the secretary of the club. The men constituted themselves as members of the governing council of the National Club for Sporting Games (*Al-nadi al-ahli lil-al'ab al-riyadiyya*). For the next two years, the governing council occupied itself with the procurement of funds, the acquisition of land, and the construction of the club building. Meanwhile, the members had decided to change the club's name to the National Club for Physical Culture (*Al-nadi al-ahli lil-riyada al-badaniyya*).[81] The change was made at the suggestion of Amin Sami Pasha, who argued that the new name was a more all-encompassing construction. The opening ceremony for the club was held on February 26, 1909.[82]

The establishment of the National Club for Physical Culture is a highly noteworthy event in the annals of nationalist historiography.[83] It is usually described as a step in the natural development of Egyptian nationalism. For example, 'Umar Bey Lutfi's enthusiasm for establishing the sporting club was said to ensue naturally from his earlier involvement in the nationalist cause. The progression here was from the founding of the Higher Students Club in 1905 by Lutfi and Qasim Amin, with the encouragement of Mustafa Kamil, to more mature organizations like a national sporting club or political party. The focus of historians of nationalism on the level of founding fathers and institutional development—conceived quite strictly—has obscured the sea change that the desire to translate and create a new kind of institutional life signified in epistemological and material terms. Following are some of the questions buried by conventional political history's refusal to attend to seemingly trivial cultural matters: What was at stake for Egyptian men as *men* in the founding of a national sports club alongside a student political club? What kinds of shifts in local cultural practices and conceptual fields were signaled and shaped by this new institution? What sorts of translations and transformations of subjectivity were necessary for and necessitated by the installation of this new institution and its practices within the Egyptian social and cultural fields of the early twentieth century? And what did Al-Nadi al-Ahli mean for Egyptian politics?

In the shifting language of the time one finds some clues as to how to recontextualize the establishment of Al-Nadi al-Ahli. The change in the name of the club to emphasize physical culture was indicative of the process I referred to in the preceding section whereby the concept of al-riyada was being redefined to answer for a perceived problem of the modern subject. It is not surprising that the recommendation for changing the name came from Amin Sami. Amin Sami, like Mustafa Kamil, Qasim Amin, and 'Umar Lutfi, was educated in France.[84] The culmination of his interest in taxonomy and genealogy was represented in his magnum opus, a two-volume work on the geography and history of Egypt.[85] This resituating of Egypt within a scientifically elaborated encyclopedic framework was tantamount to an existential project, for if nations were to persist in modernity nothing less than modern proofs would suffice. Similarly, the precise definition of al-riyada and the accurate labeling of the activities that would take place in the new national club were crucial to its continued existence in the future.

In a speech given at a meeting of the General Assembly on February 6, 1919, roughly a month before the major student demonstrations that sparked Egypt's first nationalist revolution, the president of Al-Nadi al-Ahli, Abd al-Khaleq Tharwat, interpreted for the audience the motives behind 'Umar Lutfi's establishment of a national sporting club.[86] He suggested that the idea for the club emanated from a desire to build solidarity among the students and graduates of Egypt's higher schools. He was worried that as a group they would disperse, after graduation in particular, because of professional and personal preoccupations, if not by geography. He also worried that they spent all of their leisure time at coffeehouses or secluded at home. He imagined solving two problems with the creation of a sports club: the lack of political solidarity and the lack of physical activity among Egypt's next generation of leading men. The upheavals of the following months demonstrated that he succeeded, perhaps far beyond even his own imaginings.

The desire for a national sporting club speaks to a number of problems that Egyptian social reformers had begun to confront as early as the 1870s or even the 1830s, when the main conceptual problems were related to the nature of the link between state and society forged by modernization. But over two decades into a colonial occupation, the central conceptual problem became how to construct modern subjects in a not-so-modern society. One possible solution that gained adherents was the concentration of reform efforts on the body itself. The mantra of a sound mind in a sound body was not a mere rhetorical device but the stuff of nation building. By the end of the nineteenth century, although al-riyada could still be used to refer to a kind of psychic and spiritual disciplining, it was well on its way to being reconfigured to connote exclusively a corporeal location of self-disciplining. The normative force of al-riyada as an ethical and ascetic concept was harnessed to the very material and aesthetic project of building national bodies.

The early history of the institutionalization of al-riyada on a state level through the educational system suggests an initial ambivalence about including physical education in the national curriculum, but it was quickly overcome.[87] The first time any mention was made of physical education was in the curriculum for a teacher's training program from 1895.[88] This plan was, in a sense, the product of the educational reorganization attempted by Cromer's colonial administration.

After a meeting of the High Consultative Committee of the Department of Public Instruction on January 30, 1895, a board was established to reorganize Dar al-'Ulum (Teacher's college). The timing of these changes coincided with the colonial takeover of the Ministry of Education, which, ostensibly as part of fiscal austerity measures, had been reduced to a subdivision of the Department of Public Works. The resulting program of study formulated by the special board of the High Consultative Committee added a section to the third year on theories of education, which was divided into "General Issues in Education," "Physical Education" (*tarbiyya jismiyya*), and "Mental Education."[89] The tarbiyya jismiyya course explored topics with titles like "The Significance of Physical Education," "Objectives," "Physiology," "Methods of Improving Health," and "Physical Culture" (al-riyada al-badaniyya).[90] In the following year, physical education was added to the list of subjects for schools attached to the Department of Public Instruction. It seems to have been implemented only on a trial basis, since examination in this subject was contingent on permission first being obtained from the department.[91] In 1897, physical education became a more regular part of school life and included a final examination graded on a scale of twenty points — similar to subjects like *tafsir* and *hadith*, grammar, history, hygiene, and foreign languages.[92]

This move by the state dovetailed with the discourse on physical culture being articulated at the time by Egypt's reformist elite. In 1899, *al-Hilal* applauded the government for realizing the importance of al-riyada al-badaniyya and instituting it as part of the curriculum in its schools.[93] This endorsement follows the long discussion continuing from earlier issues exploring the links between "Exercise and Society."[94] This particular passage references Demolins and other unnamed "scholars of civilization" who have studied the character of the English and concluded that their energy, drive, and patience for work all came from their deep investment in exercise and sports. Nevertheless, that the press continued to pressure the government to increase its support of physical education in schools and sports in clubs throughout this period and into the 1930s and 1940s suggests that the state was never seen to be doing enough to institute al-riyada as an essential mechanism for molding Egyptian bodies to a modern world.

An institution founded a few years after the National Club, in part as a reaction to the limitations of the state, was the National Olympic Committee. The committee would play a major role in the cultivation and internationalization of the aspirations of Egyptian athletes, especially in the period after the First World War. (I discuss Egyptian participation in the Olympics and the role of the committee at length in chapter 5; here, I simply wish to locate it as another point within the expanding discourse of physical culture.)

Prince Umar Tusun, a major patron of al-riyada, announced his plan to form the Egyptian Olympic Committee (EOC) in a letter to Muhammad Pasha Said, president of the Council of Ministers, on September 6, 1913.[95] He requested the appointment of two delegates, one from the Ministry of Public Instruction and one from the Ministry of War, which was apparently the procedure in other countries. The minister of public instruction, A. Hikmat, recommended the appointment of A. H. Sharman, the principal of the Saidiyya Secondary School and the inspector of physical education for the ministry.[96] After some prodding from Muhammad Said, the minister of war, Ismail Sirry, finally nominated Mackintosh Bey, assistant to the adjutant general.[97] The constitution of the EOC announced the formation of the committee on January 19, 1914, in Alexandria, with Prince Tusun as its president.[98] In addition to the two government representatives, the members included Secretary General Angelo Bolanachi, Treasurer Amin Yahya Bey, Ziwar Pasha, Ishaq Pasha Husayn, 'Umar Pasha Sultan, and Saifallah Pasha.

Prince Tusun's rationale for founding an Olympic committee in Egypt (as well as for his encouragement and financial support of Boy Scout troops in Alexandria) emanated from his conviction that sports was a unifying element and a crucial factor in any nation's development.[99] In the 1920s Umar Tusun became a celebrated figure in the Egyptian press as a model of masculine citizenship. His picture appeared often in the context of praise for his philanthropic work on behalf of the poor, the young, athletes, refugees, and others.[100]

Conclusion

The reality of the effendiyya's anxieties about their national manhood at the end of the nineteenth century was undeniable. The reasons were many and complicated, ranging from the local to the global and from the past to the future. Foremost were the subjugation of Egypt to British occupation and the formation of an anticolonial nationalism that was simultaneously a political, ethical, and aesthetic movement. This was symptomatic of the fact that the nature of colonial occupation was not only a matter of military and economic domination; it was equally and perhaps more insidiously a question of psychological domination.[101] As this chapter has shown, however, the terms of effendi masculinity could not be reduced to an interiorized state: it was in fact quite explicitly an exteriorized and material formation.

Historians of Europe have demonstrated how works like those of Demolins were emblematic of a perceived crisis of ruling-class masculinity, a crisis which became prevalent in the last third of the nineteenth century. Domestic challenges arising from the working classes, women, and "unmanly men" joined with a sense of weakening imperial power to generate numerous critiques, plans, and programs for the rejuvenation and remasculinization of the individual and national bodies.[102] In the context of Egyptian history, this same preoccupation with the rejuvenation of society through the disciplining of male bodies could arguably be shown to have had an Islamic genealogy; nevertheless, the trajectories of these discourses of caring for the self were inextricably intertwined in colonial modernity even while being represented as polar opposites.

Although Western anxieties about emasculation and degeneration were coeval and interrelated with the Egyptian ones, in Egypt's history and historiography alike the colonized elite have been legible only as blind imitators, as self-conscious rebels, and, in the more nuanced language of revisionists, as bricoleurs who had no recourse but to strategically borrow and indigenize Western notions like national honor, character, body, and physical culture. In light of colonial modernity, wherein the two parts— colonialism and modernity— are viewed as mutually constituted, the crisis of English masculinity no longer appears as mainly a response to social pressures from within and the discourse of effendi masculinity as mainly a response to factors from without; rather, it becomes possible to speak of the colonial encounter as generating a cultural field of hegemonic masculinity within which and against which particular national identities vied for definition, status, and influence. That complex field of interrelations was simultaneously reworked in colonial and nationalist discourses as a system of hierarchical and discrete cultural bodies divided into a bifurcated model of modernity in which there were clear originals and copies, centers and peripheries. Effendi masculinity appropriated and redeployed concepts generated by the colonial encounter with Britain through a process of radically reconceiving an exclusively Egyptian past as a means of making a claim on a politically constrained present and a nationally conceived future. This modernist project, however, remained incomplete and was contested and resignified, as we will see in the following chapters.[103]

4

ASSOCIATION

———

Scouting, Freedom, Violence

The projects of Edmond Demolins and Mustafa Kamil were contradictorily identical and different because of their location on opposite sides of the colonial divide. The young men whom Kamil sought to cultivate were charged with the additional responsibility of liberating themselves and their nation from the young men who were the object of Demolins's study and admiration. I pursue the paradox further here by recounting the story of a quintessentially imperial organization that was at once deeply foreign and homegrown: I situate the history of the Boy Scouts within and between the contexts of the emerging global youth movement and Egypt's anticolonial struggle during the interwar period.

With the onset of the First World War, Egypt entered a historiographical black hole, and unfortunately my book maintains the silence. Not much is known of Egypt in the period between 1914 and 1918 except the major political developments taking place there.[1] The British occupiers imposed martial law and severed Egypt's formal historical ties to the Ottoman Empire after the Ottomans entered the war on the side of the Central Powers. As a result, after more than thirty years of having an ambiguous legal status, Egypt was finally annexed to the British Empire as a protectorate. In substantive terms, this simply meant that there was no longer a reason for the occupying power to hide its effective control of the state behind the veil of advisers. As it was no longer an Ottoman province, Husayn Kamil, a member of the Muhammad Ali dynasty whom the British picked to replace the recalcitrant Khedive Abbas II in 1914, was granted the title of sultan. He died suddenly in 1917, and the throne was presented to his brother, Ahmad Fuad.

When the war ended, the Ottomans surrendered and the empire was ultimately dissolved; the Egyptian cultural and political scenes, which had taken so many of their cues from Istanbul, were irrevocably altered. As the preceding chapters have suggested, the changes were indeed underway throughout the nineteenth century; nevertheless, the total erasure of an Ottoman political horizon, which had defined the landscape of most Arabic speakers of the region for four hundred years, was a momentous occasion.

While the effendiyya had begun negotiating the terms of an exclusively Egyptian identity in the late nineteenth century with the rise of nationalist politics, the aristocratic class of Turkish speakers was still circulating within an Ottoman cultural orbit. No matter how much integration may have taken place in the preceding decades through marriage and other alliances contributing to the formation of an Egyptian territorial and high-cultural specificity, the existence of Istanbul as an independent seat of a venerable royal and religious tradition still managed to carry considerable symbolic weight, if not command an affective loyalty.[2] The imminent vanishing of the Ottoman dynasty impressed upon the descendants of Muhammad Ali once and for all the importance of at least appearing to identify with Egypt and to cultivate an affective relationship with Egyptians.[3]

One constituency to which the new monarchs of Egypt would provide patronage in an attempt to demonstrate their national character was the youth of the effendiyya. The recently crowned Sultan Fuad established Egypt's first indigenous Boy Scout troop in the fall of 1918. This would be one of Fuad's many symbolic gestures aimed at promoting the legitimacy and Egyptianness of the Muhammad Ali dynasty. The troop was composed of fifty students selected from the Sultaniyya Secondary School. Each student was furnished with a Boy Scout uniform altered to invoke the local national context: along with the traditional tan uniforms and red bandanas they were appointed with dark *tarbushes* bearing the crescent symbol of Egypt. The new sovereign of Egypt spared no expense; in addition to the uniforms, all of the necessary equipment for conducting Scouting activities was imported from Europe.[5]

Egyptians had begun seeing these strange boys in uniforms marching through their city streets before the First World War. These troops were all composed of boys from the foreign resident communities in Egypt. Their public appearance in increased numbers and frequency as the war approached spurred a group of Egyptian nationalists led by Ja'far Wali Pasha to launch an effort to start a local troop. The outbreak of war and the

British imposition of martial law derailed their efforts: any public assembly of five or more people was outlawed and punishable by imprisonment.[6]

The prewar youth culture of colonial modernity—although somewhat tarnished by the brutalities of the Great War, as we will see below—was vigorously promoted by different interests in the context of renewed nationalist agitation in Egypt. Robert Baden-Powell's philosophy of Scouting[7]—he saw it as a regenerative process restoring to men the qualities of manliness diminished by modern civilization—had been hailed by Egyptian reformers before the war and was again upheld as a useful model for cultivating nationalist youth after the war.[8] The masculinist agenda underlying Scouting was redirected from being a corrective to modernist excess to nation-building and anticolonial strategies. Nationalists and the Palace viewed Scouting as a site through which national identity and a sense of belonging and loyalty could be constructed. The performance of one's Scouting activities, such as dressing in uniform, marching and chanting in unison, and so forth, was meant to create *within* the Scout a point from which his duties to the nation and the monarch would flow naturally.[9]

In reading the original rationale behind the creation of the Boy Scouts in Britain, Egyptian advocates of Scouting surmised that even Westerners put only so much stock in the ability of schools to cultivate men.[10] The project of rearing the self-reliant, courageous, and disciplined young man required by the nation had to be undertaken within supplementary spaces. This was especially true in a place like Egypt, where schooling was limited to a very small percentage of the population. In the prewar discussions, the Scouts were put forward as a vehicle of social reform. Scouting, it was argued, should aim to bring within its fold all boys, those in school and those roaming the streets.[11] The promise of reforming individual male bodies and molding a new generation for national service seemed to be a crucial factor in the initial attempts to establish an Egyptian Scouting organization. The Egyptian idea of the Boy Scouts was, from its inception, conceived as a pedagogic space in which the nation and its modernity would be produced. Moreover, through its mission to strengthen the body, develop the mind, and build individual character, Scouting was another location within the broadening physical culture field that seemingly addressed and activated the masculine subject-in-formation.[12] However, the Scout, as we shall see, was also an open container, an always-incomplete subject whose ends were never fully determined by a singular political rationality.

"A Paedocratic Regime"
BOY POWER AND THE REVOLUTION OF 1919

With the onset of the revolution in Egypt in 1919, the Royal Scouting movement was forced to halt temporarily, as many of its members joined the student demonstrations and were consequently expelled from their school and troop. A group of student leaders met in late September 1919 to discuss the formation of what they considered to be the first truly Egyptian Boy Scout organization. On April 4, 1920, they announced the establishment of the National Scouting Society in Cairo. The timing of Sultan Fuad's launching of the Royal Scouting movement and of the students' meetings to organize their own Scouting organization demonstrates both the significance attached to the idea of the Boy Scouts and its reappropriation by Egyptians as a local national phenomenon. The contours of this process of localization shaped and were shaped by the political context.

Sultan Fuad's move is not surprising considering his desire to influence the trajectory of the nationalist movement. Marius Deeb suggests that there was also major competition between Fuad and his relative, Prince Umar Tusun, during the last years of the war as they both sought to control the formation of the Wafd.[13] The Wafd, the major political party in Egypt until the revolution of 1952, had begun as a delegation advocating self-determination and insisting on the right to represent Egypt at the Paris Peace Conference. Fuad begrudgingly backed Sa'd Zaghlul to head the delegation as a move to counter Tusun's own ambitions.[14] Tusun was purportedly the originator of the idea that Egypt should make its case for independence at the peace conference and laid the groundwork for Zaghlul's meeting in November 1918 with Reginald Wingate, the British high commissioner in Egypt.[15] Unfortunately for Tusun, in addition to Fuad's opposition to him, Zaghlul felt that, given Tusun's rancorous history with British officials, his participation would only encumber the process of obtaining a hearing for an Egyptian delegation.[16]

At the meeting, Wingate expressed skepticism at the Wafd's plan to travel to London to present Egypt's case for independence in preparation for the peace conference in Paris. (At this time the Wafd had not formally constituted itself as such and was composed only of Zaghlul and two other members of the defunct Legislative Assembly, Abd al-Aziz Fahmi and Ali Sha'arawi.) Wingate cited among other reasons for his surprise and disbelief Egypt's immature public opinion and, correspondingly, the delegation's lack of a truly representative status. Immediately after this meeting, the Egyptian Wafd was formed as an official body to represent the national right to self-determination, with Zaghlul as its president and four other members in addition to the two mentioned above.[17] The group launched a major petition campaign throughout the country to seek the people's mandate and thereby prove to its colonial masters that the Wafd had national support to negotiate for Egypt's future. When the British recognized that the nascent party's expansion might mobilize a "mass movement" for independence, they forced the Ministry of Interior to issue orders to obstruct the campaign.[18]

In December 1918 the British military authority in Egypt rejected the Wafd's application for permission to travel to London. Events developed quickly after that. The pro-Wafd prime minister, Husyan Rushdi, resigned, the Wafd stepped up its agitation for recognition, and the British responded heavy-handedly. The arrest and subsequent exile of Zaghlul and his colleagues to Malta in 1919 sparked large urban student demonstrations in March and April as well as other uprisings throughout the country soon afterward.[19] The arrival of the Milner Mission in December, ostensibly to inquire into the causes of the unrest, was met with strikes, demonstrations—including the famous one led by Egyptian women— and a strictly enforced boycott. The Wafdist Central Committee, formed on April 11 to direct matters in the absence of Zaghlul, urged Egyptians not to have any contact with the members of the mission. One sign of the success of the boycott is the narrow range of testimonies recorded by the Milner Mission: they were mostly from English and other European residents of Egypt. The political scene resumed a level of calm as the Wafd finally entered into negotiations with Milner in London in July 1920.

The gendered and sexualized language of the English reactions to the revolution of 1919 was remarkable. In his account J. W. McPherson, an officer in the Cairo City Police, used phrases like "epidemic of impotence" and "humiliating events of this year of shame" to characterize the significance to the British of a mass native revolt. The obverse of such statements was that by rising up Egyptians had succeeded in reclaiming their masculinity. McPherson would not have seen it that way. He felt that the English showed weakness by hesitating and were thoroughly and embarrassingly trounced as a result. It was a time of decision:

> What the Egyptian wants really, though all may not know it clearly, is to be governed—the want is instinctive and hereditary and a splendid fellow he is when well led, as witness the behaviour beyond all praise of the natives who helped us in the war. It is not in my competence to say

whether it is for us to govern him, or to leave him to himself, however disastrous the result; but I think Roosevelt's advice was sound, "Either govern or clear out." . . . if we wish to put a term to this protracted shame and to avoid an ultimate calamity on a bigger scale we had better act soon for we cannot indefinitely feel about amongst the breakers without going on the rocks.[20]

The decision Britain made two years later was to grant Egypt a form of nominal independence (see below). The political uprising of Egyptian men was deemed a personal affront to the honor of British colonial officials. The refusal to participate in the Milner Mission's inquiry was a further insult, as it belied the gentlemanly conduct of imperial politics.

Offensive in the extreme were the tactics employed by the natives. The Wafd had deployed student activists and young professionals (effendiyya) as shock troops to ensure the noncooperation of the population. The effectiveness of these young men in resisting colonial power and exposing its incivility can be deduced from the mocking tone of contemporary observers. J. M. N. Jeffries, a British journalist traveling through Egypt at the time, filed several articles filled with what can only be described as a hysterical scolding of Egyptian nationalists. An excerpt of his report from Tanta after so-called riots there resulted in the deaths of some British soldiers reads as follows:

> Like most other places in the country, it has of late suffered from a paedo-cratic régime, that is to say, rule by boy students of the town, encouraged and stimulated by a well-known group of wirepullers. They have seen to it by house-to-house visits and intimidating letters that their elders and betters shall not express any opinion contrary to their own, and in a number of cases have obliged them to take a boycotting attitude towards the Milner Commission. These so-called students have indulged themselves in their usual sillinesses, spitting on the shadows of passing British officers, hissing at them in their most natural tones, scrawling on the walls near the camp: "Down with the Commission!" "God curse Milner!" "God rash the dog Milner!" and like phrases, but they assume another importance when the children rule.[21]

These youthful political actors, denounced for their infantile and animalistic behavior by this British observer, were simultaneously valorized in nationalist discourse.

The language of the nationalist portrayal is also interesting for its telling details of the gendered politics of anticolonial struggle. The revolution seemed to crystallize a new set of criteria for determining who could become a legible citizen-subject, and how, within Egypt's emergent national public sphere. The longer process of reconfiguring masculinity along bourgeois lines threaded through and shaped the terms of this form of political subjection.

In his account of the revolution of 1919, Abd al-Rahman al-Rafi'i depicted a very interesting scene of student activism that indexes the changed nature of politics and its middle-class vector as well as a normative masculine subject. The students had organized a group of marshals (*al-shurta al-wataniyya*), identified by red armbands, in order to police and regulate the course of the demonstrations and meetings.[22] After the demonstrations of March 11, which had been marred by unruly behavior resulting in property damage, the student organizers wrote to the Arabic and foreign language press calling on Egyptians to respect the limits of proper political protest and apologizing for the excesses of their less civilized compatriots.[23]

The participation of the unruly, unrespectable subjects (*al-ghawgha'*) is not explored in any detail but appears only in passing and has thus been easy for later historians to overlook.[24] Forming part of the collective Egyptian nationalist consciousness today, partly via Rafi'i's text, is the importance of the role played by students in staging the revolution. As I will argue more fully in the final chapter, what was briefly made to appear in this account was not simply the repressed other of an increasingly hegemonic bourgeois masculinity but a constitutive exclusion through which the (particular) universality of the Egyptian modern was maintained. The appearance of these students on the national political stage entailed the exclusion of other kinds of actors and other kinds of scripts, to the extent that effendi masculinity became synonymous with the national past and future.[25]

The inscription of the domain of national politics as a limited and limiting space underwritten by bourgeois masculinist norms was not unique to Egypt. The central consideration is the specific ways in which an exclusive Egyptian political subjectivity was shaped in colonial modernity. The interwar politics of youth as it overlapped with organizations like the Boy Scouts formed a pedagogic and performative site of subject formation. It affords an invaluable vantage point from which to regard the working out of Egypt as a simultaneously inclusionary and exclusionary process after the revolution of 1919, one wherein a particularly universal kind of allegiance to, or identification with, the national state was produced alongside a host of hybrid others.[26]

Youth and National Identity
THE POLITICS AND PUBLICITY OF SCOUTING

After its foundation, the National Scouting Society (NSS) competed with the Royal Egyptian Boy Scouts Association (REBSA) for troops. The principals of the Khediviyya and Sultaniyya schools, J. M. Furness and Muhammad Khalid Hasanayn, established REBSA and were its president and vice president, respectively. Competition to control the political field — the leitmotif of the relationship between the Wafd and the Palace for the next three decades — was evinced here in an interesting way. The troops that formed in government schools like 'Abidin, Tawfiqiyya, and Khediviyya joined REBSA; by the end of 1920 it had registered thirteen troops.[27] The organization attempted to hobble the competition by petitioning the Ministry of Public Instruction to mandate membership in REBSA of any Boy Scout troops that would be established at government schools in the future.[28] The charter of REBSA explicitly rejected a national characterization, probably in order to attract the various foreign troops in Egypt to its fold.[29]

There was growing interest in Scouting among students at private religious and minority schools as well. Troops were established at the Coptic, Iranian, and Ilhamiyya schools, in addition to others. Following its mission to include as many boys as possible,[30] the NSS encouraged the Manual Trades Workers Union to support a troop in Bulaq.[31] Troops of the NSS were established also in numerous provincial capitals, including Alexandria, Port Said, Suez, Tanta, Damanhur, Benha, Al-Mahalla, Kafr al-Shaykh, Al-Ismailiyya, Qina, Luxor, and Girga.

One of the most enthusiastic bases of support for the movement was the urban Nubian communities. Scouting may have given this minority group a purchase on Egyptian national identity. A publication of the Nubian community heralded the Nubian Boy Scout Troops as the pride of Egypt and the marker of their community's renaissance.[32] The Cairo Nubian troop was singled out for praise for being among "the largest, best-prepared, and most active" in the movement.[33] In fact, this Nubian troop was still active at the end of the 1930s.[34]

Ironically, especially if one belonged to the Wafdist nationalist branch of the Scouting movement, the establishment of Boy Scout troops was one of the recommendations of colonial administrators searching for ways to impede the growth of political consciousness among Egyptian youth. One of the Milner Mission reports on the educational system made the following recommendations: "Headmasters and other masters should be urged in all possible ways—through games, athletics, inter-school competitions, reading-clubs, etc. etc. to enlarge the outlook of boys, to foster a spirit of loyalty to the school, and to lay the foundation of self-reliance, public spirit and co-operation. In this connection we attach great value to the Boy Scout movement, which is now starting in Egyptian schools."[35] Countering the influences of home and street by a proactive youth policy on the part of colonial administration was a major theme running through the reports on education. Furness, the headmaster of the Khediviyya Secondary School who helped found REBSA, may have been inspired to do so because of certain preconceptions of effendi masculinity: "It was essential, in his opinion, that something should be done to help fill the lives of young men, after their school days ended, with more social amenities and to raise the standard of civilization in the social life of the higher classes. Better education would counteract the present baneful influence of mother and servants upon children. What was required was education in the humanities: merely social and ethical training."[36] The very old trope of dangerous harem influences was still circulating and used in this case diagnostically, ending with a prescription for the "social and ethical" reformation of effendi masculinity.[37] Although the motivation behind each position was anything but similar, colonial administrators and nationalists alike saw the Boy Scouts as a mechanism for the production of a proper political and ethical subject.

The subjection that one British official desired of young Egyptian masculinity was to an idea of permanent tutelage, of deferred self-government:

> As far as training of character is concerned, they had not got the type of teacher who regarded it as his duty to train character. One of the reasons was the rigidity of the code that regulated all education matters. In order to get the best type of teacher, you need to pay them more. The only solution which Mr. Wells saw was to bring out a band of men from England, trained under one dominating personality at home, and then to let these men take their pupils right up through the Elementary, Primary and Secondary Schools. At present, there was no encouragement for teachers to consort with pupils in after-school hours: for example, in organizing excursions, debating societies, games, etc.[38]

What Wells, an administrator at the Ministry of Education, pragmatically articulated was a vision of the duplication of the ostensibly well-rounded, that is, self-regulating, subject of liberalism in Egypt, with the difference that this could be accomplished only through the "dominating person-

ality" of an English mentor.[39] The impossible ideal underwriting the recommendations of these officials was the willing submission of the Egyptian
subject, which could be brought about only through a masking of colonial
relations by fabricating a myth of independence.[40] The new subject would
owe its existence and thus its allegiance to the power granting it the status,
however incomplete, of being free and sovereign. Such a power could not
be British or Egyptian; rather, it describes a network of relational force
fields generated by the apparatuses of colonial modernity, including such
practices as Scouting. Accordingly, the docility of this subject in relation
to colonial or nationalist claims would remain uncertain, conditioning the
grounds on which political contestation would take place.

The colonial and nationalist agendas, with their different and contradictory political aims, were equally implicated in the project of delimiting the particularity of Egyptian identity. The bourgeois effendi, whether
denounced or valorized, emerged as the modern subject par excellence of
Egypt. It was the recognition, at some level, of the powerful attraction
the promise of modernity had for the effendiyya that motivated leaders of
the nationalist movement to reinterpret colonial symbols like Scouting.
They would quickly find that this was a difficult strategy to sustain—and
not because the colonial rulers were better players. Rather, the bourgeois
nationalist pursuit of cultural hegemony as a political objective consistently snagged on the problematic position of the people. Despite regular rhetorical deployments under cover of identity and unity, the political
economy of colonial, class, and gender relations ensured that the people
could not be squared with the effendi—the most viable and intelligible
subject of nationalist politics.[41]

In the early twenties, the membership of the NSS was estimated at
around seven thousand students. In Alexandria, Prince Tusun organized
the city's different troops into one society under his leadership and patronage. At one point, the Cairo and Alexandria bodies were joined, but
soon after, Prince Tusun disbanded his organization, and the NSS followed
suit. Apparently, despite funding from both societies, the supervision of
the various troops proved impossible. Some troops were reported to have
taken on an explicitly militaristic agenda and even armed themselves.[42] By
the end of the decade the only remaining society was the one headed by
King Fuad. It was difficult to establish the details of how this monarchical
monopoly was achieved, but if one were to connect it to the developments
in the formal political context, an explanation of sorts emerges.

The NSS was active during the heyday of the Wafd Party in the first half
of the 1920s. The final return of Sa'd Zaghlul from exile, the unilateral

British declaration of Egyptian independence, along with the promulga-
tion of a constitution on April 19, 1923, which made Egypt a parliamentary monarchy, formally altered Egypt's subordinate status and for a brief
while held the promise of a new beginning.[43] However, Egypt's sovereignty was still seriously compromised by the terms of the treaty signed in
1922. Britain had retained control of matters relating to Egypt's defense,
minorities, foreign interests, imperial communications, and the Sudan.
It also continued to exercise influence in most other domestic matters
through its advisers to the government and through the Palace. This chi-
merical resolution to the Egyptian problem created a situation in which
the Palace and the leading party, the Wafd, were in constant conflict over
the exercise of power within a sphere that was, in a sense, preshrunk. This
deferred sovereignty constrained the domain of politics and ensured a
continuous state of crisis.

As a result, in the second half of the 1920s the Wafd found itself in a
seemingly never-ending struggle with either the Palace or the British
Residency or both. In 1928, after other relatively unsuccessful attempts by
the Palace to destroy the Wafd and by the British to control it, the Palace
managed through a political scandal to unseat the Wafd, to eventually
suspend the constitution, and to usher in a period of almost uninterrupted
authoritarian rule for the following seven years.[44] During this period, the
image of a youthful vanguard instructing their failed elders was held out
as a hope for a better future. In the cartoon reproduced here as figure 4,
the linkage between student politics and national honor is made through
a reversal of the normal pedagogic roles.

The political message of this cartoon was directed just as much at the
national leaders as at the radical effendiyya of the revolutionary period,
who by the early 1930s were beginning to be viewed as an old guard elite.
The cartoon suggests that the generation of 1919 had, by the end of the
twenties, long forgotten their political goals and even needed to be reminded of the meaning of national honor.[45] Meanwhile, the reactionary
forces of the Palace and its supporters expanded their territory, occupying
such sites as the Boy Scouts.

In a cartoon from two years earlier (figure 5), the prominent intellectual,
writer, journalist, and politician (he was a founder of the Constitutional
Liberal Party), Husayn Haykal is depicted as having already pawned his
honesty, reliability, credibility, and honor and now seems ready to sell his
last quality: masculinity. Understandably, the conventional description of
the politics of this period (until the mid-1930s) is framed within a narrative of lack and failure. This is true whether the framing was by contempo-

4. The Arabic word in the image is "honor." The first line of the Arabic caption (not shown) reads, "Students vs. Teachers." The second, "Young Pupil — True you are professors of medicine, law, and philosophy . . . but honor is something else. So you all listen up for the first lesson!" *Ruz al-Yusuf*, March 21, 1932, 7.

raries or by historians of various stripes — liberal, nationalist, or Marxist.[46] According to one perspective, the development of Egyptian nationalism along liberal lines was doomed to failure because it was encumbered both by the presence of reactionary forces and by the lack of a suitable social basis for growth:

> The political reasons [for the failure of the "liberal experiment"] were the presence of the British and of the King. Liberal growth is a tender plant that needs the proper political atmosphere in order to flourish, and that plant was smothered before it could grow. It would be more correct to qualify the period 1922–1936 as an abortive attempt to give birth to liberal institutions, for while the framework for the institutions was there it was hemmed in by so many restrictions as to render it unworkable. . . . As long as the Egyptian government was forced to defer to the monarch, and the monarch was subservient to the occupiers, no stable government could develop.[47]

Even the heroic efforts of leaders like Zaghlul were not enough to forge a liberal polity when faced with a society that was not quite fully in the

5. The first line of the Arabic caption (not shown) reads, "What remains!!" The second, "(The newspaper *al-Siyasa* in its latest issues has plummeted to the lowest of the low.)" The third, "Dr. Husayn Haykal— How many cents will you give me for the only thing I have left?" *Ruz al-Yusuf*, April 19, 1930, 9.

modern age: "They had to *cope* with a society that was only just beginning to slough off the skin of Ottomanism and pan-Islamic traditionalism and to think in terms of national interests and patriotism" (emphasis added).[48]

Partha Chatterjee has demonstrated how this focus on formal politics in the history and historiography of non-Western nationalisms has served simultaneously to render the narrative of lack or failure coherent and to obscure other domains of the political.[49] It is within those repressed domains that one can locate both the differences of nationalisms within colonial contexts and a shared epistemological ground with "Western universalism."[50] Refocusing the historical lens on the performance of Egyptian middle-class masculinity through the discourse of Scouting, for example, illuminates a field of political and social becoming in which the question of failure is displaced, because, rather than presupposing an exemplary model and searching for an originary moment, the historian is redirected to mapping a series of beginnings that were always already interconnected spatially and temporally.

The activities of the Boy Scouts received much celebratory attention in the press in the years after the revolution; this remained true even after the explicitly nationalist societies ceased to exist. Muhammad Effendi Tawfiq Nasim launched the first Egyptian Boy Scout magazine in April 1921.[51] It published articles and pictures covering the activities of the various troops, the annual jamboree, and sports. The visit of Baden-Powell to Cairo occupied much of the print space in the second issue.[52] The magazine also included didactic pieces examining backward customs that were in need of reform.[53] Moreover, news and pictures of the Scouts appeared in the pages of all the major and minor papers and magazines of the time.[54]

That the emergence of the Boy Scouts onto the national stage was a contested process is undeniable. The attempts to monopolize the symbolic capital of this branch of the youth movement were always political; the practice itself, however, sheds light on the workings of power on a number of levels. Each side tried to impose its reading of the proper public display of the Scouting spirit. The Royal Boy Scouts Association, ostensibly leaning toward an international outlook for the movement, charged that public opinion viewed Scouting unfavorably because of all the unauthorized troops marching in disorderly fashion through the streets with the sole aim of creating a noisy spectacle.[55] The organization went as far as to seek exclusive rights from the Ministry of Interior to the wearing and exhibiting of the Scout uniform and insignia.[56] Which public mattered to the royal association is a relevant question because there were other reports of a public opinion that viewed the parades of these young boys favorably, even with pride. Although the different sides (Wafd-Palace-British) had begun to presume the existence of a generic public, they were entirely imbricated in a larger process of actually constructing, delimiting, and controlling this new sphere of representation. The appearance of Scouting troops in public ceremonies, parades, and competitions became a regular feature of Egyptian urban life after the revolution of 1919. These forms of representing and enacting identity were that much more important and contested when the project of nation building became more of a reality and consequently more complex in the years after 1922.

It does not seem so strange, then, that the groups of young men and boys marching in uniform received so much coverage in the press. These kinds of public performances were usually carefully staged and were attended by many politically important personalities. At one such event, the annual Boy Scout festival in Cairo in 1924, the nation's modernity was elaborately staged through a juxtaposition of signs that reflected a movement forward in material and spiritual terms and at the same time demonstrated cultural rootedness.[57] The festival was held on the grounds of

Al-Nadi al-Ahli, the national sporting club established in 1907. In what seems to have been the main pavilion of a set of exhibition sites, the various troops displayed their handicrafts. The Royal Waqfs troop attracted the most praise for weaving a carpet of Persian design. Other troops presented the wares of the various crafts in which they specialized: carpentry, copper work, sewing, cooking, and so on. While the occasion and setting of the performance expressed a modern, global cultural form, the individual displays and objects indexed local and regional traditions. And none other than Sa'd Zaghlul himself was there to inspect the products of the Scouts' labor.[58]

The presence of Zaghlul at this event was notable for several reasons. In January he had been elected the prime minister of independent Egypt's constitutional government — "the first fallah Egyptian to occupy that position."[59] It was often argued that what set Zaghlul apart from the other political leaders of the time and made him popular was his ability to connect with the masses. This connection was usually attributed to his allegedly peasant roots, and even the British participated in this characterization. The following is excerpted from a sketch of Zaghlul that appeared in the *Manchester Dispatch* during the period of the revolution and was supposedly read by the Milner Mission en route to Egypt: "Saad Zaglul Pasha is sixty-one years old, and for forty of them has been an outstanding figure in the politics of his country. Tall, massive, and of commanding presence, the Pasha reflects in his manner the intense earnestness and sincerity of his mind. The suggestion has been made that he is a survival of the old-time powerful faction of Pasha landowners. That is, of course, absurd. Zaglul is himself a Fellah. To this day his brothers labour on their lands amid their Fellaheen neighbours."[60] Even though Zaghlul never tilled the land and in fact eventually became a relatively large landowner, the construction of an authentic populist image was important beyond the narrow tactical concerns of the Wafd. In his use of language and his comportment Zaghlul struck a figure recognizable to Egypt's majority peasant population and to most urban dwellers: the *ibn al-balad*.[61] The term *ibn al-balad* could be translated as "native son." As a category of identity it connotes, among other things, a homegrown product. Zaghlul's biography, which was disseminated widely through literature and the press, indexes the appropriation of the ibn al-balad as national and maps the production of the national as the legitimate performative space of this figure.[62] The grafting of this popular notion of masculinity onto nationalist discourse was a clever political move.

The symbolic value of aligning the image of Zaghlul (the ibn al-balad) with these Boy Scouts should not be read simply in terms of instrumental political tactics. Indeed, Zaghlul and the Wafd were aware of their dependence on the popular public personality of "Sa'd" for their political successes—especially as the memories of revolution receded and their battles with the Palace, the British, and their major party rival, the Liberal Constitutionalists, intensified. No matter how popular Sa'd became, the Wafd were forced to operate within a context of constant political intrigue: Zaghlul was forced to resign within a year of assuming the position of prime minister, and the first parliament was dissolved by King Fuad on December 24, 1924.[63] Analyzing the Scouting movement in terms of the formal political context could tell one much about the new uses of the street in anticolonial struggle; it could disclose something about student movements and nationalism; and it could reveal a layer of previously unexamined cultural politics. But this means asking the kinds of questions that historians have engaged for quite some time now in their exploration of topics ranging from political parties and class formation to women's history. Although the answers might be interesting, they would not compel historians to revise much their picture of Egyptian history as primarily a story of national becoming.[64] Furthermore the questions about politics—understood as a tangible field of agonistic competition for resources and power—constrain the historical field of vision such that polyvalent practices like Scouting are reduced to a dynamic of domination and resistance.

If read in terms of the formation of a modern subject and the reconfiguration of masculinity, it becomes possible to glimpse in Scouting other meanings as well as suppressed domains of the political. Thus, in order to grasp the full significance of a new cultural form like the Scouts, the reading of this moment in the Egyptian past must not only push the boundaries of one's understanding of the political, but also attend to the aesthetic and the ethical. In other words, the meaningful nuances of the modern form of the nation and masculinity are located elsewhere, beyond the Wafd-Palace-British triad.

Plural Objects
YOUTH, SCOUTING, NATION, AND MASCULINITY

Even contemporary observers did not always read the practice and representation of Scouting as a performance with only one meaning. For one observer, it exhibited the advancement of the sons of the Nile Valley, allowing all "to raise their heads high among foreigners." [65] On the other hand, the utility of Scouting was related to Egyptian parents as an activity "nourishing the body so that it may endure the strains of the mind." [66] Bodily exercise was most important for the young urban effendis who were destined for a sedentary life. Scouting also taught self-reliance, a principle fundamental to successful manhood and the accomplishment of great deeds. This version of normative masculinity is linked by the anonymous observer to the general national good by invoking the voice of the beloved national hero Sa'd Zaghlul, who said, "Scouting keeps the student from having to think up diversions because he has no spare time to waste uselessly without doing something that would yield a beneficial return for him and his nation." [67] In other words, Scouting categorically requires one to be productive while reproducing a national manhood that evokes pride in fellow Egyptians. This assessment of Scouting invoked its advantages for a nationalist pedagogy while also highlighting its benefits for the physical and moral development of the individual.

When the vision of Scouting as a site of national and individual subject formation is foregrounded, a remarkable continuity appears in the traditionally turbulent politics of the interwar period. The 1930s are usually represented as the decade in which parliamentary government eventually failed and popular forces began to organize under radically different banners—fascist, Islamist, communist. [68] But the discourse of Scouting, with which both fascist and Islamic positions engaged, in fact points to a continuity with the twenties in their basic terms of articulation, even though those terms were being reformulated to accommodate the changing social and political context. As the state became the province of the king, his allies, and the British, the expanding effendi class was hard hit by the global depression of the early thirties. In organizations like the Shubban al-Muslimin (Young Men's Muslim Association, modeled on the London-founded Young Men's Christian Association), the Ikhwan al-Muslimin (Muslim Brotherhood), and Misr al-Fatat (Young Egypt) some of these men ostensibly found a different and more welcoming kind of community. [69] Yet the difference in how these groups actually perceived politics and its subject was at best perfunctory. [70]

One of the ways in which the difference is normally asserted is by locating a shift in political and cultural discourse from a secular territorial nationalism toward pan-Arabism and pan-Islamism. [71] During this period, there were indeed signs of such a change even in the discourse of Scouting. For example, there were attempts to make the idea of the Scouts more indigenous by retracing their lineage within Arab and Islamic genealogies. In an article titled "Scouting and the Arabs," the unnamed author relocates the origins of the philosophy underwriting Scouting to the ancient Arabian Peninsula.[72] He argues that historically the Arabs completely embodied the ideals of Scouting and also trained their children in its ways. Hasan al-Banna, the founder of the Shubban and the Ikhwan, participated in this discussion. His aim was to install Scouting squarely within an Islamic tradition.

In an article entitled "Scouting and Islam" that Banna wrote for the monthly *al-Muntakhab* in 1939, he outlined the objectives of Scouting: to develop the individual on physical, emotional, moral, rational, and social planes.[73] Then he asks, "Isn't that why Islam came?" At this point, he takes the reader on a quick tour of Islamic history to demonstrate the affinities between Scouting and Islam. He ends with a hagiography of the original über-Scout: the Prophet Muhammad. The *hadith* — "You have a duty to your body" — is repeated and resignified within a modern discourse of *riyada*. It is reported that Muhammad said this to 'Umar (a successor to the Prophet). Muhammad himself exemplified this rule in his person: "He . . . was indeed a model of the perfect creation: a sturdy build, strong muscles, powerful energy, and a mighty will constituted his noble body."[74] He excelled at horse riding, archery, and wrestling. He was also generous, compassionate, and wise. In short, Muhammad was the exemplary Scout. Banna concludes, "Anyone who has read the rules of Scouting . . . and also knows the principles, commandments, and spirit of Islam, knows how Scouting fits within Islam."[75]

The interpretation of the rise of the Muslim Brotherhood as a challenge to the liberal and the conservative political positions in Egypt during the 1930s (and more so in the 1940s) tends to accept the terms of political difference articulated by contemporary actors. The conceptual grid for the elaboration of an Islamic understanding of Scouting that was nonetheless recognizable by others was one shaped by the struggle between the colonial state and nationalists. That the nexus between the nation and a modern masculine subjectivity also formed the horizon for the political project of the Muslim Brotherhood was articulated by its supreme guide, Hasan al-Banna, in a tract that appeared in the group's newspaper on August 31, 1934:

> You saw in the previous article that the Society of Muslim Brothers was at the forefront of productive societies with regard to public works and benevolent foundations: from mosques, schools and committees of charity and piety, to lessons, lectures, speeches, sermons, and clubs dedi-

cated to both word and deed. However the nations in struggle [*al-umam al-mujahida*] who face a new renaissance and are passing through a serious period of transition and who desire to build their future lives on a solid foundation that would guarantee to the ensuing generation comfort and happiness and who demand the restitution of denied rights and pillaged [*maghsub*] honor are in need of a different structure than these. [These nations] are in utmost need of self-formation [*bana' al-nufus*], construction of character [*tashiid al-akhlaq*] and the impression of their sons with a proper masculine disposition [*taba' abna'ha 'ala khuluq al-rujula al-sahiha*] in order for them to persist when an obstacle stands in their way and overcome the difficulties that confront them. Man is the secret of the life of nations and the source of their renaissances. The history of all nations is a history made by men who are the most outstanding in strength of self [*al-aqwiya' al-nufus*] and will power. The strength or weakness of nations is measured by their capacity [*khusubatiha*] to produce men who possess within themselves the conditions of proper masculinity. I believe—and history supports me—that it is in the power of one man to build a nation if his masculinity is in order [*in sahat rujula-tuhu*]. It is also in his power to destroy a nation if this masculinity was heading in the direction of destruction rather than construction.[76]

The echo of the Scouting philosophy we have already encountered is loud and clear.

Before the attempt to absorb Scouting philosophy into an Arab-Islamic history, there were those who anticipated the rise of a dangerous militarism and questioned the wisdom of taking the Boy Scouts as a model for the rearing of Egyptian youth. Where in society did this critique originate? The horrors of the First World War had convinced many around the globe of the folly of blindly accepting civilizational advice from Europe. *Al-Muqtataf*, which, as we have seen, had wholeheartedly endorsed looking to the West for guidance in matters of customs, manners, and science, had also supported the expansion of the Scouting movement in Egypt. From the latter part of the nineteenth century into the twentieth, *al-Muqtataf* was the unrivalled site of the translation of European culture for educated Arabic readers. But after the war it too began to question the assumption that everything Western was naturally superior. The nexus between patriotism and militarism was one gift of European civilization that was subjected to interrogation.[77]

The debate over the desirability of Scouting was initiated in late 1924 by a minor entry tucked away at the back of the magazine in a section called "Commending and Criticizing" (*al-taqriẓ wa al-intiqad*).[78] It announced the launch of a new Scouting magazine in Iraq and briefly mentioned in closing *al-Muqtataf*'s reservation about the practice: "Iraqi Scouts—We are pleased that the Scouting movement in Iraq has matured to the point that it requires its own magazine. . . . We used to consider Scouting to be highly beneficial and we were the first to write about it and to coin this name [*al-kashafa*]. However, now we fear it prepares people for mass warfare [*harb 'amma*], which would destroy the human race."[79] In April 1925, *al-Muqtataf* published a letter it had received from the Iraqi Boy Scouts objecting to the paragraph on the grounds that it was not fair in interpreting the original intent and honorable principles guiding the movement.[80]

In making his argument, the author of the letter quoted the last two lines of the original *al-Muqtataf* entry. He then responded to the two points raised by the journal, the value of Scouting and its putative relationship to militarism. On the first point he argued that if one actually studied the situation, there would be no way to deny the benefits of Scouting to the individual and to society; he continued, all of the activities of the Boy Scouts were aimed at teaching boys self-reliance and developing in them a commitment to helping others. On the second point, he cited the Boy Scouts charter as evidence that there was no connection between the principles of the movement and militarism and in order to demonstrate that it in fact endorsed the complete opposite, cooperation and coexistence.

Al-Muqtataf's reply was swift and pointed.[81] The journal argued that principles and rules in themselves meant nothing in the realm of action. It gave the example of Christianity, which professed an even clearer injunction than the Scout Creed to love others and end human atrocities, as evidence of the meaninglessness of principles in the face of man's primordial inclination to war. Those principles did not stop the European nations from slaughtering each other because they did nothing in the decades prior to blunt that natural human instinct and desire for war. The only way to prevent such barbarities from recurring was to distance children from all signs and symbols of militarism and war, of which Scouting, *al-Muqtataf* asserted, was a perfect example.[82]

Observers sympathetic to the Scouting movement in Egypt engaged in another type of criticism. This particular critique appeared in a piece that reviewed the history of the Egyptian Boy Scouts on the occasion of their attendance at the twenty-first anniversary celebration of the founding of the Scouts in Britain.[83] In general, the author argued that the idea of Scouting was initially acted upon in good faith, as it was born out of the nationalist struggle, but soon corruption and scandal came to sully the movement.

Its popularity, according to the article, was undeniable. It seems Scouting had become a fashion of sorts for the new middle class (effendiyya). Everyone knew who the Scouts were from their uniforms, music, and parades. Soon books were being written about them, and poems were being composed in praise of Scouting. It also became a commodified practice: "The 'Scouting trade' spread everywhere. There was a proliferation of advertisements in newspapers for stores selling tools for Scouts and equipment for troops—for tents, cookware, bedding, etc." [84] Although the author does not make the connection explicit, it was in the commodification of Scouting that some of the potential for and actuality of corruption lay. He noted later in the article certain troops were established only as fraudulent schemes to make money or as a desperate means to acquire any form of material gain, from food and drink to clothes.

Other forms of corruption were also identified. Somewhat salaciously, the author alluded to incidents in faraway camps at night where "the character of young boys was perverted." [85] And distorting the Scouting mission altogether, some troops were formed simply as fronts for terrorist organizations. [86] After surveying these failures in the movement, the author then proceeded to ascribe them to a general Egyptian inability to absorb the proper spirit of Western cultural forms. Scouting in Europe and America was practiced in a fundamentally different manner. Tawfiq Effendi Habib, the author of *Boy Scouts* (*Fityan al-Kashafa*), was cited as an authority. In the final chapter of his book Habib compared the Egyptian Scouts to European and American ones and concluded that the Egyptians were Scouts in name and appearance only (in their "tan uniforms and multicolored bandanas"). Most of them, according to Habib, could not even put on their uniforms properly, much less explain the principles of Scouting. The reason for disparaging Egyptian Scouting becomes apparent as the anonymous author draws the article to a close. He was pleased that many of the troops founded in the aftermath of the revolution had disbanded by the end of the 1920s. He concluded that they had brought about their own death, and for the nation their demise was a good thing. Although his anti-Wafdist position was never explicitly stated, he reveals much by choosing to structure his analysis so that the end of the nationalist troops appeared as self-destruction. In this way, it was not necessary to document the battles between the nationalist and royalist Scouting societies. Indeed, nowhere in the article did the author mention that at the time he was writing the Palace had finally managed to gain the upper hand in its perennial struggle with the Wafd. According to this author, it was simply a time for rebirth under the patronage of King Fuad and the Ministry of Education, who apparently had committed to establishing troops in every government primary school and assigning trained Scoutmasters to them. The delegation attending the Boy Scouts jamboree in London was a sure sign of the advancement of Scouting in Egypt — now that those who genuinely grasped Western civilization were in charge. The royalist leanings of this author were evident. Nevertheless, his desire to make the Scouts conform to an apolitical and disciplinary ideal that he believed existed among their Western counterparts is worth further exploration.[87]

Fixing the Real
YOUTH, SOVEREIGNTY, AND THE POLITICS OF PERFORMANCE

The importance of Scouting as a pedagogic site for hegemonic masculinity and national identity continued to grow symbolically, if not numerically, in the 1930s.[88] King Fuad and the British took renewed interest in the movement as its political potential assumed new vectors. For Fuad, the Scouts presented an opportunity to market his son and heir-apparent, Prince Faruq, to the nation. The British viewed the increasing pan-Arab character of the Scouts with suspicion, if not trepidation. Against, or in spite of, these interests, the reproduction of youth through the performance of Scouting would continue to pose challenges to its formulation as a disciplinary technique.

The 1930s were inaugurated globally with the expansion of the Great Depression, and in Egypt, additionally, with the rise of Isma'il Sidqi's autocratic government.[89] The first half of the decade was characterized by government coercion — which included police repression, press censorship, and legal chicanery — and popular opposition, which resulted in hundreds of deaths and thousands wounded. One historian of this period notes that the configuration of politics around an axis of coercion and resistance established a pattern of political violence that Egypt has continued to experience up to the present.[90] Within this context, young men, particularly students, were seen as increasingly important actors. Alongside the Boy Scouts, new groups emerged that explicitly sought to organize young men for religious, cultural, and political activities. The Muslim Brotherhood grew out of the Young Men's Muslim Association (YMMA) that Banna had helped establish in 1927. The Brotherhood eventually created its own scouting troops, or *jawwala*, in 1935, although they had in practice existed from the beginning as athletic groups within the YMMA.[91] In 1936 the Wafd set up a paramilitary youth organization, the Blue Shirts, to counter the growing influence of Ahmad Husayn's Green Shirts, paramilitary members of his society Misr al-Fatat, established in 1933. Except for the YMMA, the other youth groups eventually faded from history or mutated into other kinds of organizations in the 1940s.

The establishment of these groups has most often been offered as evidence of the turn in Egyptian nationalism toward violence or toward supranational identification and a more traditional outlook.[92] Describing these groups only in terms of political nationalism reiterates nationalism's exclusive narrative of modernity, wherein the indexes of success and failure, deviance and normality are narrowly self-referential. From the perspective of youth and masculinity, it is possible to see that something else was also going on. In order to regard this supplement historically, it is necessary to read between the lines, problematize the archive, and vigilantly refuse the insistent overtures of the nation.[93]

The Royal Boy Scouts Association renewed its efforts in 1931 to become recognized by the government as the official, exclusive representative body for all Egyptian troops.[94] In their petition to the government they included a report on the state of Scouting in Egypt, which concluded that there were too many disparate troops (Egyptian and foreign) operating independently and that they needed to be connected on a national level. They proposed their own organization to assume the responsibility of uniting the various troops under one national body. They argued in a letter to the Public Security Department that official government recognition would help stamp out troops sponsored by organizations with hidden agendas or nefariously seeking to attract public attention. They emphasized the fact that officially sponsored Scouting had proven itself in other countries to be an effective vehicle for the production of good (that is, docile) male citizens.[95] A letter from Chief Scout Baden-Powell himself commended Furness for seeking government recognition and suggested that it was the only way to make the movement work for the advancement of the nation.[96]

The recurring theme of fixing the organizational hierarchy of the Boy Scouts is an important one. Behind the drive to regulate the troops was a desire to suppress elements deemed unruly and dangerous. The earlier withdrawal of Prince Tusun from the organizational role he had assumed apparently did not put an end to the existence of rogue Scouts. For some troops marching in uniform was not an end in itself. Historians have noted that youth were not always simply pawns to be manipulated by their political elders.[97] Even when they are treated as a political force in their own right, the story is nonetheless always told in terms of the nationalist struggle or of the class struggle, and so on.[98] This is not a call for telling a more accurate story of Egyptian youth by adding more domains of practice. Rather, I am suggesting, on the one hand, that the narrative and practical constructions of youth as a category were fundamentally political and from their inception imbricated in other stories and, on the other hand, that the formation of youth as a subject constantly challenged the capacity of narrative to represent them. The identification and the desire to regulate rogue Scouts, rather than pointing to the actuality of their deviance, signals the existence of disjunctive political positions, at times pro-Wafd, at times pro-Palace; moreover, these two poles of politics did not exhaust the possibilities of Scouting or its "futures past," its potentialities at different points in time. There were certainly local and global dynamics, for example, which shaped other political, aesthetic, and ethical vectors in Scouting that went unrecorded in the national archive.

One of the distinguishing aspects of politics, ethics, and aesthetics in the 1930s was the global phenomenon of paramilitary, fascist-styled youth organizations and the urban street violence they popularized. The violence alluded to and associated with certain strands of the Egyptian Scouting movement was ambivalently registered in the historical sources from this period. Analogous to — perhaps resulting from — the process of designating the nonbourgeois participants in the demonstrations of the revolution in 1919 as uncivilized rogues was the construction of violence in the 1930s as a flexible boundary marker between the domains of respectable masculinity and its Other. It was flexible because, although all sides on the political playing field used violence, the liberal discourse of the times required maintaining an official public distance from the acts themselves.[99] Indeed, the ability to determine the line between sanctioned and unsanctioned violence was long a basic objective in any claim to sovereignty. In Egypt the process of establishing sovereignty created a zone between the colonial and the national state wherein hybrid, nonmodern others were produced. These were subjects deactivated as intelligible beings in the terms of the new order.[100]

Naturally, the inclination to control the threat of the perceived crypto-Scouts can be read at face value as a genuine challenge to public order or even as a tactical move against an attempted Wafdist resurgence. The return of the Wafd to power under Mustafa Nahhas in January 1930 lasted only for a period of six months. The government that replaced the Wafd was led by Isma'il Sidqi, who, in conjunction with the Palace, worked to rule Egypt without parliamentary or constitutional guidance for the next three years. There were popular demonstrations, assassination attempts, and guerilla attacks against this tyranny throughout the country aimed at toppling the Sidqi government and the king and demanding the return of the Wafd. Students played a leading role in orchestrating this political violence; the attempt to regulate the Boy Scouts was, in an immediate tactical sense, part of that context.[101] The threat these rogue boys posed was also to the symbolic order underlying the political and cultural hegemony sought by all parties: the Wafdists, the king, and the British. This was evinced in a proposal to the Ministry of Interior in 1931 in which Furness and Hasanayn laid out a schedule of penalties for nonsanctioned troop activity.[102] The first offense was to be made punishable by a fine not to exceed one Egyptian pound. For a second offense, the masquerading Scouts were to be subject to seven days' imprisonment and the confiscation of their dangerous weapons: uniform and insignia.

Finally in 1933 King Fuad, feeling more confident and viewing the Boy Scouts as the means to advance a new royal agenda, accepted the Furness–Hasanayn proposal and issued a royal decree placing the newly constituted umbrella organization, the National Association of the Egyptian Boy Scouts, under the patronage and supervision of the government.[103] New statutes were decreed and published in the *Journal Officiel* on April 27 announcing the formation of the National Association of the Boy Scouts of Egypt. Two Palace cronies—or henchmen, as they were popularly perceived[104]—Zaki al-Ibrashi Pasha, director of the Royal Waqfs, and Hasanayn himself, would serve as its president and vice president, respectively.[105] Two days later a grand ceremony was held before a large audience to install Prince Faruq as the Grand Scoutmaster of Egypt; in attendance were Egypt's elite, headed by the king, and many foreign diplomats.[106]

The whole month of April seems to have been filled with Scouting-related activities, which explains in part the move by Fuad to governmentalize the movement. Earlier in the month, the British were quite perturbed by the unannounced (to them) visits of Iraqi and Palestinian Boy Scout troops.[107] Since colonial officials in Baghdad and Jerusalem had failed to give advanced warning, neither the British Residency in Cairo nor the Palace had sufficient time to influence the itinerary of the visitors. The Iraqi and Palestinian Scouts attended numerous tea parties of the wrong sort, all of which were recorded by the secret police.[108] The most sensitive segments of their itineraries were the Palestinian troop's reception by the Wafdist stalwart Makram 'Ubayd, their visit to Sa'd Zaghlul's grave, and the party thrown in honor of the Iraqi Scouts by the YMMA.[109] These connections among the Wafd, foreign Scouts, and the Brotherhood bothered the colonial authorities and convinced Fuad to take action, but perhaps even more worrisome were reports suggesting that Young Egypt (whose leader, Ahmad Husayn, was reputed to idealize Benito Mussolini) was also trying to find recruits among the Boy Scouts.[110] Notwithstanding their shared mistrust of other political actors and their overlapping interests, the Palace and the British were not natural allies, as some historians have asserted.

The Residency, for example, was divided on the political implications of King Fuad's attempt to rein in the Scouting movement.[111] Percy Loraine, the acting high commissioner, was pleased that Article 3 of the constitution of the National Association of the Boy Scouts defined it as a nonreligious, nonpolitical organization. The Oriental secretary, Walter Smart, who was always willing to see the worst, was convinced the king was up to something:

> In view of Art. 3 of the first decree it would have been better to have avoided such a political appointment as that of Zaki-al-Ibrashi. Muhammad Khalid Hassanein, Inspector General of Modern Sciences at the Azhar, is also one of the Palace fold. Neither of these two appear to have particular qualifications for directing Boy-Scout movements in their normal directions. Neither have probably ever taken any exercise in their lives or had anything to do with sport. The King obviously wants to use the Boy-Scout Movement for his own purposes, and the appointments and the installation of Prince Farouk as Grand Scoutmaster is indicative of this attitude.[112]

Smart did not elaborate on the king's "purposes" in taking charge of the Scouts. R. Campbell, Smart's colleague and a much more astute and subtle observer of Egyptian politics, reformulated his crude reading of the king's actions. Although Campbell espoused views about Fuad's intentions similar to those of Smart, he crafted his assessment in such a way as to situate the king's decision within a general rubric of statecraft: "We do not, as far as I know, know whether there were not good reasons, arising out of the non-organization of the [Egyptian] Boy Scouts, which made it desirable for the [government] to organize them under its own authority (as I believe the French [government] did with the French Scouts) and putting them under the [Ministry] of Public Instruction. Though personally, on principle, I feel that all Boy Scouts should be kept on as unofficial a basis as possible. I dare say that this cannot work satisfactorily in Egypt. I can quite imagine that some official direction is necessary here."[113] On one level Campbell suggested that the conditions on the ground may have in fact warranted governmental intervention, and he even aligned it with accepted European practice rather than ascribing it to the inevitable whimsy of the Oriental despot.

Campbell went on to proffer another explanation of the situation, one which seemed to take the king's actions at face value: "It seems to me to be a natural and proper thing for H. M. to take the lead of the movement. H.M. is keen on Education . . . and in 'le sport' and outdoor activities."[114] Even if this had been the case, which he did not believe it was, Campbell suggested it as a possible reading, conveying his political acumen: rulers' actions potentially signified beyond their intentions. He made the connection between intention and action more explicit by aligning it with another sometimes seemingly disconnected pair, sports and politics:

> No doubt there enters into his thoughts the idea that the more the young Egyptian occupies his mind with physical training and outdoor pursuits, the less prone he will be to fill the otherwise idle moments with the disturbing amusement of rather "hare-brained politics." If so there's a lot to be said for this on general grounds, and if thereby H. M.'s convenience as monarch is suited, and this has not been absent from his thoughts, we must not lose sight of the decent motive and its good effects. He may even [have] thought that the thoughts of possible future Prime Ministers may gradually be turned from other methods of filling idle moments and their damaging consequences. Moreover if H. M. had taken fright at the recent use of the Boy Scouts from Iraq and Palestine for political purposes by prominent Wafdists and the vista that this opened out, I cannot blame, but on the contrary commend him. Even if it is only eye-wash, the Sovereign does stand here for something above politics and is by way of being the symbol of all non-politics in Egypt.[115]

Projecting a British conception of "the Sovereign" onto Egyptian politics, wherein the king had not achieved such a transcendent status, Campbell's aim was to reiterate the importance of keeping good relations between the Residency and the Palace. The Wafd was clearly the political actor to watch and to constrain when necessary. Campbell's assessment of the king's actions reveals a subtler dimension of colonial liberalism, one in which good government often meant the foreclosure of avenues that could lead to the formation of a politically active civil society. Hence, the extension of the sovereign's control over the Scouting movement in Egypt was a necessary step in keeping it within the ostensibly harmless symbolic realm of "non-politics" and countering the attempt by other forces to push it into an overtly political one. In concrete terms, Fuad himself, having been outmaneuvered in the past by the Wafd and other popular forces, saw another opportunity to assert his influence over the youth movement. The timing also seemed ripe, as the youth movement drifted away from Wafdist control and the king's son neared maturity.

Prince Faruq's swearing-in ceremony as Egypt's Grand Scoutmaster on April 29 was received well by the press. The provincial weekly newspaper *al-Minya* reported on the induction in its issue of May 13: "The day of the Prince and the Boy Scouts was a joyous occasion for all of Egypt. That day Egypt celebrated her Crown Prince dashing boldly into the arena of practical life for the first time, declaring his leadership of the youth and pledging his commitment to that position. Leadership [can] create something [*al-wujud*] from nothing [*al-'adam*] and revive in the youth of Egypt a belief in the future."[116] The article's review of the kind of active life the prince was beginning conveys some of the nuances of the competing narratives of national identity in Egypt in the 1930s. By becoming the leader of the Scouts, the article maintained, Faruq had chosen a path that would "inspire in youth feelings of generosity, courage, manliness, and an attachment to and love for the nation." The rest of the article is given over to similar panegyric prose except for one interruption to insert Faruq into the dynastic line inaugurated by his great-great-grandfather Muhammad Ali. Appeal to the genealogy binding the monarchy to the history of Egyptian nationhood had become a truism by this point. But young Faruq was indeed the darling of the Egyptian public.[117] The sense of hopefulness projected through public performances like the ceremony and the press coverage surrounding it produced an image of Faruq as the promise of a better future in an increasingly pessimistic political environment. The article noted that Faruq, the "new miracle," was sure to be the most "wonderful verse" in all that had been written about the House of Muhammad Ali.

The installment ceremony was also front-page news in the nation's major daily, *al-Ahram*, a paper that claimed to have a nonpartisan political stance. The lead article took the opportunity to explain the importance of strong monarchies to the birth, health, and prosperity of nations. It queries where Egypt would have been without the house of Muhammad Ali, asserting that the monarch represents and guides the nation toward unity, rising above politics "to drive the ship of state" to peace. Through-

الثمن خمسة مليمات   ١٥ أبريل سنة ١٩٣٧   العدد السابع

الدَّليل
في الكَشْف

يحررها بعض شباب
الكَشافة الوطنية المصرية بالقاهرة

صاحب الجلالة ملك مصر المحبوب وكشافها الأعظم

6. As late as 1937, four years after the installation ceremony and a year after Fuad ascended the throne, the portrait of the prince as Grand Scoutmaster was still making the front page, even if it was in a Scouting magazine. At least for awhile and posthumously, Fuad's investment in building symbolic capital seemed to pay off. "His Majesty the Beloved King of Egypt and her Grand Scoutmaster." *Al-Dalil fi al-Kashf*, April 15, 1937, cover.

out the history of nations, the article argued, one could see how monarchs brought a people together under one banner, citing the House of Savoy in Italy, Peter the Great in Russia, and the Bourbons of France. The other article on the front page gave a detailed account of the proceedings of the festivities on April 29. The display of Scouting activities accompanying the swearing-in ceremony was very reminiscent of the gathering in 1924 with Sa'd Zaghlul in attendance. This exhibition was also held on the grounds of Al-Nadi al-Ahli. During the ceremony, Faruq was presented with the Egyptian Scouting staff — the top of which was crowned with the head of a jackal, the ancient Pharaonic symbol (*wa's*) of power and authority.[118] His every utterance and every movement were noted with adulation; when he descended from the royal gallery to inspect the Boy Scout troops, his walk was described as that of a man exhibiting manliness and courage.[119]

King Fuad and his Palace supporters were not the only ones who saw the potential for political gain in supporting the Boy Scouts. As the British views cited above attest, the Wafd was involved in the guidance of the Egyptian Scouting movement in what it considered the proper direction. The politicization of the Boy Scouts movement in Egypt along anticolonial and anti-imperialist lines was a source of some anxiety for British officials in Egypt and elsewhere, but it did not necessarily correspond to antimonarchical positions.

The activity of Egyptian Scouts in Palestine was of particular concern to the British. An intelligence report from August 3, 1933, recorded the activities of the Khalid Ibn al-Walid troop that summer.[120] They were allegedly engaged in propaganda work in the countryside around Nablus, instructing the villagers on the evils of transferring lands to Jewish buyers. Furthermore, they were encouraged to seek the mediation of national bodies as opposed to the authorities of the British Mandate.

The impressive spying done by the Central Intelligence Department of the British Mandate government in Palestine recorded an interesting speech by Akram Zu'aytir, who was a founding member of the Palestinian Istiqlal Party that had been formed in 1932 on a pan-Arabist platform.[121] Zu'aytir pointed out the necessity of recognizing colonial difference in the future makeup and mission of Scouting in Egypt:

> The Egyptian boy scouts visited Nablus on the 30th July. About 200 young men and the boy scouts of Nablus received them on the way. After lunch, Akram Zueitar delivered a speech in which he referred to efforts to divide the Arabs and called the Egyptians the leaders of the Arab nation.

He welcomed the boy scouts and wished them to become a strong military organisation—*not boys like those of Baden-Powell*, but young men
who would save the country and enjoy the confidence of the people. They
were under the rule of tyrants and every day witnessed a new form of
persecution. If they united and became powerful they could oppose their
oppressors. . . . One of the Egyptians, in replying, spoke of Moslem solidarity, and said that in order that they might overthrow the present rule
they must unite in thought and in deed; they must be under one banner,
be one strength and seek independence.[122]

Zu'aytir was in no uncertain terms encouraging the Egyptian Scouts to
reassess their vision of Scouting given the conditions of external oppression under which both of their nations suffered. In a colonial situation, according to the Palestinian activist, it was not enough to be satisfied with
simply being symbolic *of* something, like Baden-Powell's boys, who ostensibly represented the glory of their imperial nation. On the other side
of the colonial divide, the very right of representation had yet to be established.

With the proliferation of pan-Arab bourgeois connections in the 1930s,
the tactical political work that King Fuad hoped the Boy Scouts would do
was often attenuated and contradicted by the broadening of the political
both geographically and in terms of the social, cultural, and everyday conditions within which actual boys were shaped.[123] Nevertheless, as the following report from another leg of the Boy Scouts' tour illustrates, certain
things, however ephemeral, could be achieved by the careful working of
cultural symbols:

> The party attended a tea-party held in their honour by the Young Men in
> Bethlehem.[124] At this reception Eissa Al Bandak delivered an address of
> welcome wherein he emphasised the ties which unite Egypt to Palestine,
> and made allusion to the Pharonite [*sic*] movement and asked the Scouts
> to do without that idea, because it separated them from the Arabs. In his
> reply Abdul Wahab Al Najjar[125] stated that the movement referred to by
> the speaker is only vouched for by few persons in Egypt and abroad who
> are of little influence. He then cheered King Fuad and his Heir and the
> Arab unity and wished the Arabs to obtain their national hopes.[126]

One could read Abd al-Wahhab al-Najjar's concluding salute to his king
and prince as simply pro forma in the same way it was repeated in countless other public performances, from ceremonies and sporting events to
published news reports and poetry. In those instances, as in Palestine, the

presence of spies and censors had become an accepted reality. But why should Najjar make this honorific gesture in a context that seems to be highly critical of tyrants and oppressors? It may have been obvious to him that there was a spy among them. But perhaps, by 1933, the paradoxical idea of the Egyptian nation as a natural and historical formation was one in which the descendants of Muhammad Ali were seen to have a constitutional role. And it was precisely through the repetition of hailing the sovereign through performative spaces like the Boy Scouts that that history was naturalized. While it may be a stretch to argue this for 1933, there are indications that the public relations offensive started by Fuad and continued by Faruq when he attained the throne in 1936 managed for awhile to successfully align the sovereign with the ambitions and aspirations of the youth.[127]

Conclusion

The unintended consequences of a youthful masculinity hailed into being by diverse techniques and institutions of power are not the stuff of history. And this is understandable, for history must make some broader sense to be communicable and relevant. Nevertheless, in this chapter, while trying to map a particular discursive terrain, I have insisted on the importance of making visible those moments of slippage in order that the process of subject formation not appear fixed or reduced to given determinations.

The expansion of the physical culture discourse through institutions like the schools, the National Sporting Club, and the Boy Scouts — even if one views them as insignificant because of their limited reach within Egyptian society — sheds light on a global cultural process taking place in the 1920s and 1930s. In that sense Egypt was no different from India, China, Britain, or France. Nonetheless, the colonial context of Egyptian modernity was relevant to that process, and not only because of the political and economic domination usually implied by the colonial. As David Scott has theorized, the compulsion to be modern afforded no alternative — this was an epistemological (and psychological) condition of social and political survival.[128] Yet Scott does not explore, beyond the writings of a certain intellectual elite, the cultural practices of that modernity, its mechanics of conscription, or its gendered constitution.

I have argued here and in chapter 3 that physical culture and youth organizations were two technologies of producing modern masculine Egyptian subjects, but with complicated and often unpredictable vectors. Ideological variations aside, the modern subject of riyada secured in part the condition of possibility for a new politics of representation and a reconceptualization of sovereignty within a reorganized national, regional, and (as we will see better in the following chapter) international geography. The repetition of this subject would in turn constantly reintroduce the possibility of performative failures and potential resignifications.

5

GAMES

International Culture and Desiring Bodies

As the case of the Boy Scouts suggested, the 1920s and 1930s were marked by the simultaneous expansion of national and international culture. This paradoxical formation, in which one was also many, is little understood because the historical treatment of the interwar period, freighted by the Eurocentric teleology of horrific political and cultural failure, has focused almost exclusively on the radicalization of nationalism and particularly on its fascist implications. That focus, however warranted it may have been, has occluded a fascinating chapter in the interconnected and asymmetrical emergence of contemporary bodies—individual, national, regional, and global.[1] Moreover, the historical privileging of national cultures as being hermetically formed has tended to obscure the colonial origins of the unequal forms of representation institutionalized after the Second World War in international bodies such as the United Nations and the World Bank. Mandate Palestine is an example of a place where the tendency of international relations to reduce the world to comparable units has made for an intellectually unsatisfactory historiography,[2] but even in ostensibly less problematic national locations such as Egypt, the recognition of its national form, by internal and external bodies, has hidden away in that collaborative act of affirming identity a multitude of difference.[3]

In this chapter I explore that work of identity and difference, of the many in the one, in terms not of unsightly or abject bodies but of the very bodies, masculine bodies, on which the modern Egyptian nation staked its unique and universal value. I argue on the one hand that the national form that achieved cultural and political hegemony in Egypt after 1919 did so through a process of constant and repeated comparison on a global stage of racialized and gendered bodies. On the other hand, conceiving the subject performatively reveals the limits of nationalist and internationalist formations of culture while illuminating the existence of a constellation of bodies situated in varying, uneven relations to one another and, at times, within the one.

In the history of effendi masculinity that I have been recounting, the desire for a new social body was shot through with the simultaneous desire for a new physical body. The colonial conditions within which that desire was shaped profoundly affected the form and content of the bodies that were ultimately produced. In other words, the national and effendi bodies became sites of signification bearing the marks of their particular history as well as the burden of a universal future. Yet even though those conditions were largely inescapable they were subjected, through the working of anticolonial nationalism and, perhaps more important, through the workings of everyday cultural practices, to creative adaptations.[4] The figure of the effendi that appeared in the critical political discourse of the 1930s, for example, was often represented as the object of popular mockery. When viewed only within that field the figure seemed to be waning as a possible social subject. The effendi as a middle-class subject of everyday spaces and practices, however, was a polyvalent figure evincing a complex instance of the social performative, to the extent that even as entry into the social required an embrace of the modern, the ideological interpellations (discussed in the previous chapter) were always only partial and potentially reversible.

In this chapter, the implications for a colonized people of participating in the emerging international sporting arena are examined in juxtaposition to the everyday practices of physical culture (*al-riyada al-badaniyya*) developing locally during the interwar period. Beginning with a forgotten—mainly because it never happened—historical event, the first African Games, I explore various perspectives on Egyptian participation in international competition. I pose the question of the stakes involved in public exhibitions of physical prowess for colonial and anticolonial positions and, in search of answers, come back to consider the fate of the first African Games. Viewing the new performances of the colonized body at multiple levels, namely, on international, national, and local sports stages, provides crucial insight into otherwise overlooked arenas of interwar history. It illuminates the processes of subject formation and nation building as mutually constitutive acts without reducing the one to the other, demonstrating their specific materialization or embodiment within a racialized and classed colonial modernity. These stages of performance, therefore, are global, overlapping, and moving planes on which the relationships among body, subjectivity, and national culture might be reconsidered by reflecting on the location of desire between colonial modernity and the everyday.

A Games Ethic
STATES (OF) BECOMING MODERN

In 1965 Brazzaville, the capital of the recently independent Republic of the Congo, hosted the first Pan-African Games. Twenty-eight nations were in attendance. But the well-hidden, dusty, and rarely visited Ahmed Touny Museum of the Egyptian Olympic Committee in Cairo tells another story of the games.[5] In a locked display case copies of invitations, posters, and medals silently contest Brazzaville's claim to having held the first Pan-African Games. As if preserving a moment that was frozen in time, like a freeze-frame interrupting a cinematic narrative, the objects on display tell of the readiness of Egypt, of the port city of Alexandria in particular, to host the African Games in April 1929. One can almost see and hear the processions of the opening ceremony when suddenly the music fades and the image blurs. Lest the museum visitor be forced to conjure catastrophic earthquakes or hordes of barbarian invaders, a sign affixed to the showcase obviates any need for speculation about the cause of the event's sudden dissolve. According to the sign, the great imperial powers Britain and France decided at the last minute it would not be in their interest to have a bunch of African youth gather in the same place at the same time, so the games were canceled by colonial fiat. In short, Alexandria "held" the very first African Games, but thanks to imperial anxieties no one attended. Africa would have to wait until the postcolonial era, three and a half decades later, for its first real continental games, while forgetting this other first, faded out by colonial history.

As I mentioned in chapter 3, the Egyptian Olympic Committee (EOC) was formed in 1914, but its activities were suspended for the duration of the war. The EOC was reactivated after the war and was able to field a team in 1920 to participate in the Olympic Games in Antwerp. This first Egyptian delegation to the Olympics was composed of a football team, two competitors each in track and field and gymnastics, and one each in wrestling, fencing, and weightlifting.[6] Their showing was for the most part unremarkable, and the athletes won no medals. Nevertheless, preserved in the Egyptian National Archives is a picture of the team that accompanies

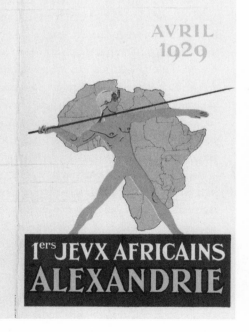

7. Invitation to the First African Games. TNA: PRO CO 554/77/7.

(below)
8. Invitation to the First African Games. CIO: JREGI-AFRIC-ALXDR 205627/SD5.

a report on the games by Angelo Bolanachi, the general secretary of the EOC.[7] Bolanachi became a regular focus of attacks in the press for the poor performance of the Egyptian team and for what was seen as the general lack of commitment by the EOC to fielding and preparing a strong team; the faultfinding became even harsher after another lackluster performance in Paris in 1924.[8] These public criticisms also targeted (and illuminated) bodies that had begun to take shape in the four decades preceding the war: the sporting establishment, bourgeois masculinity, and Egyptian national identity.

A year before the next Olympic Games, an Egyptian writing under the penname Abu Muhammad described the nexus of sports, masculinity, and national identity.[9] He began by framing the two Egyptian appearances at the 1920 and 1924 Olympics as "a comedy performed on European world stages."[10] The author placed the blame squarely on the shoulders of Bolanachi, who was faulted for not providing the athletes with proper guidance. In short, the article depicted Bolanachi as essentially incapable of such guidance in that it required someone who could inspire a nationalist consciousness in the athletes. The fact that he was Greek rendered this impossible. The author correlated an athlete's will to succeed in international competition with the awareness that one was representing one's nation. He ascribed great importance to this representative aspect of the athletes' performance and recommended the appointment of one or two Egyptians alongside Bolanachi (whose contribution to the advancement of sports in Egypt did not go unacknowledged) in order to cultivate a nationalist consciousness among athletes.

Abu Muhammad's description of the Olympics as a large stage for the dissemination of nationalist propaganda partially explains the significance he placed on the embodiment of nationalist consciousness.[11] He contended that the Olympic Games were viewed by participating nations as an opportunity to exhibit the level of their advancement in culture (*hadara*) and character (*akhlaq*).[12] The bodies competing against each other were signified and differentiated by a flag or uniform, but the bodies themselves signified and differentiated nations through degrees of success or failure. Within this field of competing signs and signifiers, bodies and nations, the author concluded, "Our representatives must be the players with the best skill and the best character."[13]

Abu Muhammad was echoing earlier sentiments about national identity being integrally connected to Egypt's performance in the international sporting arena. A critical article evaluating the prospects of the Egyptian team on the eve of the Paris games of 1924 reviewed the country's dismal showing at Antwerp in 1920 and expressed hope that the present team would change the image of Egypt left behind by the preceding delegation.[14] The author faulted the EOC for not supporting the athletes financially; apparently they were not allocated enough funds to find decent lodgings or even to eat. But the main concern of the writer was not the deprivation of the athletes so much as what the Europeans thought about Egypt as a nation. Reflecting his own assumptions and expectations of civilized behavior, he projected the conclusion that Europeans had drawn after seeing the nearly destitute Egyptian team at Antwerp. They most certainly thought that "Egyptians are still walking around naked like the rest of the peoples of Africa," and "they must have ascribed to us all kinds of savage behavior."[15] At least for this author, the very material ways in which Egyptian bodies were displayed at the Olympics also implicated him in a shared metaphorical space with the athletes, which he read along racial and national lines. The delimitation of the boundaries of that national space and the articulation of the identity within it involved the continuous repetition of these occasions, in which similar performances of honor and shame drew and redrew the lines between "us" and "them."

Acknowledging the slightly improved performance of the team in Paris, one author observed optimistically "that little was a lot in the eyes of others, and moreover it was a palpable sign that Egypt had started to move forward."[16] The same author went on to elaborate how the performance of Egypt at the Olympics reflected on all Egyptians. He explicitly identified it as a problem—in the sense of a complicated issue requiring care and attention—of patriotism (*qawmiyya*). He implored those in charge, the EOC, to form the best team possible and to give the members all the necessary training in order to carry out successfully their duties as national representatives. He depicted the athlete's body as a resource to be used in the struggle for gains in symbolic capital, to use a concept from Pierre Bourdieu. These gains were to be made in the international market of the sporting arena. The returns, whether sweet or bitter depending on the levels of investment, were shared by every Egyptian since what was ultimately at stake was the image of an entire nation. He also figured the body as a weapon and the sports field as an international battlefield: "We must enter the Olympic field with instruments fit for battle and not be left defenseless in the face of an armed enemy."[17] To be "left defenseless" was tantamount to defeat and dishonor.

The problem of national honor was indeed a central issue in the case of the first African Games. Alexandria was selected to host the regional games at a meeting of the International Olympic Committee (IOC) in

Paris in July 1924.[18] Pierre de Coubertin, the founder of the modern international Olympic movement and the president of the IOC from 1896 to 1925, wrote in a memorandum to all the national committees, "The time has come for sport to advance to the conquest of Africa, that vast continent which it has as yet hardly touched and to bring to its people the enjoyment of ordered and disciplined muscular effort, with all the benefits which flow from it."[19] These benefits were well known to interested parties in Egypt, though framing sport as another conquest would be a source of significant tension, as we shall see below. Initially, the African regional games were scheduled to be held in 1927, before the next Olympics in Amsterdam, but King Fuad postponed them until 1929, arguing that the necessary preparations had not been completed.[20]

One sports commentator, Muhammad Murad, reacted angrily to the announcement of the postponement, writing, "It has become clear that we are not capable [of handling] public matters like Westerners."[21] He went on to criticize wealthy Egyptians for their "temporary enthusiasm" and short-term memories. Murad contended that the same class of people who selfishly and single-mindedly pursued the accumulation of capital in the present was in the past supportive of the Egyptian "sports renaissance."[22] The past invoked here must be that of the revolutionary period between 1918 and 1924. There was a frenzy of activity in the sporting arena during that time, as the famous Egyptian historian Rafi'i recounts: "The 1919 revolution was influential in spreading the sporting spirit to *shabab* and non-*shabab* [to the young and the not young]. Previously it was confined to the narrowest circle. [After the revolution] the *shabab* and their supporters began to form associations and clubs for sports."[23] Apparently, as nationalist euphoria waned so did financial support for sports. The philanthropic generosity of their European counterparts was cited to shame the Egyptian upper class for neglecting its civic duties.

Murad mapped a complex of shame that encompassed the whole nation: "It is strange and painful, indeed very painful for [one's] conscience, that the Westerner takes more interest in encouraging these Games in our country and in other Eastern countries. Meanwhile, the Egyptian does not take interest in encouraging them in his [own] country or in other countries of the East near to that precious nation."[24] Although all of Egypt is implicated in this passage, "the Egyptian" was inscribed ambivalently. It could be read as signifying a specific classed or a generalized national subject. The first line, which expresses an intense pain ostensibly originating from a feeling of shame, sets the author apart from "the Egyptian" and signals a reading of the author as an incomplete marker of identity. In another passage, "the Egyptian" appears allusively as only one of many ways of performing a category of masculine difference, the historical boundary of which was drawn between East and West. The author asks, "Is the East devoid of men? Is it devoid of rich people, of intellectuals, of supporters of a sporting spirit? Is it devoid of the ancient spirit of the East that gave life to civilization in the East and West?"[25] The answer to Murad's questions is no; it is only that "the rich need to be reminded perpetually that the bones of their great ancestors buried in [this] hallowed ground [al-ard al-tahira] demand of them the preservation of [this] land], compassion for their grandchildren, and the raising of their heads among nations."[26] Speaking on behalf of Egypt's conscience, however much the author acknowledged the internal and external differences constituting the nation, he simultaneously homogenized those differences in a transhistorical sweep, while insisting on memory and responsibility as the grounds for identity. The question, or problem, of honor returned, then, as universally significant to all Egyptians regardless of class. Gender in this context remained a site of difference; national honor was really a question only for men to describe, display, and decide.[27]

Shifting the focus, then, to the elite decision makers concerned with national honor, I want to consider what or who ultimately derailed the first African Games. The decision to postpone the event from 1927 to 1929 could very well have been related to the perennial power struggles taking place after independence among the Wafd, the Palace, and the British—of which much has been written (including my own version in the previous chapter).[28] King Fuad might well have decided to delay the games in order to prevent the Wafd from reaping any additional gains in public opinion after their reassertion of parliamentary power in 1926. The cancellation of the games in 1929 was a clearer issue, at least in terms of who was responsible. After some vacillation, the British decided it would not be wise to bring together so many colonized subjects in one place and blocked the participation of their African colonies, thus effectively ruining the games.

Sir George Lloyd, known for his heavy-handed dealings as the British high commissioner in Egypt since 1925, viewed the decision to hold the African Games in Alexandria as a recipe for disaster in terms of British positions on the continent. Deploying a racist and imperialist logic, he recommended to the Foreign Office that it not publicly reject the games but counsel British colonial governments to decline the invitation: "The object which it [the games] seeks to promote fills me with misgiving. Subsidiary Olympic Games have in the past, notably in the Philippines in 1925, been productive of serious friction and, in the present case, they are open to the additional objection that the native races of Africa are by no means ripe for participation in such activities. Indeed the prospect of having Alexandria filled with large numbers of natives from all parts of the Continent is distinctly undesirable."[29] Part of his reasoning for not issuing an ultimatum to Egypt to cancel the games was owing to the direct patronage of King Fuad. During this period, Lloyd was at the height of his political game playing off the Palace and the Wafd. His correspondence with the foreign secretary alludes to a much broader understanding of the relationship between the games and politics as well as of the character of each. A seasoned political player like Lloyd was well aware of the practical and symbolic potential of such a gathering to assume a much more negative significance than the "naïve" members of the IOC who rallied around the games seemed to allot it.[30] Lloyd was uniquely positioned to see the games as more than a simple competition among athletes precisely because of his vantage point as a colonial official.

In a plea to Downing Street to encourage the participation of the British colonies, Lord Rochdale, a member of the IOC, wrote,

> May I conclude by saying that in my opinion these Games will, like the Far Eastern, Central American and the Latin American Games do an enormous amount of good in Africa, and especially in Egypt, and the good will be seen in the period that will follow the Games. By their enthusiasm and keenness the natives will eventually become proficient in sport and athletics of all kinds. This at any rate has been found to be the case in those countries in which the Games have already been held. And I think you will agree that for every native who becomes a sportsman, you will find one less agitator against law and order. With all the millions of natives under our rule, it seems imperative to push forward such a movement.[31]

This view of sports as a depoliticizing agent echoes the one surrounding the Boy Scouts. But just as in the case of Scouting there were colonial officials who also viewed the gathering of natives in a sports context as potentially dangerous to "law and order." Both of these seemingly contradictory readings ascribed to sports and particularly to international competitions a political significance, the core of which was concerned with the production of docile political subjects. Those involved in the day-to-day administration of colonies and subject races recognized the political importance and meaning assigned to sports in anticolonial and nationalist struggles and sought to limit contacts between "natives" from different parts of the empire.[32]

Because of its developed nationalist movement, the Colonial Office viewed Egypt especially as dangerous terrain. The officials responsible for Britain's African possessions were horrified by the idea of a Pan-African Games in Egypt. The various responses to the games from Colonial Office authorities all echoed Lloyd's opinion in one form or another. The first handwritten note on a minute sheet from February 1928 expressing disbelief that the IOC genuinely supported such an idea referred to the games as "an Egyptian scheme."[33] The second entry from J. E. W. Flood, who was in charge of Nigerian affairs, called it silly and added, "They won't get any athletes from Nigeria anyhow, and I would not have anything to do with it."[34] In the same entry, he proposed the following tack as a way of politely declining the invitation: "A line which might be followed is that athletics in the [West African] colonies are not organized on a scale sufficient to justify any official participation."

By March 9, thirteen months before the games were scheduled to begin, the Foreign Office still had not taken a position, and officials at the Colonial Office were getting a bit edgy. In order to preempt a decision by the Foreign Office, they thought about forwarding the invitation to the colonial governments themselves. Flood's note again expressed unequivocal aversion to the whole idea of an African Games: "It seems to me a totally evil show conceived in Pan-Africanism and Egyptian propaganda. I should be inclined to tell Governors not to have anything to do with it."[35] Flood's colleague G. L. M. Clauson supported this view, adding his impressions of local actors whose support for the games, he felt, were not motivated simply by an enthusiasm for sports. He described Prince Umar Tusun as "probably the most dangerous, and anti-British, man in Egypt" and referred generally to the threat to British interests posed by any Wafdist government.[36]

Finally by May 11, a decision was reached to notify the Egyptians that the British colonial governments in Africa would not be participating. The French, who had initially agreed to participate, were persuaded to reach the same conclusion "because of the risk that this '*manifestation sportive*' might assume a political character."[37] The Belgians followed suit a few months later.[38] In a last-ditch effort to salvage the games, King Fuad expanded the criteria for participation to include Europeans who had been resident in Africa for at least two years.[39] This move was accompanied by pressure from the IOC on the British, but the decision not to attend was maintained. Flood, in his characteristic tetchy tone, noted, "Quite apart from all this [logistical and political considerations] there is no sort of athletic organization yet in any of our W. A. Colonies. The people are not nearly ripe for it and it would be impossible to get any sort of representation. I think better of the British flag than to feel any pride at the thought of its being carried round an arena at Alexandria or Cairo by black men from W. Africa—who frequently would not be British subjects."[40] "Pride" and "representation" were two central concepts in the formulation of national honor. Thinking through these terms was not solely the provenance of British colonial officials.

I have noted the significance Egyptians assigned to international games and the signification through them of Egyptian national identity. The African Games offered another opportunity to reflect on the place of Egypt among nations. The promise of this major event being held within its borders signaled a step up on the ladder of progress. Some invoked Egypt's ancient history to underscore the point that sporting success was not an impossible dream for modern Egyptians since it was already in their blood. As one observer remarked, during the ancient epoch of the first Olympics Egypt's power (sporting and military) extended far and wide: "The Egyptian was the ruler of himself and others."[41]

The intersection of national honor and male bodies in competition on the playing field did not simply happen but was actively orchestrated. The attempts to do so within a colonial context were sometimes met with resistance, which only served to reinforce and naturalize the connections among corporeality, gender, and ideology in the minds of colonial and anticolonial nationalists. Nevertheless, as I argue below, access to the biographies of individual athletes complicates this picture of the coincidence of sports and nation.

Before turning to the individual athlete, I want to pursue the question of nation building within a colonial context circulating racialized images of masculinity. The EOC and the expanding sporting community in Egypt had continued to express displeasure with the appointment of Bolanachi as their Olympic representative. After the humiliating failure of the African Games but emboldened by the results of Egyptian athletes at the Amsterdam Olympics in 1928, the EOC began to agitate more vigorously for a change of representatives.

In her study "The Dictatorship of Sport: Nationalism, Internationalism, and Mass Culture in the 1930s," Barbara Keys notes that disputes between the IOC and member nations over representatives were quite common. Apparently, the selection of national representatives by the IOC was a constitutional feature aimed at ensuring the autonomy of the commit-

9. Photo caption reads, "Antwerp 1920–Opening Ceremony–The Egyptian Delegation." Credit: IOC Olympic Museum Collections.

(below) 10. Photo caption reads, "Paris 1924 — The Egyptian Team (EGY)." Credit: IOC Olympic Museum Collections.

HET EGYPTISCHE ELFTAI

11. Photo caption reads, "Amsterdam 1928 — The Egyptian Team (EGY) 4th."
Credit: IOC Olympic Museum Collections.

(below) 12. Photo caption reads, "Berlin 1936 — The Olympic Stadium during
the Opening Ceremony. Entrance of the Egyptian Delegation (EGY)."
Credit: IOC Olympic Museum Collections.

13. Photo caption reads, "Berlin 1936 — An Egyptian Weightlifter." Credit: IOC Olympic Museum Collections.

(below)
14. Photo caption reads, "67.5–75kg: Wagner, Adolf (GER) 3rd El Touny, Khadr El Sayed (EGY) 1st and Ismayr, Rudolf (GER) 2nd." Credit: IOC Olympic Museum Collections.

tee.[42] It was beyond the scope of Keys's project to show how such contests over jurisdiction were mobilized by nationalist projects and what differences obtained between colonial and colonized societies.

In a unified protest to the IOC over its refusal to change its representative, the Egyptian sports establishment declined the invitation of the United States to participate in the tenth Olympiad, to be held in Los Angeles in the summer of 1932.[43] When the Egyptian government received the invitation, the Ministry of Public Instruction asked the Egyptian Sports Federations to form a team to represent Egypt. In a joint letter to the minister signed by the various delegates, the reasons for declining the U.S. invitation and all future invitations were laid out.[44] The signatories were the heads of the football, boxing, fencing, weightlifting, and tennis federations and the representatives of the Egyptian Union of Sporting Societies, the Army Sports Association, and, the Ministry of Public Instruction. Their central objection was not to the right of the IOC to appoint its own representative but to what they believed to be the disingenuous position of the IOC in its continuing support of Bolanachi: "The Egyptian Federations and their Committees have noted with regret that the IOC did not see fit to name an Egyptian to represent it in Egypt. This leaves one to believe that the IOC reckoned that no Egyptian meeting the necessary criteria to fill the position could be found and that it was forced to make its representative in Egypt a foreigner."[45] Illustrating the colonial difference that Keys missed in her analysis, the delegates perceptively pointed out, referencing various legal statutes, that this situation could be described only as a "gratuitous injury" (*l'injure gratuite*). They maintained that in the charter of the Olympic Games (Article VII) and in the general rules (Article IX) of competition, the one stipulation for those participating under the flag of a certain country was that they be "*the nationals or the naturalized* [citizens] *of that country*." Furthermore, they argued that the very statutes (*Statuts du Conseil International Olympique*) authorizing the IOC and its membership defined the representative as originating from a country fielding Olympic teams composed solely of national competitors. They concluded that the status of Egypt as the only nation with a foreign spokesman was indeed an unjustifiable exception.[46]

This legalistic argument for the IOC's failure to treat Egypt equally was followed up with an appeal that was affective and historical. The authors invoked "a legitimate sentiment of national dignity" (and the implicit loss thereof) as the explicit justification for their decision, which also served to underscore the severity of the matter and to preempt hollow internationalist counterarguments. They followed this with a reference to "the devel-

opment of sports in Egypt" and its performance in international tourna-
ments "where the Egyptian colors were very often raised" [où les couleurs
égyptiennes ont été très souvent à l'honneur] as further evidence of the
IOC's position being nothing more than a biased attitude.

The situation remained at an impasse until the Los Angeles games were
concluded. Then the president of the IOC, Henri de Baillet-Latour, made
an official visit to Egypt to discuss the future of its membership, which
according to the rules became void with the resignation of Bolanachi.[47]
Al-Ahram, in an interview with Baillet-Latour, asked his opinion on what
had transpired between the sports federations and Bolanachi. He suggested that the Egyptian federations misunderstood Bolanachi's role and
reiterated the foundational principle of the IOC: "I ask that you tell the
readers of your newspaper that Mr. Bolanachi was not the delegate of
Egypt to the International Olympic Committee but rather the delegate
of the International Olympic Committee in Egypt."[48] Pressed on why
an Egyptian delegate had not been selected to replace Bolanachi, he responded that that was the fault of the Egyptians themselves since no one
had expressed the desire to assume his duties.

On the question of Egypt's refusal to participate in the previous Olympiad, he blamed its sporting establishment for failing its athletes and ascribed it to "bad administration . . . and the lack of maturity of Egyptian
knowledge in matters of international rules."[49] He also intimated that if
Egypt did not respect the customs of the IOC and continued along this
combative path, then its reentry as a member would be impossible. As
might be expected, Baillet-Latour's "menacing tone" was not received
very well.

A sharply worded assessment of the interview was published in a subsequent issue of *al-Ahram*.[50] The newspaper claimed that its readers were
"very shocked by the menacing tone of the president" and that it would
try in the article "to defend our injured dignity and our disavowed sovereignty."[51] The correspondent broke the situation down into four major
issues — "Mr. Bolanachi's situation, Egypt's participation in the Olympic Games, Egyptian sports administration, choosing the Egyptian delegate" — and replied to each one, demonstrating Baillet-Latour's disin-
genuousness.

In the first instance, the argument was essentially that times had changed
and there was no shortage of good men in Egypt to take Bolanachi's place.
Second, it was the IOC who violated the rules and made Egypt's participation in the Los Angeles games impossible; additionally, the exclusion
from future participation was a small price to pay "as long as our dig-

nity would be saved." Third, the count's only knowledge of Egypt was through his representative, Bolanachi, and it was in his interest to depict Egypt as being immature. Finally, to the extent that Egypt's liberty and sovereignty continued to be trespassed, the nation would progress in the sports arena on its own with or without a delegate of the IOC.

Ultimately, the two sides settled the dispute, and an Egyptian delegate, Muhammad Taher Pasha, a nephew of the king, was elected in 1934.[52] The IOC representative from Austria, who recommended him, described Taher as a "true sportsman." Included among his good qualities were an education that was "entirely European" and "an enormous fortune." He was also the president of the Automobile Club.[53] That same year Bolanachi became the IOC delegate for Greece. Although one shouldn't overstate the importance of this victory for Egypt in the international arena, it is nevertheless quite revealing how national honor and dignity were deployed in this dispute. During the 1930s racialized and masculinist rhetoric became increasingly prevalent on the international stage as it became the privileged site in which national identities were compared, contested, and constructed even as it emerged simultaneously as a discrete space of exchange and interaction among continent-hopping cosmopolitans.[54]

George Mosse notes in the European context how the modern transformation of masculinity, which he associated with the rise of the middle class, was co-opted by the nation in the latter years of the eighteenth century and throughout the nineteenth.[55] He also points to a gap between national and everyday notions of masculinity that one might read as the space of ethical and aesthetic practices. He alludes here to the way in which the political gradually occupied that space during the interwar period with ultimately tragic conclusions: "The willingness to sacrifice for an ideal was always latently present, but in daily life and in its social function, masculinity reflected a moral stance — the practice of manly virtues — rather than single-minded national or political commitment. And yet, after the Great War, masculinity as a national and political symbol reached its climax. The ideal of masculinity was close to the heart of fascism, which, together with communism, was about to become the most fateful political movement of the interwar years."[56] There were similarities to Mosse's description of the symbolic shifts in masculinity in the nationalist appropriation of sport in colonial Egypt, but there was also a "world of difference."[57] The spaces inhabited by Tusun, Taher, Bolanachi, Coubertin, and Baillet-Latour were inflected by differences of political power and, in the case of Bolanachi, a diasporic history. But what of the athletes represented by these men? What worlds did they inhabit?

Between the National Modern and the Everyday

Ironically, the colonial political machinations that were responsible for the failure of the African Games did not incur as much criticism as the initial decision to postpone them in 1926. In part, this was because of the euphoria that followed the performance of the Egyptian team at the 1928 Olympics and in part the controversy over replacing Bolanachi.[58] In Amsterdam, the Egyptian wrestler Ibrahim Mustafa became the first athlete from Africa to win a medal in the history of the modern Olympics.[59] He won the gold after defeating his German opponent in the light-heavyweight class.

After his victory, the picture of Mustafa's half-nude body became a regular image in the popular press. In fact, the propulsion of Egypt into the pantheon of nations that had won a gold medal emboldened the launching of new sports magazines during a harsh economic climate.[60] One of these was *al-Abtal* (Champions), a sports supplement to the popular weekly *al-Musawwar*, which was started in 1924. The first issue of *al-Abtal* appeared on December 17, 1932. The masthead announced the magazine's editorial staff as having been drawn from the *crème de la crème* of athletes. The cover of issue number 8 featured a black-and-white photograph of Mustafa in a shirtless, flexed pose.

Inside was a two-page spread recounting Mustafa's life and his rise to international prominence as an athlete; wittingly or unwittingly the biography mirrors the trajectory of another subject's renaissance: the Egyptian nation.[61] In an uncharacteristic move, the biography recounts the humble origins of the champion.[62] It noted that Mustafa's exact birth date was unknown because of the ignorance of his illiterate parents. Emphasizing their poverty, the article revealed that the father did not enroll Ibrahim in a government or a *kuttab* school as a child. In this social and cultural context, the biography continued, a birth date was not deemed to be worth remembering.[63] Mustafa for some reason was certain that he was born in 1905, and he remembered having "visions of strength" from his earliest days. His movement from humble and ignorant origins to a heroic and cultured present was similar to and different from the progress insistently charted by contemporary accounts of modern Egypt's own history. The peculiar temporality of the nation also enabled it to claim a prior history that was rich and glorious. Accordingly, the identity of Mustafa's biography and the nation's could only ever be partial.[64]

Mustafa's first encounter with sports of any kind was watching weightlifters competing informally and showing off in front of a stand that sold

15. The new phenomenon of exhibiting seminude male bodies for a public audience did not seem to attract censure, which may have been the result of over three decades of discursively joining physical culture, masculinity, nationalism, and modernity. The cultural field for producing and visualizing a bare muscular corporeality had been patiently ploughed and planted as part of the general cultivation of Egypt's modern gendered subject. Ibrahim Mustafa, "The World Wrestling Champion." *Al-Abtal* 8/1 (February 4, 1933), cover.

sugar cane juice near his home in Alexandria. He observed them for a while before joining in and eventually surpassing them all. Another account of his life, which also depicts the arena at the juice stand, locates his first experience of sports elsewhere. According to the sports historian Al-Sayyid al-Faraj, Mustafa was apprenticed to an Armenian carpenter when he was eight, and he used to watch from the roof of the shop when the members of the Armenian sports club next door came out to the courtyard to wrestle and lift weights.[65] When he was about eighteen and his athletic promise had become obvious, his boss, Mehran Garabadian, an influential member of the Armenian community in Alexandria, secured admission to the sports club for Mustafa and three fellow apprentices. Faraj also notes that the young Mustafa was inspired by watching the popular strongman show of Abd al-Halim al-Misri in Alexandria.

The biography in *al-Abtal* suggests that his entry into wrestling started on the streets horsing around with his peers, until a group of sports enthusiasts started a makeshift club they named Al-Nadi al-Ahli al-Iskandari (The Alexandria national club) in 1921. It was essentially a hut on the beach. Mustafa joined and became one of the club's best wrestlers. Wanting to exhibit his talents to a wider audience, the club organized a tournament for boxers and wrestlers from the Alexandria region in the Rashid Gardens. In this match, considered Mustafa's official debut as a wrestler, he faced a trained opponent, the Greek wrestler Mitso Dandia.

Mustafa lost that match, but this taste of competition and his popular appeal ('atf al-gamahir) only inspired him to train harder. The experience also got him noticed. Soon he was being trained by Bianchi, a well-known coach at the Italian sports club Ballistra. According to al-Abtal, "It was not difficult for Bianchi to mold [Ibrahim] into a new creation because of his naturally strong and docile body and his simple and modest character." [66]

His training produced results: he was selected to represent Egypt at the 1924 Olympics. Unfortunately for him, Mustafa was one of those athletes who suffered from the negligence of the EOC (see above) toward the members of the delegation. The description of Mustafa's experience in Paris is quite poignant. He was given shoes that were not fit for wrestling and a uniform made of flimsy material that ripped easily. Al-Abtal explains that no one in charge expected him to get beyond the first round. As it turns out, he made it to the semifinal round and lost because his feet kept slipping and he was constantly preoccupied with trying to hold up his torn uniform. The author recounts that Mustafa cried after this defeat. The humiliating loss affected him so much that he withdrew from the match to determine third place.

Although the biography is sympathetic, it does not comment on how badly Egypt let Mustafa down. After returning from Paris, he was forced by financial pressures to quit training and devote all his time to earning a living. Before the next Olympic trials, he was fortunate to be taken under Bianchi's wings again and qualified for the Amsterdam Games of 1928. Mustafa defied all odds yet again, reaching the final round this time and capturing the gold medal. After his victorious return from Amsterdam, he was rewarded with a job in the municipality, and, owing to his tremendous popularity, he started attracting students from the next generation of wrestling aspirants.

In a previous issue, al-Abtal had featured the hulking figure of the then-famous Sayyid Nusayr on its cover.[67] Nusayr had won a gold medal in weightlifting at the Amsterdam Olympics. His biography in the magazine gave his birth date as August 31, 1905. Unlike Mustafa, Nusayr was born to what must have been a relatively prosperous peasant family in Shubar, a village in the Delta province of Gharbiyya. A much more illustrious genealogy was provided by the British physical culture magazine *Superman*, which did a four-part feature on Nusayr's life as a buildup to the Berlin Olympics in 1936:

> Shortly after the death of the Prophet Mohammed, his fanatical followers rode out from the Holy City in the deserts of Arabia to conquer and convert unbelievers by fire and sword. These fierce horsemen swept everything before them. They drove back the Christian powers as far as Vienna, on their way from Constantinople: while by way of North Africa they entered Spain and the south of France. One of their leaders, Moussa Ibn Nosseir by name, made himself a powerful prince in Spain. He ruled there as a despot until his enemies intrigued against him at the court of the Caliph . . . at Constantinople. They whispered that Moussa Ibn Nosseir was planning to throw off the power of the Caliph and make himself an independent prince in Spain. Influenced by these rumours, the Caliph ordered Ibn Nosseir to travel to Egypt. In this country, then, he settled down and founded an influential family, whose descendants are well known in Egypt to-day — one of them being El Saied Nosseir, Amateur Heavyweight Weightlifting Champion of the World.[68]

What this passage lacks in historical accuracy it makes up for in the fantastical inscription of Nusayr's life as a descendant of the once-noble Arab race. The Egyptian rendition of his biography was rather tame in comparison, signaling a qualitative difference in the extent to which athletes could be the subjects of heroic narratives.

Nusayr's father enrolled him in a government school in Tanta, where he also attended secondary school. He was apparently the strongest and most able athlete in both schools. His interest in weightlifting was aroused, perhaps somewhat ironically, while he was attending a saint's festival, the *mawlid* of Al-Sayyid al-Badawi.[69] Nusayr, like Mustafa, attended a performance by Abd al-Halim and, according to his biography, was transfixed and transformed by the strongman's "incredible muscles and astonishing body." As the "spirit of Abd al-Halim penetrated Nusayr," he knew immediately what he wanted to become.[70] The desire to have Abd al-Halim's body drove Nusayr to seek out others like him, and he discovered quickly that there were many bodybuilding and weightlifting enthusiasts in Tanta alone. His school encouraged him by establishing a weightlifting club.

Nusayr never obtained his high school diploma but was given a job at the Ministry of Agriculture in 1927. When he returned with an Olympic gold medal the following year, he was promoted to the "Inspectorship of Games" in the Egyptian army. After leading Egypt to a team victory at

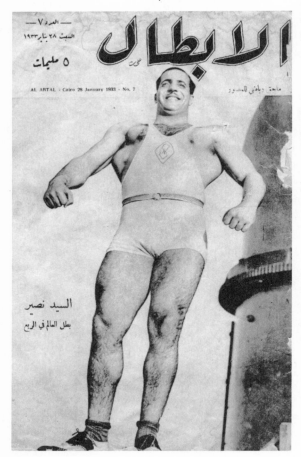

16. The successful display of Egyptian muscle internationally was a more immediate condition of possibility for the proliferation of more revealing photographs of male bodies in major and minor publications in the late 1920s and 1930s. Al-Sayyid Nusayr, "The World Weightlifting Champion." *Al-Abtal* 7 (January 28, 1933), 4–5.

the European Championships in Luxembourg in 1931, he was appointed to the Ministry of Education in recognition of his contribution to the nation. The celebration of Nusayr's triumphs on the world stage had inspired even Egypt's poet laureate, Ahmad Shawqi, to compose an ode to him entitled "The Esteemed Conqueror of the West."[71]

Shawqi's poem, *Qahir al-Gharb al-'Atid*, was recited at a celebration organized by the governor of Cairo (it seems with the patronage of King Fuad) in December 1930. Nusayr had just returned from his first individual European championship competition in Munich, where he defeated ten heavyweight lifters, all of whom weighed more than he did and were more experienced.[72] The poem was composed in an ironic tone that could not have been lost on the audience. The praise Shawqi heaped on

Nusayr for his unrivaled physical strength was doubly undermined by his probing of the meaning of strength and endurance in everyday life:

Oh Great Conqueror of the West, you filled it
    With praise of Egypt on the lips, beautifully.
You overthrew a hand with almost the force
    Of strength to lift into space, an elephant.
He who created iron and its strength
    To your hands made the iron pliable.
You wrested it, weakened its resistance
    On the ground you grabbed it, it clinked and rattled.
Why is the iron unbending, yet you do not cease
    To it you read, do you recite the revelation?
The crisis intensified and its tribulation descended
    With your force [*rukn*] strike its force until it bends.
Samson you are, its forces [*arkan*] dug in
    Among its forces stroll, to eliminate.[73]

The remainder of the poem was structured as a series of questions to Nusayr, querying if he had ever carried other weights, which Shawqi defined as the burdens of daily life. He concluded that these are vastly heavier than any piece of iron. The crisis that was inexorably approaching and growing stronger was like the trials of life that seemed to be compounded with time. Responsibility for others, debt, longing, suffering, betrayal were the forces that must be faced in the biggest challenge of all—living. Hence, the force of physical strength was ultimately inadequate for conquering life, or the West, because as in the case of Samson, it was ephemeral.

It is possible to read Shawqi's tongue-in-cheek eulogy of Nusayr as an intervention in the ancient discourse of al-riyada ("culture," "cultivation," "care" with human and nonhuman targets) and its popular reinscription over the preceding four decades with a distinctly corporeal significance. The "popular" that Shawqi was reacting against here was not some traditional folk custom but the very modern practice of physical culture (al-riyada al-badaniyya). His poetic refusal to celebrate its resultant modal subjectivity should be a clue to the existence of varied middle-class tastes and judgments regarding the new cultural forms that had become popular in the interwar period. The ambivalence around this figure of riyada within the Egyptian cultural landscape was also symptomatic of the unevenness of and tension between capitalist and colonial modernity.

A Beautiful Body
PHYSICAL CULTURE FOR EVERYONE AND EVERYDAY

In the early 1930s *al-Riyada al-Badaniyya* (Physical Culture), another magazine born of the rising popularity of physical culture in Egypt (and other Arabic-speaking lands), sponsored an annual contest for ordinary people called "Beautiful Bodies" (*al-ajsam al-jamila*).[74] The magazine solicited pictures of people in bathing suits so that the physical development of the contestants could be measured and judged. Only men seem to have responded.[75] Photos of men wearing swimming trunks, bikinis, fig leaves, or nothing at all while striking bodybuilding poses were printed in the magazine each month during the year, and a winner was picked. Sometimes the letter that accompanied the picture was also printed. The attached letters were often testimonials to how the contestant's reading of *Physical Culture* and following of its advice, moral and physical, had lifted the person from a life of weakness and either helped him achieve a body he was proud of or placed him closer to the ideal. The contestants were drawn from all over Egypt and the wider Arabic-speaking region; some entered multiple times. The first six contestants appeared in the issue for October 1932; among the six contestants pictured in the issue for March 1933 were physical culture enthusiasts from Iraq and Jordan. The occupation of the participant from Jordan is noted: Director of Telegraph and Post, Amman.

The magazine framed the photos of young and regenerate men as symbolizing both the past and the future; the bodies portrayed in them bore the traces of a once-glorious Egyptian and Arab past that could be recaptured if those bodies were proliferated on a national and transnational scale.[76] Enabling the reproduction of these bodies was the mission of *Physical Culture*, and implicit in that desire was a modernist temporality. Although the photos in the "Beautiful Bodies" competition were presented and read at the time as signs of a rebirth of Egyptian and Arab masculinity, this renaissance was always nothing more than a future possibility of which the individual expressions of corporeal strength were mere harbingers. What it would take to completely transform Egypt, Egyptians, and Arabs into independent, self-constituting subjects was never fully articulated. Ibrahim 'Allam described the role of sports journalism in this process and at this liminal stage as a surreptitious agent for the introduction of the modern into nonmodern spaces. In an intriguing framing of his own and ostensibly of *Physical Culture*'s project as agents in "the age of communication [*murasala*]," he wrote, "Truly, communication is the magical force [*al-quwa al-sahira*] that flows into environments deprived of the features of modern civilization [*al-madaniyya al-hadira*] and nourishes them, alleviating their impoverishment and malignancy." [77] In addition to offering a glimpse of the importance the purveyors of the physical culture discourse ascribed to themselves and their medium in Egypt's modernist aspirations, this quotation illustrates how civilization appeared in their field of vision.[78] (One can imagine Shawqi, with his narrower definition of culture, objecting at this point.)

The bodies on display in the contest contrasted sharply with a society that was always found wanting. Consistently overshadowing the beautiful regenerate bodies were the ugly degenerate bodies of the majority. Ninety-five percent of the male population was declared to be overweight or underweight and lacking in masculinity: "Among these [men] of small bodies, short stature, and weak builds one does not see masculinity except in the . . . thin line that has been left above their lips, as if there were no difference between masculinity and the absence of masculinity other than a moustache." [79] The alchemy of sports journalism in ameliorating a civilizational lack was paralleled by the practice of sports, which would cure the individual body. Unlike the ambiguous future of civilization, exercise promised more concrete gains: "If we [like the West, prioritized exercise as a basic need after food, drink, and sleep], we would make great strides towards our independence, more than what we have gained in half a century. We need health, social progress, and a proper view of masculinity and life in order to obtain our national aspirations." [80] Given the social landscape of Egypt in the 1930s, it is a wonder that national rejuvenation could be thought of in terms of the generalization of a program of physical exercise. In part, this was indeed a testament to how far removed the articulation of an Egyptian bourgeois culture was from the politico-economic reality of the vast majority of the population. But *Physical Culture* was deeply ingrained in the habitus of an emergent social category that dominated culture and politics of the period.

The distance from Egyptian reality, or from the lives of the majority of Egyptians, implied in the very articulation of a discourse of physical culture did not mean there was a distance of differentially classed bodies from one another. The expansion during the interwar period of an Egyptian urban middle class, which formed the readership of *al-Riyada al-Badaniyya*, was accompanied by a major increase in rural to urban migrations. The population of peasants in urban centers grew at unprecedented rates after 1929. The propinquity of peasants and the effendiyya and a growing desire by the effendiyya to distance themselves from the

17-1-17-6. "Beautiful Bodies
Competition," *RB* (March 1933), 25–26.
Pictured counterclockwise (from page
25) are "Beautiful Bodies" contestants
nos. 31) Abdallah Effendi Sabari in
Baghdad; 32) Ahmad Hasan Effendi;
33) Muhammad Ali Isma'il. Pictured
clockwise (from page 26): 34) 'Izz al-Din
Sulayman Effendi; 35) Mazhar Effendi
Jalal; 36) Hasan Effendi al-Jundi.

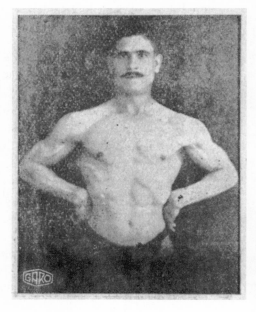

heinous bodies of the peasants, who populated the everyday spaces of urban life, may well have conditioned this seemingly disconnected discourse. In the difficult economic and political climate of the 1930s, the physical culture discourse was a means by which the emergent social category of the effendiyya, desiring a rupture from its origins, sought a new kind of cultural capital. Yet precisely because of the political economy of colonial modernity, in order to conceive individual and national sovereignty it was necessary to imagine a future national landscape populated with regenerate bodies.

Contrary to the standard positioning of the effendiyya in historical narratives as a class that either was or sought to be representative of the nation, I find that the articulation of the physical culture discourse from the second half of the 1920s onward demonstrates an ambivalence toward that nation. To put it bluntly, laying claim to an ugly national body was not a desirable position; furthermore, it was because that body was made up of sickly, nonsovereign parts that independence had been so elusive for the past half century. Even though there was a desire for a representative voice, which is clearly demonstrated in the political involvements of the effendiyya, the normative subject of the riyada discourse and desire for a particular kind of corporeal beauty evinces an uneasy identification with the nation as it was.

Even if in retrospect the proposed cure appears inadequate, there is a lesson to be learned from the diagnosis. In what way was the Egyptian national body considered to be sick? The problem was located at the very bases of its birth and its reproduction, making the national characteristic of the body dependent on the way it was gendered and sexualized. In a telling article entitled "The Fate of Weak People," Mukhtar al-Jawhari, one of the editors of *Physical Culture*, made an argument that connected weak male bodies to individual, marital, familial, and national happiness or lack thereof.[81] Beauty and strength were presented as the most important distinguishing features between the sexes.[82] When they were joined by mutual attraction and marriage, what resulted was the happiest of households. Since the family (*al-usra*) was the most important unit (*wahda*) of society, it also became "the angel of a nation's life." Not just any family qualified for angelic status; it had to be the "proper [conjugal] family" based on strong males and beautiful females. The male was the more essential and indispensable part of the equation; a woman without a beautiful face could compensate for it by possessing a beautiful body or soul. If she failed on those counts as well, then she could rely on her natural "feminine wiles" (*fitnat al-unutha*).

Conversely, although a weak man could achieve some material success owing to the prevailing conditions of civilization, a rational woman would not choose him as a conjugal partner. She knew he lacked the physical strength to protect her and to defend himself; the strength of character that would guarantee his fidelity and her happiness; and the "strength of will and relentless determination that would secure for her and her children a comfortable lifestyle."[83] The man of strength, on the other hand, was capable of everything and failed at nothing, and this was mainly because his basic constitution was different. He was happy in his skin, in simply being (*yajidu al-saʿada fi mujarrid al-wujud*). But given the pedagogic mission and profit motives of the magazine, the futures of weak bodies were not constructed as terminal, and the diagnosis of deficiency came with a course of treatment.[84] As we will see in a more detailed analysis of this long-running publication in the next chapter, a regime of caring for the self could lead to the recovery of masculinity.[85]

Conclusion

The politics of the African Games, the two brief biographies of Egyptian Olympic champions, and the proliferation of a magazine like *Physical Culture* illustrate a number of points about national identity, masculinity, and culture. On the discursive level, a more confident representation of a muscular Egypt was conditioned by the revolution of 1919 and the achievement of an independence of sorts in 1922. For contemporary commentators, the alignment of national identity and honor with muscled bodies was enabled by the extension and popularization of weightlifting and wrestling throughout the country combined with the extraordinary success of Egyptian wrestlers and weightlifters in the widening arena of international sports competition. On the other hand, the evidence of the arena in front of the juice stand and the club on the beach point to an entirely different, though overlapping, popular level of participation than that represented by the expanding formal fields of sports activities through schools, clubs, and associations.[86] On the subjective and everyday levels, the biographies of Ibrahim Mustafa and Sayyid Nusayr and the mere existence of Beautiful Bodies contestants serve to complicate the neatness of a national (and nationalist) mythology and add nuance to the workings of colonial power in the new era of internationalism.

I do not mean simply that highlighting the economic constraints on these subjects disrupts nationalist and internationalist discourses; that

ذكرى وفاة بطل للمصارعة المرحوم عبد الحليم بك المصرى

نشر هذه الصورة قبلنا واجبنا الصحاق نحو الفقيد الادب والرياضة المرحوم
عبد الحليم بك المصرى بطل المصارعة فى مصر واحد اذكرى ذلك البطل

راحت هناك اشاعة بوفاة الرياضى المشهور وبطل مصر المعروف فى المصارعة
حسن بك على الطويل اثر مصارعته الاسدوالحقيقة أن هذه الاشاعةعارية
عن الصحة وان الأسد لم ينل منه مأذى ولا يزال حسن بك حيا يقوم

18. The national recuperation of Abd al-Halim's powerful body is perhaps best attested to in this public recording of his death, signifying that his life was far more meaningful than the living and passing of a mere carnival performer. "Commemorating Wrestling Champion the Late Abd al-Halim al-Misri." *Al-Nil al-Musawwar* (October 7, 1926), 24.

form of critical interruption was already taking place everywhere in the 1930s.[87] Nor do I mean to suggest that their stories represent some other popular, more authentic reality. Indeed, given the archives available for Egypt, accessing the consciousness of these figures is nearly impossible;[88] however, their biographies, photos, and letters do contain some clues as to how the lives of Mustafa, Nusayr, and the many other physical culture devotees might be extricated from an exclusively national framework and resignified. The desire to possess muscular bodies alludes to an affective domain that was overdetermined. The love of nation might have played a role here at some point in the matrix of desiring a perfect body; however, their constitution as desiring subjects for whom body image assumed a new signification seems to demand other kinds of explanation. The fashioning of a modern self in Egypt during the first three to four decades of the twentieth century is a story most often told in terms of nation or class. These categories cannot account for the particular desire exhibited, for example, by Mustafa and Nusayr. Both were said to have been especially moved by the vision of Abd al-Halim's muscular body, even though it was established that their love of sports had begun at an early age — and in Mustafa's case had developed through his observation of the exercises of Armenian boys and men.

Abd al-Halim's traveling body was a trope in which disparate and overdetermined desires for muscular corporeality could be pinned on one unified national longing for strength. Without dismissing the nationalist mapping of Egyptian bodies, it is conceivable that a different economy of desire became operative through the course of Egypt's interpolation into the world economy and subjugation by a colonial power. For Egypt, colonial modernity certainly meant a subordinate relationship in capitalist developments of the sporting field; nonetheless, the masculine subject of riyada was a highly visible figure on the interwar cultural landscape in part because of its simultaneously universal and particular possibilities within nationalist, internationalist, and individualist agendas. It is impossible to say much about what it meant for Mustafa, Nusayr, and all the other ordinary men to desire muscular bodies, but what that specific kind of desire meant in the history of the modern masculine subject in Egypt may yield to further inquiry.

6

COMMUNICATION

Sex, Gender, and Norms of *Physical Culture*

By the 1930s a genealogy of Egypt's participation in sports through time was popularly available. Its modern manifestation was represented as a significant dimension of national rebirth; it was a site of the restoration of Egyptian manhood. Some thought the Egyptian rediscovery of sports occurred during the First World War, when it came to be seen as more than mere child's play. According to the sports editor of *al-Ahram*, Ibrahim 'Allam (a.k.a. Juhayna), it was the act of actually witnessing sports played by the forces of the British imperial army that transformed its meaning for Egyptians.[1] "We saw" that even at the worst points of the war the occupying forces engaged in sports; then "we understood" that it was a powerful means of constituting a bond between the state and the people.[2] As noted previously, in this discourse the history of the contemporary revival was located equally in ancient Egypt and Islam.[3]

But recent history was also invoked as a more familiar and apparently more popular narrative by the 1930s. There is a scene in the comedy film *al-Riyadi* (The Sportsman) (1935) in which the heroic genealogy of Egyptian football is recounted as a contrast to the less glorious present.[4] The scene is set in the locker room of a local Alexandria team, Athletic, after its loss in a match against the foreign team RSM. The Bey (the owner of the club) enters and, finding his players dejected, immediately launches into what is ostensibly a pep talk delivered in classical Arabic. He invokes the days not long ago when Egyptian football was renowned for its *majd wa fakhr* (glory and pride) as a prelude to his prediction that those days would, through hard work and effort, return. As the Bey exits, the dialogue returns to a colloquial register and one of the players despondently retorts, "Magd wa fakhr? That was a long time ago. The days of Higazi, Salem, Adel Riyadi [?], and Abaza." These players from the teens and twenties were already markers of a golden age in the mid–thirties.

The process of constructing a useable history of modern practices and modern actors was a diffuse effort during the interwar period. By the 1930s it was simultaneously taken up by scholars, journalists, artists, filmmakers, doctors, and others who focused on all manner of everyday practices as the repertoire of an Egyptian modern. A good example of this engagement with the relationship between modernity's history and present was the monthly sports magazine *al-Riyada al-Badaniyya* (Physical culture). It attempted to intervene in the cultural life of Egypt at a time when the push forward into the promised future of freedom and progress seemed to have stalled ten years after the revolution and five years after the first parliament. The interventions were on a number of issues and at several levels, all of which intersected at the question of sex.

On the one hand, *Physical Culture* elaborated an explicit discourse of sexuality as a site of identity and desire and, on the other, critiqued the same through intensive rounds of didactic lessons on self-discipline. In order to grasp this combination of the proper, the prurient, and the pedagogic, it may help to think of the magazine as an event, which 'Allam's heralding of an age of communication invites. It represented the culmination or maturation of the physical culture discourse in Egypt both through its formal structure, which gathers within its purview a wide range of topical issues, and through its content, which illustrates a significant reach and depth. In a sense, that climax of form and substance in a discourse on bodily discipline, desire, and self-constitution could not but be represented by scantily clad models spread on the cover of nearly every issue. The future beckoned, and even if Egyptian women could not yet occupy the position of these models, modern life and its consumers had to be consistently nourished in order to persist. In this regard, *Physical Culture* is an important artifact of the urban material culture of the emergent effendiyya as it illuminates a pivotal moment in its subject formation; through this text one catches a glimpse of an intimate, though public, renegotiation of the terms of survival for the subject of effendi masculinity in colonial modernity.

Physical Culture is also compelling because in addition to its national circulation it maps a diasporic and transnational geography for modern, middle-class Arabic culture.[5] While no circulation figures are available, the provenance of the magazine's letters to the editor, for one, suggested an impressive distribution.[6] The intended audience was the emergent

19. That the images in magazines of scantily clad female bodies were primarily those of noticeably "foreign" women during this period indexes the particular way in which the physical culture discourse in Egypt had come to be gendered and sexualized. The national reframing of muscular masculinity since the late nineteenth century opened a space for the public display of seminude Egyptian male bodies while simultaneously foreclosing it to women on the grounds of that very same masculinity; for example, masculinity's condition of possibility in colonial

modernity was the expulsion from itself, or abjection, of femininity. Thus, rather than tradition or Islam barring images of Egyptian women's bodies from the new public culture it was a specific historical configuration of nationalism and physical culture—both quintessentially modern forms of constructing subjects heavily mediated by new technologies of communication. Female swimmer, *RB* (December 1934), cover.

effendiyya class of professionals, government civil service employees, men occupied in the new business trades, and their spouses and daughters. The magazine was read in every major city and in several smaller towns throughout Egypt. Beyond Egypt, it had readers in Sudan, Palestine, Jordan, Lebanon, Syria, Iraq, and Bilad al-Arab (the Arabian peninsula). The magazine seemed to circulate even among the Arab diaspora in far-flung places like Brazil, Gambia, Sierra Leone, and Bombay.

In Cairo (the most historically verifiable segment of the magazine's readership) the urban geography that was the proximate setting for the birth of *Physical Culture* had changed dramatically. The street on which the Jawhari brothers established their physical culture institute in 1927 was a major artery in the heart of modern Cairo. By the beginning of the First World War the city had, through the expansion of habitable land created by the construction of the first Aswan Dam in 1902 and an extensive tramway system by 1917, experienced significant growth in terms of built space. But not until after the war did Cairo truly become a major city in terms of population and geography. The demographic expansion of Cairo's population, matched by a startling expansion of its built space, created new administrative and policing concerns as well as new ways of imagining the city (I explore these subjects extensively elsewhere).[7] Additions to the urban landscape and urban culture included new kinds of establishments: department stores, movie theaters, and theme parks.[8] There was also an expansion of the number of cafés and nightclubs. The tramway system enabled the geographic growth of Cairo and transformed physical movement within the city into an entirely new practice for all classes; by the end of the war, the system served seventy-five million passengers a year.[9]

Physical Culture, the brainchild and business venture of the lawyer Muhammad Fa'iq al-Jawhari and his brothers, Mukhtar and Ra'uf, formed part of a socially expansive and variegated interventionist agenda emerging in the last years of the 1920s. By the end of 1927 the three brothers had opened the Physical Education Institute (*ma'had al-tarbiyya al-badaniyya*). In the same year, the Young Men's Muslim Association, complete with its own athletic facilities, was established not far from their location at 28 Sharia Fuad in Cairo.[10] The following year the brothers launched *Physical Culture*. Its focus was the care of the body—a literal translation of the Arabic expression *al-riyada al-badaniyya*. Under this rubric, the editor, Muhammad al-Jawhari, made it the magazine's mission to educate the Egyptian reading public about sex, love, and physical beauty. Although the figure of the nation made regular appearances as a legitimizing trope, the magazine represented a much broader modernist project and was intensely conscious of its role as a new technology in the process of modern self-fashioning and of heralding the future.

Sex and Colonial Modernity

In 1919, after four tumultuous years of war which saw enormous deprivation at home and the disappearance of the four-hundred-year-old Ottoman Empire of which Egypt had been a part, larger numbers of the new effendi middle class asserted themselves in the political and cultural spheres with renewed vigor, especially as opportunities within the eco-

20. Sharia Fuad, ca. 1930s. Photo, Lehnert and Landrock Collection (Oriental Art Publishers, Cairo); dates given in store catalogue are 1930–36.

nomic sphere expanded less rapidly.[11] The energy and momentum of the revolution of 1919, which had brought Egypt a nominal form of independence from British rule in 1922, quickly gave way to old problems. Egypt was still compelled to prove itself worthy of total self-determination. New cultural and political agents among the effendiyya began to contest the elites' claims to being the rightful representatives of the nation. One of the modes in which this contest was carried out was pedagogy. During the interwar period there was a marked proliferation of conventional educational institutions as well as independent print and other media dedicated to the dissemination of nationalist and modernist lessons.[12] In this vein the new magazine *Physical Culture* displayed a keen interest in sex education (*al-tarbiyya al-jinsiyya*). The appearance of "sexuality" as an object of pedagogy in Egypt was coincident with global economic crises and may to some extent index the beleaguered condition of middle-class effendi masculinity as the economy worsened, political negotiations stalled, and contentious women were running amok.[13] At the same time, the reiterations in *Physical Culture* of what was a proper sexual subjectivity and how to attain this normative condition were culturally productive in ways that were subtle and never fully predictable. Nevertheless, the difference between a colonial performance of masculinity and sexuality and a contemporaneous metropolitan one is difficult to locate, especially when the former was fully engaged with coeval Euro-American discourses of physical culture and sexuality.

Joseph Massad's recent elaboration of sexuality in the Arab context attempts to correct for drawbacks to Eurocentrist and Orientalist perspectives on cultural formation, which, as he argues, have constrained understanding of the mutually constitutive work of colonialism and modernity.[14] Sex played a boundary-making role in the delineation of such seemingly natural binaries as East and West, barbaric and civilized, deviant and normal. Despite Massad's attention to the colonial birth of sexuality, the Arab engagements with it often appear as a simple case of internalization of an epistemology imposed from elsewhere.[15] The pioneering works of Ann Stoler, Mrinalini Sinha, Antoinette Burton, Philippa Levine, and others have begun to recast the old imperial history and some of the more recent social histories that have maintained, wittingly or unwittingly, national frames of reference for apprehending a historical past that was if anything characterized by an unprecedented global connectedness of humans, nonhumans, and ways of knowing.[16] Within such a history, conceived as a series of networks and flows, the production and dissemination of cultural—as well as economic, political, and biological—forms can no longer be regarded as moving from an originary center to the periphery but must be traced along different axes. Those lines of interconnection would increase in density from the late nineteenth century through the first half of the twentieth. Thus, for interwar Egypt, as for modern societies everywhere, the cultural politics of sexuality and masculinity cannot be understood in isolation from the imperial social formation, which was materialized through the simultaneous circulation and containment of differentiated bodies (of humans and nonhumans, of ideas and microbes) within and between national and imperial territories.[17]

As Massad has demonstrated, the power to accelerate, limit, alter, or stop the flow was unevenly distributed across the globe, and hence the experience of the colonial (and postcolonial) would never be the same in London and Cairo. Furthermore, the coloniality of this space was not so much the outcome of singular events—military conquests, occupations, settlements, treaty negotiations—as it was shaped by repeated performances of, among other things and practices, gendered and sexualized subjectivities. *Physical Culture* represented one such performance.[18] Although the asymmetries of politico-economic relations between colonies and metropoles determined the primary direction of cultural traffic, the distances between the translation, dissemination, and reception of the "borrowed object" left room for revisions and rewritings.[19] Nonetheless, the power differential of colonialism entailed costs in metropoles and colonies that were sometimes inversely related. I will suggest at the end of this chapter that one such cost was recursively transferred to life forms whose precarious existence could not be reproduced through pedagogy, represented in the new media, or contested in the new public sphere.

Although a distinct disciplinary project of physical culture did emerge in Egypt between the 1890s and 1920s, the argument developed here does not rest on a correspondence between discourse and psychological internalization. My inquiry views the formation of a subject of physical culture — a global rhetorical and material strategy — as an ongoing process of normalization, which in Egypt in the 1930s appeared to have snagged on unresolved questions of sovereignty and rights, both of the individual and of the nation.[20] *Physical Culture* is a generative source to consider in this regard, as anxieties of moral failure and didactic responses permeated the text, while at the same time it was marketed via the very terms of that failure: sexually suggestive images and the proliferation of deviance talk. The subject denominated here as an effect of physical culture was thus a nominalist entity but all the same it was a concrete formation that housed numerous possibilities while also occulting others.[21]

Theoretically, the subject of modernity performatively shaped through discourse is never fully materialized anywhere; accordingly, this historical example from Egypt is best viewed as a snapshot of the kinds of rhetorical and practical strategies that were deployed in a particular society seeking to stabilize the relationship between words and things as the future seemed at once increasingly present and an elusive hope. The particulars of Egyptian physical culture gained their specificity from a colonial universalization of the modern form as a possibility everywhere. Such a conception of space and time informed the interwar production, differentiation, organization, and representations of individual and national bodies (for labor) around the globe.[22] *Physical Culture* as pedagogy and performance represented a refusal, without necessarily constituting an act of resistance, of the colonial difference[23] that located places like Egypt in the space of the non-modern or not-yet modern; this disavowal animated the magazine's simultaneously moralistic and salacious character and conditioned both the possibility and impossibility of future subjects.

Building Bodies, Modernizing Desire, and Fantasizing Sovereignty

A Self to Call Modern

How was the modern fantasy of a self-governing body inflected by Egypt's location in an imperial social formation? In *Physical Culture*, one could use labels like masculinist, patriarchal, and heterosexist—not to mention classist and racist—but these should be avoided for now in order to bypass the conventional referent of such signifiers: the history of a Euro-American social order. This is easier said than done given the magazine's self-conscious mimicry of the terms, logics, and vision deployed by metropolitan social scientific discourses. In the next two subsections I trace the major themes in *Physical Culture* as they relate to norms of gender, sexuality, and the body. In the final section, I explore some ways in which this source may be coaxed to yield other histories of the modern that were inhibited or suppressed by the terms of power forming the subject in colonial modernity.

Physical Culture began publication in 1929 and continued through the early 1950s. The last issue of the magazine that I have dates from October 1940, but in that issue the editor set forth his plan to launch an expanded version of the magazine in the following year.[24] It is likely that the longevity of this sports magazine—at a time when the life span of a new periodical often did not exceed a few months—was due precisely to its treatment of a controversial subject like sex. The magazine was organized into scientific sections presenting articles on health, sports, and sex (*abhath sihhiyya, abhath riyadiyya,* and *abhath jinsiyya*) and into fictional and autobiographical sections presenting stories and letters from readers concerning love and marriage.[25]

The majority of the articles that pertain to sex, including the letters and stories, can be grouped along an axis that spans the distance between permissible desire and correctable deviance. From the hundreds of letters published I reproduce one that features all of the ingredients the magazine required in a successful recipe for the refashioning of self:

Dear Cupid,

I am a young man twenty-three years of age who is a foreigner in these lands. I began my working life at sixteen, that is, at puberty, and I used to think a lot about increasing my knowledge of the second sex at that time. Since then,

*sexual feelings have been raging through me. However, I was so shy my heart
would start beating rapidly at the thought of speaking to a girl, even if it were
just polite conversation. I slept in my own room and after my parents locked all
the doors I'd spend the nights staying up. Some nights I'd stand at the window
after midnight hoping to find women passing by alone or accompanied by a
young man. If my wish were fulfilled, then I'd curse them both for their freedom and for enjoying [their] love safe from the eyes of censors. Then my blood
would boil and I'd become like a madman. I sought freedom. Not much time
had passed with me in this state before I was struck with fits of coughing, my
body grew thin, and my eyes became hollow. I attracted pity from the family.
I was always nervous about doctors prescribing too much medication with no
benefit, so I traveled to Cairo with its renowned doctors and stayed for nearly
six months.*

These are the tortured opening lines penned by "A.Y.D." (Arabic initials
alif-ya-dal) in a long letter dispatched from "the extreme western border of Sudan," sent to *Physical Culture*, and published in March 1936. The
young man's epistle, titled "A Voice from Unknown Africa," occupied
more than three pages of the letters section called "What Would You Do
in This Situation?"[26] A.Y.D.'s letter was one of many from readers with
similar concerns about love, sex, and intimate relationships published in
the magazine during the course of the highly unstable 1930s.[27] Indeed,
during different phases of its life span, the magazine featured multiple
letters sections in the same issue; for example, appearing alongside "What
Would You Do in This Situation?" was a "Health Advice" section fielding
questions on exercise, masturbation, venereal diseases, and so forth, with
answers proffered by none other than "Hippocrates."

In the letter from "Unknown Africa," A.Y.D. continued by elaborating
for readers the depths of his moral depravity and the resultant physical
suffering he endured.[28] The young man averred that he was able to find
his way back to the straight and narrow only when he started reading
Physical Culture. A concerned friend had mailed him some back issues of
the magazine from 1933 and 1934, while he was hospitalized for a lengthy
period after contracting a severe case of gonorrhea:

> I started to read through it and quickly fell in love with it. When I
> could finally leave the hospital, I was filled by this truthful idea [*al-fikra
> al-sahiha*] about life. I read a lot about harmful habits and the excesses
> of sexual relations; I found in front of me a guide to show me the way—
> through honest information about the second sex, which I had been
> yearning to learn. I left the hospital in better health, and I made the issues

of *Physical Culture* my first priority. I used to read it every day, mastering the exercises. I got used to showering in cold water daily followed by a massage and sunbathing in the nude. My health improved and my weight increased from 122 pounds to 134 in less than two months. I also made friends who would play sports and take long walks with me.[29]

Although the author of this letter appeared to have resolved his sexual crisis through the ingestion of new knowledge about sex and the practice of alternative physical activities, he remained in an ethical dilemma. Before becoming ill, he believed he had impregnated a woman he was in love with and with whom he was obviously having a sexual relationship. After an initial period of confusion and as the news of her pregnancy began to spread, they agreed (according to the author it was a mutual decision) to keep some distance between them. In fact, the author claimed his lover insisted that he move on and seek another companion. Being ever so compliant, this was how he found himself in the hospital with gonorrhea. After leaving the hospital he learned that his lover had delivered a black (*ʿabd*) baby who had "a broad nose like the uncircumcised [*qalalif*] and eyes like the devil" — most definitely not his son:

> Here is where I ask you for the answer, Mr. Cupid, or the honorable male readers — not females — to the [question]: Is it correct to subscribe to Schopenhauer's philosophy, mentioned in the November 1935 issue of your magazine, on women, their wiles, shortsightedness and ignorance — that all that was given to women in terms of talent are cunning and deception in order to be wooed and courted; she does not strive for the capacity to benefit humanity [*al-insaniyya*], rather to extract from a man an expression of interest in her so that she can reign over him. I ask you for a reply to this problem of mine. It will determine what I will do with this woman. Present [the problem] to them. Tell them that I haven't forgotten that my relationship with her was illicit, but they need to overlook whether it was licit [*mashruʿa*] or illicit [*ghayr mashruʿa*] and look at the issue from the perspective of a purely sexual relationship, which, if it takes hold of a young man, leaves him no room to think about what is licit and illicit. So, does a woman deserve all of our respect and reverence and does she deserve that we submit our hearts to her in love and trust her with this love or with our offspring? Answer this question, dear sir, for it is the source of my problem, my confusion, and my misery.[30]

Normally the responses of the readers and Cupid's own evaluation of the situation would appear in the following issue of the magazine. Unfortunately, I did not have access to a copy of *Physical Culture* from April 1936, so the reactions to A.Y.D.'s situation must remain a mystery for now.[31] Nevertheless, it is safe to say that, compared to others, the richness of this letter in terms of detail must have provoked a massive response from readers.

This raises the basic question of why people would engage the problems of strangers through this medium. Although it is beyond the scope of this study to offer a satisfactory answer, it may be safe to say that the novel system of awarding prizes for the best advice served as an adequate incentive to some. It was Cupid's role as the forum moderator to select the best solutions or analyses of the preceding month's problem and to award their authors prizes ranging from one Egyptian pound for first place to various publications relevant to physical culture for second, third, and so on.

There were nearly a thousand responses to a situation that was far less interesting than the one above, a case of marital infidelity in which the wife wanted to know from the public if she should stay with her cheating husband, whom her family was pressuring her to leave. The majority (790) enjoined "Mrs. S" to persevere and to patiently reform her husband's ways by making herself more attractive to him. One hundred eighty-five respondents did encourage her to leave her husband.[32] Readers' letters came from far and wide; one Abu al-Abbas Ahmad al-Attar from Bombay was awarded fifth prize for his opinion. First prize went to an unnamed male reader who confessed to having been in her husband's shoes; he advised her to remain the devoted wife and to try to obtain a transfer for her husband so they could move to another town.[33]

In the first few issues published after this letters format was introduced in 1931, the editors ran the following explanatory note about the new forum, which they labeled "A Parliament for Readers": "Do the people . . . around you understand you and do they provide you with compassion and support when you need it? If your answer was in the negative then you are in need of Cupid. He is ready to serve you in times of confusion, pain, and unhappiness."[34] Mrs. S, like numerous others, certainly felt that her family did not understand her and turned to this virtual community of strangers for compassion and support. According to the editors, Cupid answered most of the letters privately, and only the most complicated problems were published. Indeed, the problems were sometimes too complicated for this "Parliament" to resolve.

In the same issue in which A.Y.D.'s letter was presented to the *Physical Culture* audience, the readers responded to a young woman's problem from a previous issue. Very briefly, this young woman had developed intense feelings for a female classmate during their school years together. When the classmate went on to get married, she discovered that what she was feeling must be love since she had never been attracted to any of the boys she knew and since the thought of her friend being betrothed to a man appeared to her to be an utterly devastating loss. In this case, which Cupid called a "psychological problem deserving study and analysis," none of the responses were deemed to be a useful solution, and most were dismissive of her situation. Cupid does add that several young women wrote about how they could "understand her psyche" and offered their consolation.[35]

Talking Sex, Translating Sexuality

A primary concern—it would not be an exaggeration to say an obsession—of the magazine evident in practically every issue was the problem of abnormality and the possibility of straight sex. In general, the domain of supposed sexual deviancies was delimited according to *Physical Culture*'s mission to promote sex education; the targets were most often masturbation and venereal diseases.[36] Medical expertise, foreign and Egyptian, was regularly marshaled to demonstrate the harms of sexual activity outside of the legitimate bonds of marriage.[37] Dr. Fakhri Faraj and Dr. Sabri Jirjis became household names and images through the frequent appearances of their articles and interviews in the magazine.[38]

In an interview conducted in 1932 Faraj was presented to the readers as a pioneer in Egyptian medicine who had long advocated and worked for sex education.[39] He launched his crusade in 1921 with a lecture at the Egyptian University, which apparently was not well received. For years after, the only venue at which he was allowed to lecture about sexual health issues was Ewart Hall of the American University in Cairo.[40] He was not prevented from publishing extensively, and eventually he became a regular contributor to *Physical Culture*. He had written several volumes on female sexuality, reproduction, prostitution, venereal diseases, the woman question, and sexual impotence.[41]

When the interviewer asked whether his efforts had made a difference, he admitted that at both the government and popular levels only limited progress had been made. In a report on the spread of prostitution and ways to combat it, a report he had submitted to King Fuad and to the first Parliament in 1924, he recommended that sex education programs be instituted in government schools. His plan was partially implemented by the Ministry of Education: lessons on plant and animal reproduction were

21. (left) Dr. Fakhri Faraj. *RB* (December 1932), 7 and (right) Dr. Sabri Jirjis. *RB* (December 1932), 8. The dissemination of images of professional men, of experts in a field, represents another genre of publicizing the effendi as a source of bourgeois masculine authority, as a mimetic figure of the instance of nation.

added to the primary school curriculum, but the human reproduction component, which was meant for secondary schools and university, was not incorporated. Although he performed what he termed his civic duty (*wajibi al-ijtima'i*) through the public lectures he delivered at the American University, he acknowledged that the audience was not the mass of the population.

For the masses, especially the young, cases of sexually transmitted diseases were on the rise.[42] According to Faraj, the increase was commensurate with their total ignorance about sex: "I am probably not exaggerating if I said that they don't know any of its details except for what is [necessary] to fulfill their sexual cravings. They are not different in this respect from their companions — wild animals."[43] Despite the state of sexual ignorance in which the majority of Egypt's (peasant) population found itself, Faraj expressed his abiding confidence that "the spirit of Egypt's intellectual renaissance" and "the spirit of [its] leap forward" could not but address this problem too. He cited anecdotal evidence of doctors in the provinces who were imbued with this spirit and who were undertaking on their own initiative programs to educate the people about sex and sexually transmitted diseases.

Although the politics of sex education was not addressed directly in the interview, it did rear its head when Faraj mentioned in passing opposition from "the guardians of public morals." According to the editor, the magazine was constantly subjected to erroneous charges of encouraging immorality.[44] Muhammad al-Jawhari introduced his editorial comments a few months after the interview with Faraj by reflecting on the historical case of the European Wars of Religion as an example of fighting for a cause—of the principled assault. He contrasted this to the attacks on the magazine, which he deemed hypocritical because of their intentional misrepresentation of its educational mission to enlighten people about the dangers of abusing their bodies sexually. It is when one wonders who was doing the attacking—since they go unnamed—that the example drawn from European history becomes intelligible. Unlike the Wars of Religion, wherein questions of belief were ostensibly at the heart of conflict, the editor of *Physical Culture* was suggesting that his magazine was being attacked in the name of religion by people who should and did know better. In other words (words that went unuttered), Islam was being twisted to meet ends that were not necessarily Islamic.[45]

Even the American University was not impervious to the reach of the guardians of public morals. Faraj was taken to court for a lecture he delivered there (presumably) in 1931 about the need to revise personal status codes to reflect the advances of modern civilization. Although I was unable to discover the specific charges, it is likely from the context that he was accused of offending the revealed religions. After the court acquitted him, the lecture was serialized in *Physical Culture*, with a preface emphasizing the good doctor's courage in carrying out his civic duty.[46] The radical aspect of Faraj's lecture seemed to lie in his criticism of the Eastern Christian authorities for their antiquated approach to divorce and inheritance rights. Although only the Catholic Church was named in his critique, his call for a unified civil code on personal status issues implicated Copts and Muslims as well.[47] This was clearly a controversial position to uphold at that time, but it did not necessarily correspond to a belief in gender equality.[48] His major concern, as an expert on venereal disease, was the consequence to society of women who became prostitutes or bad mothers simply because of insufficient legal safeguards that did not prevent their impoverishment in cases of death or divorce.[49]

On the issue of equality between men and women, he expressed indignation at those who would even pose such a question and accused them of living in a fantasy world. Ostensibly, the little political responsibility women already had was a burden too heavy for them. Echoing late nineteenth-century discourse on motherhood, Faraj points to Egyptian men marrying foreign women as a sign of the failure of Egyptian women in their nationalist duty to raise sons with good nationalist values.[50] In any case, according to Faraj, nature and biology had already invalidated the very possibility of equality. For motherhood was a natural right given only to women, one through which they had power over others: children, husband, family. Because men could never possess this right they were denied that route to power.

As a medical expert assessing women's mental and physical capacity, Faraj granted that there was the potential for a certain level of equivalence with men if these aspects were allowed to develop. The problem was that such development would undermine the biological basis of personhood and contradict the social aspects of the woman's role as spouse and mother. Practicing sports that resulted in building musculature, for example, could introduce masculine elements into her body that would affect her chances for marriage, her sex life, and her reproductive ability. Only properly feminine activities such as tennis, calisthenics, and jumping rope were recommended.[51] Higher intellectual pursuits were to be stopped upon marriage since a good mother was more beneficial to society than a smart woman; after all, there was no dearth of smart men to undertake intellectual efforts. Medical science could show that the tensions caused by excessive intellectual exertion would hinder the woman's capacity to be a good mother or even to become a mother.

The creeping masculinization of women and the threat this posed to social order was a phenomenon that deeply concerned the Egyptian middle class, including the feminists who sought to challenge the status quo. As Margot Badran points out, although education was one of the areas in which Egyptian feminists had made major gains, by the mid-1930s there was growing unease about the inability of educated women to fulfill their roles as mothers and daughters. So much so that even feminists articulated the need for more home economics courses and supported the Ministry of Education's establishment of so-called schools of feminine culture in 1938 as an alternative route after girls finished primary school.[52] On the other hand, the family was an arena in which feminists had failed to achieve any real advances, but in the 1930s they shifted strategies from seeking change through legal reform to instructing women on ways of running a more efficient household and of obtaining better conjugal relations with their husbands. Badran explains this move in terms of economic need and political expediency:

> By the late 1930s middle-class women had broken into new professions, entering the workplace in significant numbers and often competing with men for jobs. The influx, which made many men uneasy, was exacerbated by the persisting economic recession. As working women came under increasing attack as wives and mothers who neglected their home and "natural" roles, feminists stepped up the discourse on the importance of women's family roles. This was by then a familiar strategy of feminists in promoting new opportunities for women in society; it was especially expedient in the 1930s with the rise of Islamist conservatism. Through a focus on women's traditional roles their fragile gains in the workplace might be protected and the way paved for future advances. Advice on making the family function more smoothly and the household oper-ate more efficiently could also help women employed outside the house shoulder their new double burden.[53]

The fear of women's denaturalization was not just a question of the failure to fulfill roles, as Badran suggests. There was a more fundamental ques-tioning of the boundaries between masculinity and femininity that was brought to the foreground by the factors Badran identifies but whose im-plications were problematic for both men and women. The political car-toons of this period satirize both the masculinization of Egyptian women and the emasculation of Egyptian men. Men were depicted as fighting (poorly) on two fronts to maintain their honor: against persistent colonial relations and the feminist onslaught. Women are depicted mainly as fight-ing Egyptian men for trivial gains. The figuration of the political context is shot through with explicitly gendered tropes. In the cartoons I have tracked from the early 1920s to the late 1930s, it is possible to get a sense of the growing unease over women becoming more like men (culminating in corporeal sameness—a fact attested to by a highly publicized sex-change operation).

The perceived sense of women's growing identity with men as an un-natural occurrence was not represented simply as a critique of the femi-nist movement. Implicit in the satirical images were anxieties about men's ability to lead the new nation to complete freedom and to lead the new middle-class households—based on companionate marriages—to hap-piness. Against this critique of middle-class masculinity, *Physical Culture* stood as a response and a program for the rehabilitation of Egyptian men.

22. The postindependence field of gender politics is showcased here with many levels of interpretation possible, the most obvious being the backlash against the vocal feminist movement. The Arabic sentence in the image reads, "Women Lead the Men." The first line of the Arabic caption reads, "Women advance and men regress." The next line: "Ms. Huda Sha'rawi issued a general call for the ladies to look into the question of Sudan." *Khayal al-Zill* (October 30, 1924), cover.

The other regular contributor to the magazine's pedagogic mission, Dr. Sabri Jirjis, offered his expert knowledge on abnormal and deviant sexuality. He was introduced to the readers of the magazine in August 1931 as a new volunteer member of the *Physical Culture* family. Jirjis practiced at the venereal disease clinic in Bani Suwayf, south of Cairo.[54] The editor described him as a young sportsman (*shab sbur*). A letter from the good doctor followed the introduction. He praised the magazine for its dual mission of bringing physical culture and sex education to the youth of Egypt. About physical culture, he wrote, "Its share in the prosperity of European states is well known, and its influence in molding the character of [their] youth is evidently clear. We perceive it everyday when we read the news of pilots, swimmers, and athletes. It has, thanks to God and serious effort, begun to penetrate the hearts of boys and girls in this country."[55] Jirjis, it turned out, was extremely well read in contemporary European theories on sexuality and sexual disorders. Indeed, one of the reasons he desired to join *Physical Culture*'s "virtual family" was his search for a venue in which to present his Arabic translation of the oft-cited study from 1905 by the Swiss sexologist August Forel, *The Sexual Question (al-Mas'ala al-Jinsiyya)*.[56]

23. While the problematization of Egyptian feminism is evident here, situating this representation against the backdrop of effendi masculinity—partially sketched in this book as a project of national rejuvenation—offers another perspective. The presuppositions of the satirical image are thereby made legible in a way that suggests an emerging yet incomplete national subject, wherein something as ostensibly natural and basic as gender becomes confused. The Arabic at the top reads, "After Huda Sha'rawi's Meeting." At the bottom: "The Masculinization of Women and the Feminization of Men." *Khayal al-Zill* (November 6, 1924), 8–9.

Jirjis noted the resistance to sex education in Egypt and commended *Physical Culture* for staying the course: "Sex education, despite the newness of research on it in Europe, has taken major strides in the last few years such that today it has become a science with its [own] rules and principles. However, in Egypt, tradition—or say a false shame—has prevented us from producing a reformer, an intellectual, or a parent who would discuss with his children sexual matters scientifically and truthfully." [57] The effect of this pedagogic neglect was utter "moral chaos": "Until you [*Physical Culture*] advanced onto the field—[where] previous weak attempts were crushed and died in their cradles without anyone noticing—and continued fighting and struggling in an environment [*wasat*] not acclimated to revolting against tradition [*al-thawra 'ala al-taqalid*], until you

السيدات ولعب كرة القدم

24. The Arabic sentence in the image reads, "The Ladies Playing Football." The first line of the Arabic caption reads, "A few years ago some ladies established a club for playing tennis." The second line: "We were recently informed that some of the leaders of the feminist revival are thinking about forming a team to play football and others for wrestling, boxing, and tug-of-war!!!" *Ruz al-Yusuf* (November 24, 1927), cover.

25. Again, beyond the obvious satirization of Egyptian feminism, what is interesting in this and the previous cartoon is the presupposition that sports and femininity were incommensurable at the point that the latter crossed some imaginary boundary that not only threatened to blur into masculinity but simultaneously to undo it violently. "In the World of Women's Sports." *Al-Matraqa* (April 15, 1928), back cover.

(في عالم الرياضة البدنية عند السيدات)

26. *Ruẓ al-Yusuf* (February 14, 1928), cover. The original caption for this image read, "The Feminist Revolution and Its Three Principles." Each principle is attached to one of the represented scenes: (*clockwise from top*): "freedom, fraternity, and equality."

بقية الازواج بعدالزواج   معظم الازواج بعد الزواج   قبل الزواج

27. That life had become tantamount to men's emasculation through women's selfishness in marriage rounded out the critique of feminism. Another reading is that the story being told here and through the other images was not of life at all but of *a* life that remained precarious nearly six decades after its birth, a modern life for which new fantasies of men and women, of masculinity and femininity, were being inscribed, debated, edited, and disseminated faster and more widely by the 1930s. The Arabic phrase in the image reads, "The Story of Life." The Arabic captions read (*from right to left*), "Before Marriage," "Most Marriages after Marriage," and "The Rest of the Marriages after Marriage." *Misr al-Haditha al-Musawwara* (October 9, 1929), 21.

emerged victorious through the force of the truth, the conviction of the believer, and the steadfastness of the confident. Meanwhile, the columns on sex education in your magazine became the principal [source] that a young man can read and benefit from rather than just be entertained. That, I swear, is a major victory in a short time."[58] Aside from the blatant self-serving flattery, Jirjis's letter points to the emergent relationship between medical science and social reform. His contributions over the years would illustrate the quest for a scientific cure to the persistent sense of uncertainty about the future of the national community. With the progress of time, ambiguities surrounding Egypt's political and cultural identity only seemed to proliferate; securing a proper order in the domain of gender and sexuality became all the more important. Through the course of the 1930s and especially in the 1940s, better theories and better science were seen as the key to resolving protracted social and political crises.[59]

Supplementing his medical knowledge, Jirjis employed a critical social science lens to achieve a better view of the relationship among sex, gender, and social progress. He revealed the intellectual tools available to him in an article entitled "On Politics and Political Economy."[60] He began by explicating the difference between the two: "Power and wealth were always the two objects targeted by politics. However, political economy [al-iqtisad al-siyasi] is a science that studies the different conditions of [groups of] people, and all of its theories are based in history, statistics, and observations. Its aim is to determine laws for organizing production and distribution of products, for the division of labor, and for the social regulation of peoples in terms of public health, population (over or under), and rates of birth and death (increase or decline)."[61] He proceeded to identify a glaring absence in political economy, one which he labeled "natural history" — by this he meant the history of the body and psychology as they related to sex and reproduction. This lacuna undermined the ability of political economy to produce solutions for the imminent population crisis. He next traced the roots of eugenics to Malthus and theories of rational selection, agreeing with the current view that people like the Chinese posed a threat to humanity's future if they continued to overbreed. Jirjis advanced his support for sex education and women's rights on a social Darwinist basis.

Jirjis rejected what he termed the traditional tendency to explain any strange or extraordinary social developments with an injunction to "examine women" (ibhath 'an al-mar'a). Women were not left out of the equation altogether, but the starting point, according to Jirjis, should be to "examine the sexual impulse" (ibhath 'an al-dafi' al-tanasuli). Such an investigation was warranted, he maintained, since desire and emotion (ahwa' wa 'awatif) were more common determinants of human action than reason and logic, the sexual impulse being the most powerful. The role of women was essential here in connecting sex to the social and political. Only through the liberation of women (tahrir al-mar'a) would society advance. Reversing Faraj's argument, Jirjis maintained that making women equal partners with men in social life by encouraging their participation in work and by granting women the right to vote and be elected, the sexual relationship would necessarily be transformed as her object status was eliminated. Moreover, as the sex act duly became elevated out of the depths of selfish lust and was redirected at smart reproduction, it would be aligned more with the social good.[62]

Jirjis's writing on sexuality and deviance exemplified the work *Physical Culture* did to help bring about the normalization of heterosexuality as a key to Egyptian modernity. Essential to this goal was the constitution of society as an object that could be acted upon by its localization in the individual human body, namely, in the male sex.[63] The male subject of Egyptian modernity had been problematized since the late nineteenth century as lacking the proper qualities of masculinity. After a lull in the discourse around the revolutionary years following 1919, Egyptian masculinity as it returned in the pages of *Physical Culture* faced a new, endangered future, sapped by excessive masturbation and the contraction of venereal diseases.

The magazine concentrated its critique on forms of deviance (*al-shudhudh*) resulting from what it considered a lack of masculine self-control or will power, that is, the individual's exerting of excessive sexual energy, either upon himself or with a partner of the opposite sex (prostitution was a favorite object of criticism). More monstrous forms of deviance were left lurking in the shadows. For example, the figure of the cross-dressing male performer, the *khawal*, who seems to have made appearances even at elite wedding parties as late as the 1930s, was never treated explicitly in this discourse.[64] One possible explanation for this absence is that even though a scientific discourse of sexual problems (inversion, third sex, and so forth) was available to Egyptian social commentators, the homegrown difference represented by the perceived traditional khawal defied the broader language of modernity. It appeared only as a passing, unnamed reference.[65]

Jirjis did write about homosexuality as a form of sexual deviance. His article "Homosexuality" (rendered as *'ishq al-jins*) from March 1933 was part of a series he wrote entitled "Psychosexual Illnesses" in which he presented translated excerpts of Forel's *The Sexual Question*.[66] In fact, he seems to have coined the expression *'ishq al-jins* to capture the scientific significance of "homosexuality" as an illness deserving of public sympathy and serious medical attention and care.[67] He also addressed the desire for same-sex marriage in his article "Prostitution and Civil Marriage."[68] His objective here was to advocate for the legal recognition of a system of heterosexual marriage based on love between two companions (*rafi-qan*). In the case of those "afflicted with same-sex desire," for whom there was no marriage provision within law, he ventriloquized Forel's argument, that as long as there was no injury to a third party and as long as neither of the partners was "normal," then the law should simply overlook them; in other words, let them live out their (literally sick) fantasies as long as they didn't spread their disease.[69]

In short, sex education and a rational regime of caring for the self were prescribed as the way to achieve proper gender relations and a healthy sexuality. Even homosexuality, a deviation from the person's nature, could be averted through this program.[70] The magazine was ambivalent in its advocacy for the prohibition of prostitution, mainly because it recognized that demand created supply in this instance. This also explains why the problem of prostitution was often routed through the discourse on marriage and sexuality. In "Prostitution from a Medical Perspective," an unnamed expert on venereal diseases disagreed with those calling for a ban on official prostitution, arguing on the one hand that there was no correspondence between rising numbers of socially transmitted diseases and prostitution and, on the other, that a sudden prohibition would cause more harm than good.[71] Another article blamed the misogyny inherent in the laws for the failure to curb prostitution; it attacked as "social cowardice" the implementation of laws that punished only one partner and highlighted the complicity of male lawmakers with male clients of prostitutes.[72] Ultimately the magazine's position was one of promoting self-help; the resolution to these social problems lay in the cultivating of properly disciplined subjects.

Striking about these engagements with contemporary European theories on sexuality is their blatant disconnection from Egyptian social and sexual realities. The absence of the multitude of laboring bodies — women, khawal, peasant — in this presumably modern discourse is only one, perhaps extreme indicator of how the emergence of the effendi as a representative masculine subject depended on the suppression or erasure of other disruptive figures. However striking it may be, this pattern of exclusion and inclusion was not specifically Egyptian and neither was the lack of fit or the distorting distance between categories of knowledge and their subjects and objects. This was the work of colonial power in the constitution of the modern subject the world over. The difference between metropole and colony was surely a matter of politico-economic asymmetry, but that alterity had to be figured somehow in the prevailing liberal discourse to effect its own historical legibility while simultaneously keeping open the possibility of emancipation into, and identity with, the modern.

Conclusion
REMAINING TO BE TOLD

Caring for the body was the prescribed program of a reforming elite that sought to produce desirable subjects in a social context populated by disturbing reminders of a presumably surpassed order, a past time. This was a different project from the explicitly nationalist formulations of physical culture derived in preceding decades, formulations which resulted in the expansion of physical education in schools, the development of a sporting establishment (local and national clubs, teams, and associations), and the emergence of internationally competitive athletes. *Physical Culture* was, quite literally, in another sort of business. Its address was within a capitalist commodity space and to an emergent social category characterized by its imbrication with global cultural forms. Sex, as we have seen, was a normalizing conduit in the reforming of Egyptian masculinity and femininity to align with modernity.[73]

On the one hand, *Physical Culture*'s assemblage of texts—letters, articles, stories (not discussed here), and photos—points to a pedagogical project that sought to normalize a global bourgeois conception of heterosexuality and its attendant gendered subject for a national project; on the other hand, read critically, it may illustrate a creative adaptation of that discourse to the local conditions of colonial modernity. The hybrid nature of *Physical Culture*, as a material object, between the pedagogic and the performative becomes intelligible only when desire, the colonial, and the modern are situated as a part of and apart from the Egyptian social reality of the interwar period. In other words, this object—as magazine with pages, text, and images and as a particular discourse of sexuality and self—existed in tension with both the local and the foreign, stood for and against normative sexuality, circulated in spaces that were at once colonial, national, and diasporic, and produced a virtual transnational field of desiring subjects and discursive engagements with unpredictable outcomes. Accordingly, the discourse of gender and sexuality that took shape in the pages of *Physical Culture* and was fostered by it was not willed into existence solely through the interests of the editors and authors of the magazine. Furthermore, the full significance of that discourse would be missed if it were viewed exclusively as the determinations of a transformed political economy. Neither can its emergence be explained through ahistorical psychological states of anxiety or crisis. It was through continuous repetition in forums like *Physical Culture* and movement through various social and spatial networks that the terms of a corporeality, gender, and sexuality overlapped, producing by the 1930s an ostensibly seamless normative sphere of bourgeois heterosocial and heterosexual life—but one that seemed eternally precarious.[74]

Other possibilities of imagining Egypt's past present themselves only when its particular subject—effendi, nationalist, masculine, modern, and so forth—no longer appears as a historically foregone conclusion. For example, the historical translation of desire into respectable heterosociality and -sexuality which came to define the culture of the effendi in the interwar period might be made legible historically without eliding the fact that it was only one possible representation of sexual desire, one possible worlding of love—albeit a complex and vulnerable one. Indeed it was in the very slippage between moral and immoral (acts, images, and thoughts) that *Physical Culture* managed to stake its claim to Egypt's modernity. Scantily clad foreign cover girls and bare-chested local muscle men were juxtaposed to narratives and epistolary tales of libidinal excess, all of which were used in a pedagogic mission—perhaps sincere, perhaps not—to produce the necessary bodies for a sovereign Egypt of the future. Nevertheless, the charges of immorality leveled at the magazine for its sexual rhetoric also hint at the supposed unanticipated use of the magazine for other ends.

Physical Culture might still reveal more than the existence of this somewhat predictable space between modernist intentions and acts, pedagogy and performance. Another historical question to this source could have been about the silence of its bourgeois fantasy that was ironically the outcome of a boisterous colonial program to police homosexuality. Was the discourse of physical culture serving as a "masquerade that has screened away something more"?[75] An answer to this question about the veiled and the silent must necessarily be speculative, but it can be shown at a minimum the norms that organized access to the truth of the discourse. By extension, recognizing suppressed histories in this discourse requires thinking beyond the norm.

The realm of bourgeois masculinist fantasy represented by *Physical Culture* conforms to and confounds Judith Butler's rearticulation of the relationship between gender and the norm in terms of the emancipatory "work of fantasy" that attempts "to rework the norms by which bodies are experienced."[76] The performativity of gender reads quite differently and is at cross-purposes in a colonial context.[77] The gendered discourse of physical culture in Egyptian colonial modernity was a bodily investment in advancing a broader claim to humanity that was paradoxically both more inclusive *and* more exclusive than in the preceding era. The new national public sphere of citizen subjects was indeed informed by a universality that at least promised another world from the previous religio-political order with its paternalistic and patriarchal hierarchies. However, the burden of producing the human central to realizing this modern order was compounded and consistently deferred by the colonial.[78]

Within this constellation of figures—colonizer, colonized, citizen, universal human—the particular histories of Egyptians who fit neither within this system nor within the construction of the prior order of despots and aliens were subject to erasure. An example of the historical repetition of modernity's silences is my own marginalizing to a footnote of the fragmentary sighting of the khawal (alluded to above). Indeed, in this case the khawal did not even bear its proper name but was subsumed under the category of *'awalim*: female entertainers who sang, danced, and played instruments at weddings and other ritual occasions.

The occasion for this appearance was a monthly advice column, "The Tales of Venus" (*ahadith finis*), in *Physical Culture* for August 1932. The special topic for the month was "The Wedding Night" (*laylat al-dukhla*). Venus, in a highly satirical and bourgeois moralistic tone, set out to expose the vanity and excessive folly of all classes—but specifically of women—when it came to marriage celebrations. The potential for disorderly conduct of various kinds was persistently underscored. After narrating a series of untoward happenings at weddings that she had attended over her lifetime, ranging from the competition among women to be the best-looking to fights over trivial matters, Venus arrived at the most scandalous and most prevalent wedding phenomenon: the 'awalim, in her ironic words, "the most important group upon which a wedding celebration depends."[79] Venus cautioned against inviting this lowliest of life forms into respectable homes because of the 'awalim's foul language and their even fouler deeds, the most brazen of which could be the seduction of the groom. Venus went on:

> But the strangest of all was when I attended a wedding where I happened to be seated near the 'awalim. My gaze landed on one of them with her ambiguous [*munakkara*] shape and unpleasant face. She ended up talking to me without pause about one thing or another until she asked me about the gown I was wearing and just as I was about to answer her, with all politeness of course, one of my acquaintances whispered in my ear advising me to distance myself from this woman because she was . . . watch out . . . a man! I was stunned by her words and left him angrily. I went to

28. Postcard dated December 18, 1906. From Max Karkegi Collection. The Arabic in the image reads, "In Egypt, *khawal*," and the French caption reads, "Eccentric cross-dressing dancer."

the hostess and told her that it was absolutely improper of her to allow
a man entry into a gathering of women. I was beyond shock when I saw
that she was bemused by what I had said and then replied that there was
no need for all this anger since the *'alima* or the *'alim* that I was talking
about although biologically differed completely from the biology of our
sex, he was closer to [being] a woman than he was to a man.[80]

In spite of Venus's apparent shock and indignation, it is telling that no
memory of men dressed as women in performance could be recalled under
its proper name, that her language could not accommodate this difference.
Was this because *khawal* as signifier had already undergone its second semantic transformation: first, from slave and servant, as it appeared in the
medieval lexicon *Lisan al-'Arab*, to male performer in drag by the nineteenth century, then to "faggot," as the term is derogatorily used in Egypt
today?[81] Perhaps. But can one historicize and critically grasp this specific
failure of language beyond its signifying practices within the emerging
global discourse of sexuality?

Given Jirjis's approach to homosexuality as an illness, reflecting the way
it was treated in Europe, it seems that the object field for gender normativity had begun to crystallize in interwar Egypt as medical practitioners
and others earnestly advocated a relatively protestant approach to sex and
marriage. Indeed between the rare discursive deployment of homosexuality and the frequent performative reiterations of heteronormative masculinity and femininity, the spectral presence of the cross-dressing khawal
as late as the 1930s sheds light, however faint, on another terrain of gender, sexuality, and sociality that was in the process of rapidly receding.

In the exchange between Venus and the host of the wedding, one might,
by straining, hear a whisper of the unspeakable of colonial modernity:
otherwise gendered lives that were seemingly intelligible but were in the
process of being moved from the domain of the real to the unreal, indexing perhaps the loss of their purchase on communal norms that had ensured their persistence in the past. Additionally, rather than producing the
conditions for a resignification with the aim of expanding the purview of
the human, the colonial genealogy of gender as a norm conditioned and
reproduced by the apparatuses of modern regulatory power has consistently narrowed the confines of the subject and foreclosed possibilities for
subjective proliferation.

Put this way, the disappearance and return of the khawal in twentieth-
century Egypt pushes to the forefront the imperial context in which
norms of gender and sexuality were constituted in both metropoles and

colonies, first and third worlds, and presently in the global North and South. One should be attentive to the historical specificities of the moments mapped by these loose spatial designations, but conceiving the relational dynamic of gendered subject formations across these spaces can productively complicate performative theories and extend the range of history. It does so by inquiring into the asymmetries of power that effect the material conditions for the iterability and potential resignification of norms governing the subject. The effect of colonial modernity in Egypt — overcoming simply being — was implicit in the vanishing sociality of the cross-dressing khawal, but the category was not extinguished altogether. Indeed, following Butler, it was the occasion for a resignification that momentarily allowed posing a question that cannot be answered: Who are you? Although it is only in the interstices of questions and answers that were intelligible, in penumbral corners and for fleeting moments, between the lines of a quintessentially modern text that one might virtually dwell with the silent other, that possibility, however much a chimera, might bespeak other beings and other dwellings in time.

A first reading of *Physical Culture* suggests a profound sense of lack, an identity deficit the text aimed to ameliorate, which situates the magazine squarely within discourses of national culture and alternative modernity. Indeed, viewed through these lenses there is little new to be learned from this impressively long-running magazine, which reiterates the tired moralistic rhetoric of contemporary reformers from Tokyo to New York, except with an Egyptian difference. When the numerous articles, letters, translations from French and English, and the commentaries on them are recontextualized within the imperial social formation which made questions of gender and sexuality intelligible, the contours of a shared colonial modernity emerge. An essential feature of such a modernity was the formation of a universal subject, which entailed the attempted straightening of the world. However, the specificity of the discourse of physical culture in Egypt lay in its disavowal of colonial difference, and it was precisely through this negation that the terms of future subjects were defined and their limits fixed. Accordingly, the return of the pathologized object of sexuality did not manifest itself in claims to identity, as in the West, but was characterized by a silence and supposed absence from the public sphere.

7

FASHION

———

Global Affects of Colonial Modernity

On October 29, 1932, a major celebration was held at Ankara Palace in honor of Turkish Republic Day. The Turkish leader Mustafa Kemal Atatürk had invited foreign dignitaries and the local elite to the evening festivities. Among the distinguished invitees was the Egyptian ambassador, Abd al-Malik Hamza Bey. He arrived dressed in his formal regalia topped off by the symbol of Egyptian (and, up to 1925, Turkish) officialdom—the *tarbush*.[1]

Atatürk greeted the Egyptian representative coldly and ordered him to remove the tarbush while in his presence. When Hamza Bey hesitated, Atatürk barked an order at one of his servants to demand from the guest his tarbush. In order to avoid a diplomatic incident, Hamza Bey acceded to the will of the Ghazi.[2]

In spite of the Egyptian diplomat's effort to avoid controversy, the event escalated into an incident through, it seems, the provocation of the British press. Two weeks after the fact, the *Daily Herald* carried a report detailing the affront faced by the Egyptian ambassador in Ankara. Only after the publication of that article did the Egyptian press and public come to learn about "the tarbush incident." Suddenly there were calls for action, including the severing of relations with Turkey. The incident was immediately framed as a question of national honor.

The prominent Egyptian historian Yunan Labib Rizk recently surveyed the coverage of the tarbush incident as it was reported in *al-Ahram*.[3] Although Rizk suggests that there were different "sectors of opinion in Egypt"—that is, pro- and anti-tarbush—the possible cultural meanings of these positions are subsumed by the larger, ostensibly more significant story of international relations between Egypt and Turkey after the First World War. Although the international as context and as refigured object in the interwar period is important to my argument, as will become evident, my aim is to investigate the question of dress not simply for what it symbolized but also for how it participated in the performative constitution of a new cultural order on the level of competing and comparable national subjects, which in turn engaged actual social and individual bodies seeking to fashion themselves. In other words, in the twentieth century, as dress became a question of fashion that spread across competing and sometimes conflicting temporalities (Islamic, national and international, traditional, modern), it produced cultural tensions and anxieties that were textually represented and afford a novel perspective on the subject of effendi masculinity, affect, and alterity. The fact that there were different public opinions about the tarbush suggests at the very least that identity was open to debate and not a given. On the one hand, I use the question of dress as a lens through which to view the shifting, contradictory, and contested relationships between individual and national identity within the times of fashion, and, on the other hand, I regard dress as a crucial site in an ongoing process of working out Egypt and its subject in colonial modernity.[4] That work paradoxically engendered a simultaneous delimitation of Egypt's particularity and its generality while also opening a space for creative adaptations.

Others' Modern
TURKEY, EGYPT, BRITAIN, AND THE
NEW ORDER OF NATIONS

Since the tarbush incident was instigated by him, one way of beginning the discussion is to look to the figure of Atatürk. Mustafa Kemal's efforts to forcefully Westernize Turkey are well known.[5] Among his most famous dictates are the banning of the veil and the codification of a secular state.[6] Perhaps less well known is his banning of the tarbush in November 1925.[7] In Egypt this act touched off a flurry of heated discussion on the merits and demerits of the tarbush that flared up periodically for well over a decade.[8]

The monumental actions of Mustafa Kemal, which continue to animate cultural and political life in contemporary Turkey, came on the heels of other significant world-historic events.[9] At the end of the First World War, France and Britain divided up the Arab provinces of the Ottoman Empire they had not previously occupied: Syria and Lebanon went to France, Palestine and Iraq to Britain.[10] The Treaty of Sèvres in 1920 essentially completed a process of the slow stripping away of the sovereignty of the defeated Ottoman state.[11] Meanwhile, guerilla forces displayed their contempt for this dispensation, and Kemal assembled a national army of resistance in the Anatolian heartland. Over the next three years, through the exercise of military will and diplomatic negotiations, the dissident faction led by Kemal successfully procured the Treaty of Lausanne (July 24, 1923), which affirmed Turkey's national sovereignty and control of most of the territory it had lost in 1920.

The events that unfolded in the theater of war and the restructured field of international relations from 1914 into the 1920s, particularly those involving the defeat and dismemberment of the Ottoman Empire and the creation of the Turkish republic, had far-reaching and conflicting implications for the political and cultural spheres of life in Egypt. Unlike Atatürk's widely publicized wresting of independence from foreign occupiers, the independence Egypt was granted by a unilateral British declaration on February 22, 1922, was relatively hollow. The treaty's loopholes—areas of strategic interest in which the British retained control—would remain a source of discontent and agitation for three decades. The political situation in Egypt during this period is usually characterized as a perennial struggle for power among three major parties—the Wafd, the king, and the British. As the contests over the political sphere oscillated among these three poles, other struggles were waged in the seemingly separate cultural sphere about such seemingly trivial matters as the proper headdress for men.[12]

Within these debates, set against the backdrop of a self-conscious internationalized political order and absent national sovereignty, the tarbush was alternately celebrated and pilloried depending in part on the position taken toward culture. When culture was conceived hermetically and as ontologically unique, the tarbush appeared to be indispensable to national identity; when culture was regarded as always already a site of difference and hybridity, the change of headdress was viewed positively. A third stance assumed vis-à-vis culture melancholically regarded it as a contemporary dystopia, and the passing of time, conceived as rupture, with subsequent ethical implications, became the object of concern over and against superficial objects like the change of headdress. The first two positions, which conceived of culture spatially, deemed the international and recognition within it fundamental to the working out of a national Egypt and by extension its proper subject.[13]

The international here, as seen from the Egyptian perspective, assumed more than the institutional form embodied by the League of Nations or the numerous other organizations, commissions, and conferences to which Egypt sought and gained representation.[14] It was the metaphorical gold standard of national value: recognition in the international was an ineluctable stage of national consciousness.[15] Even by the last third of the nineteenth century the effendiyya exhibited a growing appreciation of Egypt's need to measure up to standards that were deemed not in its power to determine.[16] In the debates on dress that took place in the interwar period, the international appears as the familiar political order of sovereign nations as well as a site of forming cultural subjects.[17] On this view, the international, while formally manifested in the constitution of distinct sovereignties at the level of states and law, becomes intelligible to the extent that similarly distinct or comparable formations of culture and its proper subject could be determined. That process of determination— presumably a key to national identity, and, I contend, to sovereignty— was paradoxically possible only within a system of mutual recognition in which Self and Other, internal and external, were inextricably linked.

There would always be ample disagreement about the best way to achieve recognition. Accordingly, in the 1920s the tarbush could simultaneously be a sign of the modern and the traditional, the civilized and the savage, the national and the foreign, the masculine and the effeminate. In the 1930s, the nationalist meaning of the tarbush acquired surplus value, so to speak, through the expansion of consumerism and a new politics of youth.[18]

As the form of headdress worn mainly by the effendi class of men, the tarbush was most consistently the signifier of an ambivalent bourgeois masculinity. That the tarbush became a contested site as the cast of characters involved in the production of cultural meaning expanded was not coincidental. The examples from the preceding chapters show that the proliferation of new cultural practices such as sports incorporated players from a broader social base into an interwar public culture, wherein the gendered subject of Egyptian modernity was resignified.

The redefinition of the political and cultural relationship between Egypt and its once-imperial overlord, now an autonomous, detached republic, was necessarily freighted with the different outcomes of their international and local struggles for national sovereignty, which included a reevaluation of historical symbols of Ottoman masculinity.[19] The political and economic mediation of the West (which went back at least to the intervention of Britain in 1840 on behalf of the Ottomans to discipline the

29. Sewing the inner lining of the tarbush. Photograph (c. 1940s) from Max Karkegi Collection.

30. Pressing the tarbush into shape. Photograph (c. 1940s) from Max Karkegi Collection.

overly ambitious governor of Egypt, Mehmed Ali) quietly became a cultural mediation as well by the twentieth century, as the prior axes linking Cairo and Istanbul were intercalated and eventually usurped by the Cairo-Paris-London axes.[20] The tarbush incident represented the vanishing horizon of the former. In another version of the story with which I began this chapter, Abd al-Malik Hamza Bey was given permission by Mustafa Kemal to remove his tarbush to be more comfortable. Apparently it was very hot in the palace halls that evening, and Mustafa Kemal was simply being a gracious and thoughtful host who knew that Egyptian diplomatic protocol required the wearer to keep the tarbush on until invited to remove it. This version of events eventually became the official line that formally closed the tarbush incident.

After the initial outcry in Egypt, in which voices were calling for the severing of all ties with Turkey, positions on the tarbush incident largely reflected the views of the two poles that had emerged in the preceding years: the pro- and anti-tarbush camps. Admirers of the Turkish model of modernization, who were also generally anti-tarbush, were willing to wait for another explanation of the incident. Supporters of the tarbush, which had become recoded during the First World War as a specifically Egyptian nationalist symbol through its public expression of opposition to the British, read the incident as yet another example of Egypt's Turkish-blooded leaders compromising its national honor.[21]

This schema of positions is admittedly simplistic and should be read as awkward shorthand used to designate a much more complex field of cultural debates, politics, and subject formation. For example, the proponents of the Western-style hat were not always anti-tarbush, and defenders of the tarbush were not necessarily anti-hat; and those who wore turbans occupied a position that could be labeled rejectionist, uncertain, unaware, or simply disinterested. It is in the details of individuals' experiences with the politics of headdress that the irreducible realm of subject formation as a relationship of self to self, an aesthetic and ethics, becomes legible.

A series of cartoons published in Ruz al-Yusuf gives some indication of how the shifting political horizons were broadly perceived among liberal-leaning effendiyya. The first cartoon reproduced here, depicting a meeting between Percy Loraine, who had just been transferred from Cairo to Ankara, and Mustafa Kemal on the surface portrayed the intimate and physical ties linking national honor, power, and masculinity. Turkey under the leadership of a great, or at the very least a real, man did not suffer affronts to its honor or sovereignty like Egypt, whose leadership was by implica-

31. The first Arabic caption (not shown) reads, "Here and . . . There!! (Many fear that Sir Percy Loraine will wreck his assignment in Ankara thinking that Ankara is . . . Cairo!)" The second: "Secretary of the English Embassy — Yes sir, it's the Honorable Sir Percy Loraine, the new English Ambassador. The Ghazi Mustafa Pasha Kemal: Listen . . . Tell that man to sit

properly or take his stuff and get out. Make it clear to him that here is not like there [*hina mish zayy hinak*]." *Ruz al-Yusuf* (August 28, 1933), back cover.

tion lacking virility and manliness. The political backdrop to this critique was the rise of the authoritarian government of Isma'il Sidqi in 1930.[22] As the second and third cartoons bluntly suggested, Sidqi courted the high commissioner for British support in keeping his unpopular government in office. The aim of this gendered and sexualized critique was in part to expose the profound weakness behind Sidqi's reputation as a strongman. More generally, as the cartoons and the furor over the tarbush incident reveal, also at stake in the question of national sovereignty for Egypt was the question of identity, figured as the possession of masculine virtues, primarily honor.

When these texts are read more for what they do than for what they say, the circulation of figures like Hamza Bey, Sidqi, Atatürk, and Loraine — as well as the news about them and caricatures of them — assume a different significance. It was precisely the possibility of movement and the space it inscribed — what might be termed the international scene of national subject formation — that helped constitute a new norm of gender, which I have variously labeled bourgeois masculinity, national manhood, and

32. The Arabic caption (not shown) reads, "The cinemas in Cairo to show a film of the Prime Minister's travels. It is expected that said film will demonstrate the extent of Sidqi's success in achieving love and support of the country. And this is a scene from the new film portraying His Excellency's success with the English!" *Ruz al-Yusuf* (May 9, 1932), cover.

effendi masculinity. As the previous chapters show, the three discursive fields had distinct yet overlapping genealogies whose relationship depended on the historically variable interrelations of capital and empire. In the Egyptian context, effendi masculinity was a condensation of the other two fields, bourgeois masculinity and national manhood, which existed in a relationship of temporal and spatial tension.

The onset of global economic depression in 1929, which hit Egypt severely by 1931, unleashed a new wave of nationalist critique that has been associated by Israel Gershoni and James Jankowski with the emergence of a generation of activists representing a broader social base and with older disillusioned reformers, both of whom turned toward Arab and Islamic sources of identification and away from the West. This conception of the new effendiyya of the 1930s, with their traditionalist outlook (which facilitated a supra-Egyptian nationalism), is reductive and fails to

33. The first Arabic caption (not shown) reads, "The press has mentioned that doctors advised His Excellency the Prime Minister to travel to Vichy to seek treatment." The second: "Dr. Percy Loraine — Forget Vichy. London is for you . . . you'll find on Downing Street, number 10, a doctor named Dr. MacDonald! It's true that he's a bit greedy in his demands, but there's no one else who understands your illness like him." *Ruz al-Yusuf* (June 13, 1932), cover.

account for the ways in which masculinity and sovereignty continued to depend on an international formation for their intelligibility at home in the nation, a formation that included the West as a constitutive element.

The cartoons and the diplomatic episode illuminate a differentiated field of modern masculinity whose intelligibility and reproduction were still contingent on the implicit affirmation of the international. Such masculinity was also contingent on the denial of environmental determinism. Regardless of historical differences, geographical specificities, and politico-economic asymmetries, engendered in the interwar conception of the international was a shared perception of modern culture's publicity. The latter also implied a common grammar of political expression and a common subject of politics. Nevertheless, when that generic form of the public and masculinity was infused with national, religious, and individual sentiments the meaning of modern culture appeared as anything but universal. The representation of Atatürk, for example, as the exemplar of masculinity, modernization, and nationalism in the post-Ottoman world did not go unchallenged.

As the following sections demonstrate, the intricacies of interwar public culture as it pertained to subjectivity, bodily aesthetics, and politics cannot be understood within the exclusively national framework into which all objects were increasingly fixed.[23] Neither can they be understood by merely expanding the frame of reference to include broader sources of identification without a proper accounting of the relations between the subject and culture and between culture and modernity. The very concepts of national honor and identity were reproduced within an international scene of culture formation, political struggles, and negotiations; indeed, they were contingent on and only intelligible within an international scene. Accordingly, the subject of effendi masculinity emerged between and betwixt the notions of territory and sovereignty presupposed in the conventional historical accounts of Egypt's modernity.[24]

Dress and National Honor
PRELUDE TO AN ARGUMENT

The question of national honor and dress in the Egyptian context is usually associated with the debates about veiling and the condition of women that were set off in the modern era by the publication of Qasim Amin's *Tahrir al-Mar'a* (Women's liberation) in 1899.[25] The historiographical neglect of the fashioning of modern masculinity has limited comprehension of this highly significant moment in the history of gender in Egypt. Situating the question of dress in the broader contexts of colonialism, modernity, and subject formation gives one a better understanding of how the early debates about the veil were initiated by masculine anxieties about power and self-rule (or the lack thereof). Self-rule could mean the right to self-determination in a geopolitical sense, but I focus on the significance attached to governing one's individual self according to a new perception of subjectivity underwritten by the modern grammar of enlightenment and performed within the imperial social formation or the nascent international.[26] Implicit in this rubric of self, as I have outlined in the preceding chapters in relation to physical culture, is a certain sense of having the right to fashion an individual identity; such a right to the self was also linked to the government of others. This right could also be perceived or rendered as a problematic force pushing against an external body or against the collective will and collective identity, according to the political context. In either case, the ability to govern the self and others posed the question of sovereignty outside its traditional domain, namely, within the emerging global cultural formations of dress and gender.

The first signs of an Egyptian sartorial refashioning were most evident perhaps among the new Arabic-speaking officer corps that was expanded during Sa'id's reign (1854–1863). Although Egyptian peasants had been conscripted in large numbers in Muhammad Ali's efforts to create a modern army in the first quarter of the nineteenth century, it was only under Sa'id that Arabic-speaking Egyptians were allowed to rise to the rank of colonel. During this period also the dress of both officers and soldiers, which had followed patterns set by the Ottoman imperial tradition, began to change.

Ehud Toledano's work on this neglected period of Egyptian history (the reigns of Abbas and Sa'id), which he terms the forgotten years, hints at how the relationship between the opening of new opportunities for the sons of Egypt's rural notables in government and military service and the change of dress this required spoke to a transformation of self and cultural identity.[27] Although he does not put it in these terms, Toledano's argument suggests that while the change in notions of personhood, as enacted through dress, was not viewed as a threat by the Ottoman-Egyptian elite or as a basis for opposition by the aspirants to elite membership during the middle years, it did condition the grounds for thinking in terms of national identities. He analyzes the social divide between the elite and nonelite produced and represented through language, dress, etiquette, and modes of using and moving through space and notes that the desire to cross that divide eventually gave rise to an oppositional consciousness. About the newly promoted and newly dressed, he writes, "The tensions that existed between them [Arabic-speaking officers] and the other more senior officers constituted one of the main factors behind the events of the 1880s that led to the 'Urabi Revolt. At mid-century they were still making their first steps up the steep ladder towards becoming full-fledged members of the Ottoman-Egyptian elite."[28] In the middle of the nineteenth century a shift in aspirations of social mobility was palpable among Egyptians, and it began with the symbolic crossing of the threshold of elite culture.[29]

A powerful example of the transformation of self that a change of fashion enabled is given in the memoirs of Ali Mubarak (1824–1893).[30] Mubarak is usually cited as one of the towering figures of the nineteenth-century Egyptian renaissance for his contributions to state building and public works in his various capacities as an engineer, administrator, and educator. He was also the author of the famous encyclopedic work *al-Khitat al-Tawfiqiyya*, which mapped the physical and political geography of Egypt in the nineteenth century. This work has been a valuable source for social, political, and urban historians of Egypt and Cairo. Rarely commented upon is his autobiographical entry in volume 9 of the *Khitat*.[31]

Mubarak recounted the story of his return home to his village of Birinbal after fourteen years' absence.[32] When he arrived there was a brief yet crucial moment in which his mother failed to recognize him: "I knocked on the door. A voice said, 'Who's there?' I said it's your son Ali Mubarak. Fourteen years had separated me from my mother, without her seeing me or hearing my voice [even once]. Perplexed, she got up and came to the door. She looked and she stared. I was in my French military uniform, outfitted with my sword and [officer's] regalia. She kept asking the question until she [finally] realized it was me. Then she opened the door and hugged me; overwhelmed, I fell into her [arms]."[33] This episode may seem an altogether minor one, but the fact that this keen observer of the distinct features of the Egyptian landscape bothered to report it suggests that Mubarak attached significance to the return home that went beyond the emotional reunification with his mother. The key to reading this event lies in the material objects of distinction. The momentousness of the initial reception accrues just as much or even more from Mubarak's military uniform as from the long years of separation. Within the new logic of self-fashioning, the momentary lack of recognition by his mother caused by his changed appearance serves to reaffirm in Mubarak's mind and in that of his audience that he had truly transcended his peasant roots.

Another episode Mubarak depicted in the text reaffirms that for him and many like him the movement out of peasant garb into European-style military dress was a quite noteworthy and positive change in the conditions of a once-difficult life. Mubarak described an audience with Abbas Pasha (r. 1848–1854) in which he was given the commission of schools' inspector. After the announcement of his promotion, he was informed of the punishments he could expect if he failed to carry out his new duties honestly. In addition to being stripped of rank and benefits, there was to be a form of public shaming. Shaming seemed to weigh the most heavily on Mubarak's mind, perhaps because it condemned the guilty official to wearing peasant clothing and to living out the rest of his life as a peasant.[34] After swearing to carry out his commission, he was accorded his new rank and decorated with the appropriate medals: a silver half-crescent moon and a gold star encrusted with three diamond stones. He brought this scene to a close by telling the reader that his induction had left him happy.[35]

After the British occupation of Egypt, dress and manners became politically charged sites of cultural contestation in which for the first time it was often thought that the very essence of Egyptian identity was at stake. The expanding domain of print culture, including books, newspapers, and magazines, was a primary locus for public debates on matters of clothing and comportment, themes that were as inchoate as the public itself in the years leading up to the occupation. A particular fear by the 1890s—before veiling became the seemingly all-consuming focus of cultural debate—was of the younger generation, who had come of age knowing nothing other than colonial rule, adopting European styles of dress and self-carriage without comprehending the reasons behind European progress and superiority.[36]

Al-Ajyal (The generations) of July 3, 1897, featured an article titled "Blind Imitation" with illustrations of an urban *flâneur*. The urban dandy mixed and matched the several pieces of the two suits he owned to make it appear he was wearing a new outfit every day. The illustrations showed a young effendi in various poses set against the backdrop of an urban geography that would have been familiar to the properly bourgeois (and to aspirants) as the place to promenade. In the first image, he is standing at a street corner dressed in one of his suits, wearing a tarbush, and holding a cane tucked under his right arm. He seems either to be contemplating crossing the street or just idly observing the goings-on within the shopping arcade on the other side. In the second illustration he is seated at an outdoor café dressed in a different combination. His left arm is propped on the table, and he is resting his head in the palm of his hand while a small turbaned man busily shines his shoes; the expression on his face suggests he is lost in some private reverie. In the third illustration he is standing next to a man who is wearing a *gallabiya* and turban (apparently the shoeshine man) and is attending to a donkey while the effendi stands with his hands in his pockets, cane slung over his right arm, smoking a cigarette and staring indifferently off into the distance. In the next image he is paying off a carriage driver. In the fifth illustration he is having his picture taken. His pose is carefully drawn here: he is standing with his right arm resting on a tall stand seemingly built for that purpose, and in his hand are his gloves and cane; his left hand rests on the back of an armchair; his left leg is bent slightly and crosses in front of his right, forming a forty-

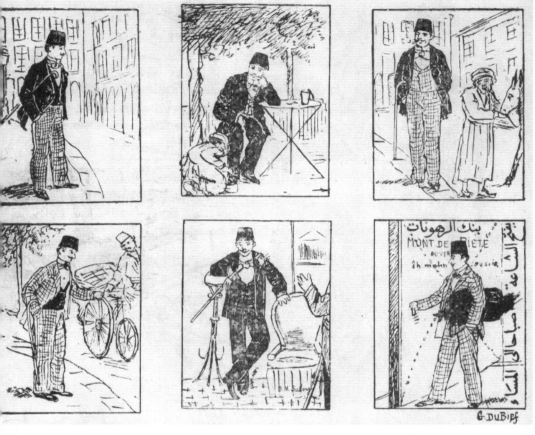

34. "Blind Imitation." *Al-Ajyal* (July 3, 1897), 36.

five-degree angle. All of this unproductive posing was his undoing. The reader sees him for the last time carrying one of his suits under his arm as he enters a pawnshop.

The article criticized the many young Egyptians who "were under the illusion" that imitating the look and behavior of Westerners was tantamount to genuinely understanding what it was to be modern and civilized.[37] In fact, moral and material bankruptcy was the inevitable end of such superficial appropriation of Western styles of dress and life. Another reading is that an Egyptian living within lower- to middle-class means could not sustain the patterns of consumption that participation in the new urban culture increasingly demanded.

Yet another dimension seems possible when the illustration is read slightly apart from the accompanying text. Through the striking of certain poses, the body of the mimic man was made to represent a new masculinity.[38] The images illustrated the repertoire a man must acquire in order to inhabit this new subjectivity, which, I emphasize, was not being rejected.[39] Rather, the author of the article enjoined a cautious and knowledgeable mediation of the modern terms of masculinity. His objective for writing was to encourage the reader to examine the reasons for European cultural, political, and economic domination. Missing from the illustrations are scenes of productivity on the part of the exemplar of Egypt's future. Although the man in the gallabiya is in fact working, he was figured only marginally as a representation of the past and thus in a sense as unrepresentative of the potential Egyptian being imagined here. In other words, the nation and modernity could be secured only through a reproduction of this new figure of bourgeois masculinity. Yet an unexamined adoption of the signs of modernity not only signaled "blind imitation" — that is, an unsuccessful attempt at being modern — but posed grave risks for the imitator, one of which was financial ruin.

A few months later, *al-Ajyal* delved further into the topic of dress and mimicry and its implications for Egyptian society.[40] The anonymous author reiterated his criticism of men's imitation of European dress as harmful but added that women's unbridled consumption of Western fashions, the focus of this article, was having an apocalyptic effect on the whole of Egyptian society. Men were admonished for affecting a Western style when they did so from a class position that could not sustain such a habit and when that habit was not grounded in a deeper understanding of Western culture. What that deeper understanding consisted of becomes evident later in the author's analysis of women's consumption. But first, the material and metaphysical costs of being overly attentive to the body's adornment were underscored generally with a poetic interruption from a "wise Arab poet":

> Oh servant of the body how you suffer in its service
>   Do you demand gain from what is a loss?
> Attend to the soul and the perfection of the virtues
>   For you are by the soul not by the body human.[41]

The "ancient" poet contrasts the baseness of submitting to corporeal desires with an ethical praxis that elevates man from the state of nature to a higher plane of existence. The moral injunction in the poem did not actually flow with the argument in the text. The split between the body and soul as the grounds of caring for the self was clearly not the emphasis; unlike the poet, the author of the article did not view investments in the body as categorically without virtue. While imported products and cultural practices were deemed central to Egypt's subjugation, they were also conceived of paradoxically as vital to its liberation. Nonetheless, by grafting the Arabic tradition of wisdom literature represented by this quatrain onto the problematic of being in the modern world, he attempted to adapt and familiarize the terms of an otherwise foreign materialist critique of colonialism.

The author developed his critique by focusing on evolving consumption patterns among women, specifically in the realm of fashion, that he felt threatened to undo, as it were, the very fabric of Egyptian society. An act as simple as wearing a corset could be "a major cause leading to the ruin of many households, the fall of honorable families, the affliction of disastrous calamities on the majority of humanity."[42] In fact, according to the author, "The danger exceeds the limits of the imagination."[43] As in the case of men who mimicked the West, the problem was most germane to women of *al-tabaqa al-wusta* (the middle class).

The author's critique was built on four interacting levels: the individual, the family, nation-colony, and empire. He connected these nested domains through the mechanism of uneven economic exchange. He linked the potential ruin of families resulting from the recent desire of Egyptian women to imitate Western women with the continued subordination and exploitation of the Egyptian and Eastern economies by Europeans. He faulted the new generation of girls and women whose desire for European styles of dress pushed them to make unreasonable demands on their fathers and husbands. He argued that the contemporary middle-class woman was still under the impression that clothes made the individual special and set her above others of her sex: "She does not realize that it is the rational woman [*al-mar'a al-'aqila*] who is made beautiful through her virtue and made whole through knowledge and refinement."[44] Ostensibly, education would erode the competition among women to be the most fashionable by exposing the harmful force driving that competition, envy, and by teaching women to engage in more productive activities.[45] The proof of the beneficial effects of education was found in the lives of their Western counterparts, who were rational women and who were like Egyptian women in most respects except that "not a single one of them lived beyond their means."[46]

Many studies of the social and political implications of this rescripting of women's domestic roles in nationalist discourses of the late nineteenth century and early twentieth now exist.[47] Few have paid attention to how the redefinition of femininity was constitutive of a new national manhood or bourgeois masculinity — the discursive field I have labeled effendi masculinity.[48] Critiquing the sartorial excesses of Egyptian women was only one of the many ways nationalist men and women sought to produce the modern subject deemed necessary to quite literally populate the space of the nation, in which the boundaries between private and public were being redrawn in line with political and cultural engagements with colonialism.[49] The masculinist response to the perception of Egypt's and Egyptians' degenerate position in colonial modernity is illustrated in this article, especially as the critique moves from the individual to the family.

Here the author cited the strain that women's excessive consumption had on marital relations. The husband's inability to meet his wife's (and daughters') material desires called into question his masculinity. Furthermore, the mother's desire for expensive clothes was evidence of her irrational approach to household management and a sign of her inability to provide her children with proper guidance. This could affect her daughters adversely when it came time for them to get married. If they exhibited the same desire to consume, they could scare off the few eligible bachelors there were, most already having spurned marriage because of its cost and the dearth of rational brides.[50]

The author's next move made it clear that consumption as such was not being critiqued. Women's purchase of expensive clothes, even if it went beyond their means, would not be so negative — in fact, it would be a positive act — if "textile factories were spread throughout the length and breadth of Eastern countries."[51] If that were the case, then Eastern capital would remain in Eastern hands and enrich the East instead of the West.

The author explained how the draining of Eastern capital in this way had gendered consequences. Men, who were the public face of Egypt, paid the price of women's unthinking consumption of fashion. The continued economic exploitation of the nation daily reinforced the impotence of its men in resisting foreign penetration: "This money that we spend randomly doubtless winds up in the hands of Europeans who are laughing at us, who look down upon our intellect and who drain us of our wealth *through strange tricks like these*."[52] The "strange tricks," for this author, referred not to the mysteries of exchange value in commodities, which veiled the real relations of production, but rather to the circulation of capitalist desire obscuring the colonial relations of power.[53] This peculiar organization of commodities could override rational self-interests and undermine nationalist aspirations.[54] The magic of expansionist capitalism was so powerful that it was capable even of compelling Eastern women to endanger their physical well-being for the sake of fashion. The author argued that most Western dress was unsuitable for Easterners, but this was especially true of the corset; he marshaled scientific testimony to prove its insalubrious nature.

The nationalist male had a duty to demystify these crafty strategies intended to exploit, humiliate, and subordinate his people. Public textual interventions into matters of dress would continue through the following decades, with both men and women participating. The debates became almost exclusively focused on the place of the veil in modern Egyptian society. As the number of men wearing European-style clothing grew steadily during that period, and the suit and tie became a commonplace in the urban landscape of the 1920s, men's imitation of Western dress seemed to become a nonissue. One might argue that the disappearance of contention around the suit took place in an inverse relation to the growing recognition of the validity of the claims of the effendiyya to represent, or speak for, Egypt — in an address that was at once national and international. The revolution of 1919 to a certain extent galvanized this claim and was embodied by Sa'd Zaghlul and the Wafd Party.

The achievement of only nominal independence in 1922 generated the conditions for a renewed cultural criticism centered on men's dress.[55] The nationalist representatives' failure to secure Egypt's sovereignty was variously analyzed as a question of modernity.[56] Mustafa Kemal's radical modernization policies in fully independent and sovereign Turkey touched off a new wave of public debate about men's attire that reengaged questions of modernity, tradition, gender, national identity, and freedom.

"The Perfection of Masculinity" or Dressing for the Times?

In 1925 Fikri Abaza, the editor of the cultural magazine *al-Musawwar*, explained his decision to evaluate the implications of Mustafa Kemal's social policies.[57] He claimed that those policies were highly relevant to Egyptians since "Egypt is still tied to Turkey in many ways: in terms of religion, kinship, and Eastern traditions."[58] His criticism of Atatürk's prohibition of the veil and the tarbush and legislation of European dress echoed the turn-of-the-century critics in calling for a deeper understanding of what it meant to be modern but differed in the particulars. In his opinion, national renaissance required a commitment to mass education and other unstated fundamental social reforms. Addressing leaders and intellectuals, he concluded, "Reforming the basic conditions of life is what is important. Outward accoutrements that do not develop or retard are best left on heads and bodies as an eternal marker of the renascent nation that has retained its traditional image, its special character. Then, the crucial factor becomes what is inside the head and chest, not what covers the head and chest."[59] In other words, becoming modern was a much more complicated process than simply imitating foreign dress or rejecting local traditions.

Abaza's consideration of modernity's proper constitution and its relationship to tradition was taking place against the backdrop of a specific political struggle in Egypt sparked by the new Turkish republic's abolishment of the caliphate in 1924. Most *ulama* and palace supporters in Egypt favored the restoration of this highest office in Islam with King Fuad as the new caliph. The political parties spearheaded by the Wafd supported a reform of religious institutions in Egypt—from the *shari'a* as a source of legal practice to the office of the mufti—but initially avoided getting involved in the caliphate question.[60] In this context, Abaza's position could be seen as an attempt to bait the Palace into a debate on cultural modernity to expose its secularist outlook.

Abaza's problem with the Turkish model of reaching modernity was explicitly gendered. Although Abaza objected to Kemal's decree of European dress for both men and women, his reasons for each were quite different. While he did not say so explicitly, as a wearer of the suit himself, his objection to the Kemalist reforms of men's dress was registered in terms of the antidemocratic measures underlying them as opposed to some strong commitment to the preservation of traditional male costumes. In the case of women and the *hijab* (signifying here both the face veil and seclusion), his argument assumed a different course. He said, "I used to be an 'extreme conservative,' but the fierce attacks of the 'fairer sex' have gradually weakened my passionate attachment to the venerable past."[61] (The remarks that follow make one wonder what he thought about women when he was in his extreme conservative phase.) Abaza's first salvo against the Kemalist program for women's emancipation was personal. He attacked Kemal's hypocrisy by pointing to his failed relationship with his wife, Latifa Hanim, who was a model of European culture. He suggested that despite Kemal's public proclamations, in fact it was his wife's unveiling and her appearance in mixed company that led to the collapse of their marriage.

Abaza's next move was to assemble a list of European luminaries who also had cautioned against "permissive freedom for women." Some would find it interesting that Oscar Wilde appeared here alongside George

Bernard Shaw and Arthur Schopenhauer. Abaza emphasized the import of their warnings of disastrous consequences by underlining the geographical and cultural specificity of their utterances. In other words, if social failure was feared in Western Europe as a result of giving women more freedoms, then imagine what was in store for Eastern Turkey.[62]

It seems Abaza did manage to elicit a response from the pro-Palace camp. His views on the Turkish path toward modernity were denounced by the editor of *al-Nil al-Musawwar* as reactionary and shortsighted.[63] The editor of *al-Nil* did not raise the question of women's dress explicitly, an omission that may reflect the Palace's desire to support the new Turkish republic without alienating its religious supporters.[64] On the other hand, given the content of Abaza's article, the criticism was directed implicitly at his claims about women and the hijab.

The editor of *al-Nil* endorsed the Turkish project on the grounds that Turkish reformers grasped the nature of the changed world in which they lived. They understood the need to dress for the times: new clothes were required to meet the new fast-paced lifestyle. In addition to the efficiency and productivity enabled by Western dress, the author pointed to their suitability for the weather. Apparently the suit and brimmed hat could shield the wearer from Egypt's climate better than the ancient gallabiya and tarbush.

The author tried to shame Egyptian reformers (*mujaddidun*) further by asserting that Egypt, which was actually a part of Europe, should have preceded the Turks in instituting cultural changes. Then, somewhat contradictorily — relocating Egypt geographically again — he declared, "Alas, the East ambles along in its same old way." Taking a step away from the Turkish model, though, he concluded by framing the question of dress as a matter of having the freedom to choose.

In a postscript addressed personally to Abaza, the editor of *al-Nil* pointed out that the cost of a *baladi* (traditional) costume was more than double that of one of his European suits. He ended by inquiring of Abaza, "So why do you want to block the way of others to economy?"[65] The mocking query aimed to mute Abaza's call for Egypt to deal with its basic social problems before debating superficial cultural matters. What the editor of *al-Nil* failed to point out and what Abaza did not recognize in his own argument as contradictory was that the question of dress was a problem precisely because it was a deeply political issue perceived as having dire social consequences, something of which the preindependence critics were more conscious.

The fact that men's dress could still assume political significance was further evinced in the Dar al-'Ulum controversy that was unfolding as Abaza and the editor of *al-Nil* sparred on the pages of their respective magazines. In February 1926, students at Dar al-'Ulum and Al-Azhar came to class wearing suits and tarabish.[66] When Education Minister Ali Maher tried to enforce the dress code, the students went on strike, demanding the right to substitute the tarbush and suit for the turban and robe. The minister obtained rulings (*fatawa*) from the rector of Al-Azhar and the mufti of Egypt stating that the Western-style hat was un-Islamic. The students also obtained fatawa, most notably from Shaykh Muhammad Shakir, who had been deputy rector (*wakil*) of Al-Azhar.[67] Shakir argued that Islam's only prescription regarding dress was as a cover for the naked body, that Islam is a "religion of hearts and souls." The neutrality of Islam on the question of dress was confirmed, for example, in the case of Muslim converts in other cultures, who were not expected to change their outward appearances. He concluded that there was nothing wrong with dress keeping up with the times.

Similar to the prior invocation of the soul/body split through the words of the ancient poet, here students mobilized the moral and spiritual authority of the Islamic tradition in order to diminish the signifying potential of the external self even as their quest for the freedom of dress belied the importance they ascribed to aesthetics for their presence in modernity. The Ministry of Education rejected their demand and ordered the students to return to their classes or face expulsion. The students ultimately complied.[68] That students of Al-Azhar and the Arabic teachers' training college sought to alter their dress code was perhaps not terribly significant in its own right. Indeed, this incident was perhaps the last in which the turban would feature as a site of public contestation in Egypt; however, the dispute between the students and Minister Maher managed to hold the public's attention for the entire year as the discussions quickly fanned outward to include the general question of national identity, which repositioned the debates exclusively around the tarbush and the hat and along a transnational axis.

The satirical cartoon from 1928 reproduced here is an example of this shift. Mocking religious rulings on matters of proper dress, it features only the hat and tarbush as objects of debate even as the subjects are turbaned and in robes. The two *shaykhs* represented here were both prominent figures involved in the early nationalist movement, and they remained part of the political scene after the revolution in 1919. Al-Shaykh Bakhit had served as mufti of Egypt and, as mentioned above, al-Shaykh Shakir had been a wakil at Al-Azhar. The extinction of the turban, or at least its rele-

35. The Arabic heading reads, "The Shaykhs and the Hat." The first Arabic caption reads, "Al-Shaykh Bakhit—We prayed with the Afghan King and he was wearing a hat! What are we going to tell the people?" The second Arabic caption reads, "Al-Shaykh Shakir—We'll tell them that when a Muslim king wears the hat it becomes *halal*, but when we or anyone else wears it, it becomes *haram.*" *Al-Kashkul* (January 1, 1928), 20.

gation to the sphere now understood as solely religious, seemed a foregone conclusion, even in the self-designated Islamic press.

Al-Fath, a magazine representing the Islamic press, opposed the move to do away with the turban but sided with the pro-tarbush camp against the proponents of Western-style hats. It enlisted the likes of Shakib Arsalan, Ahmad Zaghlul, and Ahmad Taymur in its efforts.[69] By yoking the turban and the tarbush into one seamless Islamic history, *al-Fath* was insisting on a national identity that embraced Egypt's Arab and Ottoman past simultaneously while refusing an exclusively secular conception of modernity. The debate over headgear became an active platform from which specific claims on Egyptian modernity could be forwarded to a broader public. In the case of *al-Fath*, this entailed the rearticulation of the terms of national and masculine subjectivity in a modified Arabo-Islamic register—perhaps a searching one, in the wake of Atatürk's abolition of the caliphate two years earlier.

Arsalan's article used the visit of the Moroccan prince and anticolonial activist Muhammad ibn Abd al-Karim al-Khattabi to Europe to deliver a lesson to Egyptians on the value of customary dress.[70] He linked the shame or pride a man had in his nation's traditional fashion to colonial penetration but also to a process of willful self-fashioning. In other words, it was the total submission of Egyptian elites to European culture in the face of colonial domination that accounted for the nation's emasculation.

Arsalan demonstrated through the body of Prince Abd al-Karim that the loss of masculinity was usually self-inflicted. Contrary to some people's expectations, he claimed, the prince and his entourage were celebrated and honored in Europe for preserving the Islamic fashion of the Moroccan Rif: the turban and the hooded cloak: "They do not see themselves as less than Europeans nor do they recognize the hat and pants as signs of authority or markers of superiority."[71] Their pride in themselves and their culture was recognized and respected. Furthermore, Arsalan argued, their dress was not an obstacle to progress or to functioning in the modern world. In fact, the will to adapt to the modern world (adaptation was understood here as the acquisition of knowledge) without renouncing one's heritage, sartorial and otherwise, held the key to a genuine and complete masculinity: "The perfection of masculinity [*kamal al-muruwwa*] is through obtaining knowledge by whatever means and acquiring wisdom from whichever direction, while retaining national character and native dress [*al-mushakhkhisat al-qawmiyya wa al-aziya' al-asliyya*] so that we are not like slaves in love with imitating their masters."[72] He also registered the possibility of achieving a more physical, or martial, masculinity enabled by the respect for Islamic traditions—in this case expressed in dress. He cited the valor of the Rif Moroccans on the battlefield, where dress was not an impediment in their destruction of the mighty armies of Spain and France. Arsalan underscored this accomplishment by locating the might of their opponents on a global geopolitical scale: "[France and Spain] are not second-class states like Greece or Bulgaria."[73]

Whereas Arsalan's intervention took a broad international and anti-imperialist perspective, Zaghlul's contribution to *al-Fath*, published a month later, emphasized the local and the national. Zaghlul's response also came on the heels of another development in Egyptian sartorial politics. After the Dar al-'Ulum incident, a club named the Eastern League (*al-Rabita al-Sharqiyya*) addressed a letter to the Egyptian Medical Association (EMA) in the form of a questionnaire seeking a scientific ruling on matters of dress.[74] The EMA's reply caused a furor in the pro-tarbush camp.

The first question the league posed was asked about the health implications of wearing the tarbush versus other forms of headdress; the second was about the suitability of Western clothes for Egypt's climate; and the last regarded proper footwear. In all three instances, the EMA ruled that Western styles were superior to local ones. The tarbush was the major victim of the ruling, as it was designated completely unsuitable for Egypt's heat. In its stead, the pith helmet and brimmed hat were recommended as healthy alternatives: "We would like to point out on this occasion that the foreigners who have settled in hot countries conducted numerous medical and scientific experiments before they arrived at the clothes that they wear now, which are the most appropriate in terms of health for regions like these. This [conclusion] is also supported by several experiments carried out by respected members of this association."[75] In short, the EMA categorically endorsed what could be termed colonial fashion because it was the result of scientific testing.

This decision by an official but nongovernmental body blurred the lines between cultural representation and political representation in interesting ways. Ahmad Zaghlul, the nephew of the nationalist hero Sa'd Zaghlul, sharply denounced the EMA's decision as well as its presumption to officiate in the matter in the first place.[76] He began his criticism by revisiting the events of that year and relating them to the present controversy as a series of destabilizing moves for the nation. He recounted the Dar al-'Ulum incident and how it ended with the students returning to class humiliated after the Ministry of Education threatened them with expulsion. However, inspired by the Dar al-'Ulum students, another group of students from government secondary schools began to clamor for the right to wear the hat instead of the tarbush. In this instance Sa'd Zaghlul himself apparently advised the students, saying, "The question of dress is an issue of authentic national identity [qawmiyya mahda]. If we changed our own [style] of dress, we would change our national identity, and a people without a national identity are a people without life."[77] The author added that there were also fatwas issued by some religious leaders warning the students of evil consequences if they changed completely to European dress.

Given that the moment was so critical, Zaghlul professed his shock at the irresponsible decision of the Egyptian doctors to endorse Western dress. The moment was ostensibly one in which the nationalist symbolic value of the tarbush was being undermined by unthinking youth who were playing into the hands of those who would deny Egypt a developed national identity—and "a people without a national identity are a people without life." Zaghlul's incredulity in the face of the EMA's decision and his denunciation of it were justified since, in a sense, the very existence of Egypt was at stake.

Zaghlul continued his criticism by attacking the organization's unrepresentative status, especially when it came to such a weighty matter as changing the traditional dress of the Islamic community. The slippage between Egypt and the Islamic community seems to be a rhetorical deployment aimed at emphasizing the breadth and gravity of the action taken while simultaneously highlighting the ridiculousness of any claims to representativeness made by such an unauthorized body. He contrasted the EMA's place in Egyptian society with the "actual representatives" of the country — the *nuwwab* (s. *na'ib*, parliamentary delegate): "The *nuwwab* are the spokespersons of the nation, expressing its hopes and its pains. They know what is in its best interest and endeavor to satisfy it. At their head is the great leader Sa'd Pasha Zaghlul."[78] Consequently, Zaghlul argued, if there was in fact a public health concern about the tarbush it would have been the responsibility of the parliamentary health committee to research the matter and render a decision. But it was evident, he continued, that the question of dress was not a salient public issue except for a tiny minority of Westernized youth who lacked *al-muruwwa al-qawmiyya* (national manhood) as well as any ambition to become productive citizens. Their voices were thus negligible, and the "nation has rejected them, recognizing them as a burden on her; it has left them to play and be merry."[79]

Then he turned again to censure and shame the doctors for humoring the trivial fantasies of this insufficiently masculine constituency while there were more pressing national health concerns to address: "You did not think about your wretched peasant who suffers under the oppressive weight of sickness. You considered fashion but did not consider the condition of the villages, their filth, and rampant illness. . . . It is better for you to put aside this nonsense and [work to] uplift your nation."[80] Zaghlul's article was not just an attack on the advocates of the brimmed hat. He sought to accomplish a number of tasks through his criticism. The first move, in which he located the EMA's decision within a series of contests by youth over the proper headgear, was made to highlight the immature nature of this constituency and their demands. By playing to these demands, the EMA not only devalued itself as a responsible body but also overstepped its bounds. This was Zaghlul's most significant intervention. The identification of a social problem and its delimitation as national was the exclusive function of the new parliamentary representatives, the nuwwab, and to Zaghlul's mind the nuwwab with the greatest authority were members of the Wafd Party. The civic life of associations was thus to be confined to a consideration of questions deemed relevant by the one truly national body. This territorialization of the political and its conflation with the national were especially significant at the time since the definition and eventual control of the state were contested by formal political parties, the monarch, and the British.

In light of this heterogeneous and embattled political terrain, it is note-worthy that Zaghlul based his criticism of the hat proponents on a gen-dered concept of representation. The proper representatives of the nation and those deserving of representation were joined in forming a field of national manhood — united in this instance around the symbol of the tar-bush. Conversely, the detractors of this symbol were rendered deficient in nationalism and masculinity, and as the nation's abject they could be banned from representation.[81]

Arsalan too responded to the EMA's decision.[82] He began by summa-rizing a deconstruction of the health angle in the tarbush–hat dispute which had been performed by an anonymous contributor to *al-Muqtataf*.[83] In short, the author had tried to expose the pseudoscience behind the EMA's support of the hat, arguing that it did not really matter what was on one's head since human adaptation to heat varied depending on numer-ous factors, most importantly geography and class. Nonetheless, Arsalan added, if one were to accept the EMA's conclusion about dress and climate, then the turban was far superior to both the tarbush and the brimmed hat, from the perspective of health (it was better at shielding one from the sun or blows to the head) and in terms of practicality (it could double as a pil-low).

In a harsher tone, Arsalan dismissed the freedom-to-choose argument as extremely ignorant and superficial.[84] He said that those who maintained this position were in fact the least conscious of the meaning of life. If it meant to them the emulation of Westerners, then they should do so in all ways: "in their seriousness and perseverance, in their love for their nations, in learning, in research, in economizing, in cleanliness, in exer-cise, in taking risks, in their interest in industry and art and the incorpora-tion of these into [everyday] life, and in the ordering of their homes and their countries — none of which is dependent on the hat [they wear]."[85] By questioning their motivation and casting them as poor copies of the West-erner, Arsalan, like Zaghlul, achieved the rhetorical effect of locating the desire for the hat outside a national economy of desire and thus untenable. Its indefensibility was especially true, in Arsalan's opinion, since Egypt already had a diverse array of head coverings and adding another would have meant total chaos for Eastern dress.

In other words, if the Western hat too became a fixture of Egypt's fash-ion landscape, then how was Egypt to be recognized as distinctly Eastern? Arsalan asserted that outsiders would see an "amorphous social structure" (*hay'a ijtima'iyya khunfashariyya*). Despite the gravity of the problem,

Arsalan was ultimately ambivalent about the best way to achieve the unification of a national style of dress. He found enforcement by the sword, as in Turkey, an undesirable model.

Not all traditions can or should be recuperated. Although he did not mention it, the article from *al-Muqtataf* cited by Arsalan as evidence for dismissing the health benefits of wearing the brimmed hat had also offered a reading of difference, recognition, and the East–West divide that diverged markedly from his position.[86] The author of "The Tarbush or the Hat" made an argument about power and the institution of difference that intuited an understanding of the East as being on some levels a cultural construct, albeit one with political ramifications. All of the current anxiety around the question of dress, he maintained, emanated from a sense of powerlessness: "If it had been that we were in the position of power and prosperity and that the people of Europe and America imitated us in our food, drink, dress, and home furnishings, then it wouldn't have bothered us if were walking around barefoot or wearing the *balgha* on our feet and black rags on our heads.[87] But we are connected to peoples who have surpassed us in everything and who want to retain their distinction from us and do not want us to resemble them in our dress. It is like the master of a house who does not want his servants to dress like he dresses."[88] For this author, distinction and recognition were mediated through hierarchical relationships, and the maintenance of cultural difference through the preservation of Eastern fashion ironically became an act complicit with colonial power. The author pointed to efforts in other aspects of life to erase the distinctions between East and West, including in knowledge, wealth, transportation, household management, and home furnishings. Even as far as dress went, the tops of heads were the last remaining frontier of the (male) body that separated "us and them." Or so it would seem.

Although he spun out the implications of his argument and suggested that switching to the hat would be logically the final act in achieving identity with the European male, he did allow a large social and demographic fact to interrupt and complicate his culturalist discourse. Essentially, in a country in which nine-tenths of the population, according to the author, had never made the switch to pants, jackets, and tarbush, it was folly to expect a major change of fashion in a year or even several years. He was also pessimistic about tarbush wearers switching to the hat in large numbers without the leadership of the king. Hence, the sober reality of Egyptian modernity was such that all of the talk about turbans, hats, and tarabish was premature and consequently largely meaningless. Ultimately,

فوضى الأزياء فى مصر

يريشة رسام مصرى نابغة

الأزياء المختلفة فى مصر . أين اللباس القومى اذن ؟ . . . .

36. The confusion of modern life is acutely portrayed here in a sartorial map that offers little comfort to the lost souls that it presumes inhabit Egypt. What remains unclear is whether the nation can bring resolution to the chaos or is in fact its cause. The Arabic heading reads, "The Chaos of Dress." The Arabic caption reads, "The different fashions in Egypt. So where's the national dress?" *Al-Siyasa al-Usbu'iyya* (December 4, 1926), 19.

37. Like the previous image, but perhaps somewhat more directly, this cartoon poses the question of resolving the dilemma of modern life within the new national frame. How does one stay the same, true to one's origins, while keeping pace with rapid change? It suggests at the very least that adapting the past to the present in a meaningful way is more complex than selectively mixing and matching. The Arabic caption reads,

"The Modern Egyptian Woman: The truth that one who loses his past is lost and that everything goes back to its origins has shaped me accordingly: a union of the ancient and the modern." *Al-Matraqa* (February 12, 1928), cover.

for this critic, cultural adaptation was a historical process necessitated by asymmetries of power on an international scale. A nation that wished to overcome enslavement by another could not afford not to allow mimicry, if not encourage it. Conversely, guarding an inviolable and unchanging notion of Eastern fashion, which evinced an unself-consciously xenophobic attitude that was out of step with the times, was tantamount to dependence and domination without end. While I do not wish to diminish the value of the author's cosmopolitanism, the question still remained how a shift in attitude could bring about social or political emancipation for the vast majority of Egyptians still wearing the gallabiya and the turban and working the fields.

Dress, often dismissed as unworthy of comment by contemporary authors, was nonetheless heatedly debated because it was an important surface on which modernity was marked and through which cultural dependence and independence were simultaneously expressed. Determining a distinctively Egyptian headdress was thus essential to the gendered constitution of the post-Ottoman order of the nation-state, which had at once to be the same as and different from other nation-states. However, as seen briefly in the case of Mubarak's nineteenth-century refashioning of self, dress did not simply play surface to some mysterious deeper level of the subject.

Global Affects

Through the public expression of intimacy—in this case, the individual feelings of prominent figures in relation to fashion—the question of social reality and its transformation could be deferred.[89] The cultural work performed by public intimacy was at least threefold: it brought disparate social classes within one affective space, elided the class differences that Egypt's colonial and capitalist modernity was in the process of multiplying and intensifying, and performatively reinstated effendi masculinity at the center of the nation.[90]

Ali Abd al-Raziq (1888–1966), in Paris at the time, contributed a poignant analysis of the Egyptian clothing debates to *al-Siyasa al-Usbu'iyya*.[91] Abd al-Raziq belonged to an old landed family whose members were highly influential in the Liberal Constitutionalist Party. He was a shaykh trained at Al-Azhar and had also studied at Oxford. After his return to Egypt, he was appointed as a Shari'a Court judge in 1915. The publication of his book *al-Islam wa usul al-hukm* (Islam and the principles of government) in 1925 angered the king and members of the ulama, resulting in the revocation of his degree from Al-Azhar.[92] The political turmoil caused by the attempt to censure him included the resignation of the Liberal ministers in protest, leaving a totally pro-Palace cabinet. Perhaps his flight to France was undertaken to weather this storm. After his return, he practiced as a lawyer and went on to serve in the Majlis al-Nuwwab, followed by the Majlis al-Shuyukh. He also taught *fiqh* (Islamic jurisprudence) at the University of Cairo for twenty years.

Abd al-Raziq began the article in question, "Farewell to the Turban," by claiming that most people in the world regarded dress as being just as important as food and drink, and possibly even more so. Only a minority saw in the issue of dress no significance whatsoever. He intimated from the start that it was not only in terms of meeting basic needs that dress commanded attention but also in terms of a contested cultural terrain.

Abd al-Raziq continued by making explicit some of the ways in which dress assumed social, economic, and political significance in modern times. He argued that "the institutions of modern life" presupposed the importance of different styles of dress. In other words, each social context determined its own sartorial image, and conversely that image reflected a particular social context. This, he suggested, would come as no surprise to anyone who knew of the "fashion houses" (*buyut al-moda*) in the world's capitals and of "their influence on our economic life, on our character, and our customs."[93] All women, regardless of age, color, or class, were members of this *madhhab*, which accorded fashion a central place in their lives.[94] Men were slightly more differentiated in that there was a small minority who believed that clothes had absolutely no signifying value.

The minority opinion, according to Abd al-Raziq, rejected all the prior social and political claims made on dress and denied the transformative power that others liked to accord to it. Essentially, ugly was ugly, violent was violent, ignorant was ignorant, and there was nothing dress could do about it. They also opposed the connections made between nationalism and fashion because fashion was ephemeral, "a form that fluctuates with the fluctuation of time," while the nation was beautiful and eternally stable. Finally, they found the ascription of religious significance to dress objectionable and misguided.

Abd al-Raziq's rhetorical use of this unnamed group of men and their views on dress was metaphorical, signifying a political position that was disconnected from its social and cultural bases.[95] He argued that the truth was found between the two extreme positions and that that truth should be acceptable to both. The middle ground between those who viewed dress as an issue of primary importance and those who denied its importance was a categorical prohibition. Men could not be allowed to discuss, act on, or even think about the question of dress. Hence, in the name of mediation, Abd al-Raziq staked out political and moral grounds of his own based on the nonquestion of dress. He argued that even if the majority considered dress to be of great significance, men should concern themselves with other, more pressing issues. He did not elaborate on what those issues were or on the questions of how or by whom they would be determined.

The rest of the article was a personal testimony in which he bid farewell to the turban. He admitted that this discourse contradicted his previous statements about dress; nevertheless, because of the turban's special position within Islamic history and its "beloved status in spirit," it was deserving of a formal elegy.[96] "Even if the departed Shaykh Muhammad Abduh hated the turban and disparaged it," wrote Abd al-Raziq, there was a time when it signified a kind of social and religious virtue.[97] Moreover, it held a "special place" in the life of the author and his family.

The "noble tradition" (*turath karim*) of the Abd al-Raziq family was briefly narrated to illustrate the grand heritage of which the turban was an important symbolic marker. Although he was nostalgic for that past time and melancholic that he would not be able to pass on the turban to his sons as his ancestors had before him, he acknowledged that the time had come for it to be retired. This was true in part because the changing times had rendered the noble tradition of the turban archaic; moreover, a class he alluded to as being composed of ignorant and violent types were now its bearers. So in a wistful tone he brought his elegy to a close, literally bidding farewell to "the beloved turban."

Abd al-Raziq's article on dress and the extinction of the turban expressed a number of concerns and anxieties about his society and the place of people like himself within it. But before turning to an analysis of these issues, I want to consider another personal testimony from a different perspective. Mahmud Azmi was a noted journalist who worked with Muhammad Husayn Haykal on *al-Siyasa*. His story of switching from the tarbush to the hat appeared in *al-Hilal* in 1927, a year after Abd al-Raziq's article.[98] Azmi informed the reader at the start that he had been invited by the magazine to offer a personal account of switching to the hat. His narrative included a version of the history of the earlier tarbush-hat controversy that took the reader from the turn of the century to the author's present.

Azmi wrote that the social and political significance of dress first occurred to him during his adolescent years as a student in secondary school. He remembered it as the time when everyone was talking about Qasim Amin's recently published books on women and the veil. After listening to numerous opinions on the books and then reading them for himself, he became a staunch opponent of the veil. He recalled that he had opposed the veil mainly because of its foreign origins and its introduction to Egypt through conquest. His thinking on the issue had been guided by two questions: What constituted modest dress, and what dress was Egyptian in material and make?

Early in the century, prior to the First World War, the same sort of concern for proper national attire turned some against the tarbush. According to Azmi, some had declared the tarbush foreign and unhealthy and called for a return to the ancient Egyptian headdress. He remembered that he himself had been driven by similar reasons to reject the veil and the tarbush and had felt a powerful nationalist sentiment in doing so. However, just as his understanding of nationalism changed while he was studying in Paris, so too did his attitude toward dress.

It could very well have been the opposite: that his attitude toward nationalism changed as his appreciation of fashion changed. It is possible to read his testimony as saying that the experience of dressing differently, this very superficial act, was the cause of an intellectual and political shift. Nonetheless, in a retrospective account justifying the controversial decision to switch to the Western hat it was important that the explanation be couched in terms of nationalism. So, it was in France that Azmi had come to regard nationalism as a "feeling of pride" that one should have within oneself and not "spread on [one's] surface." [99] Consequently, the symbolic meaning of dress was also reevaluated but not erased entirely as per Abd al-Raziq's recommendation. In fact, for Azmi, dress and fashion assumed a renewed significance as signs of modernity's internationalism. He had been inspired at the time, he wrote, by the prevailing spirit of harmony and had realized that dress was one of the most visible sites expressing this new attitude. [100]

According to Azmi, this kind of cultural fusion had always been evident in Egypt. Over time, Egyptians on a popular level borrowed all manner of dress from various dominant cultures. There was, however, one item of foreign clothing that had been denied popular approval because it was the symbol of Ottoman tyranny, "the symbol of the power of Cairo and the autocratic Sultan." [101] This was the tarbush.

The tarbush, though, was not to remain a despised symbol forever. According to Azmi, the tarbush was recoded with the exact opposite signification during the war. It was resignified and repoliticized, Azmi argued, as the British imposed a protectorate on Egypt in 1914. The sudden declaration of Egypt as an unwilling supporter of the British war effort against the Ottomans had surprising ramifications on the popular level. Azmi did not refer to the tremendous human suffering caused by British exploitation of Egyptian resources and labor during this time, but surely this was a major factor in radicalizing the political landscape and preparing the grounds for the reappropriation of the symbol of Turkish despotism as a distinct sign of a more popular Egyptian nationalism.

Azmi drew a connection between the way Egyptians viewed the Ottoman–Circassian elite during wartime and the stigma attached to the hat. [102] He suggested that those who switched from the tarbush to the hat were trying to "flee from 'Ottomanism' and get closer to the protector state, or avoid the hostility of Australian soldiers." [103] He alluded to how this sartorial switching by the members of the ruling class was read by the masses as cowardice. The lack of courage, a key masculine virtue, combined with the aristocracy's alignment with the Protectorate were the two main reasons Azmi gave for the symbolic transformation of the tarbush into a marker of the authentic popular will, which was ostensibly both pro-Ottoman and Egyptian. In other words, by wearing the tarbush in public the wearer was expressing his willingness to defy the occupying forces openly, stand up to whatever humiliation he was subjected to, and restore Egypt to its proper historical place among Eastern nations.

Azmi referred to the period following the war as a *nahda*. Through this renaissance, ostensibly enabled by the new nationalist consciousness manifested in the popular uprising of 1919, Egyptians generally came to view the tarbush as a symbol of the reborn nation, an accessory essential to being modern, Eastern, and Egyptian. However, it was precisely as the nahda became an ordinary feature of everyday life (institutionalized in Egypt's new constitution and representative government), as freedom became an important principle to all, and as an understanding of sorts was reached with the British that a new space for moderate public discourse was created. Azmi was now talking about his own scene of writing.

Within this space, Azmi continued, some began to revisit the question of modern culture, and the tarbush again became a contested symbol. He depicted the climate in which these debates occurred as markedly different from the past. The most telling example of how much the times had changed was the apparent absence of accusations of blasphemy.[104] In fact, there was change everywhere. Azmi cited the progress of women, which was illustrated best by their "liberation from the veil." He noted the advances made in Turkey without religious opposition. Throughout the Arab lands there was also nahda and movements for independence.

In the Arab world, however, a split was developing, one which Azmi described as a civilizational choice: between being Arab and being modern. Some had come to the conclusion that attempts at finding common ground were futile because of the deep rift that existed between the past and the present of Islamic societies. He did not explain this further but mentioned the speed with which modern society was moving forward. Perhaps he believed that in the face of such a rapid pace of change any reconciliation with the past was impossible. He wrote that he himself had made the choice to draw on modern civilization; furthermore, he felt it was a choice society as a whole needed to make.

After delineating the historical context and illustrating the social and political significance of dress, he finally narrated the details of the precise moment in which he made the decision to switch from the tarbush to the hat. This sort of autobiographical writing was rare and yet emblematic of this period. Publicly presenting the intimate thoughts of a private person as he self-consciously embarked on making a change, of refashioning himself, was a quintessentially modernist performance. Autobiography as such was not rare in Egypt in the 1920s but giving the reader an exceptionally vivid picture of what an agonizing process a seemingly simple, ordinary act like choosing between two hats could be was unique. In other words, giving an account of oneself that exposed one's interiority publicly, if not entirely new, was still a novelty for the time.[105]

Azmi wrote that he had resolved in the summer of 1925 to put his convictions about being modern to the test. He announced to his friends and family that he would be switching to the bowler hat on the first of July. He said that he gave this date so that they would have some time to adjust to the idea.

Then he described in great detail the anxiety that overtook him when the day finally arrived for him to make the switch. As he approached the hat store on Qasr al-Nil Street, he noticed that his footsteps had gotten heavier and that moving forward was becoming increasingly difficult. When he finally reached the front of the store, he froze and found that he could not even open the door, much less enter. Eventually, he turned around and walked back in the direction he had come from. He wrote, "I noticed that I had started to accuse myself under my breath of cowardice and of still being under the influence of *al-akhta' al-wirathiyya*."[106] This phrase literally means "inherited flaws" or "weaknesses" but might be interpreted in this context to mean backward traditions.

Extirpating the inherited defects from within himself and from society was deemed a critical, indispensable step toward becoming modern. For Azmi, this project of overcoming the inertia of tradition and expunging the past took another full year. He confessed that he was emboldened by the ruling on the tarbush issued by the EMA in the summer of 1926: "I headed directly the next morning—the third Saturday in the month of July 1926—to the hat salesman, and I bought a summer hat. . . . And since that day I have been wearing the hat, alternating between different types depending on the season."[107]

From the two reactions Azmi recounted, it seems that his wearing of Western hats was received favorably, even lauded. One of his friends, whom he described as a leading Arab writer and intellectual, said the following: "Now the Easterners are beginning to think with their heads!"[108] Another friend was inspired to write to *al-Siyasa* with his own views on the headdress question. Azmi quoted from his article: "The struggle is not between the turban, the tarbush, and the hat, but rather it is a struggle between different visions of thought and taste [*suwar mukhtalifa min al-tafkir wa al-dhawq*] each of which wants to be dominant."[109] That said, the friend also sided with the Western hat and pronounced the turban and the tarbush as outmoded forms of headdress—and by extension, they symbolized obsolete forms of thought and taste.

The personal testimonies of Abd al-Raziq and Azmi richly illustrate the complicated negotiations of the effendiyya with their sartorial presence in an emergent interwar Egyptian public sphere. They also attest to a self-conscious engagement with modernity as a universal experience. The tension between the particular and the universal was most evident in the manner in which the two authors negotiated the relationship of dress and national identity. However much they differed in their positions on the question of dress, both were deeply conscious of its significance to culture, in terms of the relationship of form and content. Abd al-Raziq accepted the passing of the turban because it no longer signified a virtuous life, and Azmi was ready to adopt the hat when it seemed to him that the tarbush no longer signified emancipation. While Abd al-Raziq's reasoning was routed through an intimate knowledge of Islamic law and tradition, both men were critically engaged in translating modernist notions of self, community, and time in a historical moment when the stakes were well-nigh existential. Manhood, nationhood, progress, and even the possibility of an ethical life hung in the balance.

Abd al-Raziq's formal farewell to the turban inscribed the passing of a world in which men of religious learning had represented moral—and mediated political—authority. The cultural landscape he surveyed, from exile in Paris, had necessarily to foreclose a desire for the turban since its proper genealogy had been terminated by the social and political transformations of Egypt in the preceding decades. Although he longed to pass on this symbol of a noble tradition to his heirs, the kind of masculine personhood represented by the turban was no longer an ideal worthy of aspiration. This melancholic situation was only amplified by the politics in which Abd al-Raziq found himself embroiled and embattled; his thoughts on Islam, tradition, and authority were repudiated by the self-serving guardians of a moribund moral order symbolized poignantly by the now-meaningless turban.

Azmi's confession relating his decision to take up the Western hat repeated many of the terms of the cosmopolitanism prevalent in the international that was taking shape during the interwar period. The individual subject and citizen imagined therein represented an extension and deepening of a prior bourgeois and liberal understanding of the modern as a steady progression toward a future utopia. The past was inscribed in his story of personal transformation as part of a forward-moving trajectory and teleology, not as a site of loss. The self-constituting individual was the desired subject position of Azmi's narration. It was a subject position endorsed by science and resisted by an irrational Eastern mind. His courage in overcoming both the conservatism of his social milieu and his own internalized repression was publicly offered as testimony to the possibility of changing traditional tastes and frames of mind. The hat became the symbolic marker not only of modernity and the modern individual, but also of a possible future.

Conclusion

When the tarbush incident came to the Egyptian public's attention at the end of 1932, the cultural field had already been, in a sense, worked over to a large extent in the 1920s and was prepared for its reception. This might explain why a controversy that aroused loud outcries in late November was a dead issue by late December on the diplomatic level and in public discourse alike.[110] The cultural debates about the modernity and appropriateness of the tarbush for Egyptian men had already taken place. Its position as a nationalist icon had been secured against internal assault. Turkey and Egypt as discrete formations were firmly established with separate pasts and independent futures in a new international order. The final chapter of the tarbush story would be written two decades later with the abolishment of the monarchy.[111] Conversely, as Azmi's testimony evinces, cultural space had been created for men to wear Western headgear without renouncing their masculinity or national identity — so long as it was a private affair that did not impinge on the territory of the national public already staked out by the tarbush.[112]

Since there was no apocalyptic climax this might beg the question of what the stakes really were for Egyptian masculinity in these movements among the diverse styles of headdress during this period. In this chapter, I have been able only to hint at an answer by referring to sovereignty and masculinity as interrelated and that become intelligible as such within imperial and international social formations. It is necessary to marry the question of dress with the other sites of performance mapped in this work and to examine their interrelationships.

What one begins to see in the interwar period is the consolidation of an effendi masculinity that was legitimized through its claims on the nation and modernity and materialized through objects like the tarbush, practices like weightlifting and scouting, spaces like the sports club and the Olympics, and ideologies like heteronormativity. What one also sees in the example of headdress and the attempts to fix the meaning of turban, tarbush, and top hat to a specific ideological current is the possibility for and limit to resignification. The subject of these ideological formations — religious, secular, nationalist, liberal, royalist — was always modern, always contested, and always in a state of indeterminacy. Yet the modern subject within the Egyptian context was inflected by the liminality of its formation. The constant negotiation among and between local and foreign, traditional and modern binaries that were threaded through the question of national identity within the debates about dress illuminates the space and time of a colonial modernity from the vantage point of Egypt, which means the movement from Ottoman to republican Turkey was as meaningful an axis for Egyptian history as the movement from the colonial to the anticipated postcolonial.

The threat of being branded an outsider to religion or nation was not the only way in which the presence of the outside — or, as I have termed it, the international — shaped the subject of colonial modernity. There was a positive valence to it as well, in that no matter how it was ideologically deployed the international had become both the condition of possibility for and the limit to the proliferation of new subjectivities. In other words, the West that loomed in the era of crude imperialist politics prior to the First World War as the self-designated origin of the international and viewed almost exclusively as foreign was resignified as it became the locus of competing claims on a reordered global map. This West became at once a site of excess and constraint as a constitutive part of the interwar international formation of culture, gender, and modernity. Traveling through it actually and metaphorically were numerous lines of men and women, migrants and ministers, students and scientists, friends and foe from all corners of the world. Traversing it also were anticolonial politics, struggles for social reform, and appeals for recognition by colonized elites — all of which were inextricable from the ever-expanding global webs of knowledge production and dissemination.

Thus even if the terms of the West appear in the present as "hyperreal" in the description of Dipesh Chakrabarty, or as degenerate, violent, and in decline, as Gershoni and Jankowski read the revised Egyptian view of it in the 1930s, the West as it came to be in the interwar period was never the exclusive property of one place or one people.[113] In the assignment of different political and cultural meanings to the turban, tarbush, and top hat during the 1920s and 1930s, one sees not only the constant presence of the West but an instance of its reformation as the international. Debates by Egyptian intellectuals and reformers during the Depression about the differences between East and West, as if the two were discrete entities divided by a fundamental divergence of aims — spiritualist and materialist — might be viewed as another instance in the performative constitution of the international.[114] It was partly the feeling of anxiety over the vagaries of global interconnectedness brought home by the worldwide economic crisis that pushed nationalists everywhere to assert particularistic claims while in practice national units were becoming ever more integrated within an international network of bodies ranging from the League of Nations to population conferences to the fashion houses. Within and sometimes against that international order, culture, gender, and modernity were related and performatively reinscribed in Egypt to account for a post-Ottoman social, political, and religious order.

The three sartorial symbols and their differentiated evocations of nationalism and masculinity were situated unevenly in the international order — conditioned by the epistemic and physical violence of colonialism — wherein the subject's formation was measured against what was commonly regarded as the inescapable flow of modern time, with which Egypt was still playing catch-up. Nevertheless, within that space Egyptian identity in the interwar period was irreversibly established and the intelligibility of Egypt secured, even if these were still in the process of being formed and contested. The realization of Egypt's sovereignty appeared a mere matter of time.

The measure of modern time, to which Abaza, Zaghlul, Arsalan, Azmi, and Abd al-Raziq were beholden in their varying approaches to fashion and identity, obscured another order of asymmetries relating to dress. Falling in the shadows of the emergent spaces of the national and international was a sartorial politics that contested the very basis of the modern subject by failing to take the same measure of time.

8

KNOWLEDGE

Death, Life, and the Sovereign Other

Cairo in the interwar period, as we have seen, was a city experiencing dramatic changes on all fronts. The war had created economic opportunities for some and impoverished many others. Among the impoverished were peasants who were forced to leave their lands and move to Cairo by the tens of thousands in search of a livelihood. Within Cairo itself, there was a shifting of populations as the better-off residents of the older popular quarters migrated to newer neighborhoods like ʿAbbasiyya. Student activism opened the floodgates to new demands for freedom, political representation, and national self-determination. Drugs, crime, and prostitution were increasingly front-page issues for an expanding middle-class reading public concerned about their society's respectable image. Throughout this period more rigid boundaries were drawn between a modern, bourgeois Egyptian masculinity and a traditional, peasant masculinity.[1]

A fascinating series entitled "Lessons from Life" appeared at the end of the 1920s in the aptly titled magazine *Misr al-haditha al-musawwara* (Modern Egypt illustrated).[2] The articles in the series were published about the same time the population of Cairo was surpassing the one million mark (mainly because of the rapid increase in rural to urban migration) and growing concerns were being voiced about the concomitant rise in law and order problems. Although all of the articles are interesting for their ethnographic method and content, one is especially noteworthy for the relationship it posits among space, time, and the subject's formation: "The Quarter of Great Men and Poor, of Huts and Palaces," by ʿIsa Ghuji.[3] This mapping of the city's popular quarters (Islamic Cairo) evinced a new and self-conscious approach to seeing what was always present, but it also expressed both a fantasy and a nightmare of Egyptian modernity in the present.[4]

Ghuji began the article by explicitly invoking the scene of writing. He suggested that there were certain times when particular social phenomena became visible in ways that "should serve as a lesson that affects our senses, feelings, and all our faculties that connect to the mind and consciousness."[5] The "we" he spoke of were not abstract figures but the Arabic-speaking residents of middle- and upper-class neighborhoods: his intended audience. He explicitly located his readers as those "who live in Garden City, Hada'iq al-Qubba, al-Zaytun, and those neighborhoods that were laid out with a good sanitation system and based on the most ingenious of aesthetic principles."[6] In what seems to be a turning away from the initial didactic position, the objective of the article was further elaborated "as not a lesson or a sermon but as one 'cinematic' scene among many that viewers derive pleasure from seeing and understanding the mysteries of; as one reality among others that has come into being over the centuries and whose essence has been preserved to this day — to the twentieth century, the century of science, technology, enlightenment, and civilization. It is likely that subjects like these will affect us and touch our hearts."[7] In other words, there was indeed a lesson to be learned, but the lesson was to be gleaned from the material rather than preached to the reader — as was the general practice of other authors and texts and out of which nothing useful or beneficial was gained. In short, Ghuji believed the power of a text lay in the form as much as in the actual content that was presented; moreover, the measure of its success in forming consciousness was contingent on whether the text developed the reader's capacity to recognize mysterious forms and their temporal reality as Other.

This attention to form begins with the title, "The Quarter of Great Men and Poor, of Huts and Palaces." The existence of "great men" and "palaces," the author conceded, can be found only in the title and was used for literary effect. The actual neighborhoods of this Cairo had only "huts, hovels, caves and a horde of people" who were utterly destitute.[8] He added that the area was overrun by foreign tourists who came to Egypt each year to see its monuments and bizarre wonders (*al-athar wa al-'aja'ib*).[9] Ghuji positioned the strange manners, traditions, and "tastes" (which he placed in quotations: "*dhawq*," pronounced "*zu'*" in the colloquial) of the inhabitants of this quarter "on a different planet" and "under a different sky." According to him, any rational human being could not help but see them as an alien form of life. Their built environment was sketched as further evidence of the inhabitants' moral corruption; to the extent that they lived in the ugly ruins of Ayyubid and Mamluk buildings, they could be nothing other than what they were: trapped in an age and condition of barbarity. Again, form, that of spatial organization, was inscribed with tremendous effectivity.

Readers were cautioned to enter the quarter or alley at their peril because they faced both physical and mental harm. Upon entering, one was assured of finding screaming children and women, all fighting and running wild. Their speech was reproduced in its idiomatic original in order to demonstrate further their animalistic existence. Among other curses, a girl who has her foot on her sister's head screamed, "*uskuti ya bint talatin gazma allah yal'an abu umm gadd umm abu umm illi khilif abu umm gaddik!*"[10] The cruelty and violence of the two sisters toward one another, in speech and action, were attributed to their hideous premodern surroundings. After viewing this spectacle of female human degeneracy, and if the visitor has survived the ordeal intact, the "tour guide" suggested that the next stop might be one of the hundreds of cafés in this quarter.[11]

Here one would have hoped to find some relief from what was surely to have "caused pain," but as the gaze began to refocus the visitor saw male versions of the same monstrous life form. The first was probably the "garçon" who came to take the order.[12] The author described him as "the one with a black beard, yellow cheeks, green rag, and white eyes. His clothes were covered with so much dirt and grime that one averted one's gaze shamefully and with disgust."[13] Ghuji also drew attention to the language of the café — orders belted out by the drinks waiter and the food waiter — as if it were new and exotic: *allahu akbar, 'indak wahid 'ahwa sada* and *allahu hayy, hat wahid shay bi limon* or *haddir wahid kusa mabruma; hat wahid kurunb mahshi.*[14] As these sounds were taken in, the visitor's gaze settled on the other customers in the café, "the different faces and facial expressions." If one were observant, according to the guide, from among these mangled forms of man one could discern the existence of incredibly "original" and imaginative "mental worlds" (*'aqliyyat*). Ostensibly from the author's experience was produced a man he described as "barefoot, indolent [*markhi al-'asab*], in rags, and sitting cross-legged" waxing poetic about the politics of the day: "Italy is good. She waged war on Rome and was victorious over it. And France defeated Paris."[15]

Readers are informed that if one tired of the café then the obvious next destination was Khan al-Khalili, a section of Cairo's medieval bazaar, described as "the predator's trough" (*marbat al-faras*). Following was a description of the Egyptian merchant that would be familiar to many present-day visitors to the Khan. The merchant was depicted as notoriously dishonest even as he appeals to God (for the Egyptian visitor) and to his honor (for the foreign tourist) that his product was being offered at a price below cost. As one escaped from his clutches and headed away from Khan al-Khalili down Mashhad al-Husayni Street, one inevitably stumbled into yet another den of thieves. This time they were men of religion and beggars, represented here as overlapping categories. Making it through their carefully orchestrated gauntlet unharmed was depicted as well nigh impossible, and thus the next stop for most visitors was usually the police station.

If the visitor was one of the rare few, who, with God's help, managed to exit Mashhad al-Husayni Street, then he faced yet another nightmarish encounter. The next challenge to the visitor's moral, psychological, and physical fortitude came from charlatan saints claiming to possess magical powers and to belong to imaginary Sufi orders. They were identified by flowing robes, turbans, long beards, and shaved mustaches. They claimed to hold healing powers in their prayer beads for everything that could ail people, from heartbreak to lovesickness. The author suggested that here there was no possibility of escape: either one paid or one was accused of blasphemy. Apparently they worked in teams, and if one did not succeed in selling something to the visiting effendi another was ready to accuse him of blaspheming the supposed shaykh and religion. Then it fell to the discretion of the policeman who was summoned whether the effendi would be arrested for slandering religion in public or rescued from the clutches of the Sufi pretender. The scourge of these shaykhs was even worse for women, presumably because they were more susceptible to the promises of magic cures for their romantic ailments.[16]

Ghuji rounded out this tour of the bizarre sights and sounds of the Husayn quarter with an apt saying attributed to Ali ibn Abi Talib, cousin and son-in-law of Prophet Muhammad: "Not everything that is known is said. Not everything that is said is said in its time. Nor is everything that is said in its time heard by the right people."[17] In closing, he held out the possibility that his revelation of "hidden secrets" might fall on deaf ears. The failure to recognize and redress the problem of this other Cairo existing coevally with the modern city was potentially disastrous for Egyptian modernity; not so much because the "quarter of great men and poor, of huts and palaces" evinced a spatial anomaly in the city's modernization, but because it bespoke a discordant temporality—an everyday that put into question the very notion of a modern city in Egypt and the modernity of its subject.[18]

This chapter is offered in lieu of a conclusion to the book.[19] It tracks, on the one hand, the production of a specifically temporalized Other of the effendi and of the modern city-state, while, on the other hand, it reads against the available sources to glimpse issues of gender, the body, and sovereignty as they may have been regarded within the field of vision occupied by that Other. The Other in this instance is *al-futuwwa* and its urban domain.[20]

Defining *al-futuwwa* is no simple task.[21] Indeed, this chapter contends that the definition, classification, and location of different life forms like the futuwwa were part of a strategy of "constitutive exclusion" essential to the historical process of working out modern Egypt.[22] With that cautionary note in mind, al-futuwwa (pl., al-futuwwat) literally translates as "youthful masculinity" and is derived from the Arabic root *fatiya*, "to be young," which generates the cognates *fatan*, "young man," and *fatat*, "young woman." Historically, at least in the early twentieth century, futuwwa could thus be a form of masculinity inhabited by or inhabiting a man or woman, although the latter was less common.[23] A related concept of masculinity was the *ibn al-balad* (native son, "the good guy"). As we saw in chapter 4 in the case of the image of Sa'd Zaghlul, *ibn al-balad* was an overarching vernacular frame for proper masculinity into which the individual might or might not fall depending on his reputation; hence, a futuwwa could be considered an ibn al-balad depending on his actions, conduct, and charisma.[24]

The futuwwa of bourgeois media, literary, and scholarly concern in the interwar era was the bearer of a heavy burden: the legacy of an authentic Egyptian heroism. The luster of this "big man" of the *hara* (neighborhood) had been tarnished over the preceding decades and his influence greatly diminished, such that the futuwwa was no longer a hero and ibn al-balad but a criminal. Thus reported the press. In other accounts, the futuwwa was still a big man but tragically incapable of assimilation, or translation, within modern forms of government and subjection. For yet others, futuwwa represented a site of mourning, of the loss of a moral agency that was homegrown and honorable.

Ghuji's anxious imaginary mapping of the city was an unacknowledged model of encountering the Other for most, though not all, of the interwar discussions of al-futuwwa as an antiquated scourge on modern civilization. As part of the rise to hegemony of modern conceptions of the politi-

cal and its subject, social theory and history typically show that other
life forms, like that of the futuwwat, were rendered exceptional and ultimately obsolete. In the preceding chapters I have explored exclusively,
albeit critically, the gendered constitution of that cultural and political
power as *the* Egyptian modern. I labeled the gender norm that emerged at
the intersection of colonial modernity and nationalism as effendi masculinity, which I located in a new constellation of practices and discourses
around the desirable, modern body. The present chapter is, in part, an
effort to decenter this bourgeois hero of the modern by deconstructing the
terms of its narration.[25]

Thomas Blom Hansen's work on sources of political power in Mumbai
offers a useful framework for relocating effendi masculinity in relation to
al-futuwwa, among "competing repertoires of authority . . . organized
around the *de facto* practices of sovereignty in the name of the law, the
community and the local 'big man.' These repertoires are founded on violence, or the threat thereof, but also structure distinct, if morally ambivalent, registers of public and political agency."[26] In the following section,
the murder case of a cabaret performer serves as the launching point for
an analysis of several encounters with al-futuwwa and a consideration of
other possible formations of the modern subject and of other sites of sovereignty. By foregrounding this possibility of otherness within the same
modernity, the work of excavating al-futuwwa also implicitly presents a
method that takes one beyond the anxious foreclosures of dissonant pasts
and exclusive inscriptions of the modern — hallmarks of this period of
knowledge production and public culture, often repeated in current historical scholarship.[27]

Big, Bad, Bold Men
DELIMITING SOVEREIGNTY, FIXING MASCULINITY

A special correspondent for *al-Ahram* wrote from Alexandria on May 28,
1936, "One of the effects of the Al-Bosfur nightclub murder in Cairo is that
its circumstances have led to an interest in the problem of 'al-futuwwat'
and how much power and influence [*al-satwa*] they have in the capital and
in other Egyptian cities."[28] The murder referred to was that of a popular
singer and dancer, Imtithal Fawzi, by a band of assassins led by the failed
businessman and weight-trainer Fuad al-Shami. I argue here that this
murder can be read as an instance of a larger event, one which might be in-

scribed in the following way: a moment that irrevocably branded the public figure of al-futuwwa with the additional meanings of thug, mobster,
and nefarious villain—*al-baltagi*. This is not a conventional way of reg-
istering this moment; indeed, the modern transformation of al-futuwwa
is rarely considered as a historical event. It is not my aim here to affirm
or deny the outcome of this transformation, and I am not suggesting that
the normative conception of al-futuwwa as an Islamic ideal of masculinity
had never before taken other forms. Rather, I posit—and want to interro-
gate—a changed historical relationship in the constitution of al-futuwwa
in which the nature of history itself stood radically transformed and made
possible the new politics of national sovereignty and gendered identity
explored in the preceding chapters.

In the passage quoted above, the daily paper's use of the term *al-satwa*
as opposed to *al-sulta*—typically used to signify official authority or sovereignty—was not a neutral description of a reality that was already
given. Rather, it was an instance of the performative remaking of the
legal, social, and political, as it alluded to and restated an understanding
of the embodied and local power of the futuwwat as corrupt and criminal. The history embedded within this reiterative structure of the performative spanned a half century to over a century, depending upon which
watershed moment was chosen as the starting point: for example, the
French occupation, the establishment of Egypt's modern military, or the
building of modern Cairo. Whichever turning point animated this journalist's historical sense of the beginning of modern Egypt, by 1936 the
look of the nonmodern appeared crystal clear, and the burning question of
the day concerned the boundary of the modern. Drawing that boundary
was implicit in the performative statement regarding the futuwwat, which
also manifested a death wish. Rather than the Other's death, as might be
anticipated here, it was the effendi's own eventual death that was projected in the representations of al-futuwwa analyzed below.[29] The death of
al-futuwwa explicitly heralded by the contemporary commentators presupposed a birth, which can neither be reliably established through extant inscriptions nor entirely discounted. What was this life that presumably existed between an uncertain birth and a desirous yet doubtful death?
Can exploring such ambiguity around the life and death of al-futuwwa
push one toward other lines of conceiving masculinity and sovereignty?[30]
Identifying those lines when they overlapped with the history embedded
in this performative moment—in making the distinction between licit
and illicit authority—and when they diverged provides a more critical

vantage point on Egypt's colonial modernity, which in turn offers another angle on the limits of the performative as a theory of subject formation.

On the evening of May 22, 1936, as Imtithal Fawzi appeared on stage at the Bosphorus nightclub to perform her regular dance number, a commotion suddenly arose outside and the lights went out.[31] In the confusion this caused inside the club, Fawzi was stabbed to death with the sharp end of a broken bottle. In the ensuing investigation and press coverage of the incident, it was revealed that she had also been attacked the week before her fatal stabbing. At that time she had in fact appealed to the police for protection but was told that the police were not paid to protect the people but to solve crimes after they happened. It was also revealed that she had reported to the police that a gang of futuwwat was trying to extort protection money from her. Although it was not enough to save her life, Fawzi's accusation did make the apprehension of the gang members a relatively easy task for the police. The man who had stabbed the dancer, Husayn Ibrahim Hasan, was prevented from escaping by the other men in the nightclub. According to *al-Ahram*, he finally confessed to his part in the murder and also exposed his accomplices, whom the police eventually rounded up.

The story that was finally pieced together from the various testimonies collected by the police detectives was quite astonishing and held the reading public in thrall for several months. The mastermind behind this team of thugs, Fuad al-Shami, a clever, attractive, well-dressed, and well-built young man, had been in trouble with the law numerous times before. At one point *al-Ahram* compared his criminal mind to the best of those in the infamous gangs of Chicago. Shami had devised an extortion racket in which the dancers in his area were placed under close surveillance, and if any of them entered into a relationship with a man they would be required to pay his gang a certain fee for their protection. If they did not pay willingly, both lovers were punished. *Al-Ahram* alleged, as another example of Shami's genius, that he had egomaniacal designs to control all of Cairo. Apparently, one way he disposed of competition from other futuwwat in areas where he wanted to expand his operation was to involve the unwitting assistance of the state and the law. In one case, he wanted the protection money paid by a nightclub that was already guaranteed safety by another futuwwa. Shami befriended the rival futuwwa by giving him a suit as a present, while at the same time he had a member of his gang tell the police that clothing had been stolen from his house. The police were tipped off on the day the man wore the suit, and they arrested him for robbery. When Shami was called in as a witness on the rival futuwwa's behalf, he denied ever having known him, and the man was sentenced to a term in jail.

When Fawzi first refused to cooperate with Shami's scheme, he gave her a warning: his close friend Kamal al-Hariri was dispatched to rough her up, after which, Fawzi, still refusing to pay, sought the protection of the police. The following week, Shami arranged for her to have an accident. His men disguised themselves in *gallabiya*s and turbans, bought and consumed two bottles of *zabib*, and then set out to murder Fawzi.[32] The plan they carried out was to start a fight in the nightclub to distract attention from the dancer, at which point Hasan extinguished the lights and stabbed her with a broken bottle of the raisin liquor.

Most press accounts depicted this case as a serious indictment of the ability of the police to maintain law and order. *Al-Ahram* condemned their callous response toward Fawzi's pleas for help: "Many police officials believe that they are not charged with the responsibility of protecting the people, only the ministers and rulers. They are ignorant of the fact that the law which commissions them to protect the minister is the same law which assigns them to protect the actress; for she and the minister from this perspective are equal before the law."[33] Apparently in response to the wide press coverage of police negligence in preventing this crime everyone from the minister of interior to the chief of police for the Cairo province became involved in the investigation. The public outcry resulted in a dragnet operation to bring in all those who were reputed to be a futuwwa. In an interview following his trial, Shami made a point of blaming the media frenzy for the harshness of his life sentence to hard labor.[34] Under this same pressure, the police chief established a new unit to deal specifically with crimes committed by the baltagis and futuwwat; he modeled it on other specialized branches that investigated, for example, pickpockets, bank robbers, and car thieves. One of the new unit's first acts was to open a register to record brief biographies of every baltagi and futuwwa operating in Cairo and compile details of their profit-making rackets and their hideout locations.[35]

At this point, there are a number of directions in which a historical investigation could proceed. A study interested in crime, the law, and modern policing efforts might examine the relevant legal archives seeking to demonstrate, *inter alia*, the new responsibilities of the state and its enhanced capacity for violence. A sophisticated political history might inquire into the formation of a public sphere in Egypt, questioning the Habermasian formulation of it as a domain of rational discourse. An urban historian could fruitfully explore the spatial reorganization of Cairo from the last third of the nineteenth century onward and show how the futuwwa's increased national visibility was a product of this new geography, which effected a division along traditional and modern lines with specific spatial and social forms germane to each. A historian of gender might investigate the ways in which this case does or does not evince nationalism's claim to represent all of the subjects within its domain. Indeed, the only study I know of that has analyzed the Imtithal Fawzi case argues — by comparing the contemporary press coverage of her murder to that of murders of other female entertainers and prostitutes from earlier in the period — that the imagined community of Egypt did in fact expand to encompass more kinds of subjects.[36] Although all of these approaches would add to scholars' knowledge of this period in Egyptian history, none would force them to question their understanding of the futuwwa as thug, and consequently all would miss the opportunity to arrive at any narrative of Egyptian politics other than a certain recursive tale of political modernity. The violence of the modern's constitution in the past would be repeated in the present.[37]

I raise these hypothetical research agendas because nearly all of the previous scholarship on al-futuwwa has concentrated on the classical period of Islam, that is, the ninth century through the thirteenth. From these philological studies, one learns that its first usage dates to approximately the second century of the Islamic calendar (eighth century) but that its genealogy is extremely hazy. Some say al-futuwwa originated as a mystical path of enlightenment and righteous conduct elaborated by Sufi masters, but it could also have been the label for urban social formations of various kinds: some with highly ritualized practices focused on enhancing fraternity and conviviality, others possibly related to guilds and the artisanal trades, and still others associated with the policing of particular neighborhoods or even the distant borders of *Dar al-Islam*.[38] As a concept, al-futuwwa is contradictorily capacious, accommodating notions like chivalry, courage, generosity, and brotherhood as well as thuggery, banditry, criminality, and depravity; furthermore, it might signify a warrior, an ascetic, or a gift.

The meticulous work of Claude Cahen and other orientalists propounds a few intriguing propositions about al-futuwwa and the itinerary by which it came to Egypt.[39] The name was applied at one time or another in classical Islam to signify a path of self-cultivation, a mode of personhood, and a form of collective organization with varying religious, social, political, and economic consequences. It seems that there were always multiple histories inscribing and inscribed by al-futuwwa, its representa-

tions contingent on the location of the author historically and geographically as well as on a relationship to temporality that oscillated between
varying shades of the sacred and the profane. The high, courtly form of
al-futuwwa inaugurated by the Abbasid Caliph al-Nasir was said to have
passed on to Mamluk Egypt after the Mongol destruction of Baghdad in
1258. The institution became nearly extinct in the fourteenth or fifteenth
century, surviving only in the form of relatively weak rituals, for example,
the bestowal of the "garment of the futuwwa," which in Baghdad was apparently trousers (*sirwal al-futuwwa*).[40] Yet there are indications that preexisting popular urban groupings of young men (*ahdath*) and craftsmen
in Cairo took on aspects of al-futuwwa that ensured its reproduction in a
new context, if not in new texts, until the modern period.

Perhaps because of al-futuwwa's disappearance from the text and ambiguity in the social context, historians of modern times have treated it generally as a footnote to their preoccupation with the more serious work of
explaining the passing of traditional society and evaluating the implications of modernity in the Middle East. It is used to mark that transition
either through its seemingly obvious existence out of time or in its disappearance because of time.[41] However, al-futuwwa has yet to be narrated
as an event in its own right, with a before and after, that is more than an
effect of the temporal structure of a given modernity. My inquiry asks of
this event the following questions:[42] What is the significance of the slippage between futuwwa and baltagi, on the one hand, and the distinction
between futuwwa and effendi, on the other, for conceptions of the modern
subject and politics? Who was the public that was making new claims on
the state and that in turn the state was ostensibly trying to placate?[43] How
do gender and space figure (in) the public? How would the displacement
of the notion of al-futuwwa from the liberal discourse of law and order
change its historical and conceptual figuration, and how might this alter
our theorization of political modernity and of history?

A recent study of how the experience of modern law was narrated in
Egyptian novels of the early twentieth century alludes to another distinction through which al-futuwwa appears in modernity: speech versus writing.[44] Reading a set of texts broadly categorized in or related to the pulp
fiction genres, Elliott Colla illuminates the emergence of an ambivalent
space of representation within Egyptian modernity, one in which legal
practice and novel writing were two intertwined "mediatory innovations."
He suggests that the abstraction required in both mediations was a new
concept of society that authorized the speaking subject: police and defense lawyers, attorneys and judges. This new role of speaking for others

before the law was represented in novels as riven with anxiety over its performance. Colla relates this anxiety to a perception among the effendiyya (lettered class in Colla's translation) of "the gap between the 'enlightened' theory of modern (European) law in colonial Egypt and the often irrational and unjust practice of that theory."[45]

Of most interest to my argument is Colla's reading of a somewhat peculiar staging of this effendi ambivalence toward legal representation in the form of a memoir from the 1920s attributed to a futuwwa named Yusuf Abu Haggag.[46] Colla renders *futuwwa* as *fitiwwa* and translates the latter as "street thug" in order to be true to the colloquial register in which the memoir was composed. This is perhaps the most accurate transliteration and translation of the term in this context. However, the slippage between the formal and informal languages (marked orthographically only in transliteration) goes without comment except to reaffirm the social divide between polite and impolite society apparent within the distinction. Ironically, an anthropological study of al-futuwwa from the 1970s makes no reference at all to this distinction in speech and writing.[47] It is beyond the scope of my discussion to examine this problematic, but it would be productive to consider how the difference between *futuwwa* and *fitiwwa* might be expressed in terms of the difference between the pedagogic and performative registers of identity formation. Maintaining the tension between them may enable a translation of *al-futuwwa* that resists the object's assimilation into a universal grid of intelligibility; the semantic, semiotic, and social range of *al-futuwwa* extends beyond crime, courtrooms, and middle-class anxieties of representation, and when its translation is limited to the register assigned by its historical interlocutors alone the formation of al-futuwwa as subject is in fact lost to history.

In the 1930s it was precisely the slippery nature of the concept futuwwa as it mapped onto individual biographies, or its failure to do so, that presented a conundrum for contemporary commentators. To the police force of Cairo, still a relatively British-dominated institution even after Egypt's nominal independence in 1922, the futuwwat represented a long-standing menace, and they were presented as an obstacle to realizing the ideals of modern governance. Their authority was criminal in nature, as Russell Pasha, the commander of the Cairo police from 1918 to 1946, notes in his annual report for 1935, written at the same time as the furor over the murder of Imtithal Fawzi exploded in the press. According to Russell, there were two kinds of criminals who became repeat offenders. The first category, he claimed, he was able to understand; crime for them probably seemed the only option when the hardships of life exceeded a certain threshold of tolerance. He was less forgiving of the second category:

> There is however another class of recidivist who deserves no mercy and who forms a serious menace to public security in the cities and that is the professional rough or strong man who lives by threatening and assaulting other people. Such "osbagia" have always existed in the Ezbekia and Bab el Sharia Districts and have always given the police a lot of trouble as they are incurable criminals who are unaffected by sentences of fine which they easily pay or by short sentences of imprisonment which are no deterrent to this class of man. The existing Law on Suspects and Vagabonds is the only weapon the police have for dealing with these pests and it is, as it stands, of very little use. Last year this Command proposed to the Ministry a number of modifications of this Law to make it effective; unfortunately nothing has yet been done to improve this Law.[48]

Russell understood the first category of offenders not because of his natural sympathy for the urban poor but because it was legible within the prevailing discourse of crime and criminality.[49] And because this kind of criminal was a product of concrete social forces, the category was situated clearly within history and thus potentially transformable in time. However, the "osbagia," a term which overlaps with futuwwat, was conceived as an ontology existing timelessly, and since crime was in their blood, so to speak, they presented an intractable problem for the police and the law. Russell seems to have believed that only if the law could better recognize futuwwat then his efforts to rid the city of them would be successful.

This pragmatic approach to the supposed problem failed to register how recognition was to be achieved; ostensibly, this labor would be performed a year later with the establishment of the new crime branch and the cataloguing of all of Cairo's professional roughs and strongmen. Shami and his gang certainly fall into the category of the osbagia with whom Russell seemed to have so much trouble. But if in the aftermath of Fawzi's murder the vigorous pursuit of this kind of criminal was indeed combined with a process of classification and recording, the cross-dressing undertaken by Fuad's gang, supposedly from a modern style into a seemingly eternal futuwwa aesthetic (by donning the gallabiya and turban, a costume worn by the majority of Egypt's male population at the time) and back again, called into question the ability of colonial power to know and consequently capture and eliminate this figure.

There is an interesting parallel here with the earlier history of thugs in the Indian colonial context and local big men in the postcolonial period. In her reading of *thugee* as a performative site that resisted easy assimilation into a colonial epistemology, Parama Roy writes,

> The thug, through his capacity for disguise and impersonation and his skill at negotiating multiple and competing identities, usurps the colonizer's privilege of complex subjectivity and of movement between subject positions and thus can be read to assume some control over both the construction and flow of colonial knowledge. So he never becomes fully naturalized as the disciplinary subject or, in other words, the knowable subject, of the colonial polity. And *thuggee*, later rewritten as dacoity, continues to function within the law-and-order context in the colonial and postcolonial state formations as a trope for the unruly and unreformable energies that cannot easily be accommodated to the needs of the civilizing mission.[50]

Thugee was constituted as a problem of knowledge and then was ascribed an ontology through and against which certain groups were understood, policed, and forced to negotiate. Roy's analysis also shows continuity between the colonial and postcolonial projects of knowing and governing these subjects. Comparing Mattison Mines's ethnography of *periyar* in late twentieth-century Madras to his findings from Mumbai, Hansen suggests that local big men as sites of sovereignty may occupy points between the two poles of *gravitas* and *celeritas*, as well as straddling the two.[51] Gravitas, which characterizes the periyar, references "responsible and ostensibly law-abiding civic leadership" and points to an autonomy contingent on a reputation for good character, generosity, and efficacy. Celeritas, or the "war principle," characterizes big men whose power was built on "reputations of violence, or connections with political parties or the underworld," but those same men could also possess elements of gravitas.[52]

A brief glance at the urban map of Shami's career track points to his location closer to the celeritas pole of power. His illustrious life as a futuwwa and a rebel started out in the modest neighborhood of Al-Zahir. After being thrown out of his brother's house for failing to reform himself, Shami attempted to start his own business in Al-Zahir. He opened a small bodybuilding salon, and things seemed to go well until a group of toughs made the salon their regular hangout.[53] Eventually the gym had to close because the constant fighting between the toughs scared away all the paying members, who had become fearful for their lives.[54] Nonplussed by this setback, Shami decided to harness the surplus energy of these men and venture in a new direction. He and his men declared themselves the futuwwat of Al-Zahir.[55] They protected the owners of grocery stores, general goods suppliers, coffeehouses, and other establishments, who for the most part, fearful of Shami and his gang, willingly paid a monthly fee in exchange for the right to conduct their affairs without any trouble. Eventually, Shami felt confident enough to extend his business into the modern entertainment districts of 'Imad al-Din and Al-Azbakiyya.[56] This was when his life and career intersected with that of Fawzi. The movement of Shami's operation outward into modern Cairo and the ensuing entanglement with the state could be read as the impossible convergence of two temporalities. His self-proclaimed status as a futuwwa might have remained unquestioned, at least by the police and the law, had he limited his activities to Al-Zahir.

If Shami had not acquired the competence to pass in respectable society, effectively confusing the categories of effendi and futuwwa, then the outcry about the persistence of this (now) criminal underclass, a state within a state, might again have been less pronounced. I am not suggesting that in the person of Shami and his physical translocation in the city there is an example of the clash between tradition and modernity, but that this was one of many moments that performatively reestablished such a distinction. Ann Stoler has argued convincingly that colonialism's bourgeois cultural underpinnings be understood as fractured and located within an imperial geography that does not presume separate cultural spheres for the metropole and the colony. She shows how the colony was a central site for the production of the boundaries of a respectable whiteness: "Colonialism was not a secure bourgeois project. It was not only about the importation of middle-class sensibilities to the colonies, but about the *making* of them."[57] While Stoler's observations are about the culture of the colonizer, this same insight can be applied to the colonized. Negotiating a complicated field of racial, sexual, and spatial segregation within a colonial context, the Egyptian urban middle classes in the 1920s, and more vigorously in the 1930s, sought to fix the boundaries of *their* society by turning to the state and the law. So it was certainly a cause for alarm when the symbols of membership in a club with seemingly ever-changing rules were so easily appropriated by an outsider—someone without real qualifications.

Driving the rush to define, classify, historicize, and differentiate among the futuwwat was a sense of anxiety over the unknowability of this concept and perhaps also a desire to transform this impossible subject to an object of discipline. Underlying every attempt to capture the specificity of al-futuwwa was an inexorable sense of lack, and this was especially true in those descriptions that were seemingly the most thorough. By attaching the label to so many different types of criminals and criminality, the force of the concept was necessarily reduced. Some contemporaries understood the latter problem, but attempts to narrow the focus were beset by still other difficulties, as we shall see.

The appearance of Shami's photo in the leading national dailies, which pictured him smiling, wearing a handsome suit, and projecting a virile, assertive personality, generated searching articles in a variety of newspapers and magazines that explored the history, culture, and meaning of al-futuwwa. For example, a major portion of *al-Musawwar* for June 5, 1936, was devoted to the Fawzi case and the phenomenon of al-futuwwa. One article, written by "an expert privy to their secrets," attempts to define and differentiate among futuwwa and other types of criminal gangs.[58] This article leads with the claim that readers of the press, elite and commoner alike, came to learn of previously unknown bands of evil criminals only through Fawzi's murder.[59] But "they were known to those familiar with the heart of the city — with its alleys and narrow lanes — and the outskirts and margins."[60] This expert faults the authors of other articles on the futuwwat for mistaking the criminals' numbers, interpreting who they really are, and describing their context.

The reporter divides the criminal underworld into three categories of actors: al-futuwwat, *al-baltagiyya*, and *al-barmagiyya*. The futuwwat are billed as the oldest of these groups: "They had their own despotic state with their own heroic figures. Their neighbors, the heads of noble houses, and merchants all feared them. They maintained their evil grip through the levying of protection fees."[61] In order to validate and ground this figure in a historical reality of sorts, the author runs through a list of notable futuwwat and the neighborhoods over which they exerted their authority. There was Ibrahim 'Atiyya of Al-Husayniyya and his successor Mustafa 'Urabi; 'Abdu al-Gabbas of 'Abidin and Hara al-Saqiyin; Rizq al-Hashshash, Girgis bin Tuhtuha, and Mikhail al-'Aguz of the Coptic neighborhoods of Al-Darb al-Wasi' and Al-Darb al-Ibrahimi; al-Assiuti of Al-Zahir; al-Fishawi, the female futuwwa 'Aziza al-Fahla; al-Ziftawiyya, and so on. But he is careful to point out that theirs was a legendary reality of the past (*ayyam al-'izz wa al-jah*), of which only traces remained in the author's present. It seems that by the 1930s the great battles that had once taken place between bands of futuwwat in the hills and wastelands bordering Cairo and in the various alleys and quarters had been mostly forgotten. People no longer talked of those kinds of conflicts, except perhaps for the butchers and blacksmiths of the abattoir quarter.

Then, as if the author suddenly remembered something, he tells of sporadic fights that would erupt between two, sometimes more, futuwwat of Al-Husayniyya, Al-Bulaqa, or Al-Qabisi. The last famous incident in public memory, he says, was probably the battle between the gangs of Mustafa 'Urabi and al-Assiuti, which ended with the police intervening to save 'Urabi from a hailstorm of sand-filled bottles. He argues that it was when their evil deeds transgressed a certain limit that the colonial state unleashed its repressive apparatus to eliminate the futuwwat. The messy issues of how that limit was constituted when it was and the deals that were certainly struck between state representatives and individual futuwwa are not allowed to complicate the story.[62] It seems, though, that as much as the author wishes to relegate the institution of al-futuwwa to the dustbin of history, his memory and present reality interrupt that narrative impulse. His desire to write the futuwwat in the past tense and to contain them within the grid of the traditional city leads him to anthropology.

Before moving on to the other two categories of criminals, he pauses to present an ethnographic sketch of the futuwwat and provide a summary of traditions (*taqalid*) particular to their culture. They are represented as being autarkic and stoic; that is, they sought no assistance from outside forces or institutions like the police or hospitals. A prominent locus of futuwwa sociability was the 'ahwa, or café, a homosocial space ubiquitous in the popular quarters of the capital.[63] The proprietors of the 'ahwas, especially those on the outskirts of these neighborhoods, were male or sometimes female futuwwat. The customers were generally "thieves, vagrants, and the like," who were usually known to the police and were often enlisted by them to help in criminal investigations. The drug trade had become the major source of revenue for most futuwwat, especially those joining from among the Sa'idi (Upper Egyptian) migrants to Cairo. But not all were from the poor or *al-sa'alik*, classes; some possessed great wealth, owned land and property, and had lawyers and advisors who helped them avoid or get out of entanglements with the state.

Unsuccessful in mapping the futuwwat's history as absolutely Other, the author institutes their difference ontologically. Even as he speaks of various crossings into al-futuwwa, like those of the Sa'idi migrant or the thrill-seeking rich kid, he implies that there is an essence there unmediated by class or history. This essence must be present for the author's simultaneous projects of recognition and disavowal. It is this essential otherness that he feels is a relic; even though he knows there were still instances of futuwwa activity in his present, he desires its return to the past or to oblivion in the near future.

38. The Muhammad al-Mu'ayyad Club, early 1920s. Photo, Lehnert and Landrock Collection (Oriental Art Publishers, Cairo); dates given in store catalogue are 1922–24.

39. Café, mid-1920s. Photo, Lehnert and Landrock Collection (Oriental Art Publishers, Cairo); dates given in store catalogue are 1924–30(?).

The rest of the article overlays the urban geography of modern Cairo with the coterminous histories of nightclubs, cafés, whorehouses, gambling dens, and their protectors: "The situation of the *barmagiyya* and the *baltagiyya* developed in step with the development of the city."[64] The author associates the barmagiyya with the early growth of the entertainment district in Azbakiyya at the end of the nineteenth century.[65] He delimits the boundaries of the Azbakiyya quarter (as of the 1890s) as an area extending from Midan al-Opera to Midan Kamil (Qantara al-Dikka) and stretching from Wajh al-Birka Street to Al-Rawi'i to the edge of Bab al-Sha'riyya: "This quarter was a chain of clubs, meeting places, bars, dance halls, and gambling houses."[66] The most chic and popular section apparently ran from Midan al-Opera to Midan al-Khazindar. Its chief attractions were the Café Egyptien for music and the bars Drakatus, Veratus, and the New El Dorado for drinks.[67] He points out that the brothels, bars, and clubs in this area were initially run almost exclusively by foreign women. These women took toughs as their companions, men who came to be called al-barmagiyya. The article embeds the split between the barmagiyya and the baltagiyya within a nationalist and gendered urban chronology. As the author sees it, the history of the baltagiyya was bound up with the shifting boundaries of the city's entertainment center from Azbakiyya to 'Imad al-Din, Alfi Bey, and Fuad streets (then outward to Shubra and Al-Zahir), and from female foreign ownership to female Egyptian ownership.

For this author, as for Chief Russell, the problem in the end was not one of knowledge alone — according to the author, all the criminal elements in society were already known to the police — but one of inadequate laws and inaction. In addition to new laws designed to make arrests and convictions easier, he advocates new legislation that would make known the identity of each and every Egyptian. He suggests this could be accomplished by issuing identity cards, as was the practice in other countries. Underwriting both of these proposals was a desire to normalize what was known about the members of Egyptian society, or what the author thought he knew; in other words, through the articulation of the police and the law, the line between legitimate and illegitimate political subjects could be reasserted and the modern rescued from undesirable crossings.[68]

Ultimately, as other interventions in the debate on the proper policing of the city and the phenomenon of al-futuwwa show, it was the perceived sense of unknowability that aroused the most concern.[69] If it was possible for a futuwwa to look and act like an effendi in every way and pass as respectable, then how was one to recognize him? While the author of

40. "Cairo, Dancing girls Ancien Eldorado." Postcard dated 1909, from the Max Karkegi Collection.

41. 'Imad al-Din Street, mid-1920s. Photo, Lehnert and Landrock Collection (Oriental Art Publishers, Cairo); dates given in store catalogue are 1924–30.

"Ask Me" protests against carelessly mixing the categories of evildoers, the writer of another piece does precisely that. In *"Adrar al-madaniyya al-haditha: tawa'if al-futuwwat wa al-baltagiyya"* (The perils of modern civilization: Orders of futuwwat and baltagiyya), the author divides the criminal body into seven constituent parts, but the parts are not inscribed with the kind of historical and geographical specificity found in the previous article.[70] Here *futuwwat* and *baltagiyya* were interchangeable terms used to describe the criminal gangs involved in protection rackets, drug trafficking, and prostitution. The use of *tawa'if* in the title to group these actors is significant. In most other cases (including this article sometimes) they were grouped under the term *'asabat*, which translates as "gangs." *Tawa'if*, on the other hand, was a more ambiguous term in this period, burdened by historical connotations that invoked other supposedly dead sodalities, such as the famous artisanal guilds of Old Cairo.[71] The author signals that he is deploying this term in order to locate the actors who fall within it as part of a different social temporality. Their "specific functions," he writes, "are carried out in peace and comfort with no fear or dread, as if we were [living] in an age without rulers or laws."[72] For this author, the anachronistic presence of al-futuwwa in modernity was a stigma that threatened to pollute all of Egyptian society, to render it as if inhabiting a precontractarian state of nature. Their elimination, then, is referred to as "the purification [*tathir*] of the city."

In this article, the threat of the futuwwat to modern civilization is insistently pinned to their ability to escape the scope of the radar that normally sites temporal anomalies. The prime offenders, labeled *al-futuwwat al-wujaha'*, are distinguished from the others sartorially and physically: "They wear only chic suits and silk shirts, and most of these thugs practice *al-riyada al-badaniyya* [bodybuilding]."[73] Unlike their athletic counterparts in respectable society, they used their muscles to inspire fear in others and to profit from that fear. This typological description might as well have been cribbed from Shami's biography. Shami was quite the fashion plate and obsessively fastidious about his appearance. In an interview which appeared a few months after *Adrar al-madaniyya* went to press, Shami expressed one of his worst fears about going to prison for life: "I almost go crazy, man, every time I think about the torture that awaits . . . how will I wear a prison uniform for all those long years? Me, who could never bear to see his suit unpressed!"[74]

The next class of criminals, *futuwwat lil-ijar*, was also known for sophisticated, chic dress; they differed from the futuwwat al-wujaha' in that they worked for hire. They were able to evade the doubt and suspicion of the police because of their appearance and manners. Ostensibly, one would have to be countrified and don the gallabiya in order to fit the profile of a potential suspect in the 1930s. Making their detection even more difficult was that they had penetrated bourgeois society, particularly its younger male circles (*awlad al-ẓawat*). They are said to have profited greatly from these associations. One of their ruses involved preying on the sense of competition (particularly for lovers) among this class and convincing one that he needed protection from another.

Yet another group that stood out for its ability to pass in bourgeois society was *al-baltagiyya al-khifaf*. These men married nightclub performers and lived off the earnings of their women: "What is uncanny is that these [individuals] are very sophisticated in their dress. This is because of their desire to appear to be wealthy pashas. They are so successful in their parody that even the dandies [*awlad al-ẓawat*] are unable to rival them. Most of them have mastered [social] etiquette and are able to mix in high society, which regards them, as a result of their guise and their chic clothes, as fabulously wealthy and holders of high positions." [75]

The article ends with a call to the new King Faruq and Prime Minister Nahhas to purify the city and to restore security to "us and others like us." Almost as an afterthought, the writer adds the "poor, threatened" fallen girls among the "we." His reluctant inclusion of female entertainers among those who deserve state protection makes clear that what is really at stake is something more fundamental than public safety. Wrapping up his description of the seven criminal types, he notes ironically, "These are the tawa'if al-futuwwat and al-baltagiyya. This is modern civilization. This is modern progress." [76] The underlying desires here for the reassertion of social and spatial boundaries and the reclamation of modernity index the precariousness of bourgeois-effendi identity in and between colonial and national mappings of the city. If one brackets the ironic tone announcing this desire, another reading becomes possible, one that allows a reenvisioning of an entirely different city of multiple life forms and temporalities, such that the future horizon — where the futuwwa ends and the effendi begins — appears blurred rather than self-evident.

That blurring of boundaries between asymmetrical subjects, and concomitantly between their histories, can be pushed even further to arrive at the transformation and transfiguration of al-futuwwa in colonial modernity as a historical event. How is this possible? I can only begin to suggest an answer here, one based on the insistence that Fuad al-Shami's claims to inhabit al-futuwwa and the searching definitions of it by effendi critics do not exhaust this category conceptually. It was perhaps in a similar spirit of inquiry that the eminent Egyptian intellectual Ahmad Amin was inspired to begin studying the ancient roots of this figure, and to do so in the context of the debates of the 1930s about al-futuwwa and anxieties about the location of modernity that were percolating in the aftermath of Imtithal Fawzi's murder.[77]

Embodied Sovereignty and Modernity

In 1938 Amin delivered a lecture at the Royal Geographical Society in Cairo based on his initial research.[78] Relying mainly on Aghani's biography of Hunayn ibn Ishaq, *hamasa* and *mufaddaliyyat* poetry of the Jahiliyya (pre-Islamic) period, Sufi texts, and Ibn Battuta's fourteenth-century travelogue, he charted the concept's development from its initial polyvalence within tribal societies to a more fixed field of meaning within the medieval Islamic empires. This coalescence was attributed to the formation of urban fraternities that self-consciously articulated al-futuwwa as a code of behavior. Amin seems to recognize that the seeds of its corruption as an institution were there from the beginning. This was related to the foundation of al-futuwwa on simultaneously material and moral bases: *futuwwa madaniyya, dunyawiyya* and *futuwwa diniyya, sufiyya*.[79]

Futuwwa madaniyya signified a field of worldly action that privileged the body. Amin assigns it a genealogy that began with the Arab traditions of chivalry and courage that later intersected with Persian and Turkish martial traditions during the 'Abbasid age. The materialization of the futuwwa orders as martial bodies was further facilitated by the threat of the Crusades to Islamic civilization.[80]

Futuwwa diniyya, in Amin's rendering, signified a field of normativity and existed in opposition to the futuwwa madaniyya. He argues that there were contemporary critics of futuwwa madaniyya who based their criticism on etymological grounds, contending that the originary term *fata* was supposed to signify an ethic of kindness and compassion; it did not mean "one who strikes with a sword or knife."[81] The conservative thirteenth-century legal scholar Ibn Taymiyya was said to have objected to the trend toward adopting ritualized practices in the meetings of the futuwwat and distinguishing their appearance.[82] He issued a *fatwa* that, because they had no bases in Islam, dismissed their initiation ritual that required the initiate to drink from a cup of saltwater and also their decision to require members to wear the *sirwal*.[83] The poet Ibn al-Wardi condemned the brotherhoods on similar grounds and added aspersions of moral and sexual deviancy (*yajma'un laha al-jumu' min al-anbat wa yahdaruha al-murd wa ahl al-liwat*).[84]

Although the links are not made explicit, by delineating the contradictory origins for the conceptual framework of al-futuwwa, Amin is laying the groundwork for an explanation of why this figure disappears with the coming of the modern state and society. His analysis of the tradition of al-futuwwa seems to proceed from the recognition of a problem space that engendered, during the time of his writing (late 1930s–1940s), the growing obsolescence of a certain kind of human agency and an attendant form of authority.[85] The agency and authority were localized and embodied and did not exist apart from the relations among individuals; also, they were deeply rooted in a specifically Islamic sociopolitical and ethical tradition.[86]

Amin's scholarly gloss on the modern manifestation and transformation of al-futuwwa differs from the journalistic representations only slightly. He associates the futuwwat with specific neighborhoods in Cairo and Alexandria: "The futuwwa is customarily a gallant, noble, and courageous *shab* [young man]; he possesses *muruwwa'* and he surpasses his peers in all of these characteristics."[87] They existed as a local form of authority that saw its public expression when they headed the processions of wedding or circumcision parties, supposedly protecting them from possible attack by rival gangs of futuwwat.[88] Amin identifies their transition from relatively good figures to bad—slipping into the form of the *baltagiyya, abu ahmad* in Alexandria, and *qabadaiyya* in Syria—as a product of colonial repression and their involvement in drugs and alcohol. After relating an account from Jabarti's chronicles of an urban uprising against the French led by the futuwwat, Amin posits that the British learned from the historical experience of the previous occupiers and thus pursued successfully a policy aimed at eliminating the futuwwat through assassinations, imprisonment, and expropriation.[89]

Testing the suppleness of the term *al-futuwwa* and its ability to resist time, Amin suggests that it would be a "more fitting" and a "more beautiful" name to give to the Boy Scouts. Then, in a nostalgic tone, he dismisses the idea, saying, "What has passed will not return."[90] He also entertains its applicability to the young men of the Muslim Brotherhood, who he says distinguish themselves from their peers by publicly displaying their possession of al-futuwwa, masculinity, and good character.[91] Amin argues that although they started with the potential of assuming the mantle of futuwwa diniyya, this was obviated by the circumstances that led to their politicization and militarization. He implicitly argues here that by playing on the ground laid out by states and political parties—that is, by operating as a worldly institution—the Muslim Brotherhood not only guaranteed their own ultimate irrelevance but also, possibly even more tragically for Amin, foreclosed what might have been the last opportunity for the reinscription of an autochthonous concept of human agency, authority, and morality as relevant to modern times.[92]

In an intriguing conclusion, Amin acknowledges the appropriation of the whole world by a monstrous, organless body: "Modernity has distributed the concept and practice of al-futuwwa over several unusual [*'ajiba*] institutions."[93] In part, the strangeness of these new institutional bodies seems to lie in the fact that they did not actually possess bodies. Or perhaps it is against their possession of actual bodies that Amin attempts to rehabilitate al-futuwwa. He argues that through the creation of civil and state institutions modernity has harnessed and rationalized modes of delivering aid and assistance to people as well as the general human impulse to do good. These organless bodies—Scouting associations, hospitals, schools, universities, public works projects, labor unions, and progressive tax regimes—have rendered futuwwa bodies theoretically and practically irrelevant.

The social life and death of al-futuwwa preoccupied the thoughts of another interwar intellectual who later rose to unprecedented heights in Arabic fiction writing. The memory of this character type would always remain with him. Naguib Mahfuz's earliest depiction of al-futuwwa appeared in the late 1930s and would vary over the decades, generally reflecting the difference between the hopefulness accompanying Egypt's anticolonial struggle and the disillusionment following its postcolonial failures.[94]

In keeping with the times, the majority of the characters in Mahfuz's first published collection of short stories, *Hams al-junun* (1938), were drawn from the effendi and aristocratic classes, and the framework within which he most often situated them was a historically changing conception of sexual and cultural mores.[95] The picture of a newly sexualized, Westernized, bourgeois Cairo was offset by a few stories of the underclass and its fate within or against that exclusively modern context.[96]

In one of these stories, "Nahnu rijal" (We are men), Mahfuz recounts the tale of a futuwwa who returned to his alley after a four-year absence.[97] He had gone to work at a British army installation during the war. At first he made a fortune by trading in smuggled military provisions, but soon he was exposed and sentenced to a term in jail. His return to the alley, de-picted as a triumphal moment, was no different from the traditional rea-sons to hold an alley celebration: marriage, circumcision, or the return of a *hajj*. The brother of the futuwwa Muʿallim Gaʿda throws a lavish party with generous amounts of food and drink.[98] During the celebration, Gaʿda finds himself repeating the words "we are men" as a preamble to the in-vocation and elaboration of different moments and aspects of life: acquir-ing wealth, marriage, brotherhood, loyalty, imprisonment. He spends the entire night drinking and enters a stupor from which he does not wake. His arteries explode, and he slowly bleeds to death.

Mahfuz foregrounded the fate of Muʿallim Gaʿda with a nostalgic evo-cation of the alley and the solidarity of its members, both of which also were under threat of extinction. The jailing and return of Gaʿda was not a cause for shame or surprise, for, as the narrator asks, "What boy from the alley hasn't been to jail at least once?"[99] The shadow of the police and the political order that it represented hovered over the alley as a potentially menacing force that slowly but surely insinuated itself into the process by which the alley reproduced its distinct forms of sociability. Mahfuz scripted Gaʿda's return in the form of a last dance. Performing a stick-dance, after every drink he avowed the masculinity of his locality. In the first of these affirmations, he sang, "We are men; we are brothers. We dis-dain those who reject their brothers. We despise those who forget their origins. Long live loyalty."[100]

In the next avowal of a shared masculine identity, Muʿallim Gaʿda rec-ognized himself in the faces of those assembled and realized an important difference between his past and his present self: "He looks at the seated as if for the first time; then, he realized and said: 'We are men; the home is for women. He who stays put loses; he who dares wins. Hurry up Gaʿda; to ʿAbbasiyya Gaʿda; to the Pyramids Gaʿda; to Helwan Gaʿda; to Tel al-Kabir Gaʿda. Work Gaʿda; skill and cleverness Gaʿda. Your money has come Gaʿda; long live money.'"[101] The passage is unmistakably a geogra-phy of Gaʿda's emasculation. The dire state of his economic life before the war when he worked selling potatoes from a little cart he pushed around the neighborhood was seemingly ameliorated during the war, when he worked as a lackey for the British. He tried to justify demeaning him-self for money by drawing an ultimately unconvincing line between the female inner sphere and the masculine outer sphere. Even though the alley celebrated Gaʿda's return as a triumphal moment, it was difficult for him to reconcile his compromised masculinity in the world outside of the alley with the assurances of his well-wishers at home, inside the alley. The nexus between money and masculinity was destabilized there by the loss of al-futuwwa.[102] In Mahfuz's rendering, Ga'da's attempt to restore that stability through a reclamation of al-futuwwa — in this case through an act of generosity towards his brothers — was doomed to failure because the time and space in which the alley existed had foreclosed this possibility. As every one of his senses began to shut down, he made one last claim to masculinity and fraternity: "We are men. Celebrate, for the world smiles upon you. My money and all that I possess is for you. My fortune is your fortune. I will never forget my brothers. Long live good fortune."[103] Then he passed out and never reawakened.

In another short story about a futuwwa's return from prison, Mahfuz more explicitly foregrounded the changes in the world that made this subject obsolete. "Futuwwa al-'atuf" narrates the rise and fall of Mu'allim Bayumi al-Fawwal.[104] Fawwal had risen to some prominence working with beys and pashas in "helping them" win elections, but he soon found himself treated as a common criminal by the police and imprisoned for several years. The world he returned to had changed dramatically. In "Futuwwa al-'atuf" Mahfuz provided a time frame and specific turning points for the semi-incorporation and ultimate expulsion of the futuwwa from Egypt's modern social and political order.

When the futuwwa of his alley died Mu'allim Bayumi succeeded him. He subjugated the futuwwat of the other alleys through a series of battles, all of which he won. Before long he was dressed in silks and cashmere and holding council at a coffeehouse with his boys and his allies reviewing the neighborhood's business, that is, the protection business. After the nation's first parliamentary elections in 1924 his status reached its greatest heights. The coffeehouse became a regular stop for politicians seeking Bayumi's assistance in winning the election. After the elections, the futuwwat found themselves the object of police surveillance and crackdown. To demonstrate the power of Egypt's newfound sovereignty, the police arrested Bayumi and paraded him around the neighborhood so that everyone could see that the era of the futuwwa was over.[105]

On his release many years later, Bayumi expected to receive a hero's welcome from his men, but to his dismay no one was waiting to congratulate him and to reaffirm for him that "prison was for real men" (al-sijan lil-gada'an).[106] He found instead a reordered social world within the alley, where the old futuwwat had met with different fates: prison, migration, succumbing to work like a common person. He would also feel the effects of that change within his intimate domains: "So, the Mu'allim met his world feeling obsolete and dejected. His greatness is a painful memory

that no one has respect for. Even his wife was fed up with his impoverished condition. She left him and returned to plying her trade on Sharia
Muhammad Ali."[107] To make matters worse, he was released on condition
that he find a job within twenty days or face being rearrested on the charge
of vagrancy. He was offered a job as a taxi driver, but the position required
that he wear a suit as a uniform, and he did not have one.

None of his old effendi acquaintances to whom he turned for a loan were
willing to help him. Then, as luck would have it, walking by a *makwagi*'s
shop (dry cleaner), he spotted a suit hanging outside. No one was around,
so he stole it and wore it to work the next day. One day, a passenger he had
stopped for recognized the suit, grabbed him by the collar, and screamed
for the police. An inexplicable paralysis overtook him and prevented him
from trying to escape. Instead, before he knew what was happening, the
police arrived, and he was taken off to prison again.

In "Futuwwa al-'atuf," as in "Nahnu rijal," Mahfuz depicted the futuwwa as a figure facing extinction in terms of power and prestige, that
is, in terms of sovereignty. The masculinity of this figure was constitutive of and constituted by historically specific relations of power, which
were contingent on place, bodily strength, and reputation. Accordingly,
Mahfuz represented the diminishing importance of the futuwwa to the
life of the city and to modern life in general through the subject's gendered deformation or emasculation. In the end, Mu'allim Bayumi's social
and sexual deaths are equivalent to Mu'allim Ga'da's literal death; both
entered a paralytic state in which their futuwwa, which can now be understood as their very life force, was vacated from their bodies—social and
biological.

In both stories the alley and the futuwwa's authority within it were
plotted in relation to the city and the new form of power represented by
the British, the police, and the national parliament, which were ostensibly
underwritten by different conceptions of masculinity and sovereignty. The
hara and the 'ahwa were not neutral microcosms of the nation, city, and
parliament; they were spaces historically produced as gendered and political domains existing in contradiction to one another. In his memoirs,
Mahfuz provided an accounting of this production.[108]

Mahfuz traced the disappearance of the futuwwat to a specific event
that he thought had finally convinced the police to eradicate them. He
argued that for a time the futuwwat formed a semiofficial system that was
to an extent recognized by the government and even relied upon to maintain local law and order. In the aftermath of the bloody battle that took
place between the futuwwat of Al-Husayniyya and Al-Qabisi on July 10,

1929, the government was encouraged to disband the system altogether.[109] 'Urabi, the chief futuwwa of Al-Husayniyya, was sentenced to twenty years in jail. The case was followed closely by all the major papers.[110] Mahfuz suggested that the press perhaps gave this incident so much attention because 'Urabi was considered the most powerful, most famous futuwwa in Egypt at the time, and his fate would determine the fate of al-futuwwa itself.

Mahfuz explicitly mapped the categorical transformation of the concept, practice, and subjectivity of al-futuwwa, resulting from the government's withdrawal of recognition and its pursuit of repressive measures:

> When the system of al-futuwwat was semi-recognized by the government, the futuwwa had to possess certain characteristics like physical strength and courage — because he was engaged in continuous battles — and he had to be sharp in order to win over the people. He also had to exhibit a great deal of gallantry and manliness [al-shahama wa al-rugula]. After the dissolution of the futuwwa system, al-futuwwa transformed into "baltagi" [a rogue, thug] who wouldn't hesitate to do anything. Some of them became pimps for underground brothels operating during the Second World War. . . . But before, when the futuwwat were semi-official, they often played a nationalist role, especially during the days of the revolution of 1919. The greatest resistance the British faced on a popular level was from the futuwwat.[111]

Ultimately, the politics of al-futuwwa was irreconcilable with the modern public sphere that emerged in Egypt in the 1920s and 1930s on the heels of a new constitutional form and its claims to sovereignty. For Mahfuz, al-futuwwa demarcated a domain of politics in which a local projection of urban space intertwined with an embodied masculine subjectivity, both of which were rendered by an aggressive modern politics as being out of step with the time of the modern city and the idea of the modern man.

Is this all there was to the history of the ancient and venerable al-futuwwa? The accounts given so far, aside from being in agreement about the death of al-futuwwa, did not provide much insight into how the futuwwa as living being negotiated identity with and within the changed political and economic order of a sovereign Egypt that sought its subordination or expulsion. In the historical novel The Age of the Futuwwat: The Age of Heroism by Egyptians in the Days of Occupation, Ministers, and Pashas, the eminent Egyptian historian Husayn Mu'nis attempted to do just that. He based the character of Mu'allim Khalil on informal interviews he had conducted with a self-identified futuwwa.[112] Khalil's life history was narrated against the background of a city increasingly divided along class lines, where inclusion or exclusion was determined both by structural location and by the nationalist imaginings of place and identity. The many layers of this character, adeptly represented by Mu'nis, serve to better illuminate the drawing of those lines, the differences between and among effendiyya and futuwwat, and the contested political terrain on which those differences were ultimately played out.

According to Mu'nis, the Cairene futuwwat began to form during the middle of the Ottoman period (the late seventeenth century) in reaction to the general insecurity precipitated by the different conflicts between Mamluk households.[113] As opposed to earlier periods when succession struggles had been brief and violent, the Ottoman policy of co-optation permanently removed leaders of certain Mamluk households from government, creating an endemic state of insecurity as the abject warlords and their mercenary bands went about the country wreaking havoc. Hence the institution of al-futuwwa emerged as a necessary means of protecting the local interests of traders, property owners, and even the residents of the alleys and quarters. These troops of assassins resembling small armies were immediately hailed for their courage and bravery and, according to Mu'nis, respected because of their indigenous Egyptian origins.

Gradually they became a regular feature of urban life throughout the country. Although some of them did become thieves and bandits, this was apparently in defiance of the unwritten futuwwa code of honor. Within this moral economy, the line between protection and extortion seemed to be drawn according to whether the arrangement between providers and buyers of protection remained mutually beneficial. Those who violated the code were often subject to disciplining (usually assassination) by other futuwwat.

Despite the final elimination of the Mamluks by Muhammad 'Ali in 1811, al-futuwwa continued as an urban force with the blessing of the new ruler. Initially the British occupiers also left the institution alone, but as they began to build their police force the two increasingly came into conflict. The institution was greatly weakened by these encounters with the new rulers, at least until the revolution in 1919. According to Mu'nis, this mass movement and the popularity of Sa'd Zaghlul as a nationalist leader convinced many futuwwat to join the Wafd Party, which in effect reframed their battles with the occupying forces as anticolonial, patriotic acts.[114] This tenuous relationship to the party and the nationalist movement apparently lasted only into the first years after nominal independence was achieved in 1922. Mu'nis contends that in the end it was impossible for the futuwwat to refashion themselves to fit into the social world of parliamentary politics with its class determinations and with its claims to law and order. Continuous police raids and imprisonment of reputable futuwwat forced the institution into extinction by the 1930s and 1940s, confirming the timeline provided by Mahfuz and the press accounts.[115]

The life story recounted in this narrative, which covers a period of some forty years from the turn of the century, is that of one Mu'allim Khalil al-Jawhari. As his name indicates, his father had been a jeweler. His father had been sent to Italy and France by Khedive Isma'il in the 1860s to learn European techniques of designing jewelry. When he returned, he worked for the khedive and members of the royal family, eventually opening his own jewelry store. They lived a very comfortable life in a large house in Al-Munasara near Midan Bab al-Khalq. When the father died and the estate was partitioned, Khalil was left with very little of the previously large fortune. Having to fend for himself for the first time in his life was a frightful proposition, so when the offer came from the local futuwwa boss to work in his gang, he found himself in a difficult position.

On the one hand, he did not believe that the kind of futuwwa represented by Mu'allim Hasanain al-Dammhuji was anything but thievery (al-lususiyya) and thuggery (al-baltagiyya); it bore no resemblance to the classic institution based on honor, courage, and generosity. On the other hand, he did not feel he had much of a choice at the time, so he agreed to perform a few jobs for this boss. Khalil was recruited by Dammhuji because he was one of the biggest and strongest men in the neighborhood. Physical prowess was traditionally one of the fundamental prerequisites for becoming the leader of a band of futuwwat, which Khalil would eventually become.[116]

This ambivalent entry into a life of al-futuwwa would remain a constant source of conflict to Khalil. Although he was compelled to occupy the position, he was uncertain whether it enabled virtuous pursuits in the way he imagined the classical manifestation of al-futuwwa had. The conflict about the nature of al-futuwwa is staged in the following debate between Mu'allim Khalil and Dammhuji against the backdrop of the revolution of 1919 and the formation of national identity:

KHALIL: Why do you want to beat and harm those poor people? Isn't it possible to reach some understanding with them through tactful discussion?

DAMMHUJI: That would be like begging, and we're supposed to be futuwwat!

K: But boss, the world has changed and the country's going through a
revolution. There's a new leader named Sa'd Zaghlul and all the people
are behind him.

D: Don't be fooled! All of that is a bunch of bull! He's just like 'Urabi and
the others. There's only one master in the country and it's the British.
They are strong, superior, and a blessing.

K: Superior and a blessing? How can you say that, boss? They're enemies
of the country. We're Egyptians just like the others and we have to support the Wafd and Sa'd Zaglul.

D: Look, Mu'allim Khalil, don't confuse yourself. We're futuwwat, and
we don't respect anyone but the British, and we won't be turned into
beggars! (63)

The figure of Dammhuji represented an aberrant and increasingly obsolete tradition of al-futuwwa in which only strength and violent force guaranteed authority and respect, anything else being less than manly. This
prenationalist tradition of al-futuwwa appears to lack the ethical dimension manifested in the classical (and potentially nationalist) relations of
protection, which were ostensibly based on compassion and generosity.[117]

For Khalil, the revolution marked the reclamation of al-futuwwa, which
was now configured along a compelling new axis of politics, ethics, and
affective affiliation. In the following conversation between Khalil and his
wife, Sitt Galila, he affirms his belief in this new nationalist order and its
potential to reshape al-futuwwa:

GALILA: Khalil, I really don't think that the country will ever be able to
dispense with the fatwana.

KHALIL: No, it will. I'll never leave the order, but it is disappearing.
As I've told you, there's a new kind of fatwana in the country and it's
called the nationalist movement. It's led by a great futuwwa, a pasha
actually, named Sa'd Zaghlul.[118] I haven't seen this man, but I like him
and I hope to stand by his side. I like him because of the position he's
taken against the English. You see how the people love him madly.
Really, I come from a distinguished family and this fatwana business
doesn't suit me. (67)

Khalil would spend the rest of his life shuttling between two competing
poles of identification. As much as he claimed to be ill suited for the title
and practice of al-futuwwa as it existed, he did find in it moments of sat-

isfaction. These moments of positive identification were initially scripted within a nationalist narrative. It was as a foot soldier for the Wafd Party of Sa'd Zaghlul that Khalil redefines al-futuwwa. It was also from this contradictory position that his ambivalence about being a futuwwa and being a nationalist was amplified.[119] The following retelling of what in Khalil's mind was a heroic deed was contradicted by the Wafd as a criminal act, setting in motion Khalil's growing doubts about the new politics of the nation and the place of al-futuwwa within it.

A contingent of British soldiers on their way from 'Ataba to the Citadel halted at a *ful* stand for lunch.[120] The owner of the shop demanded to know whether they would be paying before serving them. The Syrian translator conveyed this to the officer in charge, and he arrogantly replied, "No, they won't be paying; so, what are you going to do about it?" Then he ordered his troops to take whatever they wanted, which led to a violent battle that left the shop owner severely injured. Meanwhile, Rashad "al-Qabaqibi," the son of the carpenter who owned the shop across the street, watched in horror. He quickly gathered a group of men and ambushed the soldiers. Once Qabaqibi's men managed to disarm them, most of the soldiers fled the scene. The others were tied up while Qabaqibi stripped the general down to his underwear, tied him to his horse, and had the horse drag him all the way back to the Citadel. (88–90).

Qabaqibi and his men became famous throughout Egypt for their bravery. The papers did not print anything about the incident but people all over Egypt found out that Qabaqibi gave the English a sound beating and that his men made a laughingstock of the English commander. People said it was the Wafd's doing, but the party published an announcement denying it had any connection to the Qabaqibi incident. The statement asserted that the Wafd was a political party and as such did not engage in criminal activity. Khalil was upset by the position taken by the Wafd and went to see one of the party leaders, Nuqrashi:

> KHALIL: Ya Pasha, why did the party make that statement?
> NUQRASHI: You don't know the English. They are utterly impudent, and it's very possible that they would arrest us all.
> GALILA: So what? If they arrest you a new Wafd organization will be formed.
> N: Look, Mu'allim, you mind your business and leave politics to us. (90)[121]

Although it would seem from this exchange that Khalil believed violent confrontation with the British was necessary, at other times he was less confident that this was a sound strategy. This confusion was related to his initial ambivalence about becoming a futuwwa. As much as he tried to romanticize his role as a soldier in the service of the nation, he knew that what al-futuwwa meant in his own age was radically different from its ideal form, which continued to inhabit a small yet disconcerting place in his cultural memory. Such ambivalence led him at times to agree with people like Nuqrashi that "the age of fatwana has ended, and [Egypt] has entered the age of *political* confrontation" (104).[122]

It was into the interstices of citizen and futuwwa that Khalil fell, especially as his feelings of being anachronistic intensified within the new space of the nation.[123] When the government recruited him to destroy other groups of futuwwat, the justification was always the same: they were not really futuwwat, they were mere thieves. The unreal and the illegal in these instances became legible, it seems, only because the bourgeois representatives of the nation had hailed them as such. Before Khalil's discussion with the government official who convinced him to eliminate Tawfiq al-Rabi'ai's gang for showing a lack of respect toward the nationalist leader Sa'd Zaghlul, it was apparent that he had never thought in terms of whether or not this man was a criminal or a nationalist: "We all know that he's not 'okay,' but I've never really given him much thought because his turf is far from my own. But if he's trying to go against Sa'd now, I'm ready to teach him a lesson. Actually, what I've heard about him doesn't really justify his pretense to being the futuwwa of Bab al-Khalq. We don't know whether he has the courage or manliness to justify his claim to fatwana. If Sa'd Pasha wants us to break his neck, we're ready" (115). Khalil was very conscious of the fact that his gang was being asked to participate in a political intrigue that would remove Rabi'ai, a member of the Al-Ahrar Party, from contention for the parliamentary seat for his area, thereby allowing the Wafdist candidate to win without opposition.[124] Nevertheless, he was also conscious of the fact that this could be an opportunity to help redefine the role of al-futuwwa to fit within a politics that seemed to be the exclusive domain of an elite nationalist movement (117, 183–87). Caught between the desire to remake al-futuwwa in the image of its legendary past but fit for a modern society—that is, in the service of the nation—and the desire to leave the life of the futuwwa for good to be an ordinary citizen, Mu'allim Khalil al-Jawhari moved from one battle to another until his body ultimately refused to uphold this tension, expiring from a veritable exhaustion of spirit.

Conclusion

The history of al-futuwwa as a social institution in modern Cairo remains to be written.[125] What I have tried to do in this chapter is to stage a series of historical encounters with al-futuwwa, the final one being my own. What has the logic of this encountering been?

The bulk of this book provides a critical history of bourgeois masculinity in the Egyptian context, and al-futuwwa appears, at first reading, as only a foil for the cultural politics surrounding that discourse's emblematic figure, the effendi. Indeed, from the opening encounter of Ghuji and his readers with the sights and sounds of traditional Cairo to the various media, literary, and scholarly encounters with al-futuwwa, we are offered a dense portrait of effendis translating and transforming their world. The performative remaking of effendi masculinity, and by extension the precarious reproduction of its social life as national culture, was contingent on the construction and maintenance of rhetorical, legal, and physical boundaries between the modern and respectable, on the one hand, and the archaic and disreputable, on the other. Historically, the weight of such monumental feats of subject formation and political and cultural reformation was transferred to marginal and vulnerable lives the world over, which has most often resulted in their discursive erasure or physical extinction. Yet al-futuwwa stubbornly remains a haunting presence, refusing the intermediary roles assigned it (leading to its death) in the diverse acts of translating from overdetermined and often inaccessible social and political realities into the intelligible terms of nationalism and modernity — or critical scholarly history. Revising the translation, however, meets with enormous practical, theoretical, and methodological difficulties.

The possibilities for revisiting al-futuwwa are limited by the nature and paucity of the archives in which the figure might be located. Moreover, in history the dominant disciplinary framing of the past as times passed and as continuously superceded discourages questions about the ethics and politics of an encounter, which is ostensibly the domain of anthropology, literary studies, or (recently) oral history.[126] It is, I posit here in conclusion, by dwelling on the nature of the encounter that al-futuwwa reemerges as a gendered life, a way of living, and a site of sovereignty that was the Other of effendi masculinity and bourgeois nationalism but also the subject of an Egyptian history that is always already heterogeneous in its times and spaces.[127]

Perhaps appropriately, my final example of the encounter and its multiple possibilities comes from the most poetic and faithful interlocutor of al-futuwwa, Naguib Mahfuz.[128] Mahfuz recounts an experience from his childhood. He lived at 8 Maydan Bayt al-Qadi in the Gamaliyya neighborhood in the old section of Cairo. He remembers hearing a commotion outside his home and peering out the window onto the intersection of Darb Qirmiz and the *maidan* (square). It was the spring of 1919, and the newer quarters of Cairo had just seen the first manifestations of nationalist agitation in what would come to be termed the Revolution of 1919. But the little seven-year-old boy read the scene of marching demonstrators outside his window as one of the typical processions of futuwwat he was used to seeing in his neighborhood on the occasion of weddings, circumcisions, funerals, and other feasts, celebrations, and anniversaries. Only when he asked his mother who the head futuwwa was did he learn that this was a different kind of public spectacle. Whether his mother was able to explain the difference to him at the time — that it was nationalist, and what made it so — is not clear.

This little boy, of course, went on to become one of the most prolific and undeniably the most famous of Arabic fiction writers of the twentieth century. And the character of the futuwwa would feature prominently in a number of his most popular works. Young Naguib's misrecognition of the demonstration is instructive.

It is evident from the fieldwork conducted in Cairo by Sawsan El-Messiri in the 1970s as well as from anecdotal evidence I gathered there in 2000–2002 that al-futuwwa remains an ambivalent concept in contemporary Egyptian culture.[129] However, it is routinely translated into English as "thug," "tough," or "gangster" with no qualifying explanation. Although it is impossible today to disentangle futuwwa and baltagi, hero and menace — which may have been the case for its entire career — the intersection of this figure and the conceptual field underwriting it with modernity and the figure of the effendi assured the historical transformation of both figures but guaranteed history to one alone.

To some extent recognition of this historical fate is what propelled Amin, Mahfuz, and Mu'nis to narrate the vanishing present of al-futuwwa in their different ways — in philology, literature, and memorial. The media investigations of al-futuwwa, by contrast, were less concerned with preserving its history than with announcing its death. In the end, even sympathetic accounts had to narrate the death of al-futuwwa because ostensibly the grounds for other possible conceptions of it, beyond the binary of good and evil, had been reconfigured in colonial modernity. Accordingly, the legibility of al-futuwwa as a historical subject was constrained by a liberal discourse of law and order, and its intelligibility was conditioned by the temporality proper to the processes of history: economic incorporation, modernization, urbanization, colonialism, and nationalism.

Mahfuz's reminiscences of interwar Cairo, for example, might be plumbed for historical details about the social life of al-futuwwa and the eclipse of a traditional form of masculinity. As we have seen, Mahfuz even provided a historical timeline for the transformation of al-futuwwa.[130] I do not question the truth of such accounts. But limiting historical inquiry to this kind of historicism would reduce the subject to a casualty of colonial modernity and repeat yet again the inaugural violence of the latter.[131] In other words, by folding the history of al-futuwwa into the timeline of an a priori modern, its narrative potential is elided as the events proper to it are made to serve the narrative requirements of the autobiographies of colonialism and bourgeois nationalism. Thus in young Naguib's misrecognition of nationalism as the repetition of the local futuwwa tradition, one is alerted to the foreclosed potential for a reinscription of nationalism in terms of al-futuwwa.[132] For the historian, this moment remains a potentially generative encounter to the extent that it is recognized as a time of translation, one in which fundamental categories of social, political, and cultural life were being transformed but with the outcome always remaining somewhat uncertain and incomplete.

I have pointed to what is possibly a suppressed genealogy, another translation of modernity, masculinity, and sovereignty in Egypt. Reading against the grain of the discourses that made al-futuwwa visible, I have argued it is possible to detect the trace of a moral and political alterity that was intensely local, physical, and personal. Although I can still only hint at the contours of that Other in terms of a narrative of effendi masculinity, it is evident that the distinctions of good and evil through which al-futuwwa was materialized in the past can never be more than a partial accounting of this subject. That is not to say the specific distinctions—futuwwa and effendi, futuwwa and baltagi, futuwwa and fitiwwa—are merely modern constructs, imagined boundaries produced by colonial and nationalist discourses, that can simply be deconstructed or unimagined by the postcolonial critic. Indeed the sentence beginning "al-futuwwa is . . ." has announced specific moral, political, legal, and epistemological projects prior to modernity, the condition of possibility of which was a presupposition of alterity. Furthermore, the distinctions through which al-futuwwa was assigned significance in colonial modernity were not limited to intellectual or political exercises, but, as El-Messiri's research makes evident, also constituted everyday conceptions of this figure. The spheres of the ethico-political and the everyday in and through which the futuwwa lived and inscribed a life may never be fully recoverable as subaltern experience or agency. I hope to have shown that it is important at the very least to distinguish that form of life from the various encounters of al-futuwwa in statist, religious, and other grand narratives, both classical and modern.

NOTES

Introduction

1. The most thorough biography of Kamil is al-Rafi'i, *Mustafa Kamil*.
2. Mustafa Kamil, "The Antwerp Exhibition," *al-Ahram* (August 17 [?], 1894), reprinted in Ali Fahmi Kamil, *Mustafa Kamil Basha fi 34 rabi'an*, 2:102. All translations are mine unless otherwise indicated.
3. Kamil, "The Lyons Exhibition," *al-Ahram* (July 20–21, 1894), reprinted in Kamil, *Mustafa Kamil Basha*, 2:81.
4. This is one way to read Kamil's words. There is perhaps more to the story here in his alignment of French philosophers with the East, but I do not follow that trace here. The contradictions of French empire and French liberalism would be mediated for Kamil during his brief political career (he died on February 10, 1908, several months before his thirty-fourth birthday) through intimate relations he established as a law student at the University of Toulouse and most significantly as a protégé of the editor of *La nouvelle revue*, Juliette Adam. On Kamil's relationship with Adam, see Haddad, "Mustafa Kamil: A Self-Image from His Correspondence with Juliette Adam." Also see Adam, *L'Angleterre en Egypte*. For a recent exploration of the intimate milieus of anti-imperialists like Adam in the British metropolitan context, see Gandhi, *Affective Communities*.
5. Mitchell, *Colonising Egypt*, 13. The truth effect produced by the modern technique of enframing, of which the world exhibitions were one example, exerted power through the very act of repeatedly splitting reality from its representations.
6. The use of these labels for geographical and civilizational spaces in modern times was and still is inextricable from the history of colonialism. Hereafter, the quote marks are dropped, and if it is unclear from the context, I will note in which sense I deploy the terms.

7. Kamil, *Mustafa Kamil Basha*, 2:82.

8. His disenchantment with the promise of Europe is usually said to have begun when France entered a period of rapprochement with Britain following the Fashoda incident in 1898 and was complete when the entente cordiale was agreed in 1904. Kamil then turned to the East for examples of cultural renaissance and as a site of political solidarity, which is illustrated in his work on Japan, *al-Shams al-Mushriqa* (The rising sun) (Cairo: Matba'a al-Liwa,' 1904). See Laffan, "Mustafa and the *Mikado.*"

9. His brother says that this report was the talk of the town when it was published. Kamil, *Mustafa Kamil Basha*, 2:87.

10. Mitchell notes the disgust and embarrassment felt by Egyptian visitors at the World Exhibition in Paris in 1889, for example, but he does not explore the significance of such sentiments to the operations of the new power manifested in the "world-as-exhibition." Mitchell, *Colonising Egypt*, 1.

11. The nature of the exhibition was not at issue. In fact, despite his irritation with the Belgian effort, he noted that it should serve as a catalyst to encourage the large Egyptian merchants to display their wares at international exhibitions so that people were presented with a picture of Egypt that was not one of "self-evident shortcomings." Kamil, "The Antwerp Exhibition," 2:105. He wrote the description of the exhibition as a series of letters home but with the intention of having them published, since they were sent directly to *al-Ahram*.

12. Ibid.

13. Ibid., 115.

14. The classic statement of this relationship is Said's *Orientalism*.

15. Although Kamil ultimately achieved the title of pasha, the highest Ottoman and Khedivial honorific granted to state servants and eventually to others, for many years his name remained synonymous with youthful *effendi* activism. His funeral procession (February 11, 1908) was described by Gorst, the new British consul-general: "It is worthy of notice that almost every one taking part in the procession wore a tarbush, the turban being rarely noticed, which shows that, although Mustafa Pasha exercised extensive influence among the Effendi classes, his propaganda had so far produced no perceptible effect on the agricultural class, of which the majority of the population is composed." The National Archives (hereafter TNA): Public Record Office (hereafter PRO) FO 881/9477 Egypt Correspondence of 1908, no 26 Gorst to Grey of 16 Feb. 1908. See chapter 7 for an extensive treatment of the politics of headdress. On the shifting career of his legacy in Egyptian historical memory, see Gershoni and Jankowski, *Commemorating the Nation*, 174–203.

16. Although occupied by the British military in 1882 and with most of its administrative matters in British hands by 1892, Egypt was never declared a colony of the British Empire but legally remained an Ottoman province until the outbreak of the First World War. At that time it was made a protectorate, which it remained from 1914 to 1922, at which point it was given nominal independence through a treaty that allowed Britain to retain most of its influence. That treaty was amended in 1936 to reduce the British presence to military outposts along the Suez Canal; the final withdrawal of British troops was negotiated in 1954 by Gamal Abd al-Nasser. Through the course of this book, the colonial dimensions of this period, which are not related exclusively to formal acts, will be made apparent. Standard histories of this period in English include Tignor, *Modernization and British Colonial Rule in Egypt, 1882–1914*; Marsot, *Egypt's Liberal Experiment, 1922–1936*; and Beinin and Lockman, *Workers on the Nile*.

17. This is a very basic definition, one that I complicate and elaborate further throughout the book.

18. Ramadan, *Tatawwur al-haraka al-wataniyya fi Misr 1918–1936*; Berque, *Egypt: Imperialism and Revolution*; Deeb, *Party Politics in Egypt*; Gershoni and Jankowski, *Egypt, Islam, and the Arabs*, and *Redefining the Egyptian Nation, 1930–1945*; Beinin and Lockman, *Workers on the Nile*. For an approach from a slightly different angle, see Mitchell, *The Society of Muslim Brothers*.

19. History and the everyday are discrete yet related temporalities whose interplay were crucial to the formation of effendi masculinity and will be further elaborated below.

20. Here one might note the difference propinquity and subordination to the West made in forms of experiencing modern time. For the contrast, see Harootunian, *Overcome by Modernity*.

21. A. Ghosh, *In an Antique Land*, 236. Kamil might have been perturbed to learn that Indians traveling in Britain around the same time thought Egyptians to be at a lower stage of development based on the exhibition of their culture in museums. Burton, *At the Heart of the Empire*, 46.

22. This West was just as imaginary as the East through which France, Britain, and other nations traveled, literally and figuratively, to emerge as modern. The difference lay in the signifying potentialities of each, which were conditioned by asymmetries of political and economic power; so much so, one might argue, that traveling in the intensely cathected space of the West was a journey that all, even its own ostensible inhabitants, must take to arrive at the terminus of modernity. Indeed, the recent French debates over secularism are a continuing testament to this, as

are the liberalization projects of the post-Soviet states under the tutelage of the expanding European Union. On the French debates, see J. Scott, *The Politics of the Veil*, and on liberalization projects, see Zaborowska, Forrester, and Gapova, "Introduction: Mapping Postsocialist Cultural Studies," in 1–36. For a reflection on the simultaneously real and imagined dimensions of the complementary but distinct notion of Europe over time, see Pocock, "Some Europes in Their History," 55–71.

23. The cultural forms in which this process of becoming national and modern was manifested were also markers of a bourgeois world interconnected by new commodities and social practices. For the lines of connection that might be drawn through the latter, see Esenbel, "The Anguish of Civilized Behavior," 145–85.

24. Indeed he was an unofficial emissary of the young Abbas Hilmi II, who himself had a rocky relationship with the British since assuming the title of khedive of Egypt in 1892. See Sonbol, ed., *The Last Khedive of Egypt*.

25. Although these terms are now rendered without quotation marks for stylistic reason, this does not suggest a resolution of what made them problematic. The fixity of such terms, which Spivak refers to as concept metaphors, remains a question throughout the book.

26. This formulation, unlike alternative modernity, does not suggest a derivation from some original form; rather, it is a claim on a common origin and mutual constitution, and it should not be read as the modernity of the colonized, which is a prevalent usage. While there have been many references to colonial modernity in recent theoretical and historical works, Barlow has provided the most explicit statement of its usefulness for historical analysis in her "Introduction: On 'Colonial Modernity,'" in *Formations of Colonial Modernity in East Asia*, 1–20.

27. Hegel, *The Philosophy of History*, 99, as cited in Pagden, "Europe: Conceptualizing a Continent," citation on 35. The complete sentence in Hegel reads, "It is indeed a Western world for America; but as Europe presents on the whole, the centre and end of the world, and is absolutely the *West*—so Asia is absolutely the *East*."

28. There is a plethora of other senses to modernity, but for this historical intervention in the writing of Egypt and the location of its modern subject, the doubling which makes possible the frame of colonial modernity is the most germane, to the extent that, through it, world history appears as "a complex field of relationships or threads of material that connect multiply in space-time" enabling it to "be surveyed from specific sites." Barlow, "Introduction: On 'Colonial Modernity,'" 6. The singularity of modernity means that claims to radical relativism are checked

while simultaneously opening up Eurocentric claims to universality for interrogation. A good example of this in critical practice is Shankar, *Textual Traffic*.

29. There is a theoretical distinction between a performance (an act) and a performative (the effective quality of a speech act), but for the purposes of this historical inquiry I have found it productive to blur the lines. On the definition of the linguistic performative, see Austin, *How to Do Things with Words*. On iterability, see Derrida, "Signature, Event, Context." On the performative and resignification, see Butler, *Excitable Speech*.

30. This is partially because the book, like effendi masculinity itself, while having coherence when viewed from certain perspectives and in particular moments appears in the next instance as an assemblage of fragments, which may convey a sense of the ephemeral that is ostensibly a marker of colonial modernity.

31. Since the definition of *al-futuwwa* in modern times was itself a question (one I take up in the final chapter), providing a translation at this point is doubly problematic; nevertheless, in order for the reader to have some idea of what this figure represents in terms of the argument, for now I shall render it as "protector," "tough guy," "gangster." The literal translation, "youthful masculinity," is also highly relevant.

32. The use of and departure from the Foucaultian notion of biopower and recent treatments of sovereignty are outlined below.

33. The *gallabiya* is a long, loose robe worn by a majority of Egypt's rural population and also, with continuing urban migration, in cities. The question of dress is addressed in chapters 7 and 8.

34. *Pace* Ghosh, history shows, in the lives of many figures—like Duse Muhammad Ali, M. K. Gandhi, and W. E. B. Du Bois—that while this language may have come to dominate the interactions among people of the South and between North and South, its terms were vociferously debated and changed in the process. And, depending on one's vantage point, if one belonged, for example, to a people considered to be at the lowest rung of civilizational progress, which Egyptians were not, then the whole structure—if acknowledged at all—was more evidently problematic. Moreover, some of those other languages "in which people once discussed their differences" survived in colonial modernity, albeit in significantly altered states. For example, nineteenth- and twentieth-century histories of Islamist discourses and movements of varying stripes provide ample evidence of persistently deep and broad connections among Muslims around the world. Bearing the imprint of colonial modernity,

modern Islamism may reverse the terms of Western racist discourses, but it will remain steadfast or at most ambivalent toward essentialized religious difference.

35. In A. Ghosh's *In an Antique Land* this slippage might be captured by the friendships he did in fact form with some of the Egyptian youth at his fieldwork sites.

36. Powell, *A Different Shade of Colonialism*.

37. Kamil, *al-Ahram*, December 28, 1894, 2:267.

38. Powell, *A Different Shade of Colonialism*, 217.

39. Wautenpaugh has recently argued that in Middle Eastern historiography the burden of answering for Orientalism and demonstrating an authentic source of nationalism among the region's various societies has produced a certain bent toward the "often comprador middle class" that has largely relegated it to footnotes and abjured systematic treatments of this highly significant group of historical actors. Wautenpaugh, *Being Modern in the Middle East*, 17–18, especially nn. 30, 31. While this may be true for the Eastern Mediterranean, which is the focus of his study, his only citation for Egypt is from 1987 (and somewhat disingenuous since the focus of that study was the making of a working class) and hence overlooks works like Powell's *A Different Shade of Colonialism* and Pollard's *Nurturing the Nation*, which, although not explicitly about the middle class, by deconstructing the Egyptian nationalist discourse through race and gender, respectively, also reveal its specifically classed dimensions. Nevertheless, it is true that these are not the same as the kind of systematic historical study of middle-class culture Wautenpaugh conducted on Aleppo. My own departure from these studies has less to do with mapping formations of class than with examining moments of cultural or discursive de-formation at the level of the subject.

40. This was in contradistinction to his public denunciations of British efforts to "amputate" the Egyptian national body. Powell, *A Different Shade of Colonialism*, 156.

41. Gershoni and Jankowski, *Egypt, Islam, and the Arabs*, and *Redefining the Egyptian Nation, 1930–1945*.

42. While Pharaonicism, which emphasized Egypt's ancient past as its distinctive national personality over and against its Arab and Islamic histories, was popular in the 1920s, by the 1930s and 1940s there was a return of Islam and Arabism.

43. Gershoni and Jankowski, *Egypt, Islam, and the Arabs*, 74.

44. Their entry into the world of the effendiyya was through intellectuals engaged in articulating and popularizing an Egyptianist nationalism. These were divided into major figures (Ahmad Amin [1886–1954], 'Abbas Mah-

mud al-ʿAqqad [1889–1964], ʿAbd al-Qadir Hamza [1880–1941], Muhammad Husayn Haykal [1888–1956], Taha Husayn [1889–1973], Ismaʿil Mazhar [1891–1962], Salama Musa [1887–1958]) and secondary ones like teachers, journalists, and writers.

45. As such, there would be no need to explain why certain desires and practices related to middle-class life—promenades, consumption, physical culture, café-going, and so on—bridged the generational divide. Lockman pointed to a similar limit in Egyptian historiography and proposed investigations of the "cultural-political field," by which he means "the emerging arena of cultural politics . . . that new social space in which, in the second half of the nineteenth century and on into the twentieth century, many of the issues that are still central to the cultural politics of the Arab world—modernity, tradition, cultural authenticity, liberty, democracy, nationalism, Islam, and the role, rights, and status of women—were first extensively debated in a myriad of books, periodicals, and pamphlets, but also in plays, poems, songs and other forms of cultural expression." Lockman, "Exploring the Field," 139. My book attempts to map some aspects of this "cultural-political field," while occasionally trying to peek beyond its boundaries.

46. For a more extensive critique, see Ryzova, "Egyptianizing Modernity through the 'New *Effendiya*,'" 124–63.

47. Since I refer to a different sense of ideology below, note that here I use it in the traditional Marxist sense, a deep and contested tradition. Indeed, wittingly or not, in their notion of the "feedback loop," which they use to explain the broadening of the nationalist discursive field in the 1930s, Gershoni and Jankowski reflect Marxist debates on whether ideology, although determined, could also impact the base in turn.

48. Here the reference is to its use in Gershoni and Jankowski, *Redefining Egypt*, not to Benedict Anderson's theory of nationalism as a discursive formation developed in *Imagined Communities*. *Imagined Communities* was Gershoni's and Jankowski's theoretical inspiration, but their gloss of Anderson was the cause of a protracted debate: Smith, "Imagined Identities, Imagined Nationalisms"; Gershoni and Jankowski, "Print Culture, Social Change, and the Process of Redefining Imagined Communities in Egypt"; Smith, "'Cultural Constructs' and Other Fantasies."

49. Chatterjee, *Nationalist Thought and the Colonial World*. Wedeen has recently argued in *Peripheral Visions* that this criticism is based on a failure to distinguish between the historical element in Anderson that associates nationalism with secularism and the theoretical elaboration of its modularity. While this may be true, diffusion from center to margin remains at once a historical and theoretical problem in thinking modernity and the

very rise of modular forms, which cannot be resolved by merely recuperating Anderson.

50. For a call to redeploy Marxian critiques to blast out of historiography's national straitjacket, see Wilder, "Unthinking French History," 125–43. For an example of this, see his recent work, *The French Imperial Nation-State*.

51. Althusser, "Ideology and Ideological State Apparatuses."

52. Ibid., 171.

53. For Althusser, the topographic metaphor of society as built on an infrastructure of varying modes of production that enable different forms of rule and ideology, which respectively constitute the two levels of the superstructure, is problematic because its descriptive potential has been surpassed by history: "It now seems to me that it is possible and desirable to represent things differently. NB, I do not mean by this that I want to reject the classical metaphor, for that metaphor itself requires that we go beyond it. And I am not going beyond it in order to reject it as outworn. I simply want to attempt to think what it gives us in the form of a description." Ibid., 136.

The use of the term "ideology" to demonstrate the material reality of the subject as an interpellation is not without problems. However, for Althusser there was a strategic value to maintaining the term rather than deploying some other, such as discipline, in the critical way Foucault would do shortly after the publication of "Ideology" in *Discipline and Punish*. It was a claim on the Marxian tradition, pushing from within its own boundaries to capture the paradox of subjection beyond the bind of domination and resistance, or violence and consent, which have classically presupposed an agential or sovereign subject. On the latter point, Althusser's and Foucault's work would converge. See Montag, "The Soul Is the Prison of the Body."

54. For legal, see Cannon, *Politics of Law and the Courts in Nineteenth-Century Egypt*; Brown, "The Precarious Life and Slow Death of the Mixed Courts of Egypt," and "Law and Imperialism: Egypt in Comparative Perspective"; Peters, "Islamic and Secular Criminal Law in Nineteenth-Century Egypt: The Role of the Qadi," and "State, Law, and Society in Nineteenth-Century Egypt"; and in the same issue, "Administrators and Magistrates: The Development of a Secular Judiciary in Egypt"; Fahmy, "The Anatomy of Justice," and "The Police and the People in Nineteenth-Century Egypt." For military, see Fahmy, *All the Pasha's Men*.

55. For general histories of Muhammad Ali (the Arabic form of the Turkish Mehmed Ali), see Marsot, *Egypt in the Reign of Muhammad Ali*, and

Lawson, *The Social Origins of Egyptian Expansionism during the Muhammad 'Ali Period.* For a recent reassessment of the period and its historiography, see Abbas, ed., *Islah am tahdith: Misr fi 'asr Muhammad 'Ali.* Also see the recent biography by Fahmy, *Mehmed Ali,* in the "Makers of the Muslim World" series. For factories, see Marsot, *Egypt in the Reign of Muhammad 'Ali,* and John Dunn, "Egypt's Nineteenth-Century Armaments Industry." For hospitals, see Sonbol, *The Creation of a Medical Profession in Egypt, 1800–1924.* For a revision of Sonbol's thesis, which is faulted for its linear and progressivist assumptions about modernity, see Fahmy, "Women, Medicine, and Power in Nineteenth-Century Egypt." Also see Kuhnke, *Lives at Risk.* For schools, see Heyworth-Dunne, *An Introduction to the History of Modern Education in Egypt.* For cotton, see Owen, *Cotton and the Egyptian Economy, 1820–1914;* also see Rivlin, *The Agricultural Policy of Muhammad Ali in Egypt.* For bureaucracy, see Hunter, *Egypt under the Khedives, 1805–1879.*

56. Silvera, "The First Egyptian Student Mission to France under Muhammad Ali"; and see the firsthand account by Tahtawi, *Takhlis al-ibriz fi talkhis Bariz*; Tahtawi, *An Imam in Paris: Account of a Stay in France by an Egyptian Cleric (1826–1831)*; also Euben, *Journey to the Other Shore,* chapter 4. Administrative positions had previously been the exclusive sinecures of the Turco-Circassian elite, making them a veritable aristocracy. Potentially revising this conventional understanding of Egypt under the Ottomans is Adam Sabra's recent research into the Bakri family. He has found compelling evidence that might allow one to speak of an Arabic-speaking Egyptian high elite prior to the nineteenth century. (Author's personal communication with Sabra: Cairo, July 2008.)

57. Baer, *A History of Landownership in Modern Egypt, 1800–1950;* 'Abbas, *al-Nizam al-ijtima'i fi Misr fi zill al-milkiyyat al-zira'iyya al-kabira, 1837–1914;* al-Dasuqi, *Kibar mullak al-aradi al-zira'iyya wa dawruhum fi al-mujtama' al-misri, 1914–1952;* Cuno, *The Pasha's Peasants.*

58. Fahmy, *All the Pasha's Men,* 314.

59. These concepts will appear less familiar as I follow the trail of effendi masculinity. Similar to my treatment of the terms "bourgeois" and "middle class," that of "politics," "religion," "education," and "gender" in this book does not proceed with the aim of uncovering authentic Egyptian versions or presuppose that their modern genealogies were originally European. Rather, their production in the nineteenth century as geographically bounded categories is regarded as a paradoxical effect of colonial modernity, which, as I have suggested, had as its prior condition the traversing of physical and imaginary boundaries.

60. Butler, "'Conscience Doth Make Subjects of Us All,'" 25. The stakes of

this rereading of Althusser: "Perhaps there is a possibility of being else-where or otherwise, without denying our complicity in the law that we oppose. Such knowledge will only be answered through a different kind of turn, one that, enabled by the law, turns away from the law, resisting its lure of identity; an agency that outruns and counters the conditions of its existence. Such a turn demands a willingness *not* "to be" — a criti-cal desubjectivation — in order to expose the law as less powerful than it seems." Ibid.

61. Useful here is Butler's elaboration of the distinct but mutually constitu-tive dimensions of power as subordinating and enabling: "As a subject *of* power (where 'of' connotes both 'belonging to' and 'wielding'), the sub-ject eclipses the conditions of its own emergence; it eclipses power with power. The conditions not only make possible the subject but enter into the subject's formation. They are made present in the acts of that forma-tion and in the acts of the subject that follow." Butler, *The Psychic Life of Power*, 14.

62. A useful map of this shift in intellectual itineraries is the editor Frédéric Gros's note, "Course Context," at the end of Foucault's lectures gathered in the volume *The Hermeneutics of the Subject*, 507–50.

63. Foucault, "Preface to *The History of Sexuality*, Volume II," trans. William Smock, in *The Foucault Reader*, ed. Paul Rabinow (New York: Pantheon, 1984), cited in Gros, "Course Context," 513.

64. Indeed, as Rowson notes with explicit reference to Foucault's thesis on sexuality, medieval Islamic conceptions of sex and gender were more similar to those of early antiquity in the Mediterranean region than to those of late antiquity. Rowson, "The Categorization of Gender and Sexual Irregularity in Medieval Arabic Vice Lists," 73 and nn. 61, 79.

65. Foucault, *History of Sexuality, Volume 2: The Use of Pleasure*. Also see the two lectures by Foucault, "Technologies of the Self" and "The Political Technology of Individuals."

66. Foucault, *Hermeneutics*, 448.

67. Ibid., 416.

68. Foucault defined "flattery" as the "moral adversary" and rhetoric as the "ambiguous partner" of speaking freely but also suggested a connection between the two, "since the moral basis of rhetoric is always flattery . . . and the privileged instrument of flattery is of course the technique, and possibly the tricks, of rhetoric." Ibid., 373.

69. See chapter 2.

70. Foucault, ibid., 390. The "vertical line" is complemented by the horizon-tal relationships of friendship among students, which are crucial to "re-ciprocal salvation." This aspect of speaking freely was found in the Epi-

curean circles. On a similar conception of authorization and transmission of knowledge as it pertains to political authority within the Islamic tradition, see Mitchell, *Colonising Egypt*, 80–84. As I argue in chapter 2, the political constitution of effendi masculinity was contingent on the translation of prior notions of representation and authority.

71. While this Other in political discourse might be located in racialized bodies or an Arab-Islamic tradition, in the ethical formation of self, the Other is not necessarily exterior to the subject.

72. Foucault, *Hermeneutics*, 251. The examples he lists are "Stirner, Schopenhauer, Nietzsche, dandyism, Baudelaire, anarchy, anarchist thought, etcetera." Unfortunately, he would not have time to return to the moderns except for his brief statement on the "repressive hypothesis" and outline of a research agenda in the *History of Sexuality*.

73. Gandhi makes a similar argument in *Affective Communities*, exploring the period from the late nineteenth century on as a closing window of possibility for conceiving the political as friendship, a possibility that was overshadowed and assimilated into more serious and mature movements (communism, socialism, fascism, and so on) after the First World War.

74. See chapter 3 for a more extensive treatment of this notion.

75. Linguists, literary theorists, and philosophers have productively theorized the concept of translation beyond the technical aspects of rendering one language in terms of another. That process has been shown, at once, to appear seamless and to effect entirely new or hybrid meanings, and in cases of cultural translation some level of transformation always takes place in the terms situated at either side of the equation. "Translation" is used here both in its technical sense and as signifying a cultural change; the intended meaning should be apparent in context. See Spivak, "The Politics of Translation," in *Outside in the Teaching Machine*, 179–200; for a literary meditation on translation, see Djebar, *Fantasia*; and Kilito, *Thou Shalt Not Speak My Language*.

76. Indeed here one might say that the shift Foucault observed between the early Greek and later Hellenistic-Roman iterations of caring for the self, in which the elitist and political aspects were diminished, shifted back in the nineteenth century but with its national framing complicating the narrative. The correlation of nation and subject meant that there was an inescapable political agenda, but the candid exclusivity of the ancient practices of self would be partially disguised by a generalizing rhetoric of inclusion. For example, see Weeks, *Sex, Politics, and Society*.

77. On the question of woman, see Tucker, *Women in Nineteenth-Century Egypt*; Baron, *The Women's Awakening in Egypt*, and *Egypt as a Woman*; Badran, *Feminists, Islam, and Nation: Gender and the Making of Modern*

Egypt; Nelson, *Doria Shafik, Egyptian Feminist*; Booth, *May Her Likes Be Multiplied*; M. Russell, *Creating the New Egyptian Woman*; Kozma, "Women on the Margins and Legal Reform in Late Nineteenth-Century Egypt, 1850–1882." Also see Bier, "Modernity and the Other Woman: Gender and National Identity in the Egyptian Women's Press: 1952–1967."

78. Pollard discusses the mutually constitutive gendering of home and nation in *Nurturing the Nation*. The conventional feminist historiography of Egypt, she argues, has not answered the question of why women, who were active in the nationalist struggle, were denied formal political rights after independence. In addressing this lacuna, she points to the division between the public and private spheres that is presupposed by these feminist revisions in their explanation of the eventual relegation of women to the private. Pollard suggests that in fact the home and definitions of home were central to the nationalist project from its inception, and notions of masculinity and femininity were contested and reconfigured in the process of Egyptianizing the form of the nation in terms of family.

79. Ibid., 30.

80. El Shakry, "Schooled Mothers and Structured Play: Child Rearing in Turn-of-the-Century Egypt"; and Pollard, *Nurturing the Nation*, chapter 4. On marriage, see Kholoussy, "Stolen Husbands and Foreign Wives"; and her recent monograph, *For Better, For Worse*.

81. On the latter two arenas of discursive practices, see El Shakry, *The Great Social Laboratory*; and Abugideiri, "The Scientisation of Culture."

82. Ballantyne, "Rereading the Archive and Opening Up the Nation-State"; also Burton, "Who Needs the Nation? Interrogating 'British' History."

83. In the recent writing of Ottoman Egyptian history, this trajectory seems to have been reversed by historians' revising of Egypt's nationalist narrative. However, this tendency to locate nineteenth-century Egypt within an Ottoman political and cultural orbit — while yielding some excellent historical studies of land tenure, military, law, and society and state formation that effectively revise the story of the Ottoman Empire — begins with an answer to the national question; i.e., the nationalists (and Orientalists) had it wrong about their immediate past. But they cannot explain how or why this wrong answer, which was in fact a question about the history of the modern, compelled anticolonial nationalists from the late nineteenth century on. Thus, although contradicting the nationalist emplotment, to borrow Hayden White's expression, of Egypt's past, the revision does not displace the narrative frame of modern history, which preserves the teleology of the nation. H. White, *The Content of the Form*.

84. This problem has been explored extensively in Chakrabarty, *Provincializing Europe*. However, as I argue in the first and last chapters, *pace* Chakrabarty, the project of "provincializing Europe" must situate the latter in a network of provincial formations — material and ideal — which go beyond the properly intellectual in order to undo the spell Europe has cast on the historical imagination. For a similar argument that proposes "cross-national analysis" as a means of decentering the traditional imperial framework and reenvisioning it as a network of "interrelating margins," see Boehmer, *Empire, the National, and the Postcolonial, 1890–1920*. For an earlier period and a more social and economic historical approach, see Subrahmanyam, *Explorations in Connected History*.

85. In the African context, Frederick Cooper has demonstrated the resilience of empire as a political and economic structure (that involved national groupings but was itself neither national nor international), which could be resisted but could also be the grounds for negotiating disparate interests. Cooper, *Colonialism in Question*, especially part 3. This book is sympathetic to Cooper's larger argument about the evacuation of the history of political struggles in recent approaches to colonial studies, but it also finds in the postcolonial stance a useful approach to history as not simply a disciplinary technique that produces "our" knowledge of past objects but as an asymmetrical site of subject formation.

86. Said, *Orientalism*, esp. 166–90. This aspect of Orientalism was by no means insignificant to the formation of an idea of the East in the West; Massad, *Desiring Arabs*. Although both works depend on and make explicit reference to a notion of the historical connectedness of the world, the nature of this interrelatedness remains largely one-dimensional (political) and unidirectional (West to East).

87. It is easy enough to say that the native perspective was beyond the scope of Said's work, but that would be missing the point: that alongside Orientalism, sexuality, and gender were also productive discourses through which subjects like East and West were formed *across* the colonial divide and that in that historical process hegemonies of the Orient, sex, and gender were variously opposed, adopted, negotiated, and contested. For a reading of how these complex possibilities come to light when heteronormative assumptions are suspended, see Wallace, *Sexual Encounters*.

88. What follows is partially a response to Judith Tucker's query to me (Middle East Studies Association annual meeting, Montreal 2007) about what happens to the "small voices" of history when history is written deconstructively. See Tucker's pathbreaking book, *Women in Nineteenth-Century Egypt*, for a brilliant example of Middle Eastern social history. On the problematic of assigning agency, see the now-classic essay by

Spivak, "Can the Subaltern Speak?"; also see Scott, *Refashioning Futures*, and Johnson, "On Agency."

89. The debates about narrative in historiography are too many to enter or cite in full, but my book in its entirety might be read as a quest for a post-colonial narrative. On the impossible disavowal of narrative in history, see Rüth, "The Battle of Bouvines."

90. Burton, "Introduction: The Unfinished Business of Colonial Moderni-ties," in *Gender, Sexuality, and Colonial Modernities*, 1–16; Hall, "Intro-duction: Thinking the Postcolonial, Thinking the Empire," in *Cultures of Empire*; Ann Stoler, *Carnal Knowledge and Imperial Power*. Also see Stoler's critique of Foucault's Eurocentrism in *Race and the Education of Desire*. Among the collections exploring these themes are *Tensions of Em-pire*, ed. Cooper and Stoler, and *After the Imperial Turn*, ed. Antoinette Burton.

91. Stoler, "Making Empire Respectable," 636. In this early work, Stoler's focus was on how sex and gender could work as regulatory appara-tuses in colonial governance rather than on their destabilization. Also see McClintock, *Imperial Leather*. On "biopolitics," see Foucault, *The History of Sexuality*, and "Governmentality," in *The Foucault Effect*, and "*Society Must Be Defended*." For a conceptualization of performance in terms of language and as the scene of subject formation with the poten-tial for disruption, see Butler, *Gender Trouble*.

92. Koselleck, *Futures Past*.

93. A good survey of this wide-ranging literature can be found in Stoler, "Tense and Tender Ties." For some surprising outcomes of miscegena-tion in the Indian context, see D. Ghosh, *Sex and the Family in Colo-nial India*.

94. Levine, *Prostitution, Race, and Politics*. It might be said that the mod-ern anxieties of racial mixing were transferred to colonized people; see Kholoussy, "Stolen Husbands and Foreign Wives."

95. There have been many works on this topic since the publication of *Orien-talism* (1978), mostly from students of literature and of varying quality. An interesting example is Alloula, *The Colonial Harem*. Also see Mel-man, *Women's Orients — English Women and the Middle East, 1718–1918*; Lewis, *Gendering Orientalism*, and *Rethinking Orientalism*.

96. Ahmed, *Women and Gender in Islam*.

97. Eighteenth-century Muslim reformists, motivated by different factors, did not place gender at the center of their discourse. Haj, *Reconfigur-ing Islamic Tradition*. On the publicity of this process in Egypt, as op-posed to the privacy imputed within the Indian context, see el-Shakry,

"Schooled Mothers and Structured Play," and Chatterjee, "The Nation-alist Resolution of the Women's Question."

98. Pollard, *Nurturing the Nation*. The occupation was also cast in gendered terms; see Pollard, chapter 3.

99. Ibid, esp. chapters 1, 4.

100. This is not to say that nationalists started with a blank slate, but that making the past into history (a modern disciplinary formation) involved recircuiting events through a temporal matrix in alignment with the pri-mary determinants that had seemingly catapulted the West over the East. The slow death of the Islamic chronicle and the transformation of history writing in Egypt were complete by 1920. On this point and what he terms "*effendi* historical mindedness," see Di-Capua, "The Professional World-view of the *Effendi* Historian." Also see Di-Capua, "'Jabarti of the 20th Century.'" Other studies of Egyptian historiography, studies that repeat the modernist conception of recording times past, however, are Crabbs, *The Writing of History in Nineteenth-Century Egypt*, and Gorman, *Histo-rians, State and Politics in Twentieth-Century Egypt*.

101. A voluminous literature exists that spans the disciplinary and philosophi-cal spectrum and investigates how the subject is formed of an individual consciousness. If it must be named, this study uses a poststructuralist feminist conception of the subject. The essential point to note is that when "subject" is invoked herein — as in the "subject of effendi mascu-linity" — it is always in terms of language, which, contrary to the prevail-ing common sense, is also suggestive of a social reality adhering in the temporality proper to the subject of discourse that precedes and exceeds the lives and deaths of historical individuals. In that regard, identifying the subject of empire, nation, gender, and sexuality engages the linguis-tic and the social as simultaneous enactments in which individual histori-cal actors are determined and determining but never fully and finally.

102. To some extent it is Althusser's "Ideological State Apparatuses" that are the focus of this study, in that in his essay he attempts to map the cul-tural work of persistent institutions like culture in the maintenance of the state, even as political apparatuses change over time.

103. To clarify, this does not mean only in linear time and in physical places. Rather, this book inquires into the possibility of a post-Orientalist in-scription, for example, of Mustafa Kamil's inhabiting a time of the nation for and to which he spoke that was different from the time of those who did not speak or were not heard as speaking in its name. See Bhabha, "DissemiNation."

104. Herder (1744–1803) was a key figure in the German Romantic move-

ment. Perhaps not his greatest intellectual achievement, he elaborated the significance of having and cultivating pride in German language and culture, which were a source of the nation's organic unity. Fichte (1762–1814) composed and delivered the famous and eventually infamous *Addresses to the German Nation* in the winter of 1807–08, during the French occupation of Berlin. This was merely a handful of years after Napoleon was forced to abandon Egypt by an Ottoman-British force.

105. See, *inter alia*, Williams, *Marxism and Literature*; Anderson, *Imagined Communities*; Sommers, *Foundational Fictions*; Berlant, *The Queen of America Goes to Washington City*, esp. "Introduction: The Intimate Public Sphere," 1–24; Nelson, *National Manhood*.

106. See, for example, Fanon, *Black Skin, White Masks*, and Nandy, *The Intimate Enemy*. Another approach that complicates the psychologizing of the colonial relationship explores the plurality of subjects and temporalities that were possible in colonial and postcolonial contexts. Compare Assia Djebar's various treatments of emancipation in the context of the Algerian revolution to Fanon's theorization of the dialectic of recognition and the role of decolonizing violence. See Djebar, *Children of the New World*, and Fanon, *The Wretched of the Earth*.

107. For a reading of how racism and universalism were mutually constitutive through nationalism and sexism, see Balibar, "Racism as Universalism," in *Masses, Classes, Ideas*, 191–204.

108. Compare Sinha, *Colonial Masculinity*, and Nye, *Masculinity and Male Codes of Honor in Modern France*. The colonial context is largely absent in Nye's work.

109. For a deconstruction of Fichte's *Addresses to the German Nation* that reveals its ambivalences, in particular on the true German subject, see Balibar, "Fichte and the Internal Border," in *Masses, Classes, Ideas*, 61–84.

110. Pedagogy was viewed as important in this regard by early theorists of national identity such as Fichte. Abizadeh, "Was Fichte an Ethnic Nationalist? On Cultural Nationalism and Its Double." For a concrete example, see the classic work of Weber, *Peasants into Frenchmen*.

111. For a broad overview of the issues involved, see the collection edited by Calhoun, *Habermas and the Public Sphere*. For Habermas and the early modern timeline, see Lake and Pincus, eds., *The Politics of the Public Sphere in Early Modern England*, esp. chap. 8.

112. Habermas, *The Structural Transformation of the Public Sphere*, 140.

113. Ibid., 27.

114. On the one hand this figure is fictional to the extent that its theoretical condition of possibility is a domain constituted through the idea of "universal access," which was a historical impossibility; on the other hand,

the bourgeois individual was always a subject of fiction, a subjectivity which always mapped onto historical persons only unevenly and incompletely.

115. See, *inter alia*, Weber, *Peasants into Frenchmen*; Mangan, *Athleticism in the Victorian and Edwardian Public School*; Kinmonth, *The Self-made Man in Meiji Japanese Thought*; Kasson, *Houdini, Tarzan, and the Perfect Man*; Sinha, *Colonial Masculinity*.

116. Chakrabarty, *Provincializing Europe*, and Spivak, "Can the Subaltern Speak?"

117. Spivak, "Can the Subaltern Speak?," 271–72.

118. By success here I mean the internal coherence of the concept. That this subject's political horizon of freedom continues to justify imperialist politics and animate feminist theory has been persuasively argued recently by Mahmood, *The Politics of Piety*. Compare to Spivak, *A Critique of Postcolonial Reason*. While Mahmood goes as far as to sketch the architecture of another—Islamic—process of subject formation, Spivak's critique remains at the level of deconstruction, making visible the epistemological and political limits of various representational practices.

119. For a similar perspective on the Haitian revolutionary leader Toussaint Louverture, see Scott, *Conscripts of Modernity*.

120. Latour, *We Have Never Been Modern*.

121. As I shall argue below, this is also the limit of performative theory.

122. The work of the Subaltern Studies collective is the most familiar example. Notable works from the Middle East field include Mitchell, *Colonising Egypt*; Massad, *Colonial Effects*; and Feldman, *Governing Gaza*.

123. A good overview of these issues can be found in the Prakash versus O'Hanlon and Washbrook debate: Gyan Prakash, "Writing Post-Orientalist Histories of the Third World: Perspectives from Indian Historiography," *Comparative Studies in Society and History* (CSSH) 32/2 (April 1990): 383–408; Rosalind O'Hanlon and David Washbrook, "After Orientalism: Culture, Criticism, and Politics in the Third World," CSSH 34/1 (January 1992), 141–67; Prakash, "Can the 'Subaltern' Ride?: A Reply to O'Hanlon and Washbrook," CSSH 34/1 (January 1992), 168–84.

124. The point here is not that this is an unviable historical account of the rise of liberal politics at home secured by illiberal politics elsewhere. Within a Foucaultian accounting, the subject of the former would be the more docile and disciplined by power, a proposition again at odds with histories of liberal politics wherein the subject is a priori sovereign.

125. Conversely, and this has been most effectively argued by the Subaltern Studies group, the past (which one could also see as a thing to come in terms of discipline formation) was increasingly pinned to an unstoppable

historicizing movement that assigned a place in time to all while denying the possibility of multiple temporalities. See Chakrabarty, "Postcoloniality and the Artifice of History."

126. This was over and against the explicit terms of imperialist ideologies.

127. Prakash, "The Colonial Genealogy of Society." On the desirable modern, see Ferguson, *Expectations of Modernity*.

128. Agamben, *Homo Sacer*, 128.

129. The genius of a work is often in its bearing the sign of its specific lacuna. Agamben's sometimes enigmatic references to Islam is such a sign: for example, in *Homo Sacer* he notes that Jews in German concentration camps who had lost all will to live were referred to as Muslims; in *Means without End* he tangentially references Averroes (Ibn Rushd); and in his recent work *The Time that Remains* in which he examines the messianism of Paul, he makes a passing reference to Avicenna (Ibn Sina) and to an Islamic text about the coming of the Messiah. It is especially in this latest turn in his work, seeking to demonstrate the constitutive role of a theological conception of time from Paul to Luther to Hegel and on, where the mapping of a world of thought that presupposes a bounded "Western culture" reveals its shortcoming, in the now. Another reading, following the grain, would regard maintaining the identity of the West with itself (its modern projection) as a more politically effective move for the philosophical critiques Agamben proffers of the state of exception.

130. Stoler, *Race and the Education of Desire*.

131. Esmeir, "The Work of Law in the Age of Empire," 237.

132. Esmeir notes that, however uneven, the precolonial Khedivial state did attempt to regulate the estates, which were being allocated during Ismail's reign, in terms of an unelaborated notion of justice. The agents of the colonial state entered the estates but only when violence among peasants or against officials resulted in the loss of labor and productivity. Ibid., 248–49.

133. El-Shakry, *The Great Social Laboratory*, 6.

134. There are two potentially contradictory senses to public here: as an elite sociocultural formation and as a mass. The tension between the two modern publics was an emergent historical reality in the interwar period, so I leave the distinction to be made in context.

135. Normally in social theory exclusion is related to the process of uneven economic and political development by which certain subjects are barred from meaningful participation in society and often become its abject or excluded. The notion of a constitutive outside formulated in gender theory and deployed here, however, while acknowledging the power of dominant norms to exclude, resists a repetition of that exclusion by

showing how it was not merely an outcome but constitutive of the social. On this point, see Butler, *Gender Trouble*.

Chapter 1. Imagination

1. See for example, Niall Ferguson, *Empire*.
2. A bracing analysis of the "return" of Empire as an object of study is part one of Cooper's *Colonialism in Question*.
3. In this regard, Western feminists are often silent or betray their masculinist leanings vis à vis Muslim women. See Lila Abu Lughod, "Do Muslim Women Really Need Saving?," *American Anthropologist* 104 (3): 783–90; and, Charles Hirschkind and Saba Mahmood, "Feminism, the Taliban, and Politics of Counter-Insurgency," *Anthropological Quarterly* 75/2 (2002): 339–54. The focus of this chapter is on British imperialism at the fin de siècle; the West is used as a "hyperreal" term (following Dipesh Chakrabarty) that emerged and assumed a new popularity during this age of steamships and the concomitant acceleration of contact among and between larger segments of population groups on all the inhabited continents. The other chapters implicitly track the dialectical emergence of the East while working to displace both West and East as natural divisions.
4. One of the most famous treatises unmasking the pretensions of civilized conquerors was Immanuel Kant's philosophical proposal for "Perpetual Peace" (1795). For a careful consideration of Kant and other eighteenth-century anti-imperialist philosophers, see Muthu, *Enlightenment Against Empire*. This narrow treatment of political thought however does not fully respond to the historical critique that from this period onward it was not empire as such that Europeans considered bad but bad empire. See, for example, Dirks, *The Scandal of Empire*. A very early example of Muslims' rejection of European claims to civilizational superiority is in the textual mockery found in Jabarti's account of the French occupation of Egypt at the end of the eighteenth century, *Napoleon in Egypt: Al-Jabarti's Chronicle of the First Seven Months of the French Occupation of Egypt, 1798*, trans. S. Moreh (Princeton: M. Wiener, 1993).
5. On this political field and women's symbolic deployment of empire as a feminist strategy, see Burton, *Burdens of History*.
6. For the best work on this figure as a relational construct forged within the "imperial social formation," see Sinha, *Colonial Masculinity*.
7. Çelik, "Commemorating the Empire." On the aesthetic debates around colonial architecture in India, which were resolved in the direction of a

hybrid style after 1857 but wherein the central issue was always "political effect," see Metcalf, *An Imperial Vision*.

8. Cannadine, *Ornamentalism*, p. 122. Aside from Cannadine's confused empire nostalgia — most apparent in the autobiographical appendix — his study of image and vision is problematic for more fundamental theoretical and historical reasons (of which the nostalgia is a mere symptom). For example, his deployment of Britishness as a historical construct is consistently contradicted by an implicit reference to "the British" as an object independent of analysis. It is often unclear whether he means by this reference the elite identity being re-fashioned through an expanding empire, a purely discursive phenomenon, or a natural disposition of all those inhabiting the great isles. In part, this is a theoretical problem relating to conceptualizations of identity, but it is also a historical problem with political implications, to the extent that his attempt to reconsider Britain's imperial past as an "interconnected" phenomenon fails to do anything more than recall how *the British* exported and reproduced a system of hierarchy modeled on what they experienced at home — the reader is virtually invited to imagine a warm and fuzzy pastoral scene. For a more sustained critique, see the special issue of the *Journal of Colonialism and Colonial History* 3/1 (Spring 2002) devoted to Cannadine's book: "From Orientalism to Ornamentalism: Empire and Difference in History," Tony Ballantyne, guest editor.

9. The best evidence of this was the Frenchman Edmond Demolins' study of English public schools, *À Quoi tient la supériorité des Anglo-Saxons* (Paris, 1897). An Arabic translation was made by the brother of the future nationalist leader Sa'd Zaghlul, Ahmad Fathi Zaghlul, *Sirr taqaddum al-inkliz al-saksuniyyin* (Cairo: Matba'at al-Ma'arif, 1899). Perhaps another poignant example of how influential the image of the Englishman had become by late century was the impetus behind Pierre de Coubertin's involvement in popularizing sport in France and spearheading the Olympic movement. "A nationalist who was bitterly shaken by France's defeat in 1870–71, he sought to *rebronzer* — strengthen — France by implanting what he saw as the secret to English power and success: the moral and physical training produced by public-school sports." Keys, "The Dictatorship of Sport," p. 51.

10. Kitchener was perhaps the more influential and memorable figure in Egypt. Some of the imperial tropes that have resurfaced recently in the old metropoles and in the U.S. are also making an appearance in their "peripheries." A poster from the First World War that I encountered during a particularly unguarded moment of my research in Egypt provides

a minor illustration of the uncanny accompanying the current neoliberal phase of globalization. Over the toilet in the bathroom of one of the new fashionable bar/cafés in Cairo was a stern image of Kitchener aggressively pointing and declaring, "Your country needs you"!

11. For a contemporary analysis that departs from the conception of gender identity as preexisting and that demonstrates how the field of international relations constructs masculinities, see Hooper, *Manly States*.

12. Hall, ed. *Muscular Christianity*.

13. For an analysis of how this joining of Christian principles and imperialism produced a new popular image of the imperial soldier hero during the second half of the Victorian period, see Dawson, *Soldier Heroes*, especially chapter five. On the interplay of muscular religions, see chapter five, "Moral Muscle: Masculinity and Its Religious Uses," of van der Veer's *Imperial Encounters*.

14. Mangan, ed. *Pleasure, Profit, Proselytism*.

15. For many, entranced by social Darwinism, the scale of fin-de-siècle "exhaustion" exceeded the bounds of the nation and was considered a civilizational problem. A major proponent of this view was the German doctor Max Nordau, who denounced modernist excesses in his 1892 publication, *Degeneration* (Lincoln: University of Nebraska Press, 1993). Of course, this was not the only possible response nor was it the only perspective on the state of British or European culture and society in the late nineteenth century. For a fascinating portrayal of the "intellectual revolution" of the 1890s led by the likes of Freud, Weber, Durkheim, and others against what they understood as the simplistic positivism and "iron determinism" borne of middle-class complacency, see Hughes, *Consciousness and Society*. See also Walkowitz's dazzling study of London — *City of Dreadful Delight* — as a metropolis that was regarded as rich with possibility as well as lurking with danger, where one's vision — and how one was envisioned — depended very much on class and gender as well as ethnicity. On the rhetoric of degeneration as a pervasive cultural phenomenon connected, from the 1880s on, to a new concern with "the economy of the body and the social effects of its reproduction," see Pick, *Faces of Degeneration*, especially Part III. Also see, Schneider, *Quality and Quantity*.

16. An interesting account of war artists in Egypt and Sudan that alludes to the fashioning of a masculine persona through the act of painting violence is John Springhall, "'Up Guards and at Them!' British Imperialism and Popular Art, 1880–1914," in John M. MacKenzie, ed. *Imperialism and Popular Culture* (Dover, N.H.: Manchester University Press, 1986),

p. 49–72, especially see the description of Frederic Villiers, p. 51 and
p. 54.

17. Winston Churchill, *The River War*.

18. Imperial communication and transportation were vastly improved with
the opening of the Suez Canal in 1869 and the completion of telegraph
lines to India in 1870. The expansion of British male franchise in 1867–68
was also an occasion for the rethinking of the form and content of respectable masculinity; see, Keith McClelland, "'England's Greatness, the
Working Man.'"

19. McClintock, *Imperial Leather*, p. 45. For a portrait of how families lived
empire as a social formation, see Buettner, *Empire Families*. On the increasing ambivalences of Victorian ideals of masculinity by the last third
of the nineteenth century within the contexts of changing discourses on,
and practices of, domesticity, see Tosh, *A Man's Place*.

20. Nye, *Masculinity and Male Codes of Honor in Modern France*, p. 218–19.
The concept of hegemonic masculinity is elaborated in Connell, *Masculinities*.

21. Cromer, p. 110.

22. Anderson, *Imagined Communities*. There is a purposeful slippage in this
chapter between England and Britain, as it reflects the messiness of the
gendered splitting and reconsolidation of the two as imagined communities during the period under consideration. For a sociologist's attempt
to clear up the mess by examining Englishness as a national category
at once dependent on and obscured by imperialism, see Kumar, "Nation and empire." On the work of fashioning a British identity over and
against disparate others, see Colley, *Britons: Forging a Nation, 1783–
1837*.

23. Owen, *Lord Cromer*, p. 189.

24. For a work that purports to study the "reception" of empire, see Porter,
The Absent-Minded Imperialist. Even this work, skeptical — to put it
mildly — as it is of the new cultural histories of empire and doubtful
whether "Britain *used* to be soaked in the stuff," locates a marked shift in
the conception of imperialism in the 1880s and 1890s.

25. I am thinking here of the indomitable personality of the poet and anti-
imperialist Wilfrid Scawen Blunt (1840–1922), who was an outspoken
critic of British policies in Egypt. He published several works on the political history of the occupation, including: *Secret History of the English
Occupation of Egypt: Being a Personal Narrative of Events* (1907) and
Gordon at Khartoum (1911). The political thinking of Edmund Burke
(1729–1797) and Jeremy Bentham (1748–1832) had already carved out a
space for such an oppositional stance over a century before.

26. G.A. Henty, *With Kitchener in the Soudan: a Story of Atbara and Omdur-man* (London: Blackie and Sons, Ltd., 1903).

27. J.S. Bratton, "Of England, Home and Duty: The Image of England in Victorian and Edwardian Juvenile Fiction," in John M. MacKenzie, ed. *Imperialism and Popular Culture*, p. 73–93. In some cases this literature continued to play the role of cheerleader well into the twilight years of empire. See the autobiographical musings of Cannadine, *Ornamentalism*, p. 183 and p. 193. Also see, MacKenzie, *Propaganda and Empire*, p. 199–226.

28. Guy Arnold, *Held Fast for England*, p. 83. This literary genre should be understood as forming part of a multi-pronged effort to correct for the degeneration seen to be plaguing late Victorian society. On the multiple ways in which degeneration was narrated, see Stephen Arata, *Fictions of Loss in the Victorian Fin de Siècle*.

29. Mangan, *Athleticism in the Victorian and Edwardian public school*. On the effects of this discourse read through "critical schoolboy autobiographies," see Gagnier, *Subjectivities*, chapter 5.

30. Sometimes the prizes awarded to students at elite Egyptian schools were these adventure novels. For example, third prize for "success in the Holiday Reading Competition" at the Khedivial School was a reissue of Captain Marryat's 1841 *Masterman Ready, or the Wreck of the "Pacific"* (London: George Routledge & Sons, 1898). This copy is in the author's personal collection and bears a sticker of the school's award certificate on the inside front cover; unfortunately, it seems the second owner, Mohammed Khalil el-Eidarous, rubbed out the year and name of the original student. The family name, which can almost be made out, was perhaps Abd el Kadi. *Masterman Ready* was the first stab at juvenile fiction by the retired English naval officer Frederick Marryat (1792–1848); its success led him to also write *The Settlers in Canada* (1844), *Scenes in Africa* (1845), *The Children of the New Forest* (1847), and *The Little Savage* (1848).

31. William Hicks commanded an expeditionary force sent to block the Mahdi's advance up the Nile Valley.

32. The son's quest for his father through the expedition to Sudan provides an imperial geography for his journey into manhood, with the simultaneous objectives of recovering kin, compatriots, and perhaps a new colony.

33. On the links among gender, race, class, and state health and hygiene policies at the beginning of the twentieth century, see Anna Davin, "Imperialism and Motherhood."

34. Henty, p. 55.

35. On the conflation of character and physical superiority in the justifi-

cation of the British domination of India and the different Indian responses, see Chakrabarty, "*Khadi* and the Political Man." Also see, Sen, "Schools, Athletes, and Confrontation."

36. Henty's own biography attests to the importance he accorded physical culture: "Son of the owner of a coal mine and ironworks in Wales, he devoted his life (rather like Cecil Rhodes) to compensating for a sickly childhood." MacKenzie, *Propaganda and Empire*, p. 210. For an interesting assessment of the rise of a "physical culture" consumerism and its link to imperialism in this period of British history, see Budd, *The Sculpture Machine*. On the pervasiveness of "manly masculinity" as an ideal see Mangan and Walvin, eds. *Manliness and Morality*.

37. Bhabha, "Of Mimicry and Man." Bhabha examines the contradictory career of liberalism's subject in colonial discourse about the colonized Indian. Also see, Sinha, *Colonial Masculinity*.

38. On the cultural work performed by "Christian manliness" in service of the nation and in spite of class differences, see Alderson, *Mansex Fine*.

39. An elaboration of this point in the context of empire is in Mehta, *Liberalism and Empire*; in the context of gender relations, see Pateman, *Sexual Contract*. For a revision of Mehta's periodization and what she considers his reduction of the complexities of late eighteenth-century liberal thought, see Pitts, *A Turn to Empire*; her reading of Tocqueville's transformation into a strong proponent of France's colonization of Algeria is especially instructive, p. 189–226.

40. Interestingly, and perhaps expectedly, Henty's resolution of the liberal paradox is quite different for the metropole. Gregory's ultimate return to England as a full gentleman is accomplished not through his meritorious performance but by reclaiming his aristocratic family name and legacy.

41. Henty, p. 68.

42. Caillard, *A Lifetime in Egypt, 1876–1935*, p. 16.

43. Ibid., p. 116–17.

44. Stoler's work on class, race, and sexuality in the Dutch colonies has done much to defamiliarize and complicate the category of the colonizer; see, Stoler, "Sexual Affronts and Racial Frontiers," "Making Empire Respectable," and *Along the Archival Grain*. Also see, Clancy-Smith, "Marginality and Migration."

45. MacKenzie, "Introduction," in *Imperialism and Popular Culture*, p. 3.

46. Ibid. For an interesting reading of how the American frontier, to which a large number of middle-class Britons were migrating by the last decade of the nineteenth century, was incorporated into a similar imperial rhetoric of masculinity but in order to discursively compensate for a national loss, see Windholz, "An Emigrant and a Gentleman." For a more broad-

ranging analysis of how the "outside world" was essential for a British identity and a review of some of the historiography, see Linda Colley, "Britishness and Otherness."

47. Henty, p. 213. This passage provides an interesting spin on racial theories: one that reads pale whiteness as a sign of weakness and degeneration. It indexes Henty's larger didactic point about imperial masculinity's need for rejuvenation by appropriating to itself some of the raw, natural manliness of the native. I thank Amy Zalman for suggesting this reading of the passage.

48. Ibid., p. 98.

49. On militarism and public school boys, see J. A. Mangan, "'The Grit of our Forefathers': Invented Traditions, Propaganda and Imperialism," in *Imperialism and Popular Culture*, p. 113–39, and Mangan, *Athleticism in the Victorian and Edwardian Public Schools*.

50. For the far-reaching impact the "Indian" rebellion had on the organization and imagination of empire, see Heather Streets, *Martial Races*.

51. Henty, p. 97.

52. Ibid.

53. Ibid., p. 95.

54. With a dash of Freud on fetishism and a more convincing analysis of the symptomatic relationship between the hyper-masculinity of late nineteenth-century Victorian culture and homophobia, Rutherford reads Gregory's colonial fantasy as repressed homosexual desire in *Forever England*, p. 27–32. From the context of the American Civil War, a different permutation of desire disavowed and black masculinity becomes grounds for political solidarity. See Looby, "'As Thoroughly Black as the Most Faithful Philanthropist Could Desire.'"

55. Henty, p. 152. The Khalifa was the successor to the Mahdi, who died on June 22, 1885.

56. This hierarchization of martial valor was known to Egyptians, and nationalist reformers worked, as I will show in the next chapter, to redress this affront to their national honor.

57. The constitution of fallah, black, and Dervish as racial categories in colonial discourse is a matter that requires further study.

58. Milner, *England in Egypt*. This is a second printing of the thirteenth edition, which was published in 1920 on the occasion of the negotiations for Egyptian independence. Milner, as colonial secretary, was sent to Egypt on a fact-finding mission by the British government following the 1919 revolution. Previously, from 1890–92, he had served under Cromer as the financial adviser in Egypt. In fact, Cromer went on to recycle Milner's description of the troops in his own book, *Modern Egypt*.

59. TNA: PRO FO 633/57 Parr to Sir H. Drummond Wolff of January 17, 1886. Two enclosures from the battlefield were attached to prove his point.

60. Ibid.

61. The process of editing Parr's findings on the valor of Egyptian peasant soldiers and officers brings to mind Guha's levels of discourse that subtend the representation of peasant rebellions, "The Prose of Counter-Insurgency."

62. Caillard, p. 52.

63. The noble virtues previously ascribed to savages were gradually whittled away over the course of the eighteenth century as the natives stubbornly refused to behave as they should. On the ambivalence of early American views of the savage along the lines of status, see Karen Kupperman, *Settling with the Indians*. On the gendered dimension of the shift from noble to treacherous savage, see Carroll Smith-Rosenberg, "Captured Subjects/Savage Others."

64. Henty, p. 127.

65. Ibid., p. 173.

66. Said, *Orientalism*.

67. Stoler, "Making Empire Respectable."

68. The re-negotiation of class differences through pluck and personal strength apparently took one only so far. Indeed Gregory learns in the company of Colonel Wingate and after a decisive victory against the Khalifa's forces that the title of the Marquis of Langdale had passed to him since his grandfather, uncle, and father were all dead. Henty, p. 370.

69. Ibid., p. 383.

70. Ibid., p. 384.

71. Bayly, *The Birth of the Modern World, 1780–1914*, p. 399.

Chapter 2. Genealogy

1. Foucault, *Discipline and Punish*. The French original, under a slightly different title, *Surveiller et punir*, was published in 1975.

2. Stoler, *Race and the Education of Desire*. Foucault, *History of Sexuality*. Stoler reads race in Foucault through the lectures on biopower he gave at the Collège de France in 1976, now published in the volume *Society Must Be Defended*.

3. Stoler, *Race and the Education of Desire*, 53.

4. For a nuanced reexamination of the levels of anti-imperialist resistance and activist collaborations that took shape along what many had previ-

ously considered the margins of more central political fields, see Boehmer, *Empire, the National, and the Postcolonial, 1890–1920.*

5. Bernard Lewis's entry for "*efendi*" in the *Encyclopedia of Islam* (Leiden:
Brill, 1960) suggests that it passed into Turkish use between the thirteenth and fourteenth centuries from a Greek word that meant "Lord,
Master." It was officially erased from the books as an administrative designation of rank in Turkey in 1934. In Egypt, the ritual of investiture was
reinvigorated under the monarchy and was abolished after the revolution
of 1952 brought an end to the royal house of Muhammad Ali.

6. The government, however, would remain the largest employer of university graduates for well over a century.

7. The vagaries of fixing a definition of middle-class or bourgeois identity
is explored at length — five volumes — for the Euro-American nineteenth
century by Peter Gay in *The Bourgeois Experience*; for a lucid analysis of
the problem of definition in particular, see 1:17–44.

8. Ryzova, "Egyptianizing Modernity through the 'New *Effendiya*.'" Although there are great similarities between our conceptualizations of the
effendi as a cultural marker and a culture bearer for Egyptian modernity,
Ryzova's piece, and the volume as a whole, never fulfills the promise of
the title. Egypt is indeed situated in a richer field of social, political, and
cultural history through the fascinating new research on display, featuring work on topics ranging from modernity, marriage, media, and
crime to the teaching of history. However, since analysis of the colonial
circuits of epistemological categories and of subject formation is absent
from all of the studies, with the possible exception of Hanan Kholoussy's
chapter ("The Nationalization of Marriage in Monarchical Egypt"),
Egypt always seems only to be reacting to or reinventing cultural and
political forms — usually scripted as modernity — that originated elsewhere. Consequently, a basic question that a revisionist volume on the
period of nominal independence might ask — what is the nature of sovereignty? — remains unexplored, even in contributions treating political
parties (James Whidden, "The Generation of 1919") and foreign policy
(Fred H. Lawson, "Reassessing Egypt's Foreign Policy during the 1920s
and 1930s").

9. The Oxford English Dictionary (online) definition of "familiarization"
offers an interesting example from the eighteenth century: "By familiarization we reduce the force of formidable objects." This usage resonates
with Mehta's analysis in *Liberalism and Empire* of how the unfamiliar was
domesticated (another of the OED definitions) by liberal thinkers in their
paradoxical drives to universalize their principles and to dominate other

cultures. On the production of the "effeminate babu," see Sinha, *Colonial Masculinity*.

10. A. Milner, *England in Egypt*, 326.

11. On his notion of "two patriotisms" in a future imperial state, see the reading of Milner's *The Nation and the Empire* (1913) by Ian Christopher Fletcher, "Double Meanings: Nation and Empire in the Edwardian Era," in *After the Imperial Turn*, ed. Burton, 246–59.

12. "The temporal paradox of the subject is such that, of necessity, we must lose the perspective of a subject already formed in order to account for our own becoming." Butler, *The Psychic Life of Power*, 15.

13. Milner arrived in Egypt at the end of 1919 as the head of a commission sent to hear Egyptian grievances and to investigate the cause of the disturbances that year. For an excellent mapping of the flow of gendered tropes of morality from colonial rhetoric to the effendiyya's anticolonial nationalist discourse, see Pollard, *Nurturing the Nation*, esp. chapters 3, 6.

14. For a history of civil servants in Sudan told in part through personnel files, see Sharkey, *Living with Colonialism*.

15. Indeed, history was viewed as both a burden and an obstacle to colonial policies; teaching it was for a time proscribed in elementary schools and limited in secondary schools. Pollard, *Nurturing the Nation*, 116.

16. Ibid., 98–99.

17. I use "type" here rather than "class" in order to emphasize the cross-cultural construction of this category, which emerged as much through a racialized and gendered relationship to hegemonic colonial masculinity as through internal differentiations of elites and commoners as well as differentiations among other colonized and Eastern subjects. Moreover, "type" seems better suited to account for the "citational" nature of these kinds of classifications in colonial discourse (see next note).

18. Milner, *England in Egypt*, 322–23. Notice the similarity in the following observation from another colonial situation several decades later: "Why does the effendi constitute a major problem for Iraq? The answer is that most of the political and economic problems that will confront the country in the next ten years are problems which the effendi is not yet qualified to solve. The political and administrative problems might be better left in the hands of men of the Shaikh type and of Shaikhly family, whether 'educated' or not. This type of man comes from a governing stock and is accustomed to dealing with questions of politics or administration. The effendi in general is not yet his equal in this field." Main, *Iraq: From Mandate to Independence*, 235–36. I thank Sabri Ates for bringing this reference to my attention.

19. Cecil, *The Leisure of an Egyptian Official*, 101–4. Lord Cecil served in the

colonial administration of Egypt in different capacities during the first eighteen years of the twentieth century.

20. See the exhaustive discussion by Michael Gasper in *The Power of Representation* on the ambivalent interpellation of the peasant figure into Egyptian nationalist and reformist discourses from the late nineteenth century through 1919 as a backward Other and authentic Self. In the interwar period the same figure was more aggressively deployed as a nationalist icon; see Samia Kholoussi, "*Fallahin*: The 'Mud Bearers' of Egypt's 'Liberal Age,'" in *Re-Envisioning Egypt*, 277–314.

21. The effendi as a political problem would become a more pronounced worry for the British in the 1930s as the new generation of students and graduates were again radicalized in the context of failed negotiations for complete independence and economic hardships. See chapter 3. Also Ryzova, "Egyptianizing Modernity through the 'New *Effendiya*,'" 133–36.

22. Mehta, *Liberalism and Empire*, 35–36.

23. The following quote from *The Times* of London New Year's Day edition in 1888 illustrates this point: "The old East India Company did not develop the Bengali babu—the old East India Company left the Bengali as it found him—a cringing subservient eye servant, to be made use of as circumstances or occasion required. The Crown took the Babu in hand and developed the babu into his present state of loquacity and disloyalty." Quoted in Sinha, *Colonial Masculinity*, 2. The history of the colonial encounter charted here is remarkable when compared with Milner's quotes above, for they allow one to see how late nineteenth-century colonial discourse situated the pre-occupation government of Egypt and the East India Company in an identical temporal space: that unmarked by progress. At the same time, not all progress was desirable or permissible.

24. Mehta notes the contradiction in the two approaches to knowing the other (one assumes a certain essential and impenetrable mystery of the object and the other assumes mastery); nevertheless, he argues that as political strategies of exclusion they worked in tandem to produce a singular judgment: the need for colonial guidance. On inscrutability, see Brown, "The Ignorance and Inscrutability of the Egyptian Peasantry." On infantilism, see Pollard, *Nurturing the Nation*, 73–99.

25. On the colonial "politics of educating Egyptians," see Pollard, *Nurturing the Nation*, 114–18.

26. Ali Bey Fahmi Kamil, *Mustafa Kamil Basha fi 34 rabiʿan: Siratuhu wa aʿmaluhu min khutab wa ahadith wa rasaʾil siyasiyya wa ʿumraniyya* (Mustafa Kamil Basha in 34 springs: His biography and his works comprised

of speeches, narratives, and political and cultural dispatches) (Cairo: Al-Liwa' Press, 1908) [hereafter *MKB* followed by volume and page number]. Although there are some biographical interludes, most of the volumes are devoted to reproducing speeches, essays, and editorials written by the deceased. The biography was issued in nine volumes; the following section will only treat the first three. There is a brief mention of these volumes as forming part of a larger commemorative project in Gershoni and Jankowski, *Commemorating the Nation*, 157. Another significant biography of Mustafa Kamil that I will draw on in this chapter is Al-Rafi'i, *Mustafa Kamil: ba'ith al-haraka al-wataniyya—tarikh misr al-qawmi min sanat 1892 ila sanat 1908*.

27. For a reading of the Orientalist figuring of the Ottoman period within Egyptian nationalist historiography, see Piterberg, "The Tropes of Stagnation and Awakening in Nationalist Historical Consciousness." Salmoni has recently questioned the extent to which Orientalist tropes were incorporated into nationalist historiography by drawing a distinction between school textbooks and scholarly histories: textbooks emphasized the active role of Egyptians in their own modernization during the Muhammad Ali period. Salmoni, "Historical Consciousness for Modern Citizenship: Egyptian Schooling and the Lessons of History during the Constitutional Monarchy," in *Re-Envisioning Egypt*, 164–93. Contrary to Salmoni's reading (188, 193n73), Piterberg comments not on the passive inscription of Egyptians during the Muhammad Ali period in his "curricular analysis" but on the Orientalist framing of the Ottoman period, 1517–1798.

28. As Ryzova ("Egyptianizing Modernity through the 'New *Effendiya*,'" 127–29) has noted, this was in part because the bureaucratic effendiyya were the products of and entirely subject to the state. That this form of subjection and subordination would become anti-Ottoman and develop into a specifically ethnolinguistic nationalism was not inevitable. On the implications for Egyptian society of precolonial state building and modernization, see Fahmy, *All the Pasha's Men*; Hunter, *Egypt under the Khedives, 1805–1879*; and Toledano, *State and Society in Mid-Nineteenth-Century Egypt*.

29. In the grand march forward and with the demands of the modern state for new kinds of labor, the relatively well-to-do and their children were less likely to be subjected to state violence than the majority of the population, though some of their properties were expropriated. On the scale of violence involved in effecting the nineteenth-century social transformation of Egypt and the popular responses to it, see Tucker, *Women*

in Nineteenth-Century Egypt, 135–45; and Fahmy, *All the Pasha's Men*, 97–110, 252–62.

30. I thank Khaled Fahmy for helping me to see how this distinction between the modernizing Egyptian state and the colonial state might better situate effendi subjectivity historically.

31. It is not surprising that Egypt appeared in nationalist iconography as a woman, often as one whose honor was threatened. Pollard, *Nurturing the Nation*, 181–82; and Baron, *Egypt as Woman*, 57–81.

32. On the roles of Mustafa Kamil and the Watani Party in early nationalist politics, see, *inter alia*, Al-Rafi'i, *Mustafa Kamil*; 'Imara, *Al-Jami'a al-Islamiyya wa-1 -fikra al-qawmiyya 'inda Mustafa Kamil*; Ramadan, *Mustafa Kamil fi mahkama al-ta'rikh*; and Gershoni and Jankowski, *Egypt, Islam, and the Arabs*.

33. Muhammad Farid, *'Uẓama' al-rijal: dars li-rijal al-ghad* (Great Men: A Lesson for the Men of Tomorrow), in MKB, 1:5–53.

34. Ibid., 8.

35. President George W. Bush's deployment of a similar rhetoric of winning hearts and minds in the Middle East, albeit couched in terms of democracy-building projects, did not preclude the use of violent and deadly force.

36. Colonel Ahmad 'Urabi's eponymous movement to secure better terms for Arabic-speaking Egyptians in the army in 1881 sparked a revolt at other levels, which served as the casus belli for the British invasion and occupation of Egypt in 1882.

37. On the return of this genealogy for another redefinition of masculinity in the 1930s, see chapter 4.

38. Both of these figures could also be traced back further to the culture of pre-Islamic Arabia. Caton, *"Peaks of Yemen I Summon."*

39. In a sense this chapter treats the origins of the peculiarity of modern political authority in Egypt, which Mitchell did not explore; he chose instead to examine the precolonial understandings of language and power as a contrast. Mitchell, *Colonising Egypt*, 128–60, 131.

40. Jihad is a complex concept that connotes individual and collective Muslim struggles with spiritual, social, legal, military, and political matters. Historically it has been used to describe and to mobilize for both defensive and offensive military actions. A good recent survey is Bonner, *Jihad in Islamic History*; also see Peters's useful reader *Jihad in Classical and Modern Islam*.

41. "Authority would become something both mechanical and mysterious: as certain and straightforward as the process of meaning, and equally

metaphysical." Mitchell, *Colonising Egypt*, 154. Although the modern state in Egypt may have successfully achieved this form of authority, the claimants to become its representatives have had a much more uneven career authorizing themselves. It is here that the geographical asymmetry of "colonial" power appears most pronounced.

42. On the extension of or attempts to resolve this crisis of representation within literature around the same time, see Colla, "Anxious Advocacy."

43. Baron explores the use of family metaphors in imagining a new national identity in *Egypt as Woman*. She argues that the demise of harem slavery and the extended household, on the one hand, and the adoption of the bourgeois family model among the elite, on the other, were key factors in the reorientation of Egyptian identity in the late nineteenth century away from empire and toward the nation form. Also see Pollard, *Nurturing the Nation*, for a more sustained gender analysis of family and politics in the making of Egypt.

44. Farid, *'Uẓama' al-rijal*, 9. Mitchell comments on Mustafa Kamil's attraction to the notion of self-reliance (or self-help) in *Colonising Egypt*, 108–09. Kamil was taken by Samuel Smiles's ideas about character building developed in his famous book *Self-Help*, which was translated into Arabic in 1880. He had "self-help" and other key expressions from Smiles written on the walls of the school he established in 1898.

45. Farid, *'Uẓama' al-rijal*, 24.

46. Ibid., 34.

47. Ali Fahmi Kamil, "*Sirat walidihi*" (Biography of his father), in MKB, 1:54–62.

48. He was president from 1899 to 1902. Landau suggests that his friendship with Kamil contributed to the critical stance the council took toward the British administration. Landau, *Parliaments and Parties in Egypt*, 47–48.

49. Kamil, "*Sirat walidihi*," 55.

50. The rank of *al-yuẓbashi al-thani* is between lieutenant and captain and seems almost to have been designed to fetter the rise of Arabic-speaking officers in the military and government. As the working life of Mustafa Kamil's father came to an end, other Arabic-speaking officers led by Ahmad 'Urabi rose up against this and other discriminatory practices. On the creation of the modern Egyptian army and its officer corps, see Fahmy, *All the Pasha's Men*, 239–77. For the broader context of the 'Urabi movement, see Cole, *Colonialism and Revolution in the Middle East*.

51. His full name was given to reflect nine generations of his family: Captain Muhammad Effendi Fahmi bin Ahmad bin Yusuf bin Mahmud bin Ibrahim bin Husam al-Din bin Harun bin 'Ali bin Jamal al-Din.

52. A *mawlid* is usually a celebration to mark the birthday of the Prophet Muhammad, but in Egypt and elsewhere people considered to be saintly figures are also honored, sometimes with large celebrations named for them, such as the *mawlid* of Al-Sayyid Ahmad al-Badawi in Tanta.

53. We will see again in chapter 4 that this exact marking of birth dates became a sine qua non of Egyptian middle-class modernity by the interwar period.

54. For a similar point about later nationalist historiography, see Di-Capua, "'Jabarti of the 20th Century.'" On the incorporation of the Muhammad Ali period into Egyptian historiography as an emergence narrative, see Cuno, "Muhammad 'Ali and the Decline and Revival Thesis in Modern Egyptian History." As Cuno notes, although the "decline and revival thesis" became hegemonic, this was not the only possible interpretation of that period, as the likes of Muhammad Abduh and the British were quick to point out. He also notes (107) the pivotal role of Mustafa Kamil in popularizing this history, citing a speech he gave in Alexandria on May 21, 1902 (the year of the *hijri* centenary celebration of M. Ali's accession to the governorship of Egypt), in which he expounded on "the work of Muhammad Ali that revivified the nation and advanced it."

55. Mitchell, *Colonising Egypt*, 68–69.

56. Here one might pose a counterfactual question about the kind of relationship that would have prevailed between individual and state, on the one hand, and between subject and biopower, on the other, had the British not occupied Egypt in 1882. And hence what sort of effendi would have emerged?

57. According to Ibn Manzur's medieval lexicon *Lisan al-'arab*, the *wakil* "assumes (responsibility for) the affairs of the one entrusted to him."

58. Cromer, *Modern Egypt*, 2:172–73. Emphases added.

59. Mustafa Kamil, "[French] Translation of Speech Delivered in Alexandria, May 21, 1902," in *Egyptiens et Anglais* (Paris, 1906), 255–56. Emphasis added. Note the emergence in the last third of the nineteenth century of this same general framework for plotting the beginning of modern Egyptian history in the works of Tahtawi, Ali Mubarak, and Jurji Zaydan. Cuno, "Muhammad Ali," 103, and Di-Capua, "'Jabarti, of the 20th Century,'" 431.

60. Qasim Amin is most famous for two controversial works on the role of women in Muslim societies: *The Liberation of Women* and *The New Woman*, published in Cairo in 1899 and 1900, respectively.

61. Amin's rebuttal appeared under the title *Les Égyptiens: Réponse à M. Le Duc d'Harcourt.*

62. Charles François Marie, Le Duc d'Harcourt, *L'Égypte et Les Égyptiens* (Paris: Librairie Plon, 1893). He mentions in the preface that his observations were based on his last visit to Egypt in 1889.

63. Although the book calls into question Egyptian masculinity, it never explicitly names it as such; in this period, "manliness" was still the term in use. For a discussion of the emergence of the term "masculinity" and the discursive space it labeled in the American context, see Bederman, *Manliness and Civilization.*

64. "L'idée de résistance ouverte et de lutte paraît incompatible avec leur nature." Marie, *L'Égypte et Les Égyptiens*, 15.

65. In 1840–41, the British assisted the Ottomans in defeating Muhammad Ali's forces and retaking the Syrian lands that Sultan Mahmud II had been forced to give him in 1833. The harsh terms imposed by the Treaty of London required a massive reduction in the size of the army and an end to all government monopolies (which was actually dictated by a prior agreement signed by the Ottomans in 1838 known as the Treaty of Balta Liman). At the same time, the treaty granted the house of Muhammad Ali hereditary rights to the governorship of Egypt, a right his family exercised in different forms until 1952.

66. Marie, *L'Égypte et Les Égyptiens*, 22.

67. Ibid., 27–28. This deployment of the *fallah* as uncivilized and cowardly serves to underscore the politically interested appropriations of the same figure by the British and the nationalists as the repository of Egyptian values.

68. "Le progrès dépend d'une réforme religieuse et morale qu'il n'est ni dans les traditions de l'Angleterre de provoquer, ni dans son pouvoir de déterminer." (Progress would depend on a kind of religious and moral reform that is neither in the traditions of the English to incite, nor in its power to effect.) Ibid., 262.

69. Amin, *Les Égyptiens.* In the preface, he noted that he did not have the time required to redress all of the *inexactitudes* of d'Harcourt's book. He had to limit himself to attacking "the general laws that [d'Harcourt] wanted to deduce from the events that he observed" (5–6). Amin also pointed to the questionable methods used by Europeans to gather information for their books on Egypt, which were entirely based on secondary material and what was passed on to them by their guides (18–19).

70. Ibid., 11.

71. Ibid., 19.

72. Ibid., 22.

73. Ibid., 23.

74. Ibid., 24.

75. The reassessment of state–peasant relations in the Ottoman Empire has yielded several important studies over the past two decades. See, for example, Suraiya Faroqhi, "Town Officials, *timar-* holders, and Taxation: The Late Sixteenth-Century Crisis as Seen from Çorum," *Turcica* 18 (1986), 53–82; Rifa'at 'Ali Abou-El-Haj, *Formation of the Modern State: The Ottoman Empire Sixteenth to Eighteenth Centuries* (Albany: SUNY Press, 1991); Huri Islamoglu-Inan, *State and Peasant in the Ottoman Empire: Agrarian Power Relations and Regional Economic Development in Ottoman Anatolia during the Sixteenth Century* (Leiden; New York: E. J. Brill, 1994); Chalcraft, "Engaging the State: Peasants and Petitions in Egypt on the Eve of Colonial Rule."

76. Amin, *Les Égyptiens*, 82.

77. Ibid., 298.

78. Ibid., 27. Amin does not use the word "modern" here, but his idea of linearly evolving to a more civilized future from an uncivilized past is pregnant with a new notion of temporality; in fact, he insists on its universality as he pins the process of evolution to "la loi de la perfectibilité qui régit tout l'univers" (26).

79. "The socially informed body" that Amin and Kamil inhabited was different in a whole host of ways from other Egyptian bodies, especially those of the *fallahin*. This book attempts, in part, to illustrate the production of that difference. On the concept of *habitus*, see Bourdieu, *Outline of a Theory of Practice*.

80. It seems that in this context *al-shu'ur al-watani* might be translated as "nationalist consciousness." Letter from Paris dated September 24, 1906, in Al-Rafi'i, *Mustafa Kamil*, 233–34. Kamil recommended that the prize money be used as a contribution toward the foundation of a national university.

81. *MKB*, 2:242–43. Al-Rafi'i also reproduced the schedule in his biography of Kamil.

82. A parallel discourse on the importance of mothers to the proper upbringing of children was emerging in the same period. The difference would seem to reside in the end product—the kind of subject formed. In the reform impulse that fervently targeted mother and child, the mother emerged as a relational and subordinate subject defined by her function as wife, mother, or citizen. The father–son discourse and men's reform in general sought to produce a sovereign individual subject capable of governing others. I discuss this issue for the interwar period, when there is the additional emphasis on governing oneself.

83. *MKB*, 1:107.

84. Ibid., 108.

85. Ibid., 109.

86. On kinship and nationalism, see Stevens, *Reproducing the State*. Molly Nolan asked me to think here about the language of universal rights and the different models of family occasioned by modern discourses on the nation. Although this is a very important and interesting question, I cannot pursue it here. A helpful treatment is John Horne's recent explication of how family metaphors, be they paternalistic or fraternal, may have varied according to historical context and how their "political legitimacy" depended on numerous factors, but their shared exclusionary effects beg for an analysis of images of masculinity. Writing of the American and French revolutions, he suggests, "Part of the ideological power unleashed by those events came from the way they expanded the repertory of masculine authority." Horne, "Masculinity in Politics and War in the Age of Nation-States and World Wars, 1850–1950," 23.

Chapter 3. Institution

1. El-Shakry, "Schooled Mothers and Structured Play"; and Pollard, *Nurturing the Nation*, 100–131.

2. While this point can be and has been overstated, the argument here is not about actual reform projects, which were always limited and often contradictory, but about the terms by which a trajectory of reform was normalized.

3. Bowman, *Middle-East Window*, 67.

4. Ibid.

5. Bowman was filling his book with nostalgia and justifications for colonialism just as the British ability to control Egyptian affairs was being curtailed by the terms of the Anglo-Egyptian Treaty of 1936 and the Montreux Convention of 1937, which finally abolished the Capitulations granting special privileges to foreign nationals.

6. Lane, *Manners and Customs of the Modern Egyptians*, 37.

7. I look here in very broad terms at a vastly complex history whose surface has only been scratched in the markedly different studies — both methodologically and in terms of historical perspective — of Peter Gran and Timothy Mitchell. Gran, *Islamic Roots of Capitalism*, and Mitchell, *Colonising Egypt*.

8. Tignor, *Modernization and British Colonial Rule in Egypt, 1882–1914*, 39.

9. Cole, *Colonialism and Revolution in the Middle East*.

10. The French had brought two presses with the army of invasion in 1798,

both of which they used to publish decrees, regulations, scientific studies, a newspaper, and a magazine (in French).

11. Ridwan, *Ta'rikh Matba'a Bulaq*, 41.

12. For an analysis of the types of texts produced by the Bulaq Press, see Heyworth-Dunne, "Printing and Translations under Muhammad 'Ali of Egypt." See also, Ridwan, *Ta'rikh Matba'a Bulaq*. A synopsis of the significance of this press is given by Verdery, "The Publications of the Bulaq Press under Muhammad 'Ali of Egypt."

13. The women's press has received significant attention by historians, most notably by Baron, *The Women's Awakening in Egypt*. Also see Booth, *May Her Likes Be Multiplied*.

14. Berlant, *The Queen of America Goes to Washington City*. I thank Andrew Ivaska for directing me to this reference.

15. This approach is also warranted in part because of the absence of concrete circulation data. Although in general scholars know that the immediate cause and in a sense the effect of the discourses generated by these magazines originated in the appearance of the modern effendi class, reception can be gauged only by mapping the internal structure and development of a specific discourse such as physical culture and then connecting them to other modes by which it extended into the social domain. This chapter focuses on the mapping, and subsequent chapters proceed with both strategies.

16. Whether that object was the nation could still be argued, but here an open-ended approach to the "textual performance" does not foreclose such a debate.

17. For example, see Hourani, *Arabic Thought in the Liberal Age, 1789–1939*, 245.

18. For the beginnings of such a revision of modernity's tale, see Abu Manneh, *Studies on Islam and the Ottoman Empire in the Nineteenth Century*, and Salzmann, *Tocqueville in the Ottoman Empire*.

19. *Pace* scholars who pursue alternatives to the standard, the presumption here is that an unaccented modernity is impossible. See Mitchell, "The Stage of Modernity."

20. Mitchell, *Colonising Egypt*, 65–66, 98–99.

21. Wellington was rumored to have said, "Waterloo was won on the playing fields of Eton." *Al-Hilal* (November 1, 1923), 120.

22. A number of recent studies of power in nineteenth-century Egypt are informed by the Foucaultian approach. See Fahmy, "The Anatomy of Justice" and "Medicine and Power"; Peters, "Controlled Suffering" and "Egypt and the Age of the Triumphant Prison." For the early twentieth

century and a consideration of the subject of medical discourse, see Abu-gideiri, "The Scientisation of Culture."

23. Budd, *The Sculpture Machine*.

24. Green, *Fit for America*.

25. The cognate, *rawda*, can mean a nursery for plants or children.

26. One of the most famous examples in classical Islamic writing comes from the theologian, philosopher, and Sufi Abu Hamid al-Ghazali (1058–1111 CE). Book 22, *Riyadat al-nafs*, of his magisterial work *Ihya' 'Ulum al-Din* (The revival of the religious sciences) is dedicated to the delineation of a path toward spiritual elevation through the cultivation of good character. Perhaps it was not coincidental that this work was republished in Cairo at the end of the nineteenth century (Al-Maktaba al-Azhariyya, 1317 AH). This may index the competition — as conventional historiography would have it — between secular liberal and Islamic modernist camps to redefine the conceptual landscape; nonetheless, the subject of these discourses was to be cultivated as modern. The translator's introduction is a helpful primer on the concept; see T. J. Winter, "Introduction," in *Al-Ghazali on Disciplining the Soul and on Breaking the Two Desires: Books XXII and XXIII of the Revival of the Religious Sciences* (Cambridge: Islamic Texts Society, 1995).

27. Tahtawi, *al-Murshid al-amin lil-banat wa al-banin*.

28. Attar was the subject of Gran's mistitled study *Islamic Roots of Capitalism*.

29. Tahtawi, *al-Murshid al-amin lil-banat wa al-banin*, 59.

30. Ibid., 207. On the ubiquitous nature of play in human history, see the classic work by Huizinga, *Homo Ludens*.

31. In *Colonising Egypt*, Mitchell argues that by the end of the nineteenth century the body signified political community in ways that reflected a changed relationship between society and state. He writes, "The body is no longer something composed of social groups forming its various limbs and organs. It exists apart from people themselves, as a sort of machinery. . . . Individuals are not parts of the body, but uniform particles that flow within it. The body's mechanical parts serve to channel, regulate and set in motion theses moving particles." (156) In the discourse of physical culture, the embodied self was increasingly targeted as a site of reform precisely because of its particular impact on the national body.

32. The easy crossover from *riyada* to *la'b* is an indication that *riyada* was still a malleable term; it had not yet assumed the strict definition of sport.

33. Tahtawi, *al-Murshid al-amin lil-banat wa al-banin*, 332.

34. Ibid., 391–93.
35. *Al-Muqtataf* (March 1879), 270–72, 292–95. The adjectival noun clause that *al-riyada* forms when joined with *al-jasad*, *al-badan*, or *al-jism* (all of which translate as "the body") could connote body disciplining, training, exercise, or sports depending on the usage in context. Starting in this period, the last quarter of the nineteenth century, one sees the first attempts to capture in Arabic the contemporaneous European field of discourse and practice generally labeled physical culture. My translations of *al-riyada al-jasadiyya*, *al-riyada al-badaniyya*, and *al-riyada al-jismiyya* will slip between exercise, physical culture, physical training, and sports as the context warrants.
36. *Al-Muqtataf* (March 1879), 270–72.
37. Ibid., 292–95.
38. Ibid., 294–95.
39. The context supports this translation, but a more literal rendering would be "Adults' exercise."
40. *Al-Muqtataf* (June 1, 1882), 76–81.
41. Ibid., 77. The Gezira, one of the islands on the Nile, is today the heavily populated but elite neighborhood of Al-Zamalek. At this time it was a lush, green island with only a few villas of the upper class, one of which was the mansion built by Khedive Isma'il to house Empress Eugenie during her visit to Egypt to attend the ceremonies celebrating the opening of the Suez Canal in 1869. Today, the mansion houses the main lobby, restaurants, bars, and reception halls of a Marriott Hotel.
42. The form of the nation remained ambiguous, which is why I have refrained from describing this subject as nationalist.
43. *Al-Muqtataf* (June 1, 1882), 81.
44. The call for a revitalized Egyptian masculine body was not only made in a secular modernist register. Nevertheless, as I will show in the next chapter, in other registers, too, the desirability of this call was rarely subject to debate.
45. *Al-Muqtataf* (June 1, 1882), 77.
46. In *Colonialism and Revolution in the Middle East*, Cole alludes to the male gender politics that may have been behind the bombing of Alexandria. The bombing was ostensibly in response to the alleged fanatical Muslim massacre of Europeans in Alexandria on June 11, 1882. Cole writes, "The manner in which the British diplomatic corps and press in particular transmogrified the Alexandria riot into an 'Urabist 'massacre' of the 'Christians' may have been as overtly dishonest as Elbert E. Farman, the American ambassador, thought. This interpretation of the events, how-

ever, certainly became the turning point for the Revolution, insofar as such a 'massacre' constituted a matter of honor that absolutely required a British elite trained at Eton and other public schools to respond in a 'manly' (i.e., violent) manner" (239).

47. Recent studies of colonized subjects in the metropole illustrate their complex views on the local society. See, for example, Burton, *At the Heart of the Empire*. On a most intriguing and suggestive encounter between Gandhi and London vegetarians, see Leela Gandhi, *Affective Communities*, 67–75. Although mostly speculative, it is indeed generative to think that the possibility of the uniquely Gandhian politics might be traced back to this positive association between the young Gandhi and metropolitan subjects around the gendered question of vegetarianism.

48. The exceptional criticisms of what were thought to be the lax morals of Western men and women only seemed to confirm the rule.

49. Demolins, *À Quoi tient la supériorité des Anglo-Saxons?*; Zaghlul, *Sirr taqaddum al-Inkliz al-Saksuniyyin*. See Mitchell, *Colonising Egypt*, 110–11, for a discussion of the broad dissemination and impact of this work.

50. 'Umar, *Hadir al-Misriyyin aw sirr ta'akhkhurihim*, 199.

51. On the importance of Jawish to Egypt's early period of nation building, see Lockman, "Exploring the Field: Lost Voices and Emerging Practices in Egypt, 1882–1914," 137–53.

52. Jawish, *Ghunyat al-mu'addibin fi al-turuq al-haditha lil-tarbiyya wa al-ta'lim*, 34.

53. Ibid., 37.

54. *Al-Muqtataf* (February 1891), 335.

55. For a recent elaboration of the process of redefining women's gender roles in modernity, see Abu-Lughod, "Introduction: Feminist Longings and Postcolonial Conditions," in Abu-Lughod, ed., *Remaking Women*, 3–31; also see chapter 4 by el-Shakry, "Schooled Mothers and Structured Play." For a discussion of a similar shift in the gendering of women in Iran during the same period, see chapter 3 by Afsaneh Najmabadi, "Crafting an Educated Housewife in Iran," 91–125, in the same volume.

56. This became the general argument for women's exercise at least until the end of the Second World War.

57. *Al-Muqtataf* (May 1898), 394.

58. *Al-Hilal* (August 1899, June 1900, November 1901, March 1902). Pharaonicism, the attempt to locate the roots of modern Egyptians in the ancient civilization, did not take off until the 1920s, but this is certainly an interesting precursor. This article would fit into Colla's framing, in *Conflicted Antiquities*, of archaeology as a contested site of nationalism going back to the nineteenth century. Also see Reid, *Whose Pharaohs?*

59. I take up the topic of desiring muscular bodies in chapter 5, with a focus on weightlifting and wrestling.

60. For a recent study that examines the importance of the figure of Eugen Sandow to the emergence of a muscular masculinity at the end of the nineteenth century in America, see Kasson, *Houdini, Tarzan, and the Perfect Man*, chapter 1.

61. *Al-Hilal* (November 1901), 79.

62. As we saw in the case of *riyada*, the Arabic language had not yet fixed the semantic limits of terms within the physical culture discourse emerging on a global scale at roughly the same time. A specific term for bodybuilder would not be coined until a couple of decades later, when the sport became a truly popular, institutionalized practice.

63. His was a precursor to the much more successful business, still in operation today, built by Charles Atlas. See http://www.charlesatlas.com. For a discussion of the development of physical culture and Sandow's role in the process, see Budd, *The Sculpture Machine*.

64. Al-Faraj, *Ruwad al-riyada fi Misr* (The pioneers of sports in Egypt), 30–31, 55–56, 68–69.

65. "Rabbu ajsamakum qabla 'aqulakum," *al-Hurriyya* (January 22, 1911), 1–2.

66. *Al-Hilal* (August 1, 1899), 638–43; (April 1, 1900), 393–99; (May 1, 1900), 457–61; (May 15, 1900), 492–95; (June 15, 1900), 549–55.

67. To emphasize its cultural specificity, Demolins left the English expression "self help" without translating it.

68. Demolins, *À Quoi tient la supériorité des Anglo-Saxons*, 111.

69. *Al-Hilal* (August 1899), 639.

70. "Hidden Agents in Society," *al-Hilal* (May 1, 1899), 457–61.

71. *Al-Hilal* (August 1899), 638.

72. Ibid., 640.

73. *Al-Hilal* (April 1, 1900); (May 1, 1900); (May 15, 1900).

74. This was especially true after the revolution in 1919, when Egypt gained nominal independence. The 1920s and 1930s will be the focus of the next chapter.

75. The subject who could not will be examined in depth in the final chapter.

76. This is D. Scott's formulation, developed in *Conscripts of Modernity*.

77. Demolins, *À Quoi tient la supériorité des Anglo-Saxons*, 296.

78. Kamil, *Egyptiens et Anglais*, 289.

79. This same theme, which celebrated the *shabab* as a political vanguard, would recur in Egyptian social and cultural life right up to the Free Officers' coup of 1952, when it would be reconfigured and deployed again within the new sociopolitical context. By the 1930s such youthful energy

was often a cause for concern even among the leaders of the Wafd Party. I will address this further in the next chapter. On Mustafa Kamil, see chapter 2.

80. The material for this section comes from the private archive of the National Club, and particularly from the *Mahadir al-jam'aiyya al-'umumiyya li Al-Nadi al-Ahli*, 1907–38 [hereafter *MJA* followed by the date].

81. *MJA*, February 25, 1908.

82. Two other Egyptian sporting clubs had been founded before this date: Nadi Hockey Bulaq in 1903 (which later became Al-Sikka al-Hadid) and Nadi al-Najma al-Hamra' in 1905 (which later became Nadi al-Muwazzafin, then al-Olymbi al-Iskandari). The future nemesis (on the football field) of Al-Nadi al-Ahli, al-Zamalek, was founded by a Belgian judge on the Mixed Courts in 1911 and was named the Mixed Team, gesturing toward both its international membership and the institutional location of its founder. Its name was changed to Nadi Faruk in 1944 and Nadi al-Zamalek after the revolution in 1952. The rivalry between Al-Ahli and Al-Zamalek continues to the present and marks the major rift in Egyptian sports allegiances. Even though Al-Zamalak is today a fully Egyptian club, residues of its colonial past can still be felt in people's reactions to someone who claims to be a Zamalkawi (a fan of the Zamalek team).

83. A testament to this is the recent publication of Al-Mistakawi's *Al-Nadi al-Ahli, 1907–1997: butula fi al-riyada wal-wataniyya* (The national club, 1907–1997: A leading role in sports and in nationalism).

84. In a lecture on the life of Tahtawi, Peter Gran made the important point that it was necessary to extricate him from the Orientalist narratives that continued to position his life and contributions to Egyptian history as beginning with his time in France. He explores the intellectual formation of Tahtawi before his sojourn to France to argue that a complex epistemological base was already there, onto which his experiences in France added another layer. While agreeing with Gran's major point about the way in which the *nahda* thinkers are usually conceived within a Eurocentric paradigm, a generative deconstruction of this position requires examining the nature of the cultural translations effected by these figures, whether the axis of the intellectual encounter was rural-urban, low-high culture, or East-West. This would enable a more nuanced understanding of their formation in colonial modernity while avoiding their reduction into static, one-dimensional, culturally pure figures. "Egyptian Studies as Oriental Despotism: Tahtawi as a Blank Slate in Paris," lecture delivered at the AUC School of Humanities and Social Science

Research Scholars/Fellows Seminar, October 3, 2001. An online text version is available as "Tahtawi in Paris," http://weekly.ahram.org.

85. Sami, *Taqwim al-Nil.*

86. *MJA*, December 28, 1923.

87. It was hard to ascertain in the archives whether the reluctance was on the part of Egyptian or British representatives in the Ministry of Education. However, in spite of Bowman's championing of sports education, given Cromer's efforts to trim costs wherever possible, the ambivalence was more likely of British provenance.

88. *Brugram qism al-mu'allimin al-'arabi al-tabi' li-madrasa al-mubtadiyan* 1895, 21. (Maktabat Wizarat al-Tarbiyya wa al-Ta'lim [Library of the Ministry of Education] [hereafter MWTT].

89. Ibid.

90. Ibid.

91. Department of Public Instruction Annual Report of 1896, MWTT.

92. Department of Public Instruction Annual Report of 1897, MWTT.

93. *Al-Hilal* (August 1, 1899), 638–43.

94. This is the same series discussed in the preceding section.

95. Dar al-Watha'iq al-Qawmiyya (hereafter DWQ): Mahfuzat Majlis al-Wuzara,' Sharikat wa Jam'iyyat [box 4B], Nawadi Adabiyya wa Riyadiyya, Tusun to Said of September 6, 1913. In his book, *Ruwwad al-riyada fi Misr*, Faraj dates the formation of the EOC to 1910, but he does not offer evidence of how he arrived at that date.

96. DWQ: Mahfuzat Majlis al-Wuzara,' Sharikat wa Jam'iyyat [box 4B], Nawadi Adabiyya wa Riyadiyya, Hikmat to Said of October 16, 1913.

97. Ibid., Said to Sirry of September 11, 1913, November 2, 1913, and December 9, 1913.

98. Ibid., Tusun to Said of March 4, 1914 (EOC constitution enclosed).

99. Ibid.

100. See, for example, *al-Al'ab al-Riyadiyya* 2/1 (May 23, 1923), 1.

101. For a poignant discussion of this dimension of colonialism, see Nandy, *Intimate Enemy.*

102. See the discussion in chapter 1. For a general overview of the construction of modern masculinity as an ideal form in European societies, see Mosse, *The Image of Man.* For an introduction to more specialized studies, see the useful new volume *Masculinities in Politics and War,* edited by Dudink, Hagemann, and Tosh.

103. Although the contours were different, the same unfinished projects abounded in the West as well.

Chapter 4. Association

1. An exception is Goldberg's consideration of the social and economic causes of the peasant role in the revolution of 1919, "Peasants in Revolt—Egypt 1919."

2. On the emergence of an Ottoman–Egyptian elite that gradually incorporated more of the rural notability, see Toledano, *State and Society in Mid-Nineteenth-Century Egypt*.

3. The dynasty was officially ushered from history as a political entity when the new Turkish government in opposition eliminated the sultanate on November 1, 1922, and forced the abdication of the thirty-sixth and last Ottoman sultan, Mehmet VI Vahideddin.

4. Fuad, the youngest son of Khedive Isma'il, succeeded his brother Sultan Husayn Kamil upon his death in October 1917.

5. DWQ: Mahfuzat Abidin, Jama'iyyat [box 211], Jama'iyyat al-Kashafa fi Misr, "Report of the Administrative Committee of the Egyptian Boy Scouts Association for the Year Ending 14 November 1920." Also see "Al-Kashafa al-Misriyya: Kayfa Nushi'at, Kayfa Matat, Kayfa Ba'athat" (Egyptian Scouting: How it was established, how it died, and how it was reborn), *Misr al-Haditha al-Mussawara* 5/3 (August 8, 1929), 10–11.

6. Assemblies were banned by decree on October 18, 1914. Ramadan, *Tatawwur al-Haraka al-Wataniyya fi Misr, 1918–1936*, 1:59.

7. Baden-Powell was the founder of the Scouting movement, which spread almost immediately, as troops were formed haphazardly, upon the publication of his *Scouting for Boys* in 1908. This was a revised version for boys of a military manual he had written based on his experiences fighting wars in southern Africa. There is perhaps no more glaring example of how colonial and modern selves were mutually constitutive than the life of the legendary Baden-Powell. For themes raised in chapter 1, see his earlier publication, *The Matabele Campaign, 1896; Being a Narrative of the Campaign in Suppressing the Native Rising in Matabeleland and Mashonaland* (London: Methuen, 1897). Also see Springhall, *Youth, Empire and Society*, 53–70; and MacDonald, *Sons of the Empire*.

8. "Kashafat al-Awlad," *al-Muqtataf* (June 1914), 566–67. See also *Rawdat al-Madaris al-Misriyya* 1/1 (September 15, 1915).

9. "Kashafat al-Awlad," ibid.

10. *Al-Al'ab al-Riyadiyya* 1/1 (May 16, 1923), 9.

11. *Al-Muqtataf* (November 1914), 570.

12. Ibid.

13. Deeb, *Party Politics in Egypt*.

14. Before the war Zaghlul was a minister of education and a member of the Legislative Assembly. He came from a relatively wealthy peasant family, and his career had been catapulted upward in 1896 by his marriage to Safiyya, the daughter of Mustafa Fahmi, scion of an aristocratic Turkish family and prime minister for five terms. Ibid., 39.

15. Al-Rafiʻi, *Thawra 1919*, 119–20.

16. Ibid., 120. Interestingly, Al-Rafiʻi failed to mention here Zaghlul's own anti-British reputation.

17. The four additional members were Muhammad Mahmud, Ahmad Lutfi al-Sayyid, Abd al-Latif al-Mukabati, and Muhammad Ali Alluba.

18. Al-Rafiʻi, *Thawra 1919*, 123.

19. For a detailed account of the events of the revolution, see Al-Rafiʻi, *Thawra 1919*.

20. TNA: PRO FO 848/8 "Memorandum on the Egyptian Situation" of March 25, 1920. For an account of McPherson's career as a colonial officer, see Barry Carman and John McPherson eds., *Bimbashi McPherson: A Life in Egypt* (London: British Broadcasting Corporation, 1983).

21. TNA: PRO FO 848/13 J. M. N. Jeffries, "Egypt Boy Rule: Artificial Risings," *Daily Mail*, January 30, 1920 (included in Milner Mission series). Jeffries's other reports from Egypt are incredible for the unmasked racist and infantilizing rhetoric with which he represented nationalist demonstrators. A particularly glaring example of this is his report from Qus, "Boy 'Patriots' in Egypt: Demonstrations to Order," *Daily Mail*, March 11, 1920, also in FO 848/13. See also the reports of Valentine Chirol in FO 848/24.

22. Al-Rafiʻi, *Thawra 1919*, 235–36. The British ordered the group to disband on April 18 or be subject to arrest.

23. Ibid., 196–97. These nonnormative, or nonpolitical, actions included attacking Europeans, killing soldiers, and destroying supposedly foreign-owned shops (often belonging to longtime residents of Egypt) and public utilities.

24. For a recent study of the revolution based on "colloquial" sources and analyzed using Bakhtin's notion of the carnivalesque, see Fahmy, "Popularizing Egyptian Nationalism," 243–99.

25. For a treatment of the autonomous participation of students in the revolution of 1919, which also mentions their relationship to the other problematic demonstrators, see Al-Mutallib, *Dawr al-talaba fi thawrat 1919*, esp. 45, 53.

26. For a recent work that attempts to capture the domain of politics as the

scene of everyday practices in Turkey, see Navaro-Yashin, *Faces of the State*.

27. See note 6 in DWQ: Mahfuzat Abidin, Jama'iyyat [box 211], Jama'iyyat al-Kashafa fi Misr, "Report of the Administrative Committee of the Egyptian Boy Scouts Association for the Year Ending 14 November 1920."

28. Ibid., see note 10.

29. Ibid., see note 14.

30. According to one definition, this would constitute a youth movement. Springhall, *Youth, Empire and Society*, 13.

31. This syndicate was established by the Hizb al-Watani in 1909, and it had eleven branches. The involvement of the labor unions and capitalists in the encouragement of sports and the fielding of teams grew increasingly significant by the 1920s. Teamwork and bodily discipline were valued attributes when embodied by the new industrial employee. Unfortunately, I was unable to explore the worker and the workplace as avenues through which organized sports were developed and a new approach to the body was articulated. For a glimpse of this phenomenon, see Goldberg, *Tinker, Tailor, and Textile Worker*. For a discussion of the Manual Trades Workers Union and its relationship to the National Party, see Beinin and Lockman, *Workers on the Nile*.

32. *Majallat al-Tijariyya al-Nubiyya* 1/1 (July 17, 1921), 13; 11/1 (October 2, 1921), 173.

33. Ibid. 3/1 (July 31, 1921), 46.

34. The evidence for this comes from a short biography of Abd Allah Ali Bashir, one of the founding members of the troop in 1920 and a Scoutmaster since 1928. *Al-Dalil* (February 1938), 10. On the problem of belonging and other issues faced by contemporary Nubians, see Elizabeth Smith, "Tributaries in the Stream of Civilization."

35. TNA: PRO FO 848/6, Part B.

36. TNA: PRO FO 848/6, Part B, "Evidence of Mr. J. M. Furness (Head Master, Khedivia Secondary School), 9 Jan 1920."

37. The linkage between student radicalism and "harim ladies" would be repeatedly made in British analyses of Egyptian politics. See TNA: PRO FO 371/10074, E11165, "A report on the political situation in Egypt in 1924." This is essentially a political strategy report in which colonial officials suggest the proper course to pursue in order to maintain British and British supporters' interests in Egypt. After giving brief descriptions of King Fuad and the political parties—the Wafd, the Constitutional Liberals, and the Watanists—the report discusses the influence of students and women in politics:

The students are of two kinds. The product of the Government and private primary and secondary schools and the higher colleges and the religious students of the Azhar and kindred institutions. They are all violent politicians, perhaps 80% of Wafdist or Zaghloulist complexion and the remainder Watanist. They provide an ideal medium for the spread of propaganda, and Zaghloul did them no more than justice when he named them "his soldiers." Gangs of students on motor bicycles can be dispatched at a moment's notice to round up recalcitrant electors or break up opposition meetings, and their influence permeates all classes of society.

The Harim ladies have become ardent politicians and most of the younger ones belong to political organisations of an extreme nature like the "League of Mothers of the Future." Their influence is greatest amongst the upper and middle classes and is not without effect upon the younger students.

38. TNA: PRO FO 848/6, Part B, "Evidence of Mr. Wells (Director-General, Department of Technical, Industrial and Commercial Education, Ministry of Education), 12 Jan 1920."

39. Statistical data for the rest of the interwar period points to the continuity of the British conviction that controlling education was the best way to maintain control of Egypt. Although the number of government jobs rose significantly during this period and Egyptians started to fill these new positions as well as to replace foreigners in older positions, the Ministry of Education remained an exception. The number of foreign employees of the ministry rose from 163 in 1922 to 786 in 1936, a 482 percent rise. Deeb, *Party Politics in Egypt*, 316. Employment opportunities in the police force briefly expanded after the revolution in 1919. In 1921, 31 European officers served in Cairo and 29 in Alexandria, supported by 131 and 199 European constables, respectively. TNA: PRO FO 371/7765, Allenby (Cairo) to FO Eastern Department, "Egypt, Annual Report of 1921: Chapter VI, sub-section Public Security," cited in Thomas, *Empires of Intelligence*, 39.

40. This myth was buoyed by the unilateral diplomatic move of HM Government declaring Egypt independent on February 28, 1922.

41. Unlike the metropolitan juridico-political contexts in which a similar prefiguring — of the "reasonable man" as white, male, and bourgeois — had occurred, the colonial of Egyptian modernity became a repeated and repeatable obstacle to the sustained expansion of its representational institutions in even that narrow, liberal sense. The colonial limits to institutional expansion in the broader biopolitical sense are perhaps more interesting to consider. See Esmeir, "The Work of Law in the Age of Empire."

42. *Misr al-haditha al-musawwara* 5/3 (August 7, 1929), 10–11. The militarization of segments of the Boy Scouts was probably related to the history of secret societies that began to emerge in Egypt by the end of the nineteenth century and that carried out attacks against British troops and assassinations of political figures. See Badrawi, *Political Violence in Egypt 1910–1924*; and Reid, "Political Assassination in Egypt, 1910–1954."

43. Zaghlul's initial return from exile lasted only eight months; he was exiled again in December 1921 (to the Seychelles) for threatening political violence. The British were dragging their feet in negotiating a treaty that would grant Egypt full independence, and Zaghlul in response played his populist card, delivering speeches calling for "total independence or violent death." Al-Rafi'i, *Fi a'qab al-thawra al-misriyya — thawrat 1919* (In the wake of the Egyptian Revolution of 1919), 45. He returned to Egypt in September 1923.

44. For a lively account of this period's political history, see Marsot, *Egypt's Liberal Experiment*, 73–170.

45. On the ideological disagreements among the effendiyya of the revolutionary era, see James Whidden, "The Generation of 1919."

46. For a critique of Egyptian historiography for generally "emplotting" a heroic bourgeois teleology, see Vitalis, *When Capitalists Collide*. Interesting new work that attempts to conceive of politics more broadly include Pollard, *Nurturing the Nation*, and el-Shakry, *The Great Social Laboratory*.

47. Marsot, *Egypt's Liberal Experiment*, 6.

48. Ibid., 249.

49. Chatterjee, *Nationalist Thought and the Colonial World* and *The Nation and Its Fragments*.

50. Chatterjee, *The Nation*, 13.

51. *Sahifat al-Kashafa al-Misriyya* 1/1 (April 24, 1921).

52. Ibid (May 1921). Baden-Powell was visiting Egypt in his new capacity as the Chief Scout of the World, an honor he received at the first international Scouting jamboree in 1920.

53. Disorder, sloth, and indolence were key offenses.

54. Publicity for the Scouting magazine was provided by other publications. *Al-Muqtataf* (November 1921), 503, announced the publication of the fifth issue of *Sahifat al-Kashafa al-Misriyya*.

55. See note 9 in DWQ, Mahfuzat Abidin, Jama'iyyat [box 211], Jama'iyya al-Kashafa fi Misr, "Report of the Administrative Committee of the Egyptian Boy Scouts Association for the Year Ending 14 November 1920."

56. Ibid., see note 11.

57. *Al-Al'ab al-Riyadiyya* 10/2 (April 7, 1924), 3–6. This paper presented

a four-page spread with numerous photographs of the events and the troops in attendance.

58. Ibid. In fact, his picture adorns the cover of this issue. The caption reads as follows: "This historical picture inscribes in the life of the development of nations the great and honorable head of state Sa'd Pasha Zaghlul on the occasion of the opening of the first parliament in the history of Egypt on March 15, 1924."

59. Marsot, *A Short History of Modern Egypt*, 83. Marsot uses the term *fallah* (peasant) to describe Zaghlul in order to distinguish him and his base of support from the previous rulers of Egypt, who for thousands of years were apparently considered foreigners.

60. TNA: PRO FO 848/24 Milner Mission, Cuttings from English Newspapers, *Manchester Dispatch*, November 11, 1920.

61. El-Messiri, *Ibn al-Balad*. I examine the notion of *ibn al-balad* as an ideal type of masculinity in chapter 8 within the context of a larger treatment of sovereignty and *al-futuwwa*. I consider how traditional terms of masculinity were used to mediate the modern effendi masculinity of nationalist discourse while probing the limits of both.

62. Zaghlul's life story was conducive to nationalist appropriation, as it was significantly coextensive with that of Egypt. He was born around 1859, had served on numerous national bodies from their start, and was near the end of his life when he became prime minister. He died on August 24, 1927.

63. Although Zaghlul remained highly influential in parliamentary politics, he never again held the post of prime minister.

64. Two recent works that take steps in this direction in another context are E. Thompson, *Colonial Citizens* and Watenpaugh, *Being Modern in the Middle East*.

65. *Al-Al'ab al-Riyadiyya* 10/2 (April 7, 1924), 4.

66. Ibid.

67. Ibid. This voice seems to echo Furness and Wells.

68. Ahmad Husayn's Young Egypt (Misr al-Fatat) was the main allegedly fascist element in Egypt. The term was only loosely applicable. In fact, Husayn initially expressed antifascist sentiments, and even when the group exhibited sympathy for fascist Italy, according to Jankowski's study, its commitment to fascism was never that profound. Jankowski, *Egypt's Young Rebels*, 20–21, 58–60.

69. Marsot, *Liberal Experiment*, 36, 191–92. In one of his tracts, Hasan al-Banna addresses the issue of the young effendiyya who were being forced to compromise their manhood in their quest for the increasingly elusive government appointment. See *"Hal nahnu qawm 'amiliyun?"*

in *Majmu'at rasa'il al-imam al-shahid Hasan al-Banna* (Cairo: Dar al-Hadara al-Islamiyya, 1981), 70.

70. A number of studies deal with the history and politics of these groups, among them Mitchell, *The Society of the Muslim Brothers*; Jankowski, *Egypt's Young Rebels*; Gershoni, *The Emergence of Pan-Arabism in Egypt*; Gershoni and Jankowski, *Egypt, Islam, and the Arabs*.

71. Reading the intellectual artifacts of the nationalist movement, which admittedly had become increasingly plural in the 1930s, Gershoni and Jankowski, in *Redefining the Egyptian Nation*, have made an implicit argument about the shift in the nature of the modern political subject in Egypt that is based on problematic assumptions. These are discussed in my introduction. For a different perspective on this period, see Armbrust, *Mass Culture and Modernism in Egypt*. Through a reading of popular magazines and films, Armbrust analyzes the Egyptian cultural field of the 1930s as a constant negotiation of the modern.

72. Anonymous, "Scouting and the Arabs," *al-Dalil* (February 1937).

73. *Al-Muntakhab* 36/2 (July 1939), 7.

74. Ibid.

75. Ibid.

76. Reprinted in Al-Banna, "Preparing Men," in *Hal nahnu qawm 'amiliyun?*, 68. For how this description of masculinity resonates with an earlier period, see Muhammad Farid's definition of a "great man" and Mustafa Kamil as the ideal in chapter 2.

77. Rather than as a shift or even as an instance of "creative adaptation," one might read this position as a perfect example of how *al-Muqtataf* managed to keep up with the latest trends in Europe, in this case pacifism.

78. *Al-Muqtataf* (November 1924), 464.

79. Ibid.

80. *Al-Muqtataf* (April 1925), 447.

81. Ibid., 449–50.

82. While Baden-Powell may have viewed Scouting as a means of preparing Britain's youth for an inevitable continental war, *al-Muqtataf* read it as a means of precipitating and perpetuating conditions of war.

83. *Misr al-haditha al-musawwara* 5/3 (August 7, 1929), 10–11.

84. Ibid., 10. It is not possible to pursue the commercialization angle here. For an analysis of gender in modern advertising and consumption in Egypt, see Russell, *Creating the New Egyptian Woman*. For a very interesting and impressively documented study of how consumption and production in Egypt produced different kinds of public identities at different moments, see Reynolds, "Commodity Communities."

85. *Misr al-haditha al-musawwara* 5/3 (August 7, 1929), 11.

86. As a Palace sympathizer, he was probably referring here to the Wafd's use of students in demonstrations and sometimes in performing violent acts against political opponents, but, as Tusun discovered, this could also be a reference to unassimilable local troops.

87. This desire cannot be explained solely in terms of the traditional political narrative. As we shall see in the next chapter, this type of internal critique was widely practiced in the *riyada* discourse after independence.

88. In a report to the Foreign Office, the British Residency put the number of Egyptian Boy Scouts at forty-five hundred. British and Greek troops in Egypt at the time numbered about one thousand each. TNA: PRO FO 141/705/624 of May 26, 1933.

89. Partly in order to avoid joining the chorus reiterating the exceptionalist discourse surrounding the figure of Sidqi (1875–1950), I point to how he perceived himself. In his memoirs he situated himself among a cohort that included Muhammad Tawfiq Nasim, Ahmad Lutfi al-Sayyid, Mustafa Kamil, and Abd al-Khaliq Tharwat. They were all in law school around the same time; the first two belonged to the class of 1894 along with Sidqi. Sidqi, *Mudhakkirati*, 20–21.

90. Marsot, *Liberal Experiment*, 163.

91. At the general conference of the Muslim Brotherhood in 1935, these groups were given formal status within its organizational structure. After the Second World War, Al-Banna affiliated the rovers with the national scouting association, and by 1948 they were the major force within it. Mitchell, *The Society*, 14, 200–202.

92. Marsot, *Liberal Experiment*; Jankowski, *Egypt's Young Rebels*; Gershoni and Jankowski, *Redefining the Egyptian Nation*.

93. This is, as my own narration of masculinity and nation demonstrates, no easy task. The minimum aim of this chapter is to make a case for the critical need to excavate and to preserve such a space of indeterminacy, contingency, and difference. In the following chapters, I do more to map the interstitial spaces of subject formation.

94. DWQ: Mahfuzat Abidin, Jama'iyyat [box 211], File 18/8 Jama'iyya al-Kashafa fi Misr, Furness & Hasanayn to Mahmud Shukri Pasha of August 31, 1931.

95. Ibid., attached letter to Idarat al-Amn al-'Amm.

96. Ibid., letter from Baden-Powell.

97. Marsot, *Liberal Experiment*, 163.

98. See Abdalla, *The Student Movement and National Politics in Egypt, 1923–1973*. Although his coverage of the period under study is somewhat

sketchy, this is a good example of how the youth movement is reduced to being a product of other struggles. Also see Erlich, *Students and University in Twentieth-Century Egyptian Politics*.

99. I return to the question of violence, nationalism, and respectable masculinity in chapter 8.

100. Because of the nature of the sources, I can only allude to this process here, but I explore the question more thoroughly in relation to *al-futuwwa* in chapter 8.

101. Marsot, *Liberal Experiment*, 163.

102. DWQ: Mahfuzat Abidin, Jama'iyyat [box 211], File 18/8 Jama'iyya al-Kashafa fi Misr, Furness & Hasanayn to Mahmud Shukri Pasha of August 31, 1931, attached proposal.

103. Ibid., Royal Decree of March 30, 1933.

104. Marsot, *Liberal Experiment*, 147.

105. TNA: PRO FO 141/705/624 Residency to FO of May 26, 1933.

106. Ibid.

107. These kinds of exchanges seem to have become a regular feature of the nascent pan-Arab movement. Another troop from Palestine visited Egypt later the same year. TNA: PRO FO 141/705/624 H.C. Palestine to H.C. Egypt of August 30, 1933.

108. TNA: PRO FO 141/705/624 Keown-Boyd to Smart and attached Intelligence Report of April 13, 1933.

109. Ibid.

110. TNA: PRO FO 141/498 Doss. 220, "Students. Political Activities and Strikes." Included in this file is a report on Young Egypt compiled by a spy planted in the organization by the Ministry of Interior's European Department. It was sent to the police chief in Cairo on February 18, 1934. The file contains copies of the Arabic report and its translation. In a very good history M.A. thesis on Egyptian youth culture, Aaron Jakes argues persuasively for Ahmad Husayn's ideological formation largely within the context of anticolonial Egyptian nationalism, which made him oppose Italian imperialism and, along with many colonized people, regard fascist youth movements with "cautious affinity." Jakes, "Extracurricular Nationalism: Youth Culture in the Age of Egypt's Parliamentary Monarchy" (M.A. thesis, Oxford University, 2005), 97–99. He also suggests that the best way to explain the growing militarism of Young Egypt and of urban youth in general, by the mid-1930s, was through a local genealogy of practices like Scouting. I would add that the local becomes intelligible as such only within the new international circuits of cultural production.

111. Unless otherwise specified, the information for this section comes from TNA: PRO FO 141/705/624 Residency Minutes of April 29, 1933.

112. Ibid.

113. Ibid.

114. Ibid.

115. Ibid.

116. DWQ: Mahfuzat Abidin, Jamaʿiyyat [box 211], File 18/8 Jamaʿiyyat al-Kashafa fi Misr, "Al-Kashaf al-Azam Samu al-Amir Faruq" [The Grand Scout His Highness the Prince Faruq], al-Minya, May 13, 1933.

117. This remained true during the first few years of his rule. See Salim, Faruq: wa suqut al-malakiyya fi Misr, 1936–1952.

118. I would like to thank Professor Goelet for identifying this symbol.

119. Al-Ahram (April 30, 1933), 1.

120. TNA: PRO FO 141/705/624 Smart to Graves of 15 Sept 1933, attached C.I.D. Palestine report on the visit of Egyptian Scouts of August 3, 1933.

121. The Egyptian Scouts may have been in Palestine to attend the Arab Exhibition held in Jerusalem in July 1933. Zuʿaytir mentions in his memoirs that along with the exhibition of crafts and culture from Arab countries there were demonstrations of Scouting drills. Zuʿaytir, Min mudhakkirat Akram Zuʿaytir, 1909–1935, 1:525.

122. TNA: PRO FO 141/705/624 Smart to Graves of September 15, 1933, attached C.I.D. Palestine report on the visit of Egyptian Scouts of August 3, 1933. Emphasis added.

123. This new space of politics might be considered in terms of a constant repetition of a slippage between the pedagogical and the performative, to follow Bhabha, or in terms of what Henri Lefebvre conceptualized earlier as the difference between modernity and the everyday. Bhabha, "DissemiNation"; Lefebvre, Everyday Life in the Modern World. Harootunian points to this similarity between Bhabha and Lefebvre in History's Disquiet, 53–55.

124. The "Young Men" referred to in this passage probably represented a branch of the Young Men's Muslim Association. The following year, in a handwritten memo to which he assigned the heading "Fascism," Smart reported on the Boy Scouts in Palestine becoming a greater potential threat to order than the Young Men's Muslim Association. Apparently there was a split among the Palestinian troops, over half leaving the Baden-Powell cadre and reorganizing themselves into another group with King Ghazi as their patron: "I suggested that the Palestine Govt. might try and imitate Fuad and Ibrashi who had hobbled the Egyptian Boy Scouts by putting them under Farouk etc.! Unfortunately, it is not so easy for foreign rulers to play these tricks successfully." The "tricks" of power necessary to maintain order and produce disciplined subjects were contingent, then, on a process of territorialization with marked bound-

aries between inside and outside. How this played out for the foreign rulers is now history, but the tension between the official and popular understandings of where those boundaries actually lie is still unfolding around the question of Palestine. TNA: PRO FO 141/733 Smart, Minute Sheet of June 23, 1934.

125. Abd al-Wahhab al-Najjar had become a popular author in Egypt the preceding year with the publication of his study of pre-Islamic prophets, *Qisas al-Anbiya'*. He had published another work in 1930 on the first caliphs of Islam, *Ta'rikh al-Islam: al-Khulafa' al-Rashidun*. He intended these works to be a means of resisting Christian missionary encroachments and defending Islam. In fact, Fuad's attempts to co-opt the religious establishment in the 1930s included sponsoring delegations of Azharis for travel and study abroad, and al-Najjar was a member of such a delegation to India in 1936. For a discussion of al-Najjar and the ascendancy of the *Islamiyyat* genre during this period, see Gershoni and Jankowski, *Redefining the Egyptian Nation*, 54–78. On al-Azhar, see Berque, *L'Égypte: Impérialisme et Révolution*, 529–32.

126. TNA: PRO FO 141/705/624 Graves to Smart of September 23, 1933, attached translation of report on visit of Egyptian Scouts.

127. Ramadan, *al-Sira' bayn al-Wafd wa al-'Arsh 1936–1939*, 14; Marsot, *Liberal Experiment*, 193; Deeb, *The Wafd*, 334. This by no means meant that Faruq would be able to contain the force of this movement of youth. As a dispatch from Miles Lampson to Anthony Eden in 1936 suggests, the government was unable to build the "facilities for the development of physical culture and sports for students" fast enough. Although he naïvely remained hopeful: "I am convinced that this move, though long overdue, cannot fail, if carried through, to have beneficial effects in keeping University students and school children off the streets in their leisure hours and helping them to exhaust their partisan frenzies in healthy pursuits." TNA: PRO FO 371/20102 Lampson to Eden of March 8, 1936, attached copy of "Note on the Urgent Need for Playing Fields in Ministry of Education Schools" (from Mr. Simpson, Controller of Physical Training in the Ministry of Education to the Minister of Education).

128. Scott, *Conscripts of Modernity*.

Chapter 5. Games

1. Notable exceptions have been largely in literary studies and history of the Atlantic world. See, for example, Edwards, *The Practice of Diaspora*,

and Von Eschen, *Race Against Empire*. Two treatments of nationalism in a transnational frame from elsewhere are Sinha, *Specters of Mother India*, and Manjapra, "The Illusions of Encounter."

2. Recent attempts to revise this historiography can be represented by the textbook of Pappé, *A History of Modern Palestine*.

3. As the recent failures of world trade talks attest, the power balance in international affairs has changed over time such that countries like India and China can make or break agreements on the economy, climate, etc. So the point here is not that colonial power continues into the present unaltered, but that our modes of apprehending the present — and the potential for transforming it — continue to be burdened by terms of recognition established in the colonial past.

4. The notion of creative adaptation is analogous to performativity in that it does not suggest that there was a freedom to choose willy-nilly how to be modern while at the same time it points to spaces in which people actively engaged with modernity — "an interminable process of questioning the present" — with unpredictable ends. See Gaonkar, "On Alternative Modernities," in *Alternative Modernities*, 1–23; also see Charles Taylor's essay "Two Theories of Modernity" in the same volume, 172–96. This work departs from the formulation of alternative modernities, because the ideology does not adequately account for the history of interconnections that were the condition of possibility for a common colonial modernity; in the latter, there would be no original vantage point from which to designate alternatives.

5. Most of the material housed in the museum was donated from the private collection of Ahmed Touny, who was a sportsman, avid fan, and former president of the EOC. There is a vast assortment of medals, pictures, posters, pamphlets, etc. from the various Olympic, Mediterranean, African, and Arab games from their inception. Touny was born on August 10, 1907, and died on his birthday in 1997. He was the founder of the Swimming and Gymnastics associations of Egypt.

6. An Egyptian did compete individually as a fencer in the Olympics in Stockholm in 1912. His name was Ahmed Muhammad Hasanayn, and he was studying at Oxford at the time. He went on to play a leading role in Egyptian sports and politics. In the 1930s he was a member of the EOC, president of the National Sports Club, and later president of the Fencing Club. He attained the title of pasha and served as the head of the Royal Cabinet.

7. DWQ: Mahfuzat Abidin, Jama'iyyat [box 211], al-Olymbiad al-Sabi'.

8. *Al-Al'ab al-Riyadiyya* (May 16, 1923), 11; *al-Al'ab al-Riyadiyya* 8/2

(March 1, 1924), 2–3; *al-Alʿab* 36/1 (September 17, 1926), 4; *al-Siyasa al-Usbuʿiyya* 50/1 (February 19, 1927), 31, and *passim*, 1926–27; *al-Nil* 317/7 (February 3, 1927), 20.

9. *Al-Nil* 317/7 (February 2, 1927), 20.

10. Ibid.

11. A recent dissertation on sport as a "global cultural form" relates the emergence of international spaces like the Olympics to the need for particular nationalisms to measure themselves against others. Keys, "The Dictatorship of Sport."

12. The connection between individual character, athleticism, and national identity was consistently reiterated during this period. See "al-Akhlaq wa al-riyada" in *al-Alʿab* 31/1 (August 13, 1926), 1.

13. *Al-Nil*, ibid.

14. *Al-Alʿab al-Riyadiyya* 8/2 (March 1, 1924), 2–3.

15. Ibid., 3.

16. *Majallat Misr al-haditha al-musawwara* 2/1 (November 25, 1927), 53.

17. Ibid.

18. At a meeting of the IOC in Rome in 1923, Algiers had also been proposed as a site for the first African Games. However, the governor general of Algeria rejected the idea outright, citing the lack of funds, the complicated bureaucratic and political process for securing funds that ultimately would not be granted, and the lack of preparation of the natives. IOC Historical Archives: CIO JREGI-AFRIC-ALXDR File 205627, 1ers Jeux Africains (non célébrés) Alexandrie 1929: correspondences, articles de presse, discours et publications (1924–1929), Dossier SD 1: Correspondance 1924–1929, Governor General of Algeria to de Coubertin of April 3, 1924.

19. Ibid., Dossier SD 3: Discours 1927–1929, printed sheet on the "Games of Africa."

20. Bolanachi had anticipated the postponement, citing political disturbances in 1925 and delay in completing the stadium in 1926. Ibid., Bolanachi to Baillet-Latour of December 22, 1925 and February 7, 1926.

21. Muhammad Murad, *al-Alʿab* 13/1 (April 9, 1926), 1.

22. Renaissance appeared to Egyptians at the time through a number of cultural signifiers. Sport was only one of these. As the famous statue of the woman unveiling by Mahmud Mukhtar ("Egypt's Renaissance") attests, renaissance could take the form of dressing in particular ways—and not others—which signified not only a mere historical change in fashions but also something as fundamental and profound as a shift in the political and ethical foundations of the subject (see chapter 7).

23. Ibid.

24. Murad, ibid.

25. Ibid.

26. Ibid. The phrase *al-ard al-tahira* may also be translated as "virgin ground."

27. The exclusively masculinist configuration of the formal public sphere, attested to legally in the electoral law of 1924 granting universal male suffrage, was also underwritten by the discourse of national honor.

28. Al-Rafi'i, *Fi a'qab al-thawra al-misriyya*; Ramadan, *Tatawwur*; Marsot, *Egypt's Liberal Experiment*; Deeb, *Party Politics in Egypt*.

29. TNA: PRO CO 554/77/7 Lloyd to Chamberlain of February 10, 1928.

30. Indeed this naïveté extends in other directions. As far as I could tell, documents in the IOC archive make no reference to the political suppression of the games. Rather, one gathers the impression that the failure was due to the "ignorance" of the native members of the EOC regarding proper international protocols. For example, preserved in the archive is a front-page editorial from *Le Miroir Egyptien* written by its owner, F. J. Kayat, which ridicules the EOC for seeking political explanations and trying as always to blame "'machination' imaginée on a vu la main de l'Angleterre." IOC Historical Archives: CIO JREGI-AFRIC-ALXDR File 205627, 1ers Jeux Africains (non célébrés) Alexandrie 1929: correspondances, articles de presse, discours et publications (1924–1929), Dossier SD 1: Correspondance 1924–1929.

31. TNA: PRO CO 554/77/7 Rochdale to Amery of February 2, 1929.

32. They were also very anxious about the performance of their own race within this competitive arena. See McDevitt, "May the Best Man Win."

33. TNA: PRO CO 554/77/7 Minutes of February 3, 1928.

34. Ibid.

35. Ibid., March 9, 1928.

36. Ibid.

37. Ibid., May 11, 1928.

38. IOC Historical Archives: CIO JREGI-AFRIC-ALXDR File 205627, 1ers Jeux Africains (non célébrés) Alexandrie 1929: correspondances, articles de presse, discours et publications (1924–1929), Dossier SD 1: Correspondance 1924–1929, Prime Ministry, Ministry of the Colonies to Baillet-Latour of November 8, 1928.

39. Although it was a tactical move, the king's racialized assumptions about African athletes may have also inspired his decision: "The reason of this being that it was felt that if the Games were confined to natives they might, because of their low standard of prowess, prove to be a fiasco." TNA: PRO CO 554/77/7 Rochdale to Amery of February 2, 1929.

40. TNA: PRO CO 554/77/7 Minutes of February 8, 1929.

41. *"Lamha 'an al-Al'ab al-Ifriqiyya"* (A glance at the African Games), *al-Al'ab* 3/1 (January 29, 1926), 1.

42. Keys, "The Dictatorship of Sport," 57.

43. IOC Historical Archives: CIO CNO-EGYPT-CORR: 1914–1956 (N° 71241), "Correspondence of the NOC of the Arab Republic of Egypt (EGY)," Hussein Sabry [governor of Alexandria and president of the Football Federation] to Count Baillet-Latour [president of the IOC] of February 19, 1932.

44. Ibid., Presidents and Delegates of Federations to Minister of Public Instruction, Attached to Minister of Public Instruction to Baillet-Latour of February 19, 1932.

45. Ibid.

46. The question of Bolonachi's nationality is highly complex. There was an increasing momentum during this period to define Egyptian nationality exclusively, rendering any community with access to capitulary privileges as foreign. For the buildup to this moment, see Hanley, "Foreignness and Localness in Alexandria, 1880–1914."

47. Apparently Bolanachi quit his position as the IOC delegate when he could not persuade the Egyptian Sports Federation to participate in the Los Angeles games.

48. IOC Historical Archives: CIO CNO-EGYPT-CORR: 1914–1956 (N° 71241), "Correspondence of the NOC of the Arab Republic of Egypt (EGY)," French translation of *al-Ahram* article with heading "Le Conflit Olympique," n.d., 1.

49. Ibid., 2–3.

50. Ibid., French translation of *al-Ahram* article with heading, "Commentaires du Journal Ahram sur votre Interview," n.d.

51. Ibid., 1.

52. Taher served as the IOC representative until 1968. He was apparently quite energetic in this role, and reconciliation between the two parties seems to have sped along. Owing to Taher's organizational skills, the thirty-fifth session of the IOC was held in Egypt in March 1938. As vice president of the IOC after the Second World War, Taher was also a leading proponent of the idea for an interregional games for countries bordering on the Mediterranean. It finally came to fruition in October 1951 when the very first Mediterranean Games were held in Alexandria. For the proceedings of the session in 1938, see *Bulletin Officiel du Comité International Olympique* (July 1938): www.aafla.org (accessed April 2, 2005).

53. IOC Historical Archives: CIO CNO-EGYPT-CORR Chemise 8131, Correspondance du CNO de la République Arabe d'Egypte 1914–1956, Dr. Th. Schmidt to Baillet-Latour of April 28, 1934.

54. While Bolanachi's biography attests (as does Mustafa Kamil's) to an older history of cosmopolitanism and travel, the international stage here references an interwar phenomenon characterized by a continuing collaboration but also increasing collision with the colonial. The greater frequency and diversity of bodies — institutional and human — intersecting on the international stage materialized it as a distinct space. This space was at once the meeting place of multiple nations and the nonplace of the in-between. The latter is indexed, for example, in the formulation of Taher's position as the representative of the IOC in Egypt. Indeed, glancing at the itinerary of his long career suggests a life of almost constant movement, a life which ended in Istanbul rather than Cairo. IOC Historical Archives: CIO MBR-TAHER-CORR Chemise 7255/91, Correspondance de Mohammed Taher Pacha 1934–1970. Also see Hanley's recent review of the limits of using cosmopolitanism analytically in Middle Eastern historical contexts, "Grieving Cosmopolitanism in the Middle East."

55. Mosse, *The Image of Man*, 52.

56. Ibid., 153–54. For a detailed analysis of how the liberal internationalism of the Olympic movement interacted with Nazism and Communism at the political institutional level, see chapters 4 and 5 in Keys, "The Dictatorship of Sport."

57. Variances, according to Mosse, must certainly have obtained among "the clean-cut Englishman, the all-American boy, and the ideal member of the S.S." These, however, were only a function of different kinds of ideological deployment; at the core of modern masculinity was a common complex of "virtues, strength, and aesthetic appeal." Mosse, *The Image of Man*, 180.

58. One historian suggested that the Olympic Games of 1928 did not elicit a strong response in Egypt because of the poor performance of the football team. Yunan Labib Rizk's recent survey of the *al-Ahram* coverage of those games described the reception of the athletes upon their return from Amsterdam as tepid. Rizk, "Amsterdam Olympics," *Al-Ahram Weekly* (March 7–13, 2002), 30. There were also bigger fish to fry at the time. Segments of the press were highly critical of the creeping authoritarian intentions and practices of the king, the British, and willing agents like Muhammad Mahmud. In turn, these forces were increasingly prone to unleash punitive measures against the press. The return of a Labor government in London, however, did result in the recall of the much-despised Lloyd and the promise of treaty negotiations, temporarily mitigating some of the animosity toward the British.

59. When the first African Games finally were held in 1965, it was decided to engrave the medals with the likeness of Ibrahim Mustafa. Rizk makes

no mention of Mustafa in his summary of the Olympics coverage. Rizk, "Amsterdam Olympics."

60. *Al-Mulakim* (Boxers) in Alexandria in 1929; *al-Al'ab al-Riyadiyya* (Sports) in Cairo in 1932.

61. "Our Champions: Ibrahim Mustafa the World Wrestling Champion," *al-Abtal* 8 (February 4, 1933), 6–7.

62. Humble characters were not the traditional subjects of Arabic biographies. Enabling this transgression within the biographical genre was the rapid growth of a modern popular culture during the interwar period that was powered by new technologies of the body and of communication and enacted within a globalizing frame.

63. Whether the author had read the biography of Mustafa Kamil is unknown; nevertheless, it is uncanny how the knowledge of a precise date of birth serves in both instances to mark social and cultural contexts but signifying different relations to modernity.

64. On the other hand, the authors and self-styled representatives of heritage, whether in cultural or political contexts, were quite capable of imagining and strategically employing their identity with the national.

65. Al-Faraj, *Ruwwad al-Riyada*, 67–76.

66. *Al-Abtal* 8, 6.

67. *Al-Abtal* 7 (January 28, 1933), 4–5.

68. David F. Wood, "A Strong Man's Life: El Saied Nosseir Egypt's Greatest Weightlifter," in *Superman* issues of May, June, July, and August 1936; ibid., (May 1936), 200.

69. A *mawlid* is a celebration marking the birth of a saintly figure. In Egypt, they have a reputation for being carnivalesque and were historically a source of governing anxieties, occasionally resulting in their repression. The Mawlid of Al-Sayyid al-Badawi has been one of the largest and most popular of these celebrations. The police official who commented on the need for a strong hand in handling the young effendis (see chapter 4) also wrote about the mawlids, J. W. McPherson, *The Moulids of Egypt*.

70. *Al-Abtal* 7, 4.

71. Ahmad Shawqi, "Qahir al-gharb al-'atid," *Shawqiyyat* 4 vols. (Beirut: Dar al-Kutub al-'Ilmiyya, n.d.), 2:61–62.

72. After his victories in 1930 and 1931 against Europe's strongest men, Nusayr was invited by local sports clubs and federations to exhibit his feats of strength in cities and towns throughout the continent. Apparently, the astonished weightlifting enthusiasts and others received him warmly during these demonstration tours. Wood, "A Strong Man's Life," *Superman*.

73. Shawqi, ibid. Samera Esmeir's assistance in interpreting this poem was

very helpful, although I am solely responsible for the roughness of the translation.

74. The idea for the contest seems to have been inspired by the victory of Miss Turkey, Kahraman Hanim Khalis, at the Miss Universe Pageant in 1932. "Beautiful Bodies," *al-Riyada al-Badaniyya* (October 1932), 25–31.

75. The competition was first announced in *al-Riyada al-Badaniyya* [hereafter *RB*] for September 1932. No photos from women were received, so the futile plea was repeated in the following issue with the promise of protecting the contestant's identity by not publishing her name and blanking out her face. In a later assessment, no mention is made of the original intent of the competition, and the editors of the magazine were quite pleased with how it fit in with their mission. "Beautiful Bodies Competition," *RB* (January 1934), 15–18.

76. The magazine, as profit-seeking enterprises are wont to do, hedged its bets regarding the kind of nationalism it supported. Sometimes it spoke in the Egyptian territorial nationalist voice and at other times it represented a modern pan-Arab subject.

77. Juhayna [Ibrahim 'Allam], "Egypt's Sports Revival: Between the Old and the New," *RB* (January 1934), 33. The use of "murasala" (correspondence, exchange of letters) is unusual in this context and may signify one of the first efforts to denote in Arabic a field of communications as a technology of government.

78. I am following Bederman's analysis here: "The interesting thing about 'civilization' is not what was meant by the term, but the multiple ways it was used to legitimize different sorts of claims to power. Therefore, rather than trying to reduce civilization to a set of specific formulations or points, I will be discussing it as a discourse that worked, albeit unevenly, to establish (or to challenge) white male hegemony. . . . Rather than trying to isolate commonalities about what people meant by 'civilization' — and perhaps flattening out contradictions and complexities — I will be concentrating on the different, even contradictory, ways people invoked the discourse of civilization to construct what it meant to be a man." Bederman, *Manliness and Civilization*, 23–24.

79. Ra'uf al-Jawhari, "Exercise and Us," *RB* (October 1935), 1129.

80. Ibid.

81. Mukhtar al-Jawhari, "The Fate of Weak People," *RB* (September 1934), 8–10.

82. One might contrast the rigid divisions between gender and sex established here around the idea of beauty and the more fluid understanding allowed by a figure like Tahtawi in the nineteenth century. Tahtawi de-

scribes the androgyny of boys, which makes them equally attractive to men during the prepubescent stage (*mabda' shabubiyya*), without any apparent sense of disapproval. Tahtawi, *al-Murshid al-Amin*, 39.

83. Moukhtar al-Jawhari, "The Fate of Weak People," 9.

84. Which naturally began with a regular subscription to the magazine.

85. In many instances the loss of masculinity was located at the site of male sexual weakness or impotence. See "How to Recover Masculinity," *RB* (July 1932), 11–12; (August 1932), 10–11; (September 1932), 10–13.

86. I will discuss muscles and the "popular body" more fully in the final chapter on *al-futuwwa*.

87. The standard reference for Egypt is Davis, *Challenging Colonialism*. Also see Beinin and Lockman, *Workers on the Nile*.

88. That it is not entirely impossible has been demonstrated by Ryzova's recent study of the significance of authorship in school diaries and scrapbooks she unearthed in used-book shops and flea markets — the same archive from which the stories of Ibrahim and Sayyid are reconstructed here. Ryzova, "'My Notepad Is My Friend': Efendis and the Act of Writing in Modern Egypt."

Chapter 6. Communication

1. Juhayna (Ibrahim 'Allam), "Egypt's Sports Revival: Between the Old and the New," *RB* (January 1934), 29–34.

2. Ibid., 32.

3. Hasan Kamal, "Sports Among the Ancient Egyptians," *RB* (January 1935), 7–14; Farid Abu Hadid, "Chivalry in Europe and Islam," *RB* (October 1934), 45–54.

4. *Al-Riyadi*, dir. L. Nagel and Clement Mizrahi (Sharikat al-Aflam al-Misriyya, 1935).

5. I use the linguistic rather than the ethnic label here on purpose. The flow of this discourse beyond Egypt's borders did not necessarily forge an "Arab" identity as much as it enabled the expression of middle-class concerns *in* Arabic.

6. This information was culled from the letters to the editor as well as from the magazine's data about its distribution. By 1937 *Physical Culture* had formal arrangements with agents in Luxor, Khartum, Port Sudan, Mecca, Jaffa, Akka, Gaza, Damascus, Aleppo, Tripoli, Basra, and Baghdad.

7. Jacob, "Eventful Transformations."

8. A study of department stores, goods, consumers, and modernist formations of urbanity is Reynolds, "Commodity Communities."

9. Raymond, *Cairo*, 324.

10. This was the address of the institute in 1938; I was not able to establish whether it was always in the same location. Interestingly, the YMMA continues to exist and operate in the same location while the *ma'had* has disappeared entirely, even from memory.

11. For a recent reevaluation of the conceptual and social meanings of the effendiyya as a collective and effendi as an individual subject, see Ryzova, "Egyptianizing Modernity through the 'New *Effendiya*.'" Also see Gershoni and Jankowski, *Redefining the Egyptian Nation, 1930–45*.

12. Salmoni, "Historical Consciousness for Modern Citizenship." For a study that looks at schools and the press as sites of gendered and classed instruction for the preceding period, see Pollard, *Nurturing the Nation*. For the performative possibilities engendered by the new media in particular, see Armbrust, *Mass Culture and Modernism in Egypt*.

13. I put "sexuality" in quotation marks here to signal a possible misfit in the translation into this name of a field of knowledge that was still in a nascent stage in Egypt even by the interwar period. Hereafter, the word will appear without quotes, in part because of stylistic demands, but also because the makings of sex as discourse was the sine qua non of *Physical Culture*. For another set of representations that engaged the same anxieties and in a sense paved the way for *Physical Culture*, see Booth, "Un/safe/ly at Home."

14. Massad, *Desiring Arabs*.

15. As Butler has demonstrated, internalization is never simple. The complex interplays of inside and outside in the formation of subjects cannot be reduced to a seamless function of discipline or oedipalization. In both conceptions, the subject becomes a fixed entity with little possibility for resignification. Massad's argument is also constrained by a narrowing of the discourse on sex in the Arab world for most of the twentieth century to "reconstructions of the medieval sexual life of the Arabs," a focus that obscures much of the social and cultural history written in the past decade on gender, love, marriage, reproduction, and family.

16. See, for example, Stoler, "Making Empire Respectable" and "Sexual Affronts and Racial Frontiers"; Sinha, *Colonial Masculinity* and *Specters of Mother India*; Burton, *The Burdens of History* and "Who Needs the Nation?" and *At the Heart of the Empire*; Levine, *Prostitution, Race and Politics*. While acknowledging Janet Abu-Lughod's argument about the existence of globalizing trends in other historical eras, I feel it is necessary to distinguish the period of high imperialism beginning in the last third of the nineteenth century for its compressed (faster and further) expansion of new civilizational norms bearing the stamp of one geographi-

cal area. Although the earlier Islamic conquests and empires provided similar grounds for civilizational connections, its distinctiveness was the product not of geographical projections from a center but of the stitching together of diverse peripheries. Moreover, while revisions to European imperial history rightly attempt to displace a unidirectional (metropole to colony) understanding of modern cultural formations, there were people in every society who came to believe in such a chain of transmission from the mid-nineteenth century onward. J. Abu-Lughod, *Before European Hegemony*.

17. For a recent account of these variegated interlinkages, see T. Mitchell, *The Rule of Experts*.

18. Assessing its discursive failure or success at producing a unified, authentic, masculine, and libidinal subject is not my aim here. Also, judging the performance as good or bad mimicry, as if there were an original available for comparison, is not a genuine historical concern; moreover, such aesthetic judgments were already constitutive of the social space in which *Physical Culture* circulated.

19. For a complementary analysis of similar processes, which, however, does not engage directly with coloniality, see Armbrust, *Mass Culture and Modernism*, 84.

20. See chapter 8.

21. Barlow's elaboration of historical catachresis in *The Question of Women in Chinese Feminism* is apposite here.

22. I am drawing here on Harootunian's elaboration of "co-existing modernity" in *Overcome by Modernity*.

23. Chatterjee, *The Nation and Its Fragments*.

24. It seems that the issues from the last years of the magazine's life were in fact shorter and of lesser quality, which may be explained by the onset of war and wartime conditions. I thank Walter Armbrust for bringing this to my attention. I am uncertain as to when its run exactly came to an end, but it seems not to have survived long past the Second World War; Armbrust has located issues of the magazine from 1951.

25. The section on sports was the least regular part of the magazine. I am unable to incorporate a reading of the stories' sections into this chapter, as it would require a much more extensive treatment than space will allow here.

26. *RB* (March 1936), 333–36.

27. The provenance of these letters, whether they were fabricated by the editors or genuine, is an unavoidable question. The short answer is that some of the letters may surely have been planted by the editors during slow periods or in order to generate controversy, but it seems highly un-

likely all of them were fake, given their numbers and level of personal detail. To the extent that this chapter is an investigation of the magazine's rhetorical intervention into the problem of sex rather than a social history of Egyptians' sexual practices, it is less relevant who was doing the actual letter writing; hence, the short answer should suffice.

28. The author of the letter explicitly requested that Cupid, the mediator of this epistolary forum, solicit advice on his problem only from male readers of *Physical Culture*.

29. *RB* (March 1936), 335–36.

30. Ibid., 336.

31. Although it will be unsatisfactory, based on the reactions to analogous situations, one can speculate about the solutions readers may have offered A.Y.D. They would for the most part have been very pragmatic and told A.Y.D. to move on, to forget the traitorous woman, to have his parents find him a proper partner, and to remain vigilant on his new path to good health and virtuous living.

32. These numbers indicate letters received; only a handful of letters were published. Even if the figures were highly inflated by the magazine's editors, the claims of the existence of an interested public with differing opinions about intimate issues in a stranger's life is not only intrinsically interesting but also points to an important aspect of the very constitution of the public.

33. *RB* (May 1932), 120–24.

34. *RB* (May 1931), 108.

35. *RB* (March 1936), 333.

36. This same source has been read through its visual images of women as peddling soft-core pornography in the guise of exercise and health; see Ryzova, "'I Am a Whore But I Will Be a Good Mother.'" While this may have been true and might partially account for the longevity of the magazine, the textual evidence suggests a different reality closer to its stated goals of promoting smart, modern, and healthy sexuality. That said, if the male images were read along the same erotic lines, then there was a definite subversion of these stated goals and the ideology of heteronormativity. Nevertheless, these transgressive readings would reinforce the point that norms of gender and sexuality needed to be reconstituted as a condition of possibility for a modern Egyptian subject.

37. Which marriages were suitable for modern times was also a concern, as we will see below.

38. Other contributing medical experts included Dr. Husayn 'Izzat, Dr. Muhammad Kamil al-Khuli, Dr. Muhammad Abd al-Hamid Bey, Dr. Husayn al-Harawi, and Dr. Muhammad Shahin Pasha.

39. "Sex Education: An Hour with Dr. Fakhri Faraj, The Famous Doctor of Venereal Diseases," *RB* (May 1932), 6–12.

40. Bruce Dunne discusses the role of the AUC and Faraj's lecture series in the dissemination of knowledge about sexual health as part of colonial and national efforts to civilize Egyptians; see chapter 6 of his "Sexuality and the 'Civilizing Process' in Modern Egypt."

41. Fakhri Faraj, *al-Mar'a wa falsafat al-tanasuliyyat* (Women and the philosophy of sexuality) (Cairo: al-Matba'a al-'Asriyya, 1924); *Taqrir 'an intishar al-bagha' wa al-amrad al-tanasuliyya bi al-qutr al-misri wa ba'd al-turuq al-mumkin itba'uha li- muharabatihima* (The spread of prostitution and venereal diseases in the country of Egypt and the steps that might be followed to combat them) (Cairo: al-Matba'a al-'Asriyya, 1924); *al-Tanasul fi al-hayawan wa al-insan wa al-nabat* (Reproduction in animals, humans, and plants) (I could not locate this work); *Hal tatasawi al-mar'a bi al-rajul fi al-huquq wa al-wajibat?* (Is the woman equal to the man in rights and responsibilites?); *Al-amrad al-tanasuliyya wa 'ilajuha* (Venereal diseases and their treatment) (I could not locate this work); *Al-du'f al-tanasuli fi al-dhukur wa al-anath wa 'ilajuhu* (Sexual impotence in males and females and its treatment) (I could not locate this work).

42. Given the absence of much statistical data related to sexually transmitted diseases from this period, it is very difficult to corroborate this claim. Making it his life's work suggests at least that it was a major concern of Faraj and not solely a rhetorical devise.

43. *RB* (May 1932), 9.

44. Muhammad Fa'iq al-Jawhari, "The Honorable Attack," *RB* (October 1932), 4–5. Criticism also seems to have been launched against the magazine from a third position that found the magazine's message of chastity puritanical and outdated. For a defense of their philosophy on sex education, see "Girls and Diminished Morals," *RB* (February 1935), 113–14. Essentially, the magazine maintained that knowledge about sex would encourage self-control, which was what distinguished humans from animals. An important component of their philosophy was the belief that there was a causative element to knowledge about sex, and the outcome was ultimately empowerment.

45. This reading is supported by the magazine's inclusion of religious experts alongside the medical experts to opine on issues related to sexuality and the right to research and discuss them publicly. Another likely proposition is that the editor was manipulating religion just as interestedly as his opponents in order to enhance magazine sales that depended on sexual content.

46. Dr. Fakhri Faraj, "[Part I] Why Women Have Revolted?" *RB* (December 1932), 33–38; "[Part III] Motherhood and a Social and Intellectual Life," *RB* (February 1933), 43–48; "[Part IV] The Duties and Rights of Women," *RB* (March 1933), 65–71. I was not able to obtain the issue for January 1933 and thus could not consult part II of Faraj's lecture.

47. *RB* (March 1933), 65–71.

48. For the possible repercussions of voicing too loudly a call for equal inheritance rights, see Badran, *Feminists, Islam, and Nation*, 134.

49. For another angle on this problem, see Mukhtar al-Jawhari, "Prostitution and the Problem of Orphans: How We Can Overcome [the Problems] through Proper Sex Education," *RB* (November 1932), 6–9. For a good social history of prostitution covering this period, see Emad Hilal, *al-Baghaya fi Misr.*

50. Kholoussy, "Stolen Husbands and Foreign Wives."

51. In making this recommendation he was following international standards concerning women's physical exercise that were scientifically established in preceding decades. According to the program of sessions held at the International Congress on Sports and Physical Education in Brussels in 1905, women's exercises would be discussed as "exercises propres à developper sans danger la jeune fille et la femme." DWQ: Mahfuzat Majlis al-Wuzara,' Nizarat al-Kharijiyya 4/9, Mu'tamarat (1905–1923), file 3, p. 15. Tellingly, the topic of women's physical exercise was the last entry in the program.

52. Badran, *Feminists, Islam, and Nation*, 145–46.

53. Ibid., 136.

54. This locating of Jirjis in a peripheral community added to his authenticity and authority for a mostly urban reading public. A more likely scenario was that he occasionally visited Bani Suwayf from Cairo and perhaps also offered his medical services. I thank Walter Armbrust for suggesting this reading.

55. *RB* (August 1931), 122.

56. Forel's text was originally composed in German; Jirjis based his Arabic translation on an English edition by C. F. Marshall (which edition is not clear). Forel, *The Sexual Question.* Freud's first rendition of *The Theory of Sexuality* appeared in 1905 also.

57. *RB* (August 1931), 123.

58. Ibid.

59. On the science of population, see el-Shakry, "Barren Land and Fecund Bodies." For a broad survey of the place of social science and its practitioners in discursively producing and practically managing Egypt, see Mitchell, *Rule of Experts.*

60. Dr. Sabri Jirjis, "On Politics and Political Economy," *RB* (March 1934), 15–21.

61. Ibid., 15.

62. Ibid., 20–21.

63. The use of the body as a social and political metaphor was already quite an old practice by then. Its modern use to describe national communities in Egypt can be traced at least as far back as Tahtawi's *al-Murshid al-Amin lil-banat wa al-banin*. One of the most explicit and extended treatments of the "organic body" (*jism 'udwi*) as both a metaphor for and constitutive of modern society was Ahmad Amin's *al-Akhlaq*.

64. This point is elaborated below. See Venus, "*Laylat al-Dukhla*" (The wedding night), *RB* (August 1932), 81–84. Evidence of the *khawal* as a historically important figure on the Egyptian sexual landscape at the end of the nineteenth century appears in the memoirs of Ibrahim Fawzi. See Jacob, "History and the Masculine Subject of Colonialism."

65. For a survey of expanding state powers and the policing of sexuality from the nineteenth century through the early twentieth, see Dunne, "Sexuality and the 'Civilizing Process.'" On refiguring marriage, see Kholoussy's, *For Better, For Worse*.

66. *RB* (March 1933), 30–37.

67. On the complexity of sexual terminology in premodern and modern Arabic, see Rowson, "The Categorization of Gender and Sexual Irregularity in Medieval Arabic Vice Lists," and Lagrange, "Male Homosexuality in Modern Arabic Literature."

68. *RB* (November 1933), 14–22.

69. It is hard to tell whether Jirjis believed this or was simply acting as a translator. These are Forel's words from *The Sexual Question*, 378.

70. "Sexual Deviance," *RB* (October 1934), 19–21.

71. *RB* (March 1935), 18–21.

72. *RB* (November 1936): 1008–9.

73. In terms of subject formation, it is irrelevant whether the intentions of the magazine owners were purely nationalist, capitalist, or, what is most likely, a combination of different interests. The market of possible and impossible subjects which took shape during the interwar period against a new internationalist backdrop was in itself a complex apparatus composed of material and ideological interests that were at once economic, moral, and political—teasing out one from the other being a Sisyphean challenge. The modern subject as materialized in the pages of *Physical Culture* was in fact an effect of power that was in excess of the terms of its formation. Correspondingly, the historical individuals who wrote, illustrated, produced, read, submitted to, and subverted the disciplinary dis-

course of physical culture were and were not, paradoxically, the modern subject of this technology. The subject in this sense was both a fantasy of Egyptian modernity and a real condition of its possibility.

74. The emergence of a discourse of monogamous marriage and the proper household has been traced to the 1870s, which tentatively can serve as the birth date for the ideology of bourgeois heteronormativity that silently subtended the physical culture discourse of the 1930s. Cuno, "Ambiguous Modernization," and Fay, "From Warrior-Grandees to Domesticated Bourgeoisie"; also see Pollard, *Nurturing the Nation*, 44.

75. The quotation is from Najmabadi's formulation of how the standard narration of Iranian modernity as the simultaneous and conflicted struggle to secure cultural authenticity and progress figures gender exclusively within this tension — usually marked geographically between East and West — and consequently writes out the particularities of gender's ambiguity in Iran's premodern history. In other words, histories of gender in Iranian modernity that leave untroubled the assumption of heterosexuality as a natural occurrence reproduce the "historical erasure" of figures like the *mukhannas/amradnuma* and the *amrad*. Najmabadi, *Women with Mustaches and Men without Beards*, 141.

76. Butler, *Undoing Gender*, 28.

77. Drawing on her ethnography of an Egyptian women's religious movement, Mahmood, in *Politics of Piety*, engages Butler's theorization of performativity, showing its limits when confronted with ethical practices that do not presuppose a liberal subject and a political horizon of freedom.

78. For a study that interrogates the colonial production of the human in modern law as a moment of rupture in Egyptian history, see Esmeir, "The Work of Law in the Age of Empire." Esmeir's analysis suggests that the domain of humanity became circumscribed in and through the juridical foreclosure of other domains by the time of nominal independence, which may partially explain the consistently deferred emergence of the Egyptian subject as properly human.

79. *RB* (August 1932), 82.

80. Ibid., 84.

81. Lagrange, "Male Homosexuality in Modern Arabic Literature," 197n58.

Chapter 7. Fashion

1. The *tarbush* (pl. *tarabish*), as it is called in Egypt, is more commonly known as the fez, signaling its supposed Moroccan origins. It is a brim-

less hat of red felted wool with a flat circular top and a tassel. Depending on the period, it came in varying heights, proportions, and styles of tassel. The fez was mandated as official headgear for Muslim men — except the *ulama* — in the Ottoman Empire as part of broader clothing reforms decreed by Sultan Mahmud II in 1829. In Egypt, Muhammad 'Ali had already dressed his soldiers in a version of the North African fez. For detailed information on the production, styles, and consumption of *tarabish* during the period covered by this book, see Reynolds, "Commodity Communities," 344–59. For a rereading of Ottoman reforms up to 1829 through the lens of the clothing law, see Quataert, "Clothing Laws, State, and Society in the Ottoman Empire, 1720–1829." For a comparison of the cultural significance of the decree in 1829 mandating the fez and the decree in 1925 banning it, see Baker, "The Fez in Turkey." Baker's analysis situates the movement for and against the fez within the frameworks of modernization and nationalism and relies on religious–secular and East–West dichotomies to explain these two moments in Ottoman-Turkish history. In the Egyptian case I analyze here, by looking at the gendered aspects of men's anxieties about dress, one sees that the *tarbush* makes visible a much more complex field of cultural signification.

2. The Arabic term *ghazi* is very old and in this context refers to the warriors who dwelled among Turkic tribesmen on the frontiers of Islam and launched raids against the Byzantines in Anatolia beginning in the eleventh century. A note on usage: Mustafa Kemal would be known as Atatürk (an honorary designation meaning "father of the Turks") only after a law on surnames was passed in 1934. One of the aims of the law was to promote authentic Turkish names over Arabic-derived (read: Muslim-sounding) ones. However, the image of Mustafa Kemal as the founder and emblem of a distinctively Turkish, secular cultural order circulated earlier, so I occasionally refer to him as Atatürk even in periods prior to 1934, though such usage is technically incorrect.

3. "The Ambassador's Tarboush," *Al-Ahram Weekly On-Line* 650 (7–13 August 2003), http://weekly.ahram.org (accessed December 10, 2003).

4. I have benefited in this chapter from the collection of recent approaches to the historical study of clothing and gender in a special issue of *Gender and History* 14/3 (November 2002) titled "Material Strategies"; the following articles were especially helpful: Ivaska, "'Anti–Mini Militants Meet Modern Misses,'" Carole Turbin, "Fashioning the American Man: The Arrow Collar Man, 1907–1931," and Eugenia Paulicelli, "Fashion, the Politics of Style and National Identity in Pre–Fascist and Fascist Italy."

5. The unwieldiness of the term "Westernize" as a historical phenome-

non might be thought of this way: if one unlinked it from late European colonialism and the process of mimicry it generated, then one could trace "Turkish" westernization back to the first Ottoman footholds in the Balkans in the fourteenth century. Indeed, if one rejected the imaginary lines dividing Europe from Asia and viewed the Byzantines as a continuation of Western civilization, then the timeline would have to be moved back even further.

6. For a laudatory history of the Kemalist project, see B. Lewis, *The Emergence of Modern Turkey*; for a more critical assessment, see Parla and Davison, *Corporatist Ideology in Kemalist Turkey*.

7. In fact, whereas the fez was banned by law in Turkey, the veil was restricted through administrative regulations—e.g., prohibiting it in government schools and other facilities.

8. I examine these debates in detail below, but for a helpful overview based primarily on reports in *al-Ahram*, see Yunan Labib Rizk, "Demise of the Red Headgear," *Al-Ahram Weekly On-Line* 525 (March 15–21, 2001), http://weekly.ahram.org (accessed June 29, 2007).

9. On contemporary Turkey, see the work of Gole, *The Forbidden Modern*.

10. For an overview of the political and military history of this critical period, see Cleveland, "World War I and the End of the Ottoman Order," in *A History of the Modern Middle East*, 146–67.

11. No matter how much historians revise the Ottoman story and demonstrate its active participation in the shaping of the modern world, it remains true that the empire's sovereignty, not to mention its size, was compromised from the mid-eighteenth century onward. For an optimistic assessment of the empire's ability to persist in the world had it not been dismantled, see Quataert, *The Ottoman Empire, 1700–1922*.

12. The relegation of dress to the domain of the trivial is not simply a bias of the past. Historians of Europe have only recently begun to mine this area for historical meaning; see Perrot's critique in *Fashioning the Bourgeoisie*. On the perils of minimizing culture's significance in the face of its overvaluation by right-wing politics in the present, see Duggan, *The Twilight of Equality?*

13. The argument in this chapter adds historical nuance to political theorists' recent rethinking of sovereignty beyond the conventional liberal story of contract. By highlighting the centrality of the international system of states, which began to emerge after the Peace of Westphalia in 1648, they show the constitution of mutually dependent, uneven forms of citizenship and sovereignty within global webs of imperial relations. See, for example, Hindess, "Citizenship and Empire," and Strang, "Contested

Sovereignty." This work departs from such treatments by showing that contestations over cultural borders were equally important moments in the constitution of sovereignty and the international.

14. Egypt became a regular member of the League of Nations following the Anglo-Egyptian Treaty of 1936, which renegotiated some of the terms of independence established in the declaration of 1922. See chapter 6 of this book for a discussion of the controversy surrounding Egypt's attempts to secure an Arabic-speaking Egyptian as the representative of the International Olympic Committee. For Egypt's participation in the International Geographical Union, Commission on Population, and the World Population Conference of 1927, see el-Shakry, *The Great Social Laboratory*; and for international women's groups, see Badran, *Feminists, Islam, and Nation*. For a detailed analysis of what they term "supra-Egyptianism" as the emerging framework for imagining and enacting Egypt as part of wider Arab and Islamic worlds in the 1930s and 1940s, see Gershoni and Jankowski, *Redefining the Egyptian Nation*. See the conclusion of this chapter for a critique of their treatment of "Easternism" as the loose basis of national culture in the 1930s.

15. Kurzman explores the signs of the "global within the national" in the Iranian context in "Weaving Iran into the Tree of Nations." I thank Setrag Manoukian for this reference. Also see Manela, *The Wilsonian Moment*.

16. For a somewhat different treatment of how the international was crucial to national formations, see Majnapra, "The Illusions of Encounter." A work that came out too late to consider here but with great bearing on this point is Khuri-Makdisi's *The Eastern Mediterranean and the Making of Global Radicalism, 1860–1914*.

17. For a similar argument for the postcolonial period, see Ivaska, *Cultured States*.

18. See Reynolds, "Commodity Communities." Although there is some overlap in our sources and analyses, my focus on the tarbush as a contested site of cultural signification and gendered subject formation within an international frame complements Reynolds's reading of the materiality of the tarbush in its circulation through relays of production and consumption.

19. Since I consider the kind of masculinity constituted by turban wearers (albeit tangentially) in the next chapter, the tarbush and the hat receive more attention here, although, the final section addresses the melancholic and temporal stance on culture reflected through the diminishing value of the turban.

20. As the occasion for the satirical cartoon in figure 35 indicates, Cairo-Kabul and other similar axes of the Muslim world were also being re-

drawn at this time to account for the international order emerging in the wake of the First World War and the vacuum resulting from the disappearance of the Ottoman caliphate.

21. Ironically for some, predictably for others, the tarbush was retired from active symbolic duty under accusations of embodying feudal, aristocratic, and antinationalist sentiments after the revolution in 1952.

22. Sidqi's government fell one month after this cartoon was published.

23. Timothy Mitchell's treatment of the emergence of the economy in the late 1930s is apposite here. Mitchell, *Rule of Experts*, 80–119.

24. Indeed, at some level, it was recognition of this connection that resulted in the British-controlled Council of Ministers resolutely refusing almost every invitation to participate in international congresses prior to the revolution of 1919. DWQ: Mahfuzat Majlis al-Wuzara,' Nizarat al-Kharijiyya, 4/9, Mu'tamarat (1905–1923), files 1–24. Several of the invitations that were declined were to congresses on physical education. After the revolution almost every invitation was accepted, even to the First World's Poultry Congress in the Netherlands, held in 1921. See ibid., file 19.

25. This section is mainly background to the debates over the tarbush that occurred in the 1920s. The kinds of changes taking place in the nineteenth century and early twentieth in relation to dress were dramatic and of global proportions. The revolutions in cotton production in the eighteenth century had laid the groundwork for fundamental shifts in the world economy stemming from industrialization in Britain and the consolidation of its Indian colony. The emergence of factory production of clothes and its rapid expansion at the end of the nineteenth century in Britain and the United States had a profound impact, one that reached well beyond those societies. It is impossible to consider this vast history here except in some of its discursive reverberations. In a sense, the figures of linen and the coat in Marx's elaboration of the capitalist commodity form in the first chapter of volume 1 of *Capital* constitute a historical monument to that moment. Other worthwhile sources are E. P. Thompson, *The Making of the English Working Class*, and Owen, *Cotton and the Egyptian Economy*.

26. Although in formal terms it was only after the settlements following the First World War that the states under varying degrees of colonial tutelage would be implicated in an *international* order, those terms (legal, political, economic, and cultural) were already being worked out through the various struggles as well as exchanges of knowledge which marked the imperial social formation from the second half of the nineteenth century. See Sinha, *Colonial Masculinity*.

27. Toledano, *State and Society in Mid-Nineteenth-Century Egypt*, 160–63.

28. Ibid., 178.

29. More evidence supporting Toledano's analysis is in the autobiography of Ibrahim Fawzi. On Fawzi, see Powell, *A Different Shade of Colonialism*, chapter 3, and Jacob, "History and the Masculine Subject of Colonialism."

30. It originally appeared in volume 9 of his twenty-volume work on the history and geography of Egypt, *al-Khitat al-Tawfiqiyya*. My citations are from a reprint of just the autobiographical entry, Mubarak, *Hayati*.

31. There is a translation of an extract and a brief introduction in the anthology edited by Reynolds, *Interpreting the Self*, 224–40.

32. Mubarak, *Hayati*, 21–22.

33. Ibid.

34. This form of punishment of government officials was apparently standard during the rule of the viceroys. Nassau William Senior, *Conversations and Journals in Egypt and Malta*, 2 vols. (London: Sampson Low, Marston, Searle, and Rivington, 1882), 2:85. Cited in Hunter, *Egypt under the Khedives, 1805–1879*, 84n10. Also mentioned in Toledano, *State and Society in Mid-Nineteenth-Century Egypt*, 162.

35. Mubarak, Hayati, 23.

36. The redoubtable cultural critic and anticolonialist 'Abdallah Nadim had already broached this topic in his satirical dialogue between a peasant father, Mi'it, and his European-educated son, Zi'it, in the very first issue of his weekly paper. Nadim, " 'Arabi tafarrnuj" (Europeanized Egyptian), *al-Tankit wa al-tabkit* (June 6, 1881), 7–8. Despite the use of 'Arabi (Arab) in the title, the content is specifically Egyptian.

37. The author used "Western" (*gharbi*) and "European" (*urubbi*) interchangeably in his description of non-Eastern and non-Egyptian fashions and habits.

38. In a twist from Homi Bhabha's use of this term, mimicry here had the potential of being a menacing performance for the subject and the nation rather than the colonizer. Bhabha, "Of Mimicry and Man."

39. And it is in this point that a significant difference from Nadim's time and his criticism might be located.

40. *Al-Ajyal* (October 19, 1897), 242–44.

41. Ibid., 242.

42. Ibid.

43. Ibid.

44. Ibid., 243.

45. So at least two years before the publication of Qasim Amin's supposedly

groundbreaking, controversial book *Tahrir al-Mar'a*, the education of women was already circulating in public discourse as a solution to the Egyptian question, which begs the question of Amin's celebrity status at the time and in the history of Egyptian feminism. In *Women and Gender in Islam* Leila Ahmed addressed this issue over a decade and a half ago in her memorable characterization (or, more precisely, caricaturing) of Amin as the "son of Cromer" rather than the father of Egyptian feminism, but I do not believe that linkage alone — between Amin and colonialism — explains the controversy surrounding his book's claims in favor of women's education. I would suggest that it was in the specific temporality and relational nature of his imagined female subject that one might find an answer. Despite the fact that his work merely presented a recuperated patriarchy on the Victorian model, at the time Amin's figure of the liberated woman as a necessary condition for the progress of Egyptian men was a radical proposition. Exposing the relationality of gender and projecting a cultural horizon marked by heterosocial intimacy inaugurated gender as a norm in historical time, which in turn constituted a rupture in the divine and natural times of gender that most certainly would have been an occasion for scandal.

46. *Al-Ajyal* (October 19, 1897). The potential of women to bring financial ruin on their husbands through envy and the desire to consume was also a point noted by Nadim, but without the positive valuation of Western women. Today, the misogyny inherent in these statements goes without saying, or, as Michelle Hartman notes, maybe not.

47. For Egypt, see Badran, *Feminists, Islam, and Nation*; Pollard, *Nurturing the Nation*; Russell, *Creating the New Egyptian Woman*; and el-Shakry, "Schooled Mothers and Structured Play." On representations of women in nationalist discourse, see Baron, "Nationalist Iconography," and her *Egypt as a Woman*. The literature on this subject for other geographical areas is too vast to cite here, but the work of Najmabadi on Iran is essential reading — see the bibliography of this book for a full list of references.

48. The only study I am aware of for Egypt that explicitly treats this question is by Marilyn Booth, "Woman in Islam: Men and the 'Women's Press' in Turn-of-the-20th-Century Egypt." Kholoussy's work on marriage debates and anxieties of colonial penetration into the intimate sphere is also apposite here. Kholoussy, "Stolen Husbands and Foreign Wives" and *For Better, For Worse*. For a general reference on masculinity in the Middle East, see Ghoussoub and Sinclair-Webb, eds., *Imagined Masculinities*.

49. On this point, see Chatterjee, "Nationalist Resolution of the Woman's

Question," and Chakrabarty, "The Difference-Deferral of a Colonial Modernity." Also see el-Shakry's revision of Chatterjee's inner/outer formulation for Egypt in "Schooled Mothers and Structured Play."

50. The magnitude and scope of a perceived marriage crisis, which centered on men's preference for bachelorhood or foreign brides, is explored in Kholoussy, *For Better, For Worse*.

51. *Al-Ajyal* (October 19, 1897), 243.

52. Ibid. Emphasis added.

53. On the ways in which historical differences can be made to complicate and open up the conventional story of capital's globalization through a rereading of Marx's notion of abstract labor, see Chakrabarty, "Universalism and Belonging in the Logic of Capital."

54. This early awareness of how Egyptian consumption of European fashion could be complicit with the foreign capitalist exploitation of the East continued to animate cultural criticism before the the First World War. See Salih al-Tantawi, "Real Civilization or Harmful Imitation," *al-Irshad* (February 2, 1906), 2.

55. Wilson, in her now-classic study on dress *Adorned in Dreams*, noted how debates about dress often resulted from the displacement occasioned by seemingly irresoluble political problems.

56. For the political history of this period, see Deeb, *Party Politics in Egypt*; Marsot, *Egypt's Liberal Experiment: 1922–1936*; and, for a history that includes the labor movement, Beinin and Lockman, *Workers on the Nile*.

57. Fikri Abaza came from a wealthy landed family and was noted for his Westernized appearance and secularist worldview. At the time he was a member of the Watani Party, which had been founded by Mustafa Kamil before his death. *Al-Musawwar*, which literally means "illustrated," was perhaps the magazine par excellence of Egyptian modernity in the interwar period. Its new photographic layouts represented the latest objects of cultural and technological innovation. It was launched by Emile and Shukri Zaydan as a more popular complement to their other, relatively highbrow journal, *al-Hilal*. Ami Ayalon, in his historical survey of the Arabic press, classified *al-Musawwar* as nonpolitical; he was contrasting it to the obviously political organs affiliated to one party or another and the satirical press. Ayalon, *The Press in the Arab Middle East*, 78.

58. Fikri Abaza, "Mustafa Kemal: His Triumphs in the World of Fashion," *al-Musawwar* (September 11, 1925), 2.

59. Ibid.

60. According to Vatikiotis, *The History of Egypt*, 303, the Wafd remained neutral in order not to drive the *ulama* further into the arms of the king, thereby increasing his influence.

61. Abaza, "Mustafa Kemal: His Triumphs in the World of Fashion," 2.

62. The dichotomous geography Abaza described worked by instituting a temporal difference in the relations to modernity occupied by East and West such that any hasty attempt to cover the gap could only result in a fall — in this case of Turkish society.

63. The Editor, "Between the Turban and the Tarbush," *al-Nil al-Mussawar* (February 25, 1926), 7. As far as I could ascertain, *al-Nil al-Musawwar* was a Palace-oriented magazine. A seemingly neutral article covering the radical changes declared by Mustafa Kemal had also appeared in *al-Nil al-Mussawar* (September 10, 1925), 24, a day before the *al-Musawwar* issue featuring Abaza's article.

64. At this time King Fuad was financing the efforts of the Azhari Caliphate Committee to organize an Islamic congress in Cairo against the wishes of the Wafd.

65. *Al-Nil al-Musawwar* (February 25, 1926), 7. It is not clear how he arrived at this cost ratio, but it is conceivable, given the amount and quality of material and the workmanship involved in producing a traditional costume for the elite with turban, *quftan*, *jubba*, and undergarments, that as an ensemble it was more expensive than a factory-made suit, especially in a market of diminishing demand.

66. A chronology of these events appears in the souvenir issue of *al-Musawwar* compiled by Badawi, *Shahid 'ayan 'ala al-hayat al-misriyya*, 113–38. Some of the following information was culled from this source.

67. There is a biography of him written by his son Ahmad Muhammad Shakir, who was also a prominent jurist. This reference is from Shaham, "An Egyptian Judge in a Period of Change," 441n6.

68. News of this supposedly minor incident reached as far as New York: "Western Dress in Egypt," *New York Times* (February 9, 1926), 8.

69. Arsalan (1869–1946) was an intellectual from an elite Druze family in Lebanon who was exiled during the French Mandate and lived in Geneva. He was a widely read activist who advocated pan-Islamic unity to resist imperialist aggressions, and he published frequently in the Arabic press throughout the region. His pro-Ottoman sympathies were replaced by a vehement rejection of republican Turkey following Atatürk's modernization program. Zaghlul was the nephew of Sa'd and the son of Fathi Zaghlul, who had died in 1914. Taymur (1871–1930) belonged to a distinguished Egyptian family. He was the father of the famous literary figures Muhammad and Mahmud Taymur and an author of note himself. Two of his principal works were a biography of notables, *Tarajim 'ayan*, from the nineteenth century and a collection of colloquial Egyptian proverbs, *al-Amthal al-'ammiyya*.

70. Shakib Arsalan, *al-Fath* (June 30, 1926), 14. Amir Abd al-Karim had waged a highly successful war against the Spanish in the early 1920s. It took a combined Spanish and French force to suppress his movement, which had been accomplished merely a month before Arsalan's article was published. On this trip to Europe he was most likely en route to exile on the island of Réunion in the Indian Ocean.

71. Ibid.

72. Ibid.

73. Ibid. Ostensibly, Arsalan also believed that to be defeated in the end by such major powers bore no shame and as such did not merit an explicit consideration in his argument. One could also read the reference to Greece and Bulgaria, former provinces of the Ottoman Empire, as an effort to diminish the growing cult of personality around the rabidly secularist Mustafa Kemal, the great liberator of Turkish lands from Greek armies.

74. The letter was dated May 18, 1926. The letter and the EMA's response were published in *al-Muqtataf* (August 1926), 147–48.

75. Ibid., 148.

76. Ahmad Zaghlul, "The Tarbush and the Hat," *al-Fath* (July 22, 1926), 12.

77. Ibid.

78. Ibid.

79. Ibid.

80. Ibid. El-Shakry's research on the EMA shows that it did go on to occupy itself with more socially significant issues, like population. See part 3 of el-Shakry, *The Great Social Laboratory*.

81. Women's exclusion from formal political participation (voting and standing for elections) had been decided by the electoral law of 1923, which, ironically, violated the universal suffrage provision of the national constitution that had been promulgated only three weeks prior. Badran, *Feminists, Islam, and Nation*; in particular, see the chapter entitled "Suffrage and Citizenship," 207–19.

82. Shakib Arsalan, "Healthy Clothing," *al-Fath* (October 14, 1926), 10–11.

83. Anonymous, "The Tarbush or the Hat," *al-Muqtataf* (August 1926), 140–48.

84. For an example of the freedom of choice argument, see "The Turban and the Tarbush in Dar al-'Ulum," *al-Hawi* (March 9, 1926), 5. Also see *Ruz al-Yusuf* (October 20, 1926), 1.

85. Arsalan, *al-Fath*, 11.

86. It was well known during this period that the owners of *al-Muqtataf*, Faris Nimr and the Sarruf brothers, were staunch proponents of the

Kemalist project. See Kawtharani, *al-Dawla wa al-khilafa fi al-khitab al-'arabi aban al-thawra al-kamaliyya fi Turkiyya* (The state and the caliphate in Arab discourse in the wake of the Kemalist revolution in Turkey), 33–34.

87. *Balgha* are the leather slippers, often with curly toes, that were and still are often used to symbolize an exotic and medieval Islamic East in the Orientalist imaginary. For its history as a material object in Cairo's shoe market, see Reynolds, "Commodity Communities," chap. 5.

88. *Al-Muqtataf* (August 1926), 142.

89. Long ago Martina Rieker raised the question of how to account for shifting affective domains in the interstitial zone between "Ottomanism" and "nationalism" after the abolishment of the sultanate and the caliphate. This section reflects her influence and makes a small attempt to address this large, important question.

90. One of the most compelling works to chart the relations among public intimacy, popular culture, and political change is Berlant, *The Queen of America Goes to Washington City*, which connects the rightward turn in America during the 1980s to a "privatization of citizenship" that took place in, among other locations, the realm of fantasy.

91. Ali Abd al-Raziq, "Farewell to the Turban," *al-Siyasa al-Usbu'iyya* (November 13, 1926), 17. This weekly was an offshoot of the Liberal Constitutionalist's newspaper *al-Siyasa*, which was established in 1922 and was edited by Muhammad Husayn Haykal.

92. The book raised questions about the concept of and need for a caliphate in Islam and in turn interrogated the bases of political authority. For a fuller analysis of the controversy this book sparked and its intellectual and political context, see chapter 3 of Gershoni and Jankowski, *Egypt, Islam, and the Arabs*.

93. Al-Raziq, "Farewell to the Turban," 17.

94. *Madhhab* (pl. *madhahib*) usually refers to a school of Islamic legal thought, of which there are four in Sunni Islam. His use of *madhhab* here to designate an aspect of a secular phenomenon like fashion underscored the significance he assigned to it; even if he intended it ironically, there was still an acknowledgement of significance in the parody.

95. The only distinguishing marker he cryptically attributed to the men was that they were middle-aged.

96. In his confused statement about fashion Abd al-Raziq was in good company. Walter Benjamin, who commented extensively on fashion in *The Arcades Project* and elsewhere, apparently oscillated between regarding it "as a manifestation of commodity culture" and "as the manifestation

of a long-repressed utopian desire, to be reenergized at a moment of historical awakening." Wollen, "The Concept of Fashion in *The Arcades Project*," 131.

97. Al-Raziq, "Farewell to the Turban," 17. He might have been referring to Abduh's Transvaal *fatwa* of 1903. Responding to a query from a Muslim in southern Africa about wearing European hats, Abduh answered that if the context—social or climactic—required it, then it was not *haram*. M. Canard, "Coiffure européenne et Islam," *Annales d'Institut d'etudes orientales* (Algiers) 8 (1950): 205; cited in Baker, "The Fez in Turkey."

98. Mahmud Azmi, "Why I Wore the Hat," *al-Hilal* (November 1927), 52–56. An extract from this was incorporated into another article published nearly a decade later titled, "The Hat as a Symbol of Culture: The Issue of the Tarbush and the Unity of Fashion," *al-Majalla al-Jadida* (November 1936), 17–20.

99. Azmi, "Why I Wore the Hat," 53.

100. Azmi used the word *al-tadammun* here for "harmony," which could also mean "comprising," "including," while the cognate *al-tadamun* means "solidarity." In this context, "harmony" captures the reference he was making to the growth of a new cosmopolitanism in the years leading up to the First World War, which was predicated in some circles on peaceful cultural convergence around a supposed universal modernity. For an interesting take on this moment, see Gandhi, *Affective Communities*.

101. Azmi, "Why I Wore the Hat," 53.

102. Azmi never explicitly named or categorized this group, but from the context it would have been clear to the contemporary reader to which class he was referring.

103. Azmi, "Why I Wore the Hat," 54.

104. It is very curious that Azmi thought blasphemy had been removed from the public sphere as a potentially censorious device, since it was still being wielded by members of the religious establishment to police its boundaries against intruders or rebels and was occasionally put at the service of the reigning monarch.

105. In "Postcoloniality and the Artifice of History," 9–10, Chakrabarty notes a similar difference in Indian autobiographies since the mid-nineteenth century. Most of the trappings of bourgeois individualism were indeed present in Indian novels, biographies, and autobiographies, but largely absent was the "endlessly interiorized subject" of the European context. The example he cites is from Bengal in 1932. Of course his larger argument pertains to the problematic of historical translations of cultural difference when Europe remains the "silent referent."

106. Azmi, "Why I Wore the Hat," 56.

107. Ibid. The excerpt of Azmi's confession that appeared in *al-Majalla al-Jadida* in November 1936 ended here.

108. Ibid.

109. Ibid.

110. After an exchange of secret notes between the Foreign Ministries in December, Ankara, in the absence of any further response from Cairo, decided the affair was over.

111. For an interesting story of cultural life in Egypt that takes the tarbush as a central metaphor and is told from the perspective of one of its cosmopolitan communities, see Solé, *Le Tarbouche*.

112. Azmi's case also demonstrates that one could go back to the tarbush given a different set of conditions. A humorous anecdote relates that Azmi was on a beach in Tangiers in 1947 when a Moroccan came up to him and asked what happened to his hat; apparently, in the intervening years he had switched back to the tarbush! The story was recounted by Husayn Mu'nis in *Misr wa risalatuha* and is cited in Badawi, *Shahid 'ayan 'ala al-hayat al-misriyya*, 130.

113. Chakrabarty, *Provincializing Europe*, 42–46; Gershoni and Jankowski, *Redefining the Egyptian Nation*, 43–47.

114. Gershoni and Jankowski, *Redefining the Egyptian Nation*, 47–52.

Chapter 8. Knowledge

1. Because I have focused on demonstrating the constructed nature of effendi masculinity, the figure of the peasant as a gendered subject has made only occasional appearances. Peasant masculinity was equally constructed but perhaps remained almost exclusively a negative ideological projection during the interwar period rather than becoming a site of subject formation. In the Nasserist era, the peasant would be recuperated in complex ways by state socialism as well as by oppositional movements. Indeed, a period film by Salah Abu Saif, *al-Futuwwa* (1957), captured the intricate circuits of resignification through which positive qualities of peasant masculinity intersected with modern city life, crime, and politics. For a reading of the actor playing the character of the *futuwwa*, see Armbrust, "Farid Shauqi." On the figure of the peasant in an earlier period, see Gasper, *The Power of Representation*.

2. *Misr al-haditha al-musawwara* began publication in 1924.

3. 'Isa Ghuji, "Hayy al-'uzama' wa al-sa'alik wa al-akwakh wa al-qusur,"

Misr al-haditha al-musawwara 7/3 (August 21, 1929), 6–7. Although authorship was not always attributed, most of the articles in the "Lessons from Life" series seem to have been written by the same person.

4. A good comparison would be the text *Hadith 'Isa ibn Hisham* by Muhammad al-Muwaylihi (published as a book in 1907 but serialized in *Misbah al-Sharq* from 1898 to 1900), in which the emerging present of the effendiyya and modern Cairo was the novelty under scrutiny. See Allan, *A Period of Time*; also see Mondal, "Between Turban and Tarbush."

5. Ghuji, "Hayy al-'uzama' wa al-sa'alik wa al-akwakh wa al-qusur," 6.

6. Ibid.

7. Ibid.

8. Ibid.

9. While it would be customary to translate *'aja'ib* as just "wonders," the context here suggests the transmogrification of what appears different to an outside observer into a pathological or bizarre nature of the object itself.

10. It is impossible to translate the curses without distorting their original flavor. In the quote, the girl essentially orders her sister to shut up and proceeds to call down curses on her lineage (presumably the one they both share!).

11. The author provided some statistical information here on the number of *maqahi* ([sing.] *maqha*; *'ahwa* and *'ahawi* in colloquial Egyptian). Based on the most recent census, he claimed, there were at least three hundred cafés in the Husayn quarter alone.

12. The quotations were in the original, "*al-garcon.*"

13. Ghuji, "Hayy al-'uzama' wa al-sa'alik wa al-akwakh wa al-qusur," 6.

14. Ibid. Some of the orders began with an invocation of God: *allahu akbar* and *allahu hayy*. "God is great, coffee black"; "God is life, ordering, tea with lemon"; etc.

15. Ibid.

16. The practice of *zikr*, drug-induced chanting and dancing, according to the author, is introduced in this context, but it is taken up more fully in a later article. See *Misr al-haditha al-musawwara* 13/3 (October 2, 1929); also, the relationship among drugs, a particular sub-urban geography, and the *futuwwat* is elaborated in another issue, see 9/3 (September 4, 1929).

17. *Ma kullu ma yu'arifu yuqal. wala kullu ma yuqal ja' awanihi, wala kullu ma ja' awanihi hadar ahlahu.* The saying was actually appended to the text by the editor. Ghuji, "Hayy al-'uzama' wa al-sa'alik wa al-akwakh wa al-qusur," 7.

18. Contrast this picture of urban colonial modernity with the study of London by Walkowitz, *City of Dreadful Delight*. For the London middle classes at the beginning of the twentieth century the presence of a large underclass in the East End mixing with criminal types and political radicals was a source of social and political anxiety, anxiety often displaced onto a discourse of sexual panic and projects of moral reform.

19. Since it is a matter of life and death — of the effendi and its Other — to which this chapter attends, a number of threads from preceding chapters are tied together while others are just introduced, making a proper conclusion nearly impossible. The logic of this choice of a final chapter will be made clearer in the text.

20. One might have chosen the figure of the peasant (*al-fallah*), the bandit (*al-shaqiy*), or the gangster (*al-baltagi*) rather than *al-futuwwa*, but the historical intersection of masculinity and sovereignty in the figural and actual body of the latter was, as I will show, a cause of its renewed legibility and subsequent resignification in the encounter with the effendi. As such, the mapping of the historical recognition, or misrecognition, of this Other can be generative in plumbing the limits of political modernity as a narrative of inclusion and as the exclusive location of sovereignty in the state. On the discursive production of *ashqiya'* (plural of *shaqiy*), see Brown, "Brigands and State Building."

21. When I refer to the concept exclusively, futuwwa will be written without an article preceding it, while references to a person will be indicated by the use of an article. In Arabic such a distinction is unnecessary; instances of overlap will be signaled by "al-futuwwa."

22. See the introduction.

23. The particular configuration of age, sex, and gender constituting the term's semantic limits presents a problem in itself that is beyond the scope of my investigation; suffice it to say, it is interesting to ponder how and why a term with roots capable of signifying masculine and feminine generated a form exclusively connoting masculinity.

24. El-Messiri, *Ibn al-Balad*. In her typology, an *ibn al-balad* could always become a futuwwa but not vice versa.

25. This chapter is also a segue into a new research project that will examine the discursive and everyday iterations of al-futuwwa as another vantage point from which the story of Egyptian modernity might be told and that might, in turn, retell the story of al-futuwwa.

26. Hansen, "Sovereigns beyond the State," 170.

27. For a similar critique of this period, see Harootunian, *Overcome by Modernity*. On the repetition of modernist assumptions and its implications for

the historical and literary analyses of texts, see Barlow, *The Question of Women in Chinese Feminism*; also see Latour, *We Have Never Been Modern*.

28. Similar reports on the murder of Imtithal Fawzi that portray the futuwwat to the public as characters who are not extinct, as was believed, can be found, *inter alia*, in *Ruz al-Yusuf* (May 28, 1936), 4; *al-Musawwar* (June 5, 1936), 28–29; *al-Hisan* (June 6, 1936), 4–5; *al-Matraqa* (June 6, 1936), 10.

29. Aside from the benefit of hindsight—the effendi would disappear as an official status and fade from popular discourse after the revolution in 1952—the anxiety of death (or, even more precisely, being stillborn) was, as I will demonstrate, the motor driving the frenzy of discursive activity around al-futuwwa.

30. A wide-ranging essay grounded in medieval sources but with a brief foray into modern times suggests a similar possibility albeit in a very different manner: see Irwin's "Futuwwa." Beyond the scope of Irwin's study was the significance of the colonial context to the formation of modern and nonmodern subjects and to the possibility of resignification.

31. There was extensive coverage of this case in all of the major Egyptian newspapers and magazines. Unless otherwise noted, the information for this section was gleaned from a series of articles appearing in *al-Ahram* from May 24–28, 1936. Only direct quotations are cited.

32. The *gallabiya* is a long, loose robe that was still worn by a majority of the population in the 1930s. The cut, color, material, and other variations distinguished among the class, gender, and ethnicity of the wearer. However, in the emerging public culture of the interwar period, the gallabiya became an undifferentiated marker of tradition.

33. *Al-Ahram* (May 24, 1936), 12.

34. *Al-Musawwar* (October 9, 1936), 16.

35. I was unable to verify in the archives how long this department was active and whether its records are still extant.

36. Lopez, "The Dangers of Dancing." It is unclear how he determined (102) that Fuad al-Shami confessed to Fawzi's murder.

37. For an analysis of how this problematic has burdened critique and the social sciences, see Latour, *We Have Never Been Modern*, and el-Shakry, *The Great Social Laboratory*.

38. Al-Sulami's *Kitab al-futuwwa* from the early eleventh century was probably the first formal treatment of the idea as a form of Sufi practice (*al-tasawwuf*). For an interpretation that distinguishes between futuwwa organizations and guilds, see Baer, *Egyptian Guilds in Modern*

Times; and part 3, "Turkish Guilds," of his *Fellah and Townsman in the Middle East*.

39. Some of the major texts are Cahen, "Futuwwa," in H. A. R. Gibb et al., eds., *Encyclopedia of Islam II* (Leiden: Brill Academic Publishers, c. 1960–), 961; Cahen, "Mouvements Populaires et Autonomisme Urbain dans l'Asie Musulmane du Moyen Age" (in three parts); and Cahen, "Note sur les debuts de la Futuwwa d'An-Nasir"; Massignon, "La 'Futuwwa' ou 'pacte d'honneur artisanal' entre les travailleurs musulmans au Moyen Age"; Arnakis, "Futuwwa Traditions in the Ottoman Empire: Akhis, Bektashi Dervishes, and Craftsmen"; Lapidus, *Muslim Cities in the Later Middle Ages*, 153–84. Along with Cahen, Franz Taeschner is the leading authority on al-futuwwa. Unfortunately, most of his work is in German and was inaccessible to me.

40. Franz Taeschner, "Futuwwa—Post-Mongol Period," in H. A. R. Gibb et al., eds., *Encyclopedia of Islam II* (Leiden: Brill Academic Publishers, c. 1960–), 966.

41. See, for example, Sonbol, *The New Mamluks*; Raymond, "Quartiers et Mouvements Populaires"; Berque and al-Shakaa, "La Gamaliya Depuis Un Siècle." See also Staffa, *Conquest and Fusion*; and Ghazaleh, "The Guilds: Between Tradition and Modernity." For a very different approach that treats the analogous phenomenon of *javanmardi* in the contemporary Iranian context, see Adelkhah, *Being Modern in Iran*.

42. This is only a preliminary attempt to think about the narrative possibilities available for a historical figuration of al-futuwwa. Laila Parson's forthcoming historical biography *The Making of Fawzi al-Qawuqji: An Arab Nationalist Soldier and His World* promises to break new ground on this front. On the relations among event, structure, narrative, and temporality, see Koselleck, *Futures Past*. For an eloquent example of this kind of historiography in the South Asian context, see Amin, *Event, Metaphor, Memory*.

43. Fawzi's career points to the increasingly contested nature of the public and public morality in the 1930s. In 1933, she had been arrested, tried, and fined an EGP 1.50 (equivalent to one British pound and fifty pence) on the charge of public indecency during a performance. She refused to pay the fine and appealed twice until the ruling was eventually reversed. The article ends by suggesting that her dancing at the victory party would have earned her a fine of an EGP 100! *Al-Malahi al-musawwara* 6/3 (November 7, 1933), 6–7.

44. Colla, "Anxious Advocacy."

45. Ibid., 419. For a study that demonstrates how the "enlightened" pro-

duced and depended on the "irrational and unjust" in the constitution of modern law, see Esmeir, "The Work of Law in the Age of Empire."

46. Abu Haggag, *Mudhakkirat fitiwwa* (Memoirs of a street thug), as cited in Colla, "Anxious Advocacy," 428. Colla suspects this text was written by an effendi on the margins of the literary mainstream, since similar memoirs from this period were produced under the names of outcast figures like prostitutes, orphans, and maids who were unlikely to have written their own narratives (429). Also see Booth, "From the Horse's Rump and the Whorehouse Keyhole."

47. The anthropologist Sawsan El-Messiri mapped the contemporary vectors of al-futuwwa when it converges with and diverges from a certain normative conception of the native Cairene. See El-Messiri, "The Changing Role of the *Futuwwa* in the Social Structure of Cairo" and *Ibn al-Balad*.

48. TNA: Public PRO FO 371/20126, File J7532, Annual Report of the Cairo City Police for 1935.

49. Foucault, *Discipline and Punish*.

50. Roy, *Indian Traffic*, 55–56. For an anthropological approach that both seeks the limits to and a mode of engaging and making visible the otherness of violence performed by a figure bearing resemblance to the futuwwa and *thuggee*, see Jeganathan, "A Space for Violence."

51. Mines, *Public Faces, Private Voices*.

52. Hansen, "Sovereigns beyond the State," 184–85. As we will see below, Ahmad Amin had mapped this spectrum of subject positions for al-futuwwa in the 1930s. There is a surfeit now of popular cultural treatments of the oscillation between these two points in the careers of local big men. In the United States one need only look at the treatment of the mafia and drug gangs in the highly acclaimed and popular HBO series *The Sopranos* and *The Wire* to glimpse the sophisticated ways in which this figure has returned. But one might also examine the recent film *Gomorrah* (Matteo Garonne, 2008), adapted from the controversial novel of 2006 by the Italian Roberto Saviano. In the Indian context, see the densely layered portrayal of the Mumbai underworld in the novel *Sacred Games* by Vikram Chandra, also from 2006. Why now is a question to which the answer seems practically self-evident, though it would be wrong — the state is not losing ground to other forces, but just as in the interwar period these cultural performances are perhaps signs of an emergent state. Today, this may be the security state of which many have begun to write. For one of the more thoughtful treatments of its philosophical and juridical bases, see Agamben, *Homo Sacer*.

53. According to the senior head coach of the national Egyptian weight-

lifting team, who had become interested himself in the sport in the late 1930s and became a world champion in 1950, these neighborhood workout spaces were quite common (interview with Kamal Mahjub at the Egyptian Weightlifting Association, May 19, 2002). Pictures of some of the greats of Egyptian weightlifting, including those of Mahjub, appear in his *Tadrib rafaʿ al-athqal: al-mahara al-harakiyya*.

54. *Al-Ahram* (May 26, 1936), 10.

55. This was apparently a fairly typical trajectory for weightlifting enthusiasts who found other career paths closed to them. (Interview with Kamal Mahjub; he was uncomfortable making this connection and ultimately tried to reposition the futuwwa as a heroic figure.)

56. Although signs of its declining status as an exclusive neighborhood were already evident with the rise of prostitution in the area during the First World War, when official recognition was granted to it as an acceptable area for the trade. TNA: PRO FO 141/466, File 1429 (Part I), "Report of the Cairo Purification Committee's first meeting," April 18, 1916.

57. Stoler, "Cultivating Bourgeois Bodies and Racial Selves," 90.

58. Anonymous, "Ask Me about al-futuwwat, *al-baltagiyya*, and *al-barmagiyya*," *al-Musawwar* (June 5, 1936), 28–29.

59. *Al-Matraqa* introduces them—fixed with the label *al-baltagiyya*—as a group "we had thought . . . had disappeared." *Al-Matraqa* 200/15 (June 6, 1936), 10.

60. Anonymous, "Ask Me," *al-Musawwar*, 28.

61. Ibid.

62. See below.

63. He describes these cafés elsewhere as being "traditional." Although this is one possible translation of the Arabic word *baladi*, the reader should be aware that conceptually this word envelops a complicated field of meaning in which both a spatial and temporal—and arguably a moral—alterity is figured.

64. Anonymous, "Ask Me," 29. On this other Cairo, see ʿAbd al-Wahhab Bakr, *Mujtamaʿ al-Qahira al-sirri, 1900–1951*.

65. Azbakiyya in the late fifteenth century was a wealthy suburb northwest of Fatimid Cairo, adjacent to the Nile port of Bulaq, and contained a man-made lake surrounded by the palaces of princes and leading merchants. In the nineteenth century it was absorbed into Khedive Ismail's Hausmannization projects to prepare Cairo for the grand celebrations he had planned for the opening of the Suez Canal. Janet Abu-Lughod writes that beginning in the 1880s, "with colonial rule and the influx of large numbers of Europeans, this new portion of the city was increas-

ingly marked off as a 'foreign' preserve. Azbakiyah, the center of the new city, contained over 56,000 inhabitants in 1917, of whom only under 14,000 were Egyptian Muslims!" J. Abu-Lughod, *Cairo*, 158.

66. Anonymous, "Ask Me," 29.

67. I could not find other references to "Drakatus" and "Veratus" so I cannot be certain about the transliteration. According to the author there were famous establishments known to "commoners and the elite" in other neighborhoods as well. He names 'Abidin, al-Isma'iliyya, and al-Tawfiqiyya.

68. On the concept of normalization and elite discourses of nation in the Indian context, see Chatterjee, *The Nation and Its Fragments*. Chatterjee's recent inquiry into the notion of political society as a category with greater purchase on postcolonial realities (than, for example, civil society) augurs the kind of analytics necessary to materialize al-futuwwa's transformation as a historical event and capture something of its life in the everyday. Chatterjee, *The Politics of the Governed*.

69. The murder of Imtithal Fawzi happened at a time when the bourgeois representatives of the Egyptian nation were engaged in treaty negotiations with the British to eliminate the four clauses of the declaration of 1922 allowing the British effectively to continue their control over the country. Hence, the desire to appear modern and in control was especially pronounced among Egypt's image-makers at a time of heightened uncertainty about the future.

70. Anonymous, "Adrar al-madaniyya al-haditha: tawa'if al-futuwwat wa-l-baltagiyya," *al-Hisan* 214 (June 6, 1936), 4–5.

71. For a recent history that shows the adaptive capacity and continuity of the artisanal trades and other occupations in Cairo, see Chalcraft, *The Striking Cabbies of Cairo and Other Stories*.

72. Anonymous, "Adrar al-madaniyya al-haditha," 4.

73. Ibid.

74. *Al-Musawwar* (October 9, 1936), 16. Blurring the lines further, this sartorial anxiety could index a complex economy of modern desire, as we saw in chapter 7 in terms of debates taking place during the same period among the effendiyya concerning proper headdress, masculinity, and national identity.

75. Anonymous, "Adrar al-madaniyya al-haditha," 5. One wonders in this instance whether high society consorted with the passing *baltagiyya* precisely because the passage was visible.

76. Ibid.

77. Ahmad Amin (1886–1954) was engaged during his lifetime in a project of

making sense of Islamic history in ways that would be relevant to present conditions—hence his designation as a reformer in most accounts of his life. His series of books on the Islamic past—*Fajr al-Islam* (The dawn of Islam, 1928), *Duha al-Islam* (The forenoon of Islam, 1933–36), *Zuhr al-Islam* (The midday of Islam, 1945–55), and *Yawm al-Islam* (The day of Islam, 1952)—became highly popular throughout the Arab world. His career was long and varied. He was educated as a *shariʿa* judge and taught ethics at the Shariʿa Judges School from which he had graduated in 1911. He worked at times as a translator, editor, and journalist; he also became a lecturer in Arabic language and literature at Cairo University (at the behest of Taha Husayn) and served as the dean of the Arts Faculty in 1939. He participated in Orientalist conferences in Leiden in 1931 and Brussels in 1938. For his autobiography, see Amin, *Hayati*; and in English, *My Life*.

78. A version of the lecture was published in *Majallat Kulliyat al-Adab* for May 1942; then it was expanded and published in book form a decade later: *al-Saʿlaka wa al-futuwwa fi al-Islam*. My analysis is based on the book. My reading of this text is by no means exhaustive.

79. *Al-Saʿlaka wa al-futuwwa*, 62. This classification is somewhat homologous to the ethnographic distinction between *gravitas* and *celeritas* in relation to the power of local big men.

80. There is a curious piece in the *Proceedings of the American Philosophical Society* from 1950 that evaluates and rejects all previous scholarly attempts to categorize the futuwwa organizations as a form of chivalry, arguing that the European practice was essentially different because of its basis in an entirely different social-political order, one "based on a regulated system of land grants ('fiefs')." Gerald Salinger, "Was the Futuwa an Oriental Form of Chivalry?" *Proceedings of the American Philosophical Society* 94/5 (October 19, 1950), 481–93, 491. Also see Irwin, "Futuwwa."

81. *Al-Saʿlaka wa al-futuwwa*, 71–72.

82. There is a tension here in juxtaposing Ibn Taymiyya's opposition to the futuwwa with the particular objections against a worldly futuwwa made, most likely, by Sufis. Ahmad Ibn Taymiyya was a Hanbali jurist who lived in Mamluk Damascus from 1263 to 1328 C.E. His opposition to ritual practices emanated from his desire to purify Islam of popular expressions of piety, particularly those authorized by certain forms of Sufism. Furthermore, another problem with invoking Ibn Taymiyya is that the Mamluk rulers saw him as a destabilizing force and jailed him several times; he eventually died a prisoner. This tension can be explained partly as a result of Amin's scant attention to social and political context in re-

covering a history of the futuwwa. Clearly there were political reasons for the ruling class of any city to be concerned with the formation of any kind of brotherhood with the potential for independent and forceful action. Amin leaves these other reasons unspoken, but the persistence of this problem in the nature of futuwwa sodalities will become apparent in his discussion of their fate in modern times. This is one of the clues that Amin's work is more a history of the present than a project of historical recovery; in other words, his text was deployed as an intervention in contemporary religious and cultural debates.

83. *Al-Sa'laka wa al-futuwwa*, 70.

84. Ibid., 70–71.

85. That Amin was definitely concerned about documenting certain traditions before they vanished entirely is made explicit in the introduction to his more popular work *Qamus al-'adat wa al-taqalid wa al-ta'bir al-misriyya* (Dictionary of Egyptian customs, traditions, and expressions), which he started working on at the same time as *al-Sa'laka wa al-futuwwa*. He writes, "It was seeing customs and expressions, vital and alive in my own time, begin to fade and fall out of use, such that very few were familiar even to my own sons, that compelled me to begin this work." Ahmad Amin, cited in Harlow, "Cairo Curiosities: E. W. Lane's *Account* and Ahmad Amin's *Dictionary*," 281.

86. Amin suggests heuristically that Western traditions of chivalry and philanthropy—citing the knighthood and Masonic orders—might be shown to have originated in, or at the very least have a relationship to, al-futuwwa. *Al-Sa'laka wa al-futuwwa*, 66, 75, 87–88.

87. *Muruwwa'* connotes a constellation of ideal masculine virtues—manliness, valor, chivalry, generosity, sense of honor—that when aligned within an individual (usually male) is at the very least noticeable to others. Ibid., 89.

88. Ibid., 90–91. Amin writes that if a rival gang did attack and succeeded in defeating the local protectors, the musical troop accompanying the procession would be required to sing odes in praise of the victors.

89. In Amin, *zu'ar* and *shuttar* were synonyms with futuwwat. Ibid., 93–95.

90. Ibid., 93.

91. There is some evidence that the Watani Party and the early twentieth-century secret societies that were associated with the nationalist movement might have self-consciously identified with an ethos of al-futuwwa. See, for example, Badrawi, *Political Violence in Egypt 1910–1924*, 66–68, 179.

92. *Al-Sa'laka wa al-futuwwa*, 96–98. Amin leaves to God the last word on the future of the Muslim Brotherhood. Much earlier, Amin had written

a book about the relationship of an individual's moral character to the nation using the metaphor of the organic body. Amin, *al-Akhlaq*.

93. *Al-Sa'laka wa al-futuwwa*, 115.

94. Mahfuz's novel-length treatments of al-futuwwa in *Harafish* and *Awlad Haratina* seem to be based on a different narrative impulse from that underlying the short stories written in the 1930s, which, being a non-expert on literature, I may be forgiven for seeing as the product of different historical contexts. In the postcolonial novels, the futuwwat appear as if within a discordant dreamscape, representing an impassable limit to a utopian future. In the short stories, however, the futuwwat were figured as the objects of historical memory, a counterpoint to an intolerable present, and the possibility of a different future. The novels, while fascinating, are beyond the scope of this book. For a historical treatment of futuwwa in one of the novels (that does not consider the earlier representations), see Vatikiotis, "The Corruption of *Futuwwa*."

95. Naguib Mahfuz, *Hams al-Junun* (Cairo: Maktabat Misr, 1938). The readings in this chapter are based on the sixth edition (1969).

96. An earlier darling of the new literati, one who also took a break from depicting bourgeois settings to represent the milieu of the futuwwa—but less successfully, I would argue—was Mahmud Taymur in *al-Hajj Shalabi*.

97. Throughout Mahfuz's life, the alleyways that formed the microsocial worlds of Islamic Cairo—the neighborhoods fanning out from the mosques of al-Azhar and al-Husayn—would remain an ambivalent index of the real *masr* (Cairo/Egypt).

98. *Mu'allim*, derived from the Arabic root for knowledge and knowing (*'ilm*, *'alima*), was applied in the history of Cairo's artisans to designate a master craftsman. It slipped into popular usage and continues to be used as a form of address for members of certain trades or simply to indicate a manly man or audacious woman. It can also be used ironically.

99. Mahfuz, *Hams al-Junun*, 169.

100. Ibid., 171.

101. Ibid.

102. In situations where Mahfuz wished to indicate the possession of al-futuwwa as a gift or as an undefined force inhabiting a subject, he coined the cognate *fatwana*. In order to avoid confusion, I shall continue to use "al-futuwwa" to indicate the overlap between the person and the quality.

103. Ibid., 173.

104. *Futuwwa al-'Atuf* is also the title of the collection in which the story appears. The introduction dates most of the stories from the 1930s, suggesting they had first appeared in serialized form. Several of the stories

were also published in the *Hams al-Junun* collection from 1938. "Futuwwa al-'atuf," appeared in the important literary magazine *al-Risala* 383 (November 4, 1940).

105. This chronology is similar to the one implicit in "Ask Me about al-futuwwat," *al-Musawwar* (June 5, 1936).

106. The word *gada'an* (s. *gada'*) is similar to futuwwa and *rujula* (manliness, masculinity) in that it signifies a complex of positive masculine traits ranging from generosity to honor and strength; a woman can also be considered *gada'*.

107. Mahfuz, *Futuwwa al-'Atuf*, 102.

108. Al-Naqqash, ed., *Naguib Mahfuz*. The information for this section was taken from p. 28–29 unless otherwise noted.

109. This date was cited in an account of the battle given in Abd al-Fattah, *Tarikh futuwwat Misr*, 24. Although Mahfuz remembers this event as a turning point for the institution of fatwana, it seems to have continued to pose a problem for the state as late as 1936, according to Russell's report.

110. As we saw earlier, by 1936 it was already a part of a certain collective memory and a part of a certain process of forgetting.

111. Al-Naqqash, ed., *Naguib Mahfuz*, 30.

112. Mu'nis, *'Asr al-Futuwwat*. The author wrote that he had listened and taken notes while the futuwwa narrated his life story, but he did not compose *'Asr al-futuwwat* until many years later. Given the conditions of the text's production, it is obviously a problematic representation of a futuwwa's "own" views; I use it mainly as a heuristic device. Further citations from this work will be given within the text.

113. Raymond's reading of the origins of al-futuwwat in Egypt is somewhat different. He suggests that in the seventeenth and eighteenth centuries popular militias were often manipulated by Egypt's rulers for their own interests, but they were always wary of their centrifugal potential. Egyptian chroniclers always referred to them in pejorative terms like *'usab*, *shuttar*, *zu'ar*, *ghawgha*, *'awbash*, and *harafish*, words generally signifying their low-class status and distance from respectable society. He seems to be saying that these were the terms that had come to stand in for futuwwa from some earlier unspecified period. Raymond, "Quartiers et Mouvements Populaires," 104–16. Berque claims that the futuwwa was a celebrated local figure in the traditional quarters since the eighteenth century. Berque and al-Shakaa, "La Gamaliya Depuis Un Siècle," 63–64.

114. The rare allegedly autobiographical work of the futuwwa Yusuf Abu Haggag attests to the importance of 1919 and Sa'd Zaghlul to his own development of a nationalist consciousness. This fascinating work was written in a very particular colloquial style; it was first serialized in the

weekly newspaper *Lisan al-Sha'b* starting on August 3, 1924. The articles were later collected and published in a volume titled *Mudhakkirat Futuwwa* (no publication information available). It was also reissued in the volume edited by Abd al-Fattah, *Tarikh futuwwat Misr*. Colla, "Anxious Advocacy," suggests that the *Mudhakkirat* were actually composed by an effendi. Nonetheless, it was received at the time by at least part of the reading public as an unpleasantly genuine article of nonbourgeois culture. *Lisan al-Sha'b* seems to have advertised the *Mudhakkirat* widely. See, for example, *al-Al'ab* (August 27, 1926), 2. In fact, one reader of *al-Al'ab*, Ali Bayumi, took it upon himself to write a counterbiography titled "Mudhakkirat Riyadi," which was serialized in the weekly sports paper beginning on December 10, 1926. In his words, he wished to offer a contrast between the *"rajul gentleman"* and the *"rajul roughman."* (I was unable to establish the end date for the series.)

115. Mu'nis ends his introduction with the acknowledgment that the background he presents is only a brief sketch of the futuwwa's genealogy, and he invites a serious study of the fate of this figure and the institution of fatwana in the modern period.

116. As noted, most present knowledge of what constituted the classical conception of al-futuwwa comes from works like the twelfth-century text *Kitab al-Futuwwa* by Al-Shaykh Abi Abd Allah Muhammad Bin Abi al-Mukarim (a.k.a., Ibn al-Mi'mar al-Baghdadi al-Hanbali). This text is thought to have been written during the reign of Caliph al-Nasir, who himself joined a brotherhood of futuwwat ostensibly in order to try and check their growing influence in Baghdad.

117. Again we encounter the distinction between *celeritas* and *gravitas* made in the ethnographies of local big men.

118. Mu'allim Yusuf Abu Haggag's autobiography provides a similar assessment of Sa'd Zaghlul and the student demonstrators who showed their support and resolve by putting their bodies on the line. 'Abd al-Fattah, *Tarikh futuwwat Misr*, 155–58.

119. I term this a contradictory position because, as I argued above, the futuwwa and his domain—the alley and *hara*—were not mere microcosms of the politician and the nation but formed at times an oppositional terrain of identification, politics, and ethics.

120. *Ful*, the staple dish of Egypt, consists of fava beans prepared in a variety of ways, usually stewed slowly for a long period.

121. Mahmud Fahmi al-Nuqrashi (1888–1948) was known for much of his career as a radical anticolonial nationalist or extremist. However, since he fell out with the Wafd in 1937 and given the chronological flow of the text, these incidents most likely transpired around the time of Zagh-

lul's government in the mid-1920s, when al-Nuqrashi served as deputy interior minister. Of course, his concerns about the British were not off the mark since he was briefly imprisoned for involvement in the assassination of Sir Lee Stack (governor general of Sudan) in Cairo in 1924. A less likely possibility for dating these incidents would place them in the mid-1930s, which would coincide with al-Nuqrashi's shift away from militancy as evinced by his opposition to the formation of the Wafd's paramilitary Blue Shirts.

122. Emphasis added. For Khalil's view of politics as a domain of speech as opposed to the place in which he locates himself—in the domain of action—see p. 114 of 'Asr al-futuwwat. Meanwhile, by the mid-1930s a critical bourgeois view of Egyptian politics represented it as a field polluted by illiberal, nonmodern practices.

123. He casts the Upper Egyptian in a similar relationship to time. Khalil and his futuwwat were forced to go to a village near Assiut to deal with one of his men who had been sentenced to death as a result of a *tar* (blood feud) against his father, who had died before the vendetta could be fulfilled. In this situation, Sa'idis are depicted as stuck in another time, a time incommensurate with their own, when revenge killings and other irrational acts were still prevalent (*'Asr al-futuwwat*, 132–45). A few pages later, Khalil and one of his men ponder their positions as futuwwat in terms of being on the outside of society (*mujtama'*). Interestingly, they place themselves there alongside actresses (147).

124. A fascinating political cartoon from 1935 captures this crossing of futuwwa and liberal forms of authority. It depicts Najib al-Hilali and Sir Geoffrey Corbett in tarbushes and galabiyyas locked in battle as they wield naboots (long sticks); whether they are indeed fighting or participating in a traditional Upper Egyptian dance performed by men is unclear. The issue of *Al-Ithnayn* dated July 15, 1935 (39) produced the cartoon by superimposing on a photograph of a crowd the doctored images of the two sparring officials in masquerade. This image appeared within a context of heightened criticism and anger at the Palace under the ailing King Fuad, who was increasingly dependent on the British High Commission to maintain control and to defer the restoration of the Constitution of 1923. The Palace-appointed government of Tawfiq Nasim created the Ministry of Trade and Industry and appointed Corbett as expert and technical adviser, while handing the portfolio of the new ministry to Hilali, who was already the minister of education. Casting them as stick dancers before a crowd, *Al-Ithnayn* was making a specific reference to a publicity stunt the new minister was alleged to have staged, wherein he was cheered by hundreds of fruit merchants and their workers, predomi-

nantly Upper Egyptians, during a series of visits he made to factories and wholesale markets. Read within the larger context of anticolonial and democratic political struggles, one might also view this cartoon as a general indictment of political thuggery, or the futuwwization of politics. On the new ministry, see Yunan Labib Rizk, "Born a Ministry," *al-Ahram Weekly On-Line* (September 9–15, 2004), http://weekly.ahram.org (accessed May 10, 2009).

125. As I noted above, Husayn Mu'nis makes a call for this in the introduction to *'Asr al-futuwwat*.

126. I am indebted and grateful to Samera Esmeir and Saba Mahmood, who both encouraged and aided the process of rethinking al-futuwwa. They are both formidable futuwwatan.

127. An intriguing example from history of an attempt to take account of the historian's encounter with the Others of time is Skaria, *Hybrid Histories*.

128. Naguib Mahfuz expended more intellectual labor on al-futuwwa than perhaps any of its other interlocutors. Indeed, Mahfuz's brilliant fictionalization and intimate remembrances of this figure inspired my own initial inquiry.

129. El-Messiri, "The Changing Role of the *Futuwwa*," and *Ibn al-Balad*.

130. Al-Naqqash, ed., *Naguib Mahfuz*, 30.

131. A critique of historicism along these lines is elaborated in Chakrabarty, *Provincializing Europe*, particularly in chapter 3, "Translating Life-Worlds into Labor and History."

132. I thank Arang Keshavarzian for helping me see that potential many years ago.

BIBLIOGRAPHY

National Library of Egypt Materials

Periodicals

Al-Abtal

Abu Naddara

Al-Ahali

Al-Ahram

Al-Ajyal

Akhir Sa'a

Al-Al'ab

Al-Al'ab al-Riyadiyya

Al-Amal

Al-Dalil

Al-Dustur

Al-Fath

Al-Fukaha

Al-Funun

Al-Hadara al-Misriyya

Al-Hadi

Haqa'iq al-Sharq

Al-Hawi

Al-Hilal

Al-Hisan

Al-Hurriyya

Al-Irshad

Al-Istiqama

Al-Ithnayn

Al-Jami'a al-Islamiyya

Al-Jawad

Al-Jawa'ib Al-Misriyya

Al-Kashkul

Khayal al-Zill

Al-Kifah

Kull Shay' wa al-Dunya

Al-Lata'if al-Musawwara

Lisan al-Sha'b

Al-Liwa'

Al-Majalla al-Jadida

Majalla Misr al-Haditha al-Musawwara

Majalla al-Risala

Majalla al-Shubban al-Muslimin

Majalla al-Tijariyya al-Nubiyya

Majalla al-Wafd

Al-Ma'mun

Al-Mar'a Al-Misriyya

Al-Matraqa

Misr al-Fatat

Misr al-Haditha al-Musawwara

Misr al-Jadida

Al-Muntakhab

Al-Mu'ayyad

Al-Muqtataf

Al-Musawwar

Al-Mustaqbal

Al-Nahda al-Nisa'iyya

Al-Nil al-Musawwar

Rawdat al-Madaris al-Misriyya

Al-Riyada al-Badaniyya

Ruz al-Yusuf

Sahifa al-Kashafa al-Misriyya

Al-Shahama

Al-Shaja'a

Al-Sharq

Al-Siyasa al-Usbu'iyya

Al-Taj al-Misri

Al-Ta'aruf

Al-Usbu'

Al-Watan

Books

Amin, Ahmad. *Al-Akhlaq*. Cairo: Lajnat al-Ta'lif wa al-Tarjama wa al-Nashr, 1920.

Faraj, Fakhri. *Al-Amrad al-tanasuliyya wa 'alajuha wa turuq al-waqayya minha*. No publication information.

Fikri, 'Ali. *Sa'adat al-zawjayn*. 2d ed. Cairo: Matba'a al-Ma'arif, 1923.

Goldschmidt, Arthur, Amy J. Johnson, and Barak A. Salmoni, eds. *Re-Envisioning Egypt 1919–1952*. Cairo; New York: American University in Cairo Press, 2005.

Hanafi, Ahmad Muhammad. *Al-Bahth 'an al-zawaj al-salih*. Cairo: Al-Matba'a al Yusufiyya, 1920.

Hasan, Ahmad. *Kalima fi al-zawaj al-hasan*. Cairo: Matba'a al-A'amira al-Sharqiyya, 1320 [1902].

Al-Jamal, Husayn Muhammad. *Dakha'il al-bilad aw al-rajul al-muhadhdhib*. Cairo: Matba'a al-Jumhur, 1904.

Mahmud, Mas'ud. *Al-Mar'a fi adwariha al-thalatha*. Cairo, 1925.

Al-Qirfi, Ahmad Hasanayn. *Al-'Aqd al-ijtima'i fi al-tarbiyya al-'a'iliyya*. Cairo: Matba'a al-Ta'lif, 1339 [1920].

Al-Siba'i, Muhammad. *Al-Mar'a al-jadida fi markaziha al-ijtima'i*. Cairo: Matba'a al-Sa'ada, 1921.

Government and Private Archives

Egypt. Mahfuzat Majlis al-Wuzara,' Sharikat wa Jam'aiyyat (box 4B). Abidin, Jam'aiyyat (box 211). Dar al-Watha'iq al-Qawmiyya [National Archives], Cairo.

————. Maktaba Wizara al-Tarbiyya wa al-Ta'lim. Ministry of Education, Cairo.

————. Mahadir al-Jam'aiyya al-'umumiyya li al-nadi al-ahli, 1907–1938. Al-Nadi al-Ahli, Cairo.

France. Photo and Postcard Collection. Private Archive of Max Karkegi, Vitré.

United Kingdom. Foreign Office. Series FO 141, FO 371, FO 848. Colonial Office. Series CO 554. National Archives, London.

Switzerland. International Olympic Committee. CIO CNO-EGYPT-CORR: 1914–1956 (File 71241), CIO JREGI-AFRIC-ALXDR (File 205627), CIO MBR-TAHER-CORR (File 7255/91). IOC Historical Archives, Lausanne.

Films

Al-Futuwwa. Directed by Salah Abu Sayf. Cairo: Markaz al-Sharq al-Awsat li al-Taswiq.

Al-Riyadi. Directed by L. Nagel and Clement Mizrahi, Sharikat al-Aflam al-Misriyya, 1935. Cairo: Gamal al-Laythi.

Other Published Works

'Abbas, Ra'uf. *Al-Nizam al-ijtima'i fi misr fi zill al-milkiyyat al-zira'iyya al-kabira, 1837–1914*. Cairo: Dar al-Fikr al-Hadith, 1973.

————, ed. *Islah am tahdith?: Misr fi 'asr Muhammad 'Ali*. Cairo: Al-Majlis al-a'ala li al-thaqafa, 2000.

Abdalla, Ahmed. *The Student Movement and National Politics in Egypt, 1923–1973*. London: Al-Saqi Books, 1985.

'Abd al-Fattah, Sayyid. *Tarikh futuwwat Misr wa ma'arikahum al-damiyya*. Cairo: Maktabat Madbuli, 1995.

'Abd al-Mutallib, 'Asim Mahrus. *Dawr al-talaba fi thawra 1919*. Cairo: Al-Hay'a al-Misriyya al-'Amma lil-Kitab, 1990.

'Abdelrahman, Nabila Ahmed. *The March of Woman's Sport in Egypt and the Arab Countries*. Alexandria: Alexandria University, 1996.

Abizadeh, Arash. "Was Fichte an Ethnic Nationalist? On Cultural Nationalism and Its Double." *History of Political Thought* 26/2 (summer 2005), 334–59.

Abugideiri, Hibba. "The Scientisation of Culture: Colonial Medicine's Construction of Egyptian Womanhood, 1893–1929." *Gender and History* 16/1 (April 2004), 83–98.

Abu Haggag, Yusuf. "Mudhakkirat Futuwwa." *Tarikh futuwwat Misr*, ed. Sayyid Sadiq Abd al-Fattah, 125–202. Cairo: Maktaba al-Madbuli, 1995.

Abu-Lughod, Janet. *Cairo: 1001 Years of the City Victorious*. Princeton, N.J.: Princeton University Press, 1971.

———. *Before European Hegemony: The World System A.D. 1250–1350*. New York: Oxford University Press, 1995.

Abu-Lughod, Lila, ed. *Remaking Women: Feminism and Modernity in the Middle East*. Princeton, N.J.: Princeton University Press, 1998.

———. *Dramas of Nationhood: The Politics of Television*. Chicago: University of Chicago Press, 2005.

Abu Manneh, Butros. *Studies on Islam and the Ottoman Empire in the Nineteenth Century*. Istanbul: Isis Press, 2001.

Adam, Juliette. *L'Angleterre en Egypte*. Paris: Imprimerie du Centre, 1922.

Adams, James Eli. *Dandies and Desert Saints: Styles of Victorian Masculinity*. Ithaca, N.Y.: Cornell University Press, 1995.

Adelkhah, Fariba. *Being Modern in Iran*. New York: Columbia University Press, 2000.

Agamben, Giorgio. *Homo Sacer: Sovereign Power and Bare Life*. Translated by Daniel Heller-Roazen. Stanford, Calif.: Stanford University Press, 1998.

———. *Means Without End: Notes on Politics*. Translated by Vincenzo Binetti and Cesare Casarino. Minneapolis: University of Minnesota Press, 2000.

———. *The Time That Remains: A Commentary on the Letter to the Romans*. Translated by Patricia Dailey. Stanford, Calif.: Stanford University Press, 2005.

Ahmad, Aijaz. *In Theory: Classes, Nations, Literatures*. New York: Verso, 1992.

Ahmed, Leila. *Women and Gender in Islam: Historical Roots of a Modern Debate*. New Haven, Conn.: Yale University Press, 1992.

———. *A Border Passage: From Cairo to America—A Woman's Journey*. New York: Penguin, 1999.

'Ajawi, Khaled. *Al-Haraka al-riyadiyya al-filistiniyya fi al-shatat*. Damascus: Al-Dar al-Wataniyya al-Jadida, 2001.

Alderson, David. *Mansex Fine: Religion, Manliness and Imperialism in Nineteenth-Century British Culture*. New York: Manchester University Press, 1998.

Allan, Roger. *A Period of Time: A Study and Translation of Hadith 'Isa Ibn Hisham by Muhammad al-Muwaylihi*. Reading, UK: Ithaca Press, 1992.

Allen, Bernard M. *Gordon and the Sudan*. New York: Macmillan, 1931.

Allen, Judith A. "'Mundane' Men: Historians, Masculinity and Masculinism." *Historical Studies* 22/89 (October 1987), 617–28.

————. "Men Interminably in Crisis? Historians on Masculinity, Sexual Boundaries, and Manhood." *Radical History Review* 82 (2002), 191–207.

Alloula, Malek. *The Colonial Harem*. Minneapolis: University of Minnesota Press, 1986.

Alter, Joseph. "The 'Sannyasi' and the Indian Wrestler: The Anatomy of a Relationship." *American Ethnologist* 19/2 (May 1992), 317–36.

————. "Celibacy, Sexuality, and the Transformation of Gender into Nationalism in North India." *Journal of Asian Studies* 53/1 (February 1994), 45–66.

————. "Somatic Nationalism: Indian Wrestling and Militant Hinduism." *Modern Asian Studies* 28/3 (1994), 557–88.

Althusser, Louis. "Ideology and Ideological State Apparatuses (Notes towards an Investigation)." *Lenin and Philosophy and Other Essays*. Translated by Ben Brewster, 127–86. New York: Monthly Review Press, 1971.

Altorki, Soraya. "Patriarchy and Imperialism: Father-Son and British-Egyptian Relations in Najib Mahfuz's Trilogy." *Intimate Selving in Arab Families: Gender, Self, and Identity*, ed. Suad Joseph, 214–34. Syracuse, N.Y.: Syracuse University Press, 1999.

Alwis, Malathi de. "'Respectability,' 'Modernity' and the Policing of 'Culture' in Colonial Ceylon." In *Gender, Sexuality, and Colonial Modernity*, ed. Antoinette Burton, 177–92. New York: Routledge, 1999.

Amin, Ahmad. *Al-Akhlaq*. Cairo: Lajna al-Ta'lif wa al-Tarjama wa al-Nashr, 1920.

————. *Zuhr al-Islam* [The midday of Islam]. Cairo: Lajna al-Ta'lif wa al-Tarjama wa al-Nashr, 1946.

————. *Ila Waladi*. Cairo: Maktaba al-Adab, 1951.

————. *Al-Sa'laka wa al-futuwwa fi al-Islam*. Cairo: Dar al-Ma'arif, 1952.

————. *Yawm al-Islam* [The day of Islam]. Cairo: Dar al-Ma'arif, 1952.

————. *Hayati*. al-Tab'a 4. al-Qahira: Maktaba al-Nahda al-Misriyya, 1961.

————. *Fajr al-Islam* [The dawn of Islam]. 10th ed. Cairo: Maktaba al-Nahda al-Misriyya, 1965.

————. *Duha al-Islam* [The forenoon of Islam]. 3 vols. 8th ed. Cairo: Maktaba al-Nahda al-Misriyya, 1972.

————. *My Life: The Autobiography of an Egyptian Scholar, Writer and Cultural Leader*. Translated by Issa Boullata. Leiden, Netherlands: Brill, 1978.

————. *Qamus al-'adat wa al-taqalid wa al-ta'bir al-misriyya* [Dictionary of Egyptian customs, traditions, and expressions]. Cairo: Maktaba al-Nahda al-Misriyya, 1982.

Amin, Husayn. *Fi bayt Ahmad Amin*. Cairo: Dar al-Hilal, 1985.

Amin, Qasim. *Les Égyptiens: Réponse à M. Le Duc d'Harcourt*. Cairo: Jules Barbier, 1894.

————. *Al-A'mal al-kamila.* Cairo: Dar al-Shuruq, 1989.

————. *The Liberation of Women.* Translated by Samiha Sidhom Peterson. Cairo: American University in Cairo Press, 1992.

————. *The New Woman: A Document in the Early Debate on Egyptian Feminism.* Translated by Samiha Sidhom Peterson. Cairo: American University in Cairo Press, 1995.

Amin, Shahid. *Event, Metaphor, Memory: Chauri Chaura, 1922–1992.* Berkeley: University of California Press, 1995.

Anderson, Benedict. *Imagined Communities: Reflections on the Origin and Spread of Nationalism.* New York: Verso, 1991.

al-'Aqqad, 'Abbas Mahmud. *Sa'd Zaghlul.* Cairo: Dar al-Shuruq, 1975.

Arata, Stephen. *Fictions of Loss in the Victorian Fin de Siècle: Identity and Empire.* Cambridge: Cambridge University Press, 1996.

Archetti, Eduardo P. "Playing Styles and Masculine Virtues in Argentine Football." *Machos, Mistresses, Madonnas: Contesting the Power of Latin American Gender Imagery,* ed. Marit Melhuus and Kristi Anne Stølen, 34–55. New York: Verso, 1996.

Arendt, Hannah. *The Human Condition.* Chicago: University of Chicago Press, 1958.

Armbrust, Walter. *Mass Culture and Modernism in Egypt.* Cambridge: Cambridge University Press, 1996.

————. "Farid Shauqi: Tough Guy, Family Man, Cinema Star." *Imagined Masculinities: Male Identity and Culture in the Modern Middle East,* ed. Mai Ghoussoub and Emma Sinclair-Webb, 199–226. London: Saqi Books, 2006.

Armstrong, Nancy. *Desire and Domestic Fiction: A Political History of the Novel.* New York: Oxford University Press, 1987.

Arnakis, G. G. "Futuwwa Traditions in the Ottoman Empire: Akhis, Bektashi Dervishes, and Craftsmen." *Journal of Near Eastern Studies* 12/4 (October 1953), 232–47.

Arnold, Guy. *Held Fast for England: G. A. Henty, Imperialist Boys' Writer.* London: Hamish Hamilton, 1980.

Arslan, Shakib. *Shawqi: Aw sadaqat arba'in sana.* Cairo: Matba'a 'Issa al-Babi al-Halabi.

Asad, Talal. "Are There Histories of Peoples without Europe? A Review Article." *Comparative Studies in Society and History* 29/3 (1987), 594–607.

————. "Conscripts of Western Civilization." *Dialectical Anthropology: Essays in Honor of Stanley Diamond.* Volume 1: *Civilization in Crisis,* ed. Christine Ward Gailey, 333–51. Tallahassee: University Press of Florida, 1992.

————. *Genealogies of Religion: Discipline and Reasons of Power in Christianity and Islam*. Baltimore: Johns Hopkins University Press, 1993.

————. *Formations of the Secular: Christianity, Islam, Modernity*. Stanford, Calif.: Stanford University Press, 2003.

Asad, Talal, and Roger Owen. "The Critique of Orientalism: A Reply to Professor Dodd." *Bulletin of the British Society for Middle East Studies* 7/1 (1980), 33–38.

Austin, J. L. *How to Do Things with Words*. Cambridge, Mass.: Harvard University Press, 1962.

el-Awaisi, Abd al-Fattah. "Emergence of a Militant Leader: A Study of the Life of Hasan al-Banna, 1906–1928." *Journal of South Asian and Middle Eastern Studies* 22/1 (fall 1998), 46–63.

Ayalon, Ami. *The Press in the Arab Middle East: A History*. New York: Oxford University Press, 1995.

Badawi, Gamal. *Shahid 'ayan 'ala al-hayat al-misriyya*. Cairo: Dar al-Hilal, 2001.

Badran, Margot. *Feminists, Islam, and Nation: Gender and the Making of Modern Egypt*. Princeton, N.J.: Princeton University Press, 1995.

Badrawi, Malak. *Political Violence in Egypt 1910–1924: Secret Societies, Plots and Assassinations*. Richmond, Surrey: Curzon Press, 2000.

————. *Isma'il Sidqi, 1875–1950: Pragmatism and Vision in Twentieth-Century Egypt*. Richmond, Surrey: Curzon Press, 1996.

Baer, Gabriel. *A History of Landownership in Modern Egypt, 1800–1950*. Oxford: Oxford University Press, 1962.

————. *Egyptian Guilds in Modern Times*. Jerusalem: Israel Oriental Society, 1964.

————. *Fellah and Townsman in the Middle East*. London: Frank Cass, 1982.

Bailey, Peter. *Leisure and Class in Victorian England: Rational Recreation and the Contest for Control, 1830–1885*. Buffalo, N.Y.: University of Toronto Press, 1978.

Baker, Patricia L. "The Fez in Turkey: A Symbol of Modernization?" *Costume* 20 (1986), 72–85.

Baker, William J., and James A. Mangan. *Sport in Africa: Essays in Social History*. New York: Africana Publishing, 1987.

Bakr, 'Abd al-Wahhab. *Mujtama' al-Qahira al-sirri, 1900–1951*. Cairo: al-'Arabi, 2001.

Balibar, Etienne. *Masses, Classes, Ideas: Studies on Politics and Philosophy before and after Marx*. Translated by James Swenson. New York: Routledge, 1994.

Ballantyne, Tony. "Rereading the Archive and Opening Up the Nation-State: Colonial Knowledge in South Asia (and Beyond)." *After the Imperial*

Turn: Thinking with and through the Nation, ed. Antoinette Burton, 102–21. Durham, N.C.: Duke University Press, 2003.

Ballhatchet, Kenneth. *Race, Sex and Class under the Raj: Imperial Attitudes and Policies and Their Critics, 1793–1905*. New York: St. Martin's Press, 1980.

al-Banna, Hasan. *Five Tracts of Hasan Al-Banna (1906–1949), A Selection from the Majmu'at Rasa'il al-Imam Hasan al-Banna*. Translated by Charles Wendell. Berkeley: University of California Press, 1978.

———. *Majmu'at rasa'il al-imam al-shahid Hasan al-Banna*. Cairo: Dar al-Hadara al-Islamiyya, 1981.

Baring, Evelyn, Earl of Cromer. *Modern Egypt*. 2 vols. London: Macmillan, 1908.

Barlow, Tani, ed. *Formations of Colonial Modernity in East Asia*. Durham, N.C.: Duke University Press, 1997.

———. *The Question of Women in Chinese Feminism*. Durham, N.C.: Duke University Press, 2004.

Baron, Beth. *The Women's Awakening in Egypt: Culture, Society, and the Press*. New Haven, Conn.: Yale University Press, 1994.

———. "Nationalist Iconography: Egypt as Woman." *Rethinking Nationalism in the Arab Middle East*, ed. Israel Gershoni and James Jankowski, 105–24. New York: Columbia University Press, 1997.

———. *Egypt as a Woman: Nationalism, Gender, and Politics*. Berkeley: University of California Press, 2005.

Bayly, C. A. *The Birth of the Modern World, 1780–1914: Global Connections and Comparisons*. Malden, Mass.: Blackwell, 2004.

Bean, Susan S. "Gandhi and Khadi, the Fabric of Indian Independence." *Cloth and Human Experience*, ed. Annette B. Weiner and Jane Schneider, 355–76. Washington, D.C.: Smithsonian Institution Press, 1989.

Beattie, Peter M. "The House, the Street, and the Barracks: Reform and Honorable Masculine Social Space in Brazil, 1864–1945." *Hispanic American Historical Review* 76/3 (August 1996), 439–73.

Bederman, Gail. *Manliness and Civilization: A Cultural History of Gender and Race in the United States, 1880–1917*. Chicago: University of Chicago Press, 1995.

Beinin, Joel, and Zachary Lockman. *Workers on the Nile: Nationalism, Communism, Islam and the Egyptian Working Class, 1882–1954*. Princeton, N.J.: Princeton University Press, 1987.

Benhabib, Seyla. "Feminist Theory and Hannah Arendt's Concept of Public Space." *History of the Human Sciences* 6/2 (1993), 97–114.

Benjamin, Walter. *Charles Baudelaire: A Lyric Poet in the Era of High Capitalism*. Translated by Harry Zohn. London: Verso, 1983.

Berlant, Lauren Gail. *The Queen of America Goes to Washington City: Essays on Sex and Citizenship*. Durham, N.C.: Duke University Press, 1997.

Berque, Jacques. *L'Égypte: Impérialisme et Révolution*. Paris: Gallimard, 1967.

————. *Egypt: Imperialism and Revolution*. Translated by Jean Stewart. London: Faber and Faber, 1972.

Berque, Jacques, and Mustafa al-Shakaa. "La Gamaliya Depuis un Siècle: Essai d'histoire sociale d'un quartièr du Caire." Extract of a review in *Études Islamiques* 42/1 (1974).

Bhabha, Homi. "Of Mimicry and Man: The Ambivalence of Colonial Discourse." *October* 28 (spring 1984), 125–33.

————. "Sly Civility." *October* 34 (autumn 1985), 71–80.

————. "DissemiNation: Time, Narrative, and the Margins of the Modern Nation." *Nation and Narration*, ed. Homi Bhabha, 291–322. New York: Routledge, 1990.

————. *The Location of Culture*. New York: Routledge, 1994.

————. "Are You a Mouse or a Man?" *Constructing Masculinity*, ed. Brian Wallis, Maurice Berger, and Simon Watson, 57–68. New York: Routledge, 1995.

Bier, Laura. "Modernity and the Other Woman: Gender and National Identity in the Egyptian Women's Press: 1952–1967." *Gender and History* 16/1 (April 2004), 99–112.

Blunt, Wilfrid Scawen. *Secret History of the English Occupation of Egypt: Being a Personal Narrative of Events*. New York: A. A. Knopf, 1922.

————. *Gordon at Khartoum: Being a Personal Narrative of Events*. New York: A. A. Knopf, 1923.

————. *My Diaries: Being a Personal Narrative of Events 1888–1914*. New York: A. A. Knopf, 1923.

Boehmer, Elleke. *Empire, the National, and the Postcolonial, 1890–1920: Resistance in Interaction*. New York: Oxford University Press, 2002.

Bonner, Michael. *Jihad in Islamic History: Doctrines and Practices*. Princeton, N.J.: Princeton University Press, 2006.

Booth, Marilyn. *May Her Likes Be Multiplied: Biography and Gender Politics in Egypt*. Berkeley: University of California Press, 2001.

————. "Woman in Islam: Men and the 'Women's Press' in Turn-of-the-20th-Century Egypt." *International Journal of Middle East Studies* 33/2 (2001), 171–201.

————. "Un/safe/ly at Home: Narratives of Sexual Coercion in 1920s Egypt." *Gender and History* 16:3 (November 2004), 744–68.

————. "From the Horse's Rump and the Whorehouse Keyhole: Ventriloquized Memoirs as Political Voice in 1920s Egypt." *Maghreb Review* 32/2–3 (2007), 233–61.

Bourdieu, Pierre. *Outline of a Theory of Practice*. Translated by Richard Nice. New York: Cambridge University Press, 1977.

———. *The Logic of Practice*. Translated by Richard Nice. Stanford, Calif.: Stanford University Press, 1990.

———. "How Can One Be a Sports Fan?" *The Cultural Studies Reader*, ed. Simon During, 339–56. New York: Routledge, 1993.

———. *Masculine Domination*. Translated by Richard Nice. Stanford, Calif.: Stanford University Press, 2001.

Bourke, Joanna. *Dismembering the Male: Men's Bodies, Britain, and the Great War*. Chicago: University of Chicago Press, 1996.

Bowen, Donna Lee, and Evelyn A. Early. *Everyday Life in the Muslim Middle East*. Bloomington: Indiana University Press, 2002.

Bowman, Humphrey. *Middle-East Window*. New York: Longmans, Green, 1942.

Boyarin, Daniel. *Unheroic Conduct: The Rise of Heterosexuality and the Invention of the Jewish Man*. Berkeley: University of California Press, 1997.

Boyle, Clara. *A Servant of the Empire: A Memoir of Harry Boyle*. London: Methuen, 1938.

Breward, Christopher. *The Hidden Consumer: Masculinities, Fashion and City Life, 1860–1914*. New York: Manchester University Press, 1999.

Brooks, Peter. *Body Work: Objects of Desire in Modern Narrative*. Cambridge, Mass.: Harvard University Press, 1993.

Brown, Nathan. "Brigands and State Building: The Invention of Banditry in Modern Egypt." *Comparative Studies in Society and History* 32/2 (April 1990), 258–81.

———. "The Ignorance and Inscrutability of the Egyptian Peasantry." *Peasant Politics and Violence in the Middle East*, ed. John Waterbury and Farhad Kazemi, 203–21. Miami: University Press of Florida, 1991.

———. "The Precarious Life and Slow Death of the Mixed Courts of Egypt." *International Journal of Middle East Studies* 25/1 (February 1993), 33–52.

———. "Law and Imperialism: Egypt in Comparative Perspective." *Law and Society Review* 29/1 (1995), 103–26.

Brownell, Susan. "Strong Women and Impotent Men: Sports, Gender, and Nationalism in Chinese Public Culture." *Spaces of Their Own: Women's Public Sphere in Transnational China*, ed. Mayfair Mei-Hui Yang, 207–31. Minneapolis: University of Minnesota Press, 1999.

Buck-Morss, Susan. *The Dialectics of Seeing: Walter Benjamin and the Arcades Project*. Cambridge, Mass.: MIT Press, 1990.

Budd, Michael Anton. *The Sculpture Machine: Physical Culture and Body Politics in the Age of Empire*. New York: New York University Press, 1997.

Buettner, Elizabeth. *Empire Families: Britons and Late Imperial India*. New York: Oxford University Press, 2004.

Burke, Edmund. "Orientalism and World History: Representing Middle Eastern Nationalism and Islamism in the Twentieth Century." *Theory and Society* 27/4 (August 1998), 489–507.

Burstyn, Varda. *The Rites of Men: Manhood, Politics, and the Culture of Sport*. Toronto: University of Toronto Press, 1997.

Burton, Antoinette. *The Burdens of History: British Feminists, Indian Women, and Imperial Culture, 1865–1915*. Chapel Hill: University of North Carolina Press, 1994.

———. "Who Needs the Nation? Interrogating 'British' History." *Journal of Historical Sociology* 10/3 (1997), 227–48.

———. *At the Heart of the Empire: Indians and the Colonial Encounter in Late-Victorian Britain*. Berkeley: University of California Press, 1998.

———, ed. *Gender, Sexuality, and Colonial Modernity*. New York: Routledge, 1999.

———, ed. *After the Imperial Turn: Thinking with and through the Nation*. Durham, N.C.: Duke University Press, 2003.

———. *Dwelling in the Archive: Women Writing House, Home, and History in Late Colonial India*. New York: Oxford University Press, 2003.

Butler, Judith. *Subjects of Desire: Hegelian Reflections in Twentieth-Century France*. New York: Columbia University Press, 1987.

———. *Gender Trouble: Feminism and the Subversion of Identity*. New York: Routledge, 1990.

———. *Bodies that Matter: On the Discursive Limits of "Sex."* New York: Routledge, 1993.

———. "'Conscience Doth Make Subjects of Us All.'" *Yale French Studies* 88 (1995), 6–26.

———. *Excitable Speech: A Politics of the Performative*. New York: Routledge, 1996.

———. *The Psychic Life of Power: Theories in Subjection*. Stanford, Calif.: Stanford University Press, 1997.

Butler, Judith, and Joan Scott, eds. *Feminists Theorize the Political*. New York: Routledge, 1992.

Cachia, Anna, and Pierre Cachia. *Two Alien Lives in Egypt: Land-locked Islands*. Cairo: American University in Cairo Press, 1999.

Cachia, Pierre. *Popular Narrative Ballads of Modern Egypt*. New York: Oxford University Press, 1989.

Cahen, Claude. "Note sur les debuts de la Futuwwa d'An-Nasir." *Oriens* 6/1 (1953), 18–22.

———. "Mouvements Populaires et Autonomisme Urbain dans l'Asie Musulmane du Moyen Age [in three parts]." *Arabica* 5/3 (1958), 225–50; ibid. 6/1 (1959), 25–56; ibid. 6/2 (1959), 233–60.

Caillard, Mabel. *A Lifetime in Egypt, 1876–1935.* London: Grant Richards, 1935.

Calhoun, Craig. *Habermas and the Public Sphere.* Cambridge, Mass.: MIT Press, 1993.

Cannadine, David. *Ornamentalism: How the British Saw Their Empire.* New York: Oxford University Press, 2001.

Cannon, Byron. *Politics of Law and the Courts in Nineteenth-Century Egypt.* Salt Lake City: University of Utah Press, 1988.

Caton, Steven Charles. *"Peaks of Yemen I Summon": Poetry as Cultural Practice in a North Yemeni Tribe.* Berkeley: University of California Press, 1990.

Cecil, Edward Herbert. *The Leisure of an Egyptian Official.* New York: Century Publishing, Hippocrene Books, 1984.

Çelik, Zeynep. "Commemorating the Empire: From Algiers to Damascus." *Edges of Empire: Orientalism and Visual Culture*, ed. Jocelyn Hackforth-Jones and Mary Roberts, 20–37. Malden, Mass.: Blackwell, 2005.

Chaillé-Long, C. *The Three Prophets: Chinese Gordon, Mohammed-Ahmed (El Mahdi), Arabi Pasha: Events before and after the Bombardment of Alexandria.* New York: D. Appleton, 1886.

Chakrabarty, Dipesh. "Postcoloniality and the Artifice of History: Who Speaks for 'Indian' Pasts?" *Representations* 37 (1992), 1–26.

———. "Labor History and the Politics of Theory: An Indian Angle on the Middle East." *Workers and Working Classes in the Middle East: Struggles, Histories, Historiographies*, ed. Zachary Lockman, 321–33. Albany: State University of New York Press, 1994.

———. "The Difference-Deferral of a Colonial Modernity: Public Debates on Domesticity in British Bengal." *Tensions of Empire: Colonial Cultures in a Bourgeois World*, ed. Frederick Cooper and Ann Stoler, 373–405. Los Angeles: University of California Press, 1997.

———. *Provincializing Europe: Postcolonial Thought and Historical Difference.* Princeton, N.J.: Princeton University Press, 2000.

———. "Universalism and Belonging in the Logic of Capital." *Public Culture* 12/3 (fall 2000), 653–78.

———. "*Khadi* and the Political Man." *Habitations of Modernity: Essays in the Wake of Subaltern Studies*, ed. D. Chakrabarty, 51–64. Chicago: University of Chicago Press, 2002.

Chalcraft, John T. *The Striking Cabbies of Cairo and Other Stories: Crafts and Guilds in Egypt, 1863–1914.* Albany: State University of New York Press, 2004.

————. "Engaging the State: Peasants and Petitions in Egypt on the Eve of Colonial Rule." *International Journal of Middle East Studies* 37 (2005), 303–25.

Chartier, Roger. *The Cultural Uses of Print in Early Modern France.* Translated by Lydia Cochrane. Princeton, N.J.: Princeton University Press, 1987.

Chatterjee, Partha. *Nationalist Thought and the Colonial World: A Derivative Discourse?* London: Zed Books, 1986.

————. *The Nation and Its Fragments: Colonial and Postcolonial Histories.* Princeton, N.J.: Princeton University Press, 1993.

————. "The Nationalist Resolution of the Women's Question." *Recasting Women: Essays in Indian Colonial History*, ed. Kumkum Sangari and Sudesh Vaid, 233–53. New Brunswick, N.J.: Rutgers University Press, 1997.

————. *The Politics of the Governed: Reflections on Popular Politics in Most of the World.* New York: Columbia University Press, 2004.

Chehabi, H. E. "Sport and Politics in Iran: The Legend of Gholamreza Takhti." *International Journal of the History of Sport* 12/3 (1995), 48–61.

————. "Jews and Sports in Modern Iran." *The History of Contemporary Iranian Jews*, ed. Homa Sarshar and Houman Sarshar, 3–24. Beverly Hills, Calif.: Center for Iranian Jewish Oral History, 2001.

————. "A Political History of Football in Iran." *Iranian Studies* 35/4 (fall 2002), 371–402.

Chowdhury, Indira. *The Frail Hero and Virile History: Gender and the Politics of Culture in Colonial Bengal.* New York: Oxford University Press, 1998.

Churchill, Winston, Francis William Rhodes, and Angus McNeill. *The River War: An Historical Account of the Reconquest of the Soudan.* New York: Longmans, Green, 1899.

Clancy-Smith, Julia. *Rebel and Saint: Muslim Notables, Populist Protest, Colonial Encounters: Algeria and Tunisia, 1800–1904.* Berkeley: University of California Press, 1994.

————. "Marginality and Migration: Europe's Social Outcasts in Precolonial Tunisia, 1830–81." *Outside In: On the Margins of the Modern Middle East*, ed. Eugene Rogan, 149–82. New York: I. B. Tauris, 2002.

Clancy-Smith, Julia, and Frances Gouda, eds. *Domesticating Empire: Race, Gender, and Family Life in French and Dutch Colonialism.* Charlottesville: University Press of Virginia, 1998.

Clark, T. J. *The Painting of Modern Life: Paris in the Art of Manet and His Followers*. New York: Knopf, 1985.

Cleveland, William L. *A History of the Modern Middle East*. 2d ed. Boulder, Colo.: Westview Press, 2000.

Cohn, Bernard S. "Cloth, Clothes, and Colonialism: India in the Nineteenth Century." *Cloth and Human Experience*, ed. Annette B. Weiner and Jane Schneider, 303–53. Washington, D.C.: Smithsonian Institution Press, 1989.

Cole, Juan Ricardo. "Feminism, Class, and Islam in Turn-of-the-Century Egypt." *International Journal of Middle East Studies* 13/4 (November 1981), 387–407.

———. *Colonialism and Revolution in the Middle East: Social and Cultural Origins of Egypt's 'Urabi Movement*. Princeton, N.J.: Princeton University Press, 1993.

Colla, Elliott. "Anxious Advocacy: The Novel, the Law, and Extrajudicial Appeals in Egypt." *Public Culture* 17/3 (fall 2005), 417–43.

———. *Conflicted Antiquities: Egyptology, Egyptomania, and Egyptian Modernity*. Durham, N.C.: Duke University Press, 2007.

Colley, Linda. "Britishness and Otherness: An Argument." *Journal of British Studies* 31/4 (October 1992), 309–29.

———. *Britons: Forging the Nation, 1707–1837*. New Haven, Conn.: Yale University Press, 1992.

Comaroff, Jean. "The Empire's Old Clothes: Fashioning the Colonial Subject." *Situated Lives: Gender and Culture in Everyday Life*, ed. Louise Lamphere, Helena Ragoné, and Patricia Zavella, 400–419. New York: Routledge, 1997.

Comyn, D. C. E. *Service and Sport in the Sudan, a Record of Administration in the Anglo-Egyptian Sudan*. New York: John Lane, 1911.

Connell, R. W. *Masculinities*. Berkeley: University of California Press, 1995.

Cooper, Elizabeth. *The Women of Egypt*. New York: Frederick A. Stokes, 1914.

Cooper, Frederick. *Colonialism in Question: Theory, Knowledge, History*. Berkeley: University of California Press, 2005.

Cooper, Frederick, and Ann Laura Stoler, eds. *Tensions of Empire: Colonial Cultures in a Bourgeois World*. Berkeley: University of California Press, 1997.

Coury, Ralph M. *The Making of an Egyptian Arab Nationalist: The Early Years of Azzam Pasha, 1893–1936*. Reading, UK: Ithaca Press, 1998.

Crabbs, Jack. *The Writing of History in Nineteenth-Century Egypt: A Study in National Transformation*. Cairo: American University in Cairo Press, 1984.

Cromer, Evelyn Baring, Earl of. *Modern Egypt*, 2 vols. London: Macmillan, 1908.

Cuno, Kenneth. *The Pasha's Peasants: Land, Society, and Economy in Lower Egypt, 1740–1858*. New York: Cambridge University Press, 1992.

———. "Joint Family Households and Rural Notables in 19th-Century Egypt." *International Journal of Middle East Studies* 27/4 (November 1995), 485–502.

———. "Muhammad 'Ali and the Decline and Revival Thesis in Modern Egyptian History." *Islah am tahdith?: Misr fi 'asr Muhammad 'Ali*, ed. Ra'uf 'Abbas, 93–119. Cairo: Al-Majlis Al-A'ala li Al-Thaqafa, 2000.

———. "Ambiguous Modernization: The Transition to Monogamy in the Khedivial House of Egypt." *Family History in the Middle East: Household, Property, and Gender*, ed. Beshara Doumani, 247–70. Albany: State University of New York Press, 2003.

Danielson, Virginia. *The Voice of Egypt: Umm Kulthum, Arabic Song, and Egyptian Society in the Twentieth Century*. Chicago: University of Chicago Press, 1997.

Darnton, Robert. *The Great Cat Massacre and Other Episodes in French Cultural History*. New York: Vintage, 1984.

al-Dasuqi, 'Asim. *Kibar mullak al-aradi al-zira'iyya wa dawruhum fi al-mujtama' al-misri, 1914–1952*. 1975; reprint, Cairo: Dar al-Shuruq, 2007.

Davies, Andrew. "Youth Gangs, Masculinity and Violence in Late Victorian Manchester and Salford." *Journal of Social History* 32/2 (winter 1998), 349–69.

Davin, Anna. "Imperialism and Motherhood." *Tensions of Empire: Colonial Cultures in a Bourgeois World*, ed. Frederick Cooper and Ann Laura Stoler, 87–151. Berkeley: University of California Press, 1997.

Davis, Eric. *Challenging Colonialism: Bank Misr and Egyptian Industrialization, 1920–1941*. Princeton, N.J.: Princeton University Press, 1983.

Dawson, Graham. *Soldier Heroes: British Adventure, Empire and the Imagining of Masculinities*. New York: Routledge, 1994.

Decker, Wolfgang. *Sports and Games of Ancient Egypt*. Translated by Allen Guttmann. New Haven, Conn.: Yale University Press, 1992.

Deeb, Marius. *Party Politics in Egypt: The Wafd and Its Rivals, 1919–1939*. London: Ithaca Press, 1979.

Deleuze, Gilles, and Felix Guattari. *Anti-Oedipus: Capitalism and Schizophrenia*. Minneapolis: University of Minnesota Press, 1983.

———. *A Thousand Plateaus: Capitalism and Schizophrenia*. Minneapolis: University of Minnesota Press, 1987.

Dellamora, Richard. *Masculine Desire: The Sexual Politics of Victorian Aestheticism*. Chapel Hill: University of North Carolina Press, 1990.

Demolins, Edmond. *À Quoi tient la supériorité des Anglo-Saxons?* Paris: Firmin-Didot, 1897.

Deringil, Selim. *The Well-Protected Domains: Ideology and the Legitimation of Power in the Ottoman Empire, 1876–1909*. New York: I. B. Tauris, 1999.

Derrida, Jacques. *Dissemination*. Translated by Barbara Johnson. Chicago: University of Chicago Press, 1981.

———. "Signature, Event, Context." *Limited, Inc*. Evanston, Ill.: Northwestern University Press, 1988.

Di-Capua, Yoav. "'Jabarti of the 20th Century': The National Epic of 'Abd Al-Rahman Al-Rafi'i and Other Egyptian Histories." *International Journal of Middle East Studies* 36/3 (2004), 429–50.

———. "Sports, Society, and Revolution: Egypt in the Early Nasserite Period." *Rethinking Nasserism: Revolution and Historical Memory in Modern Egypt*, ed. Elie Podeh and Onn Winckler, 144–62. Gainesville: University Press of Florida, 2004.

———. "The Professional Worldview of the *Effendi* Historian." *History Compass* 7/1 (Published Online: December 2008), 306–28, 10.1111/j.1478–0542.2008.00577.x.

Dijk, Kees van. "Sarongs, Jubbahs, and Trousers." *Outward Appearances: Dressing State and Society in Indonesia*, ed. Henk Schulte Nordholt, 39–83. Leiden, Netherlands: KITLV Press, 1997.

Dirks, Nicholas B., ed. *Colonialism and Culture*. Ann Arbor: University of Michigan Press, 1992.

———. *The Scandal of Empire: India and the Creation of Imperial Britain*. Cambridge, Mass.: Belknap Press for Harvard University, 2006.

Disch, Lisa. "Judith Butler and the Politics of the Performative." *Political Theory* 27/4 (August 1999), 545–59.

Djebar, Assia. *Fantasia: An Algerian Cavalcade*. Translated by Dorothy S. Blair. Portsmouth, N.H.: Heinemann, 1993.

———. *Children of the New World: A Novel of the Algerian War*. Translated by Marjolijn de Jager. New York: Feminist Press at CUNY, 2005.

Donovan, Brian. "Political Consequences of Private Authority: Promise Keepers and the Transformation of Hegemonic Masculinity." *Theory and Society* 27 (1998), 817–43.

Doumani, Beshara, ed. *Family History in the Middle East: Household, Property, and Gender*. Albany: State University of New York Press, 2003.

Doyle, Michael W. *Empires*. Ithaca, N.Y.: Cornell University Press, 1986.

Dreyfus, Hubert, and Paul Rabinow. *Michel Foucault: Beyond Structuralism and Hermeneutics*. Chicago: University of Chicago Press, 1983.

Duben, Alan, and Cem Behar. *Istanbul Households: Marriage, Family, and Fertility, 1880–1940.* New York: Cambridge University Press, 1991.

Duberman, Martin B., Martha Vicinus, and George Chauncey. *Hidden from History: Reclaiming the Gay and Lesbian Past.* New York: New American Library, 1989.

Dudink, Stefan, Karen Hagemann, and John Tosh, eds. *Masculinities in Politics and War: Gendering Modern History.* New York: Manchester University Press, 2004.

Duggan, Lisa. *The Twilight of Equality?: Neoliberalism, Cultural Politics, and the Attack on Democracy.* Boston: Beacon Press, 2003.

Dunn, John. "Egypt's Nineteenth-Century Armaments Industry." *Journal of Military History* 61/2 (April 1997), 231–54.

Dunne, Bruce. "Sexuality and the 'Civilizing Process' in Egypt." Ph.D. diss., Georgetown University, 1996.

Dutton, Kenneth R. *The Perfectible Body: The Western Ideal of Male Physical Development.* New York: Continuum, 1995.

Eagleton, Terry. *The Idea of Culture.* Oxford: Blackwell, 2000.

Edwards, Brent. *The Practice of Diaspora: Literature, Translation, and the Rise of Black Internationalism.* Cambridge, Mass.: Harvard University Press, 2003.

Egger, Vernon. *A Fabian in Egypt: Salamah Musa and the Rise of the Professional Classes in Egypt, 1909–1939.* Lanham, Md.: University Press of America, 1986.

Eley, Geoff, and Ronald Grigor Suny, eds. *Becoming National: A Reader.* New York: Oxford University Press, 1996.

Eriank, Natasha. "Gender and Masculinity in South African Nationalist Discourse, 1912–1950." *Feminist Studies* 29/3 (fall 2003), 653–71.

Erlich, Haggai. *Students and University in Twentieth-Century Egyptian Politics.* Totowa, N.J.: Frank Cass, 1989.

Esenbel, Selçuk. "The Anguish of Civilized Behavior: The Use of Western Cultural Forms in the Everyday Lives of the Meiji Japanese and the Ottoman Turks during the Nineteenth Century." *Japan Review* 5 (1994), 145–85.

Esmeir, Samera. "The Work of Law in the Age of Empire: Production of Humanity in Colonial Egypt." Ph.D. diss., New York University, 2005.

Euben, Roxanne L. *Journey to the Other Shore: Muslim and Western Travelers in Search of Knowledge.* Princeton, N.J.: Princeton University Press, 2006.

Fahmy, Khaled. *All the Pasha's Men: Mehmed Ali, His Army, and the Making of Modern Egypt.* New York: Cambridge University Press, 1997.

————. "Women, Medicine, and Power in Nineteenth-Century Egypt."

Remaking Women: Feminism and Modernity in the Middle East, ed. Lila Abu-Lughod, 37–52. Princeton, N.J.: Princeton University Press, 1998.

———. "The Anatomy of Justice: Forensic Medicine and Criminal Law in Nineteenth-Century Egypt." *Islamic Law and Society* 6 (1999), 340–77.

———. "The Police and the People in Nineteenth-Century Egypt." *Die Welt des Islams* 39/3 (1999), 340–77.

———. "Medicine and Power: Towards a Social History of Medicine in Nineteenth-Century Egypt." *Cairo Papers in Social Science* 23 (2000), 1–45.

———. *Mehmed Ali: From Ottoman Governor to Ruler of Egypt*. Oxford: Oneworld Publications, 2008.

Fahmy, Ziad. "Popularizing Egyptian Nationalism: Colloquial Culture and Media Capitalism, 1870–1919." Ph.D. diss., University of Arizona, 2007.

Fanon, Frantz. *Black Skin, White Masks*. Translated by Constance Farrington. New York: Grove Press, 1967.

———. *The Wretched of the Earth*. Translated by Richard Philcox. New York: Grove Press, 2004.

Faraj, Fakhri. *Taqrir 'an intishar al-bagha' wa al-amrad al-tanasuliyya bi al-qatar al-misri wa b'ad al-turuq al-mumkin itba'uha li-muharabatihima*. Cairo: al-Matba'a al-'Asriyya, 1924.

———. *Al-Mar'a wa falsafat al-tanasuliyyat*. Cairo: al-Matba'a al-'Asriyya, 1924.

Al-Faraj, al-Sayyid. *Ruwwad al-riyada fi Misr* [The pioneers of sports in Egypt]. Cairo: Al-Ahram Center for Translation and Publication, 1988.

Farid, Muhammad. *Mudhakkirat Muhammad Farid*, ed. Ra'uf 'Abbas. Cairo: 'Alam al-Kutub, 1975.

Fawzi, Ibrahim. *Kitab al-Sudan bayn yaday Gordon wa Kitchener* [The Sudan of Gordon and Kitchener]. 2 vols. Cairo: Al-Mu'ayyad Press, 1901.

Fay, Mary Ann. *Auto/biography and the Construction of Identity and Community in the Middle East*. New York: Palgrave, 2002.

———. "From Warrior-Grandees to Domesticated Bourgeoisie: The Transformation of the Elite Egyptian Household into a Western-style Nuclear Family." *Family History in the Middle East: Household, Property, and Gender*, ed. Beshara Doumani, 77–97. Albany: State University of New York Press, 2003.

Feldman, Ilana. *Governing Gaza: Bureaucracy, Authority, and the Work of Rule, 1917–1967*. Durham, N.C.: Duke University Press, 2008.

Ferguson, James. *Expectations of Modernity: Myths and Meanings of Urban Life on the Zambian Copperbelt*. Berkeley: University of California Press, 1999.

Ferguson, Niall. *Empire: The Rise and Demise of the British World Order and the Lessons for Global Power*. New York: Basic Books, 2003.

Findlay, Eileen. *Imposing Decency: The Politics of Sexuality and Race in Puerto Rico, 1870–1920*. Durham, N.C.: Duke University Press, 1999.

Forel, Auguste. *The Sexual Question: A Scientific, Psychological, Hygienic, and Sociological Study*. Translated by C. F. Marshall. New York: Medical Art Agency, 1911.

Foster, Angel M. *Sexuality in the Middle East: Conference Report*. Oxford: Middle East Centre, St. Antony's College, 2001.

Foucault, Michel. *Discipline and Punish: The Birth of the Prison*. Translated by Alan Sheridan. New York: Vintage Books, 1979.

———. "Technologies of the Self" and "The Political Technology of Individuals." *Technologies of the Self: A Seminar with Michel Foucault*, ed. Luther H. Martin, Huck Gutman, and Patrick H. Hutton, 16–49, 145–62, respectively. Amherst: University of Massachusetts Press, 1988.

———. *The History of Sexuality: An Introduction*. Translated by Robert Hurley. New York: Vintage, 1990.

———. *The History of Sexuality, Volume 2: The Use of Pleasure*. Translated by Robert Hurley. New York: Vintage, 1990.

———. "Governmentality." *The Foucault Effect: Studies in Governmentality*, ed. Colin Gordon, Graham Burchell, and Peter Miller, 87–104. Chicago: University of Chicago Press, 1991.

———. *"Society Must be Defended": Lectures at the Collège de France, 1975–1976*. ed. Mauro Bertani, et al. Translated by David Macey. New York: Picador, 2003.

———. *The Hermeneutics of the Subject: Lectures at the Collège de France, 1981–1982*. ed. Frédéric Gros. Translated by Graham Burchell. New York: Picador, 2006.

Frederick, William H. "The Appearance of Revolution: Cloth, Uniform, and the Pemuda Style in East Java, 1945–1949." *Outward Appearances: Dressing State and Society in Indonesia*, ed. Henk Schulte Nordholt, 199–248. Leiden, Netherlands: KITLV Press, 1997.

Frierson, Elizabeth. "Mirrors Out, Mirrors In: Domestication and Rejection of the Foreign in Late-Ottoman Women's Magazines (1875–1908)." *Women, Patronage, and Self-Representation in Islamic Societies*, ed. Fairchild Ruggles, 177–204. Albany: State University of New York Press, 2000.

Gagnier, Regenia. *Subjectivities: A History of Self-Representation in Britain, 1832–1920*. New York: Oxford University Press, 1991.

Galbraith, John, and Afaf Lutfi al-Sayyid Marsot. "The British Occupation of Egypt: Another View." *International Journal of Middle East Studies* 9/4 (November 1978), 471–88.

Gallant, Thomas W. "Honor, Masculinity, and Ritual Knife Fighting in Nineteenth-Century Greece." *American Historical Review* 105/2 (April 2000), 358–82.

Gandhi, Leela. *Affective Communities: Anticolonial Thought, Fin-de-Siècle Radicalism, and the Politics of Friendship*. Durham, N.C.: Duke University Press, 2006.

Gaonkar, Dilip, ed. *Alternative Modernities*. Durham, N.C.: Duke University Press, 2001.

Gasper, Michael. *The Power of Representation: Publics, Peasants, and Islam in Egypt*. Stanford, Calif.: Stanford University Press, 2009.

Gay, Peter. *The Bourgeois Experience, Victoria to Freud*. Volume 1: *Education of the Senses*. New York: Oxford University Press, 1984.

Gelvin, James. *Divided Loyalties: Nationalism and Mass Politics in Syria at the Close of Empire*. Berkeley: University of California Press, 1998.

Gendzier, Irene L. *The Practical Visions of Ya'qub Sanu'*. Cambridge, Mass.: Harvard University Press, 1966.

Gershoni, Israel. *The Emergence of Pan-Arabism in Egypt*. Tel Aviv: Shiloah Center for Middle Eastern and African Studies, Tel Aviv University, 1981.

———. "The Evolution of National Culture in Modern Egypt: Intellectual Formation and Social Diffusion." *Poetics Today* 13 (1992), 325–50.

Gershoni, Israel and James P. Jankowski. *Egypt, Islam, and the Arabs: The Search for Egyptian Nationhood, 1900–1930*. New York: Oxford University Press, 1986.

———. *Redefining the Egyptian Nation, 1930–1945*. Cambridge: Cambridge University Press, 1995.

———, eds. *Rethinking Nationalism in the Arab Middle East*. New York: Columbia University Press, 1997.

———. "Print Culture, Social Change, and the Process of Redefining Imagined Communities in Egypt; Response to the Review by Charles D. Smith of *Redefining the Egyptian Nation*." *International Journal of Middle East Studies* 31 (1999), 81–94.

———. *Commemorating the Nation: Collective Memory, Public Commemoration, and National Identity in Twentieth-Century Egypt*. Chicago: Middle East Documentation Center, 2004.

Ghali, Wacyf Boutros. *La Tradition Chevaleresque des Arabes*: Paris: Librarie Plon, 1919.

Ghazaleh, Pascale. "The Guilds: Between Tradition and Modernity." *The State and Its Servants: Administration in Egypt from Ottoman Times to the*

Present, ed. Nelly Hanna, 60–74. Cairo: American University in Egypt Press, 1995.

al-Ghazali, Abu Hamid. *Ihya' 'ulum al-din* [The revival of the religious sciences]. Cairo: Al-Maktaba al-Azhariyya, 1317 AH [1899].

al-Ghitani, Gamal. "Naguib Mahfouz Remembers." *Naguib Mahfouz: From Regional Fame to Global Recognition*, ed. Michael Beard and Adnan Haydar, 37–51. Excerpt translated by Mona N. Mikhail. Syracuse, N.Y.: Syracuse University Press, 1993.

Ghosh, Amitav. *In an Antique Land*. London: Granta Books, 1992.

Ghosh, Durba. *Sex and the Family in Colonial India: The Making of Empire*. Cambridge: Cambridge University Press, 2006.

Ghoussoub, Mai, and Emma Sinclair-Webb, eds. *Imagined Masculinities: Male Identity and Culture in the Modern Middle East*. London: Saqi Books, 2000.

Gillis, John R. *Youth and History: Tradition and Change in European Age Relations, 1770–Present*. New York: Academic Press, 1981.

Gilsenan, Michael. *Recognizing Islam: Religion and Society in the Modern Middle East*. New York: I. B. Tauris, 1990.

———. *Lords of the Lebanese Marches: Violence and Narrative in an Arab Society*. New York: I. B. Tauris, 1996.

Ginzburg, Carlo. *The Cheese and the Worms: The Cosmos of a Sixteenth-Century Miller*. Translated by John and Anne Tedeschi. Baltimore: Johns Hopkins University Press, 1980.

Goldberg, Ellis. *Tinker, Tailor, and Textile Worker: Class and Politics in Egypt, 1930–1952*. Berkeley: University of California Press, 1986.

———. "Peasants in Revolt — Egypt 1919." *International Journal of Middle East Studies* 24/2 (May 1992), 261–80.

Goldschmidt, Arthur. *The Egyptian Nationalist Party*. Cambridge, Mass.: Harvard University Press, 1968.

Gole, Nilufer. *The Forbidden Modern: Civilization and Veiling*. Ann Arbor: University of Michigan Press, 1997.

Gordon, Charles George, and A. Egmont Hake. *The Journals of Major-Gen. C. G. Gordon, C. B., at Kartoum*. New York: Houghton, Mifflin, 1885.

Gorman, Anthony. *Historians, State and Politics in Twentieth-Century Egypt: Contesting the Nation*. New York: Routledge-Curzon, 2003.

Gouda, Frances. *Dutch Culture Overseas: Colonial Practice in the Netherlands Indies, 1900–1942*. Amsterdam: Amsterdam University Press, 1995.

———. "Gender and 'Hyper-Masculinity' as Post-Colonial Modernity during Indonesia's Struggle for Independence, 1945 to 1949." *Gender, Sexuality, and Colonial Modernity*, ed. Antoinette Burton, 161–74. New York: Routledge, 1999.

Graham-Brown, Sarah. *Images of Women: The Portrayal of Women in Photography of the Middle East, 1860–1950*. New York: Columbia University Press, 1988.

Gramsci, Antonio. *Selections from the Prison Notebooks*. Edited and translated by Quintin Hoare and Geoffrey N. Smith. New York: International Publishers, 1971.

Gran, Peter. *Islamic Roots of Capitalism: Egypt, 1760–1840*. Austin: University of Texas Press, 1978.

———. "Tahtawi in Paris." http://weekly.ahram.org.eg/2002/568/cu1 .htm. (accessed May 2006).

Green, Harvey. *Fit for America: Health, Fitness, Sport, and American Society*. New York: Pantheon Books, 1986.

Green, Martin Burgess. *The Adventurous Male: Chapters in the History of the White Male Mind*. University Park: Pennsylvania State University Press, 1993.

Guha, Ranajit. "The Prose of Counter-Insurgency." *Selected Subaltern Studies*, ed. R. Guha and Gayatri Spivak, 45–86. New York: Oxford University Press, 1988.

———. *Dominance without Hegemony: History and Power in Colonial India*. Cambridge, Mass.: Harvard University Press, 1997.

Guttmann, Allen. *Games and Empires: Modern Sports and Cultural Imperialism*. New York: Columbia University, 1994.

Guttmann, Allen, and Lee Thompson. *Japanese Sports: A History*. Honolulu: University of Hawai'i Press, 2001.

Haarmann, Ulrich. "The Late Triumph of the Persian Bow: Critical Voices on the Mamluk Monopoly on Weaponry." *The Mamluks in Egyptian Politics and Society*, ed. Thomas Philipp and Ulrich Haarmann, 174–87. Cambridge: Cambridge University Press, 1998.

Habermas, Jürgen. *The Transformation of the Public Sphere: An Inquiry into a Category of Bourgeois Society*. Cambridge, Mass.: MIT Press, 1989.

Haddad, George. "Mustafa Kamil: A Self-Image from His Correspondence with Juliette Adam." *Muslim World* 63/2 (1973), 132–38.

Haj, Samira. *Reconfiguring Islamic Tradition: Reform, Rationality, and Modernity*. Stanford, Calif.: Stanford University Press, 2008.

Haley, Bruce. *The Healthy Body and Victorian Culture*. Cambridge, Mass.: Harvard University Press, 1978.

Hall, Catherine. *White, Male, and Middle-Class: Explorations in Feminism and History*. New York: Routledge, 1992.

———, ed. *Cultures of Empire: Colonizers in Britain and the Empire in the Nineteenth and Twentieth Centuries*. New York: Routledge, 2000.

Hall, Catherine, and Leonore Davidoff. *Family Fortunes: Men and Women of the English Middle Class, 1780–1850.* Chicago: University of Chicago Press, 1987.

Hall, Donald E., ed. *Muscular Christianity: Embodying the Victorian Age.* New York: Cambridge University Press, 1994.

Halstead, John. "A Comparative Historical Study of Colonial Nationalism in Egypt and Morocco." *African Historical Studies* 2/1 (1969), 85–100.

Hamouda, Sahar, and Colin Clement, eds. *Victoria College: A History Revealed.* Cairo: American University in Cairo Press, 2002.

Hanley, Will. "Foreignness and Localness in Alexandria, 1880–1914." Ph.D. diss., Princeton University, 2007.

——— . "Grieving Cosmopolitanism in the Middle East." *History Compass* 6/5 (Published online: 2008), 1346–67, 10.1111/j.1478–0542.2008.00545.x.

Hanna, Nelly, ed. *The State and Its Servants: Administration in Egypt from Ottoman Times to the Present.* Cairo: American University in Cairo Press, 1995.

——— . *In Praise of Books: A Cultural History of Cairo's Middle Class, Sixteenth to the Eighteenth Century.* Syracuse, N.Y.: Syracuse University Press, 2003.

Hansen, Thomas Blom. "Sovereigns beyond the State: On Legality and Authority in Urban India." *Sovereign Bodies: Citizens, Migrants, and States in the Postcolonial World,* ed. Thomas Blom Hansen and Finn Stepputat, 169–91. Princeton, N.J.: Princeton University Press, 2005.

Haqqi, Mahmud T. *'Adhra' Dinshwai.* Cairo: Al-Maktaba al-'Arabiyya, 1964 [1909].

Haqqi, Yahya. *Dima' wa Tin.* Cairo: Al-Hay'a al-Misriyya al-'Amma lil-Kitab, 1979.

Harcourt, Charles Francois Marie Le Duc d'. *L'Égypte et Les Égyptiens.* Paris: Librairie Plon, 1893.

Harlow, Barbara. "Cairo Curiosities: E. W. Lane's *Account* and Ahmad Amin's *Dictionary.*" *Journal of the History of Ideas,* 46/2 (April–June 1985), 279–86.

Harootunian, Harry D. *History's Disquiet: Modernity, Cultural Practice, and the Question of Everyday Life.* New York: Columbia University Press, 2000.

——— . *Overcome by Modernity: History, Culture, and Community in Interwar Japan.* Princeton, N.J.: Princeton University Press, 2000.

Harpham, Geoffrey. *Getting It Right: Language, Literature, and Ethics.* Chicago: University of Chicago Press, 1992.

Hathaway, Jane. *The Politics of Households in Ottoman Egypt: The Rise of the Qazdaglis.* New York: Cambridge University Press, 1997.

Haykal, Muhammad Husayn. *Al-Sharq al-jadid*. Cairo: Maktaba al-Nahda al-Misriyya, 1963.

Hearn, Jeff. "Theorizing Men and Men's Theorizing: Varieties of Discursive Practices in Men's Theorizing of Men." *Theory and Society* 27/6 (December 1998), 781–816.

Hegel, G. F. W. *The Philosophy of History*. Translated by J. Sibree. New York: Dover Publications, 1956.

Henty, G. A. *With Kitchener in the Soudan: A Story of Atbara and Omdurman*. London: Blackie and Sons, 1903.

Herzfeld, Michael. *The Poetics of Manhood: Contest and Identity in a Cretan Mountain Village*. Princeton, N.J.: Princeton University Press, 1985.

Hewitt, Andrew. *Political Inversions: Homosexuality, Fascism, and the Modernist Imaginary*. Stanford, Calif.: Stanford University Press, 1996.

Heyworth-Dunne, James. "A Selection of Cairo's Street Cries (Referring to Vegetables, Fruit, Flowers and Food)." *Bulletin of the School of Oriental Studies, London Institution* 9/2 (1938), 351–62.

———. *An Introduction to the History of Education in Modern Egypt*. London: Luzac, 1939.

———. "Rifa'ah Badawi Rafi' at-Tahtawi: The Egyptian Revivalist." *Bulletin of the School of Oriental Studies, London Institution* 9/4 (1939), 961–67.

———. "Printing and Translations under Muhammad 'Ali of Egypt: The Foundation of Modern Arabic." *Journal of the Royal Asiatic Society* (1940), 325–49.

———. "Rifa'ah Badawi Rafi' at-Tahtawi: The Egyptian Revivalist (Continued)." *Bulletin of the School of Oriental Studies, London Institution* 10/2 (1940), 399–415.

Hilal, Emad. *Al-Baghaya fi Misr: dirasa tarikhiyya ijtima'iyya, 1834–1949*. Cairo: Al-'Arabi, 2001.

Hindess, Barry. "Citizenship and Empire." *Sovereign Bodies: Citizens, Migrants, and States in the Postcolonial World*, ed. Thomas Blom Hansen and Finn Stepputat, 241–56. Princeton, N.J.: Princeton University Press, 2005.

Hitchcock, Tim, and Michèle Cohen, eds. *English Masculinities, 1660–1800*. New York: Longman, 1999.

Hoganson, Kristin. "The Fashionable World: Imagined Communities of Dress." *After the Imperial Turn: Thinking with and through the Nation*, ed. Antoinette Burton, 260–78. Durham, N.C.: Duke University Press, 2003.

Holt, P. M., and M. W. Daley. *A History of the Sudan: From the Coming of Islam to the Present Day*. New York: Longman Press, 1988.

Holt, Richard. *Sport and Society in Modern France*. Hamden, Conn.: Archon Books, 1981.

————. *Sport and the British: A Modern History*. New York: Oxford University Press, 1989.

Hooper, Charlotte. *Manly States: Masculinities, International Relations, and Gender Politics*. New York: Columbia University Press, 2001.

Hopkins, A. G. "The Victorians and Africa: A Reconsideration of the Occupation of Egypt, 1882." *Journal of African History* 27/2 (1986), 363–91.

Horne, John. "Masculinity in Politics and War in the Age of Nation-States and World Wars, 1850–1950." *Masculinities in Politics and War: Gendering Modern History*, ed. Stefan Dudink, Karen Hagemann, and John Tosh, 22–40. New York: Manchester University Press, 2003.

Hourani, Albert Habib. *Arabic Thought in the Liberal Age, 1798–1939*. New York: Cambridge University Press, 1983.

————. "Middle Eastern Studies Today." *Bulletin of the British Society for Middle East Studies* 11/2 (1984), 111–20.

————. "How Should We Write the History of the Middle East?" *International Journal of Middle East Studies* 23/2 (May 1991), 125–36.

Huggins, Mike J. "More Sinful Pleasures? Leisure, Respectability, and the Male Middle Classes in Victorian England." *Journal of Social History* 33/3 (spring 2000), 585–600.

Hughes, H. Stuart. *Consciousness and Society: The Reconstruction of European Social Thought, 1890–1930*. New York: Vintage Books, 1961.

Huizinga, Johan. *Homo Ludens: A Study of the Play-Element in Culture*. Boston: Beacon Press, 1955.

Hull, Isabel V. *Sexuality, State, and Civil Society in Germany, 1700–1815*. Ithaca, N.Y.: Cornell University Press, 1996.

Hunt, Lynn. *The Family Romance of the French Revolution*. Berkeley: University of California Press, 1992.

Hunt, Nancy. *A Colonial Lexicon of Birth, Medicalization, and Mobility in the Congo*. Durham, N.C.: Duke University Press, 1999.

Hunter, Robert. *Egypt under the Khedives, 1805–1879: From Household Government to Modern Bureaucracy*. Cairo: American University in Cairo Press, 1999.

————. "State-Society Relations in Nineteenth-Century Egypt: The Years of Transition, 1848–79." *Middle Eastern Studies* 36/3 (July 2000), 145–59.

Husayn, Taha. *Al-Ayyam*. 3 vols. Cairo: Dar al-Ma'arif, 1996.

Hyam, Ronald. *Britain's Imperial Century, 1815–1914: A Study of Empire and Expansion*. New York: Harper and Row, 1976.

————. *Empire and Sexuality: The British Experience*. New York: Manchester University Press, 1992.

Ibrahim, Abdullahi Ali. "Tale of Two Sudanese Courts: Colonial Governmentality Revisited." *African Studies Review* 40/1 (1997), 13–33.

Ibrahim, Hafiz. *Diwan Hafiẕ Ibrahim*. 2 vols. Beirut: Dar Sadir, 1989.

Ibrahim, Hilmi M., and Nahed F. Asker. "Ideology, Politics, and Sport in Egypt." *Leisure Studies* 3 (1984), 97–106.

Ilbert, Robert, and Ilios Yannakakis with Jacques Hassoun. *Alexandria, 1860–1960: The Brief Life of a Cosmopolitan Community*. Translated by Colin Clement. Alexandria, Egypt: Harpocrates Press, 1997.

'Imara, Muhammad. *Al-Jami'a al-islamiyya wa-ı -fikra al-qawmiyya 'inda Mustafa Kamil*. Beirut: Dar al-Qutayaba, 1989.

'Iraq, Nasir. *Tarikh al-rasm al-suhufi fi Misr*. al-Qahira: Mirit lil-Nashr wa-al-Ma'lumat, 2002.

Irwin, Robert. "Futuwwa: Chivalry and Gangsterism in Medieval Cairo." *Muqarnas* 21 (2004), 161–70.

Islamoglu-Inan, Huri. "Introduction: 'Oriental Despotism' in World-Systems Perspective." *Ottoman Empire and the World-Economy*, ed. Huri Islamoglu-Inan. New York: Cambridge University Press, 1987.

———, ed. *Constituting Modernity: Private Property in the East and West*. New York: I. B. Tauris, 2004.

Islamoglu, Huri, and Caglar Keyder. "Agenda for Ottoman History." *Review* 1/1 (summer 1977), 31–55.

Ivaska, Andrew. "'Anti-Mini Militants Meet Modern Misses': Urban Style, Gender and the Politics of 'National Culture' in 1960s Dar es Salaam, Tanzania." *Gender and History* 14/3 (2002), 584–607.

———. *Cultured States: Youth, Gender, and Modern Style in 1960s Dar es Salaam*. Durham, N.C.: Duke University Press, 2011.

al-Jabarti, Abd al-Rahman. *Tarikh aja'ib al-athar fi tarajim wa al-akhbar*. 3 vols. Beirut: Dar al-Jil, 1983.

———. *Napoleon in Egypt: Al-Jabarti's Chronicle of the First Seven Months of the French Occupation of Egypt, 1798*. Translated by S. Moreh. Princeton, N.J.: M. Wiener, 1993.

Jackson, Peter. "The Cultural Politics of Masculinity: Towards a Social Geography." *Transactions of the Institute of British Geographers* 16/2 (1991), 199–213.

Jacob, Wilson. "History and the Masculine Subject of Colonialism: The Egyptian Loss of the Sudan." *African Masculinities*, ed. Lahoucine Ouzgane and Robert Morrell, 153–70. New York: Palgrave, 2005.

———. "Eventful Transformations: *Al-Futuwwa* between History and the Everyday." *Comparative Studies in Society and History* 49/3 (July 2007), 689–712.

James, C. L. R. *The Black Jacobins: Toussaint L'Ouverture and the San Domingo Revolution*. New York: Vintage, 1989.

———. *Beyond a Boundary*. Durham, N.C.: Duke University Press, 1993.

Jameson, Fredric. *The Political Unconscious: Narrative as a Socially Symbolic Act*. Ithaca, N.Y.: Cornell University Press, 1981.

Jankowski, James P. *Egypt's Young Rebels: "Young Egypt," 1933–1952*. Stanford, Calif.: Hoover Institution Press, 1975.

Jawish, Abd al-Aziz. *Ghunyat al-mu'addibin fi al-turuq al-haditha lil-tarbiyya wa al-ta'lim*. Cairo: Matba'a al-Sha'b, 1903.

Jeganathan, Pradeep. "A Space for Violence: Anthropology, Politics and the Location of a Sinhala Practice of Masculinity." *Subaltern Studies XI: Community, Gender, and Violence*, ed. Partha Chatterjee and Pradeep Jeganathan, 37–65. New York: Columbia University Press, 2000.

Jirousek, Charlotte. "The Transition to Mass Fashion System Dress in the Later Ottoman Empire." *Consumption Studies and the History of the Ottoman Empire, 1550–1922: An Introduction*, ed. Donald Quataert, 201–41. Albany: State University of New York Press, 2000.

Johnson, Walter. "On Agency." *Journal of Social History* 37/1 (2003), 113–24.

Joseph, Suad, ed. *Intimate Selving in Arab Families: Gender, Self, and Identity*. Syracuse, N.Y.: Syracuse University Press, 1999.

Kamil, Ali Fahmy, ed. *Mustafa Kamil Pasha fi 34 rabi'an: siratuhu wa a'maluhu min khutab wa rasa'il siyasiyya wa 'umraniyya*. 9 vols. Cairo: Al-Liwa' Press, 1908.

Kamil, Mustafa. *Egyptiens et Anglais*. Paris: Perrin, 1906.

Kandiyoti, Deniz, ed. *Women, Islam and the State*. Philadelphia: Temple University Press, 1991.

———. "The Paradoxes of Masculinity: Some Thoughts on Segregated Societies." *Dislocating Masculinity: Comparative Ethnographies*, ed. Andrea Cornwall and Nancy Lindisfarne, 197–213. New York: Routledge, 1994.

Kandiyoti, Deniz, and Ayse Saktanber, eds. *Fragments of Culture: The Everyday of Modern Turkey*. New Brunswick, N.J.: Rutgers University Press, 2002.

Karlin, Jason. "The Gender of Nationalism: Competing Masculinities in Meiji Japan." *Journal of Japanese Studies* 28/1 (winter 2002), 41–77.

Kasson, John F. *Houdini, Tarzan, and the Perfect Man: The White Male Body and the Challenge of Modernity in America*. New York: Hill and Wang, 2001.

Kawtharani, Wajih. *Al-Dawla wa al-khilafa fi al-khitab al-'arabi aban al-thawra al-kamaliyya fi Turkiyya* [The state and the caliphate in Arab discourse in the wake of the Kemalist revolution in Turkey]. Beirut: Dar al-Tali'a, 1996.

Kelly, John. *A Politics of Virtue: Hinduism, Sexuality, and Countercolonial Discourse in Fiji*. Chicago: University of Chicago Press, 1991.

Keys, Barbara Jean. "The Dictatorship of Sport: Nationalism, Internationalism, and Mass Culture in the 1930s." Ph.D. diss., Harvard University, 2001.

Khater, Akram. *Inventing Home: Emigration, Gender, and the Middle Class in Lebanon, 1870–1920*. Berkeley: University of California Press, 2001.

Kholoussi, Samia. "*Fallahin*: The 'Mud Bearers' of Egypt's 'Liberal Age.'" *Re-Envisioning Egypt, 1919–1952*, ed. Arthur Goldschmidt, Amy J. Johnson, and Barak A. Salmoni, 277–314. New York: American University in Cairo Press, 2005.

Kholoussy, Hanan. "Stolen Husbands and Foreign Wives: Mixed Marriage, Identity Formation, and Gender in Colonial Egypt, 1909–1923." *Hawwa* 1/2 (2003), 206–40.

———. "The Nationalization of Marriage in Monarchical Egypt." *Re-Envisioning Egypt, 1919–1952*, ed. Arthur Goldschmidt, Amy J. Johnson, and Barak A. Salmoni, 317–50. New York: American University in Cairo Press, 2005.

———. *For Better, For Worse: The Marriage Crisis that Made Modern Egypt*. Stanford, Calif.: Stanford University Press, 2010.

Khouri, Mouna A. *Poetry and the Making of Modern Egypt (1882–1922)*. Leiden, Netherlands: E. J. Brill, 1971.

Khuri-Makdisi, Ilham. *The Eastern Mediterranean and the Making of Global Radicalism, 1860–1914*. Berkeley: University of California Press, 2010.

Kilito, Abdelfattah. *Thou Shalt Not Speak My Language*. Translated by Wail S. Hassan. Syracuse, N.Y.: Syracuse University Press, 2008.

Kimmel, Michael. *Manhood in America: A Cultural History*. New York: Free Press, 1996.

Kinmonth, Earl H. *The Self-made Man in Meiji Japanese Thought: From Samurai to Salary Man*. Berkeley: University of California Press, 1981.

Kleijwegt, Marc. *Ancient Youth: The Ambiguity of Youth and the Absence of Adolescence in Greco-Roman Society*. Amsterdam: Gieben, 1991.

Koselleck, Reinhart. *Futures Past: On the Semantics of Historical Time*. Translated by Keith Tribe. Cambridge, Mass.: MIT Press, 1985.

Kozma, Liat. "Women on the Margins and Legal Reform in Late Nineteenth-Century Egypt, 1850–1882." Ph.D. diss., New York University, 2006.

Krishnaswamy, Revathi. *Effeminism: The Economy of Colonial Desire*. Ann Arbor: University of Michigan Press, 1998.

Kristeva, Julia. *Powers of Horror: An Essay on Abjection*. Translated by Leon S. Roudiez. New York: Columbia University Press, 1982.

Kuhnke, LaVerne. *Lives at Risk: Public Health in Nineteenth-Century Egypt*. Berkeley: University of California Press, 1990.

Kulick, Don. *Travesti: Sex, Gender, and Culture among Brazilian Transgendered Prostitutes*. Chicago: University of Chicago Press, 1998.

Kumar, Krishan. "Nation and Empire: English and British National Identity in Comparative Perspective." *Theory and Society* 29/5 (October 2000), 575–608.

Kumar, Nita. *The Artisans of Banaras: Popular Culture and Identity, 1880–1986*. Princeton, N.J.: Princeton University Press, 1988.

Kupperman, Karen. *Settling with the Indians: The Meeting of English and Indian Cultures in America, 1580–1640*. Totowa, N.J.: Rowman and Littlefield, 1980.

Kurzman, Charles. "Weaving Iran into the Tree of Nations." *International Journal of Middle East Studies* 37 (2005), 137–66.

LaCapra, Dominick. *Rethinking Intellectual History: Texts, Contexts, Language*. Ithaca, N.Y.: Cornell University Press, 1983.

Laffan, Michael. "Mustafa and the *Mikado*: A Francophile Egyptian's Turn to Meiji Japan." *Japanese Studies* 19/3 (1999), 269–86.

Lagrange, Frédéric. "Male Homosexuality in Modern Arabic Literature." *Imagined Masculinities: Male Identity and Culture in the Modern Middle East*, ed. Mai Ghoussoub and Emma Sinclair-Webb, 169–98. London: Saqi Books, 2000.

Lake, Marilyn. "The Politics of Respectability: Identifying the Masculinist Context." *Historical Studies* 22/86 (April 1986), 116–31.

Lake, Peter, and Steven Pincus, eds. *The Politics of the Public Sphere in Early Modern England*. New York: Manchester University Press, 2007.

Lamphere, Louise, Helena Ragoné, and Patricia Zavella, eds. *Situated Lives: Gender and Culture in Everyday Life*. New York: Routledge, 1997.

Landau, Jacob M. *Parliaments and Parties in Egypt*. Tel Aviv: Israel Publishing House, 1953.

Lane, Edward. *Manners and Customs of the Modern Egyptians: Written in Egypt during the Years 1833–1835*. London: East-West Publications, 1981.

Lapidus, Ira. *Muslim Cities in the Later Middle Ages*. New York: Cambridge University Press, 1984.

Laqueur, Thomas. *Making Sex: Body and Gender from the Greeks to Freud*. Cambridge, Mass.: Harvard University Press, 1990.

Lash, Scott. "Genealogy and the Body: Foucault/Deleuze/Nietzsche." *The Body: Social Process and Cultural Theory*, ed. Mike Hepworth and Bryan S. Turner, 256–80. London: Sage Publications, 1991.

Lashin, Mahmud T. *Hawa' bala Adam*. Matba'a al-I'timad, 1934.

Latour, Bruno. *We Have Never Been Modern*. Translated by Catherine Porter Cambridge, Mass.: Harvard University Press, 1993.

————. "Gabriel Tarde and the End of the Social." *The Social in Question: New Bearings in History and the Social Sciences*, ed. Patrick Joyce, 117–32. New York: Routledge, 2002.

Lawson, Fred. *The Social Origins of Egyptian Expansionism during the Muhammad 'Ali Period*. New York: Columbia University Press, 1992.

————. "Reassessing Egypt's Foreign Policy during the 1920s and 1930s." *Re-envisioning Egypt, 1919–1952*, ed. Arthur Goldschmidt, Amy J. Johnson, and Barak A. Salmoni, 46–67. New York: American University in Cairo Press, 2005.

Lee, Leo Ou-fan. *Shanghai Modern: The Flowering of a New Urban Culture in China, 1930–1945*. Cambridge, Mass.: Harvard University Press, 1999.

Lees, Clare A., Thelma S. Fenster, and Jo Ann McNamara. *Medieval Masculinities: Regarding Men in the Middle Ages*. Minneapolis: University of Minnesota Press, 1994.

Lefebvre, Henri. *Everyday Life in the Modern World*. New Brunswick, N.J.: Transaction Books, 1984.

Leupp, Gary P. *Male Colors: The Construction of Homosexuality in Tokugawa Japan*. Berkeley: University of California Press, 1995.

Levine, Philippa. *Prostitution, Race, and Politics: Policing Venereal Disease in the British Empire*. New York: Routledge, 2003.

Lewis, Bernard. "*Efendi*." Entry in *The Encyclopedia of Islam*. Leiden, Netherlands: Brill, 1960.

————. *The Emergence of Modern Turkey*. Oxford: Oxford University Press, 1968.

Lewis, Reina. *Gendering Orientalism: Race, Femininity, and Representation*. London: Routledge, 1996.

————. *Rethinking Orientalism: Women, Travel, and the Ottoman Harem*. New Brunswick, N.J.: Rutgers University Press, 2004.

Lindisfarne, Nancy. "Variant Masculinities, Variant Virginities: Rethinking 'Honour and Shame.'" *Dislocating Masculinity: Comparative Ethnographies*, ed. Andrea Cornwall and Nancy Lindisfarne, 82–96. New York: Routledge, 1994.

Lipovetsky, Gilles. *The Empire of Fashion: Dressing Modern Democracy*. Translated by Catherine Porter. Princeton, N.J.: Princeton University Press, 1994.

Lloyd, George Ambrose. *Egypt since Cromer*. London: Macmillan, 1933.

Lockman, Zachary. "Imagining the Working Class: Culture, Nationalism, and Class Formation in Egypt, 1899–1914." *Poetics Today* 15/2 (summer 1994), 157–90.

————. "Exploring the Field: Lost Voices and Emerging Practices in Egypt, 1882–1914." *Histories of the Modern Middle East: New Directions*, ed. Israel Gershoni, Hakan Erdem, Ursula Woköck, 137–53. London: Lynne Rienner, 2002.

———. *Contending Visions of the Middle East: The History and Politics of Orientalism*. New York: Cambridge University Press, 2004.

Long, Roger D. *The Man on the Spot: Essays on British Empire History*. Westport, Conn.: Greenwood Press, 1995.

Looby, Christopher. "'As Thoroughly Black as the Most Faithful Philanthropist Could Desire': Erotics of Race in Higginson's *Army Life in a Black Regiment*." *Race and the Subject of Masculinities*, ed. Harry Stecopoulos and Micahel Uebel, 71–115. Durham, N.C.: Duke University Press, 1997.

Loomba, Ania. *Colonialism-Postcolonialism*. New York: Routledge, 1998.

Lopez, Shaun T. "Media Sensations, Contested Sensibilities: Gender and Moral Order in the Egyptian Mass Media, 1920–1955." Ph.D. diss., University of Michigan, 2004.

———. "The Dangers of Dancing: The Media and Morality in 1930s Egypt." *Comparative Studies of South Asia and the Middle East* 24/1 (2004), 97–105.

Low, Gail Ching-Liang. "His Stories?: Narratives and Images of Imperialism." *Space and Place: Theories of Identity and Location*, ed. Erica Carter et al., 241–66. London: Lawrence and Wishart, 1993.

MacDonald, Robert H. "Reproducing the Middle-Class Boy: From Purity to Patriotism in the Boys' Magazines, 1892–1914." *Journal of Contemporary History* 24/3 (1989), 519–39.

———. *Sons of the Empire: The Frontier and the Boy Scout Movement, 1890–1918*. Toronto: University of Toronto Press, 1993.

MacIntyre, Alasdair. *After Virtue*. 2d ed. Notre Dame, Ind.: University of Notre Dame Press, 1993.

MacKenzie, John M. *Propaganda and Empire: The Manipulation of British Public Opinion, 1880–1960*. Dover, N.H.: Manchester University Press, 1984.

———, ed. *Imperialism and Popular Culture*. Dover, N.H.: Manchester University Press, 1985.

Mahfuz, Naguib. *Bayn al-qasrayn* [Palace walk]. Cairo: Maktaba Misr, 1964.

———. *Zuqaq al-midaqq* [Midaq alley]. Cairo: Maktaba Misr, 1965.

———. *Al-Qahira al-jadida* [New Cairo]. Cairo: Maktaba Misr, 1966.

———. *Awlad haratina* [The children of Gabalawi]. Beirut: Dar al-Adab, 1967.

———. *Hams al-junun*. Cairo: Maktaba Misr, 1969.

———. *Harafish*. Cairo: Maktaba Misr, 1977.

———. *Qasr al-shawq* [Palace of desire]. Cairo: Maktaba Misr, 1987.

———. *Al-Sukkariyya* [Sugar Street]. Cairo: Maktaba Misr, 1987.

————. *Futuwwa al-'atuf*. Cairo: Maktaba Misr, 2001.

Mahjub, Kamal. *Tadrib rafa' al-athqal: al-mahara al-harakiyya*. Cairo: Dar Marjan lil-Taba'a, n.d.

Mahmood, Saba. *The Politics of Piety: The Islamic Revival and the Feminist Subject*. Princeton, N.J.: Princeton University Press, 2005.

Main, Ernest. *Iraq: From Mandate to Independence*. 1935; reprint, New York: Kegan Paul, 2004.

Manela, Erez. *The Wilsonian Moment: Self-Determination and the International Origins of Anti-Colonial Nationalism*. New York: Oxford University Press, 2007.

Mangan, J. A. *Athleticism in the Victorian and Edwardian Public School: The Emergence and Consolidation of an Educational Ideology*. New York: Cambridge University Press, 1981.

————. "'The Grit of our Forefathers': Invented Traditions, Propaganda and Imperialism." *Imperialism and Popular Culture*, ed. John M. MacKenzie, 113–39. Dover, N.H.: Manchester University Press, 1986.

————, ed. *Pleasure, Profit, Proselytism: British Culture and Sport at Home and Abroad*. London: F. Cass, 1988.

————, ed. *The Cultural Bond: Sport, Empire, Society*. London: F. Cass, 1992.

————. *The Games Ethic and Imperialism: Aspects of the Diffusion of an Ideal*. London: F. Cass, 1998.

————, ed. *Reformers, Sport, Modernizers: Middle-Class Revolutionaries*. London: F. Cass, 2002.

Mangan, J. A., and James Walvin, eds. *Manliness and Morality: Middle-Class Masculinity in Britain and America 1800–1940*. New York: St. Martin's Press, 1987.

Mani, Lata. *Contentious Traditions: The Debate on Sati in Colonial India*. Berkeley: University of California Press, 1998.

Manjapra, Kris. "The Illusions of Encounter: Muslim 'Minds' and Hindu Revolutionaries in First World War Germany and After." *Journal of Global History* 1 (2006), 363–82.

Mann, Susan, Robert Nye, et al. "AHR Forum: Gender and Manhood in Chinese History." *American Historical Review* 105/5 (December 2000), 1599–1666.

Mansfield, Peter. *The British in Egypt*. New York: Holt, 1972.

Marsot, Afaf Lutfi al-Sayyid. *Egypt and Cromer: A Study in Anglo-Egyptian Relations*. London: Murray, 1968.

————. "The Cartoon in Egypt." *Comparative Studies in Society and History* 13/1 (January 1971), 2–15.

————. *Egypt's Liberal Experiment, 1922–1936.* Berkeley: University of California Press, 1977.

————. *Egypt in the Reign of Muhammad 'Ali.* New York: Cambridge University Press, 1984.

————. *A Short History of Modern Egypt.* New York: Cambridge University Press, 1985.

Massad, Joseph. *Colonial Effects: The Making of National Identity in Jordan.* New York: Columbia University Press, 2001.

————. *Desiring Arabs.* Chicago: University of Chicago Press, 2007.

Massignon, Louis. "La 'Futuwwa,' ou 'pacte d'honneur artisanal' entre travailleurs musulmans au Moyen Age." *Nouvelle Clio* 4 (1952), 171–98.

Mayaram, Shail. *Against History, Against State: Counterperspectives from the Margins.* New York: Columbia University Press, 2003.

McClelland, Keith. "Some Thoughts on Masculinity and the "Representative Artisan" in Britain, 1850–1880." *Gender and History* 1/2 (summer 1989), 164–77.

————. "'England's Greatness, the Working Man.'" *Defining the Victorian Nation: Class, Race, Gender and the British Reform Act of 1867,* ed. Catherine Hall, Keith McClelland, Jane Rendall, 71–118. New York: Cambridge University Press, 2000.

McClintock, Anne. *Imperial Leather: Race, Gender and Sexuality in the Colonial Contest.* New York: Routledge, 1995.

McConville, Chris. "Rough Women, Respectable Men and Social Reform: A Response to Lake's Masculinism." *Historical Studies* 22/88 (April 1987), 432–40.

McCracken, Scott. "From Performance to Public Sphere: The Production of Modernist Masculinities." *Textual Practice* 15/1 (2001), 47–65.

McDevitt, Patrick F. "May the Best Man Win: Sport, Masculinity and Nationalism in Great Britain and the Empire, 1884–1933." Ph.D. diss., Rutgers University, 1999.

McLaren, Angus. *The Trials of Masculinity: Policing Sexual Boundaries 1870–1930.* Chicago: University of Chicago Press, 1997.

McPherson, J. W. *The Moulids of Egypt.* Cairo: Ptd. N. M. Press, 1941.

McPherson, John, and Barry Carman, eds. *Bimbashi McPherson: A Life in Egypt.* London: British Broadcasting Corporation, 1983.

Mehta, Uday Singh. *Liberalism and Empire: A Study in Nineteenth-Century British Liberal Thought.* Chicago: University of Chicago Press, 1999.

Melhuus, Marit, and Kristi Anne Stølen. *Machos, Mistresses, Madonnas: Contesting the Power of Latin American Gender Imagery.* New York: Verso, 1996.

Melman, Billie. *Women and the Popular Imagination in the Twenties: Flappers and Nymphs*. New York: St. Martin's Press, 1988.

———. *Women's Orients—English Women and the Middle East, 1718–1918: Sexuality, Religion, and Work*. Ann Arbor: University of Michigan Press, 1992.

———. *Borderlines: Genders and Identities in War and Peace, 1870–1930*. New York: Routledge, 1997.

Meriwether, Margaret, and Judith Tucker, eds. *Social History of Women and Gender in the Modern Middle East*. Boulder, Colo.: Westview Press, 1999.

el-Messiri, Sawsan. "The Changing Role of the Futuwwa in the Social Structure of Cairo." *Patrons and Clients in Mediterranean Societies*, ed. Ernest Gellner and John Waterbury, 239–53. London: Duckworth, 1977.

———. *Ibn al-Balad: A Concept of Egyptian Identity*. Leiden, Netherlands, 1978.

Metcalf, Thomas R. *An Imperial Vision: Indian Architecture and Britain's Raj*. Berkeley: University of California Press, 1989.

Milner, Alfred. *England in Egypt*. 1892; reprint, London: Edward Arnold, 1926.

———. *The Nation and the Empire*. 1913. London: Routledge, 1998.

Milner, Anthony Crothers. *The Invention of Politics in Colonial Malaya: Contesting Nationalism and the Expansion of the Public Sphere*. New York: Cambridge University Press, 1995.

Mines, Mattison. *Public Faces, Private Voices: Community and Individuality in South India*. Berkeley: University of California Press, 1994.

Minh-ha, Trinh T. *Woman, Native, Other: Writing Postcoloniality and Feminism*. Bloomington: Indiana University Press, 1989.

al-Mistakawi, Hasan. *Al-nadi al-ahli, 1907–1997: butula fi al-riyada walwataniyya*. Cairo: Dar al-Shuruq, 2000.

Mitchell, Richard P. *The Society of the Muslim Brothers*. London: Oxford University Press, 1969.

Mitchell, Timothy. *Colonising Egypt*. Cairo: American University in Cairo Press, 1989.

———. "The Stage of Modernity." *Questions of Modernity*, ed. Timothy Mitchell, 1–34. Minneapolis: University of Minnesota Press, 2000.

———. *The Rule of Experts: Egypt, Techno-Politics, Modernity*. Berkeley: University of California Press, 2002.

Mondal, Anshuman A. "Between Turban and Tarbush: Modernity and the Anxieties of Transition in *Hadith 'Isa ibn Hisham*." *Alif: Journal of Comparative Poetics* (1997), 201–21.

Montag, Walter. "'The Soul Is the Prison of the Body': Althusser and Foucault, 1970–1975." *Yale French Studies* 88 (1995), 53–77.

Moore-Harell, Alice. "The Turco-Egyptian Army in Sudan on the Eve of the Mahdiyya, 1877–80." *International Journal of Middle East Studies* 31/1 (1999), 19–37.

Morgan, D. H. J. "Men Made Manifest: Histories and Masculinities." *Gender and History* 1/1 (1989), 87–91.

Morgan, David. "Masculinity, Autobiography and History." *Gender and History* 2/1 (spring 1990), 34–39.

Morris, Andrew D. *Marrow of the Nation: A History of Sport and Physical Culture in Republican China*. Berkeley: University of California Press, 2004.

Mosse, George L. *Nationalism and Sexuality: Middle-Class Morality and Sexual Norms in Modern Europe*. Madison: University of Wisconsin Press, 1985.

————. *The Image of Man: The Creation of Modern Masculinity*. New York: Oxford University Press, 1996.

Mrazek, Rudolf. "Indonesian Dandy: The Politics of Clothes in the Late Colonial Period, 1893–1942." *Outward Appearances: Dressing State and Society in Indonesia*, ed. Henk Schulte Nordholt, 117–50. Leiden, Netherlands: KITLV Press, 1997.

Mubarak, Ali. *Hayati*. Cairo: Matba'a al-Adaab, 1989.

al-Mukarim, Abi Abd Allah Muhammad Bin Abi, a.k.a., Ibn al-Mi'mar al-Baghdadi al-Hanbali. *Kitab al-futuwwa*. Edited by Mustafa Jawad, Muhammad Taqi al-Din al-Hilali, Abd al-Halim al-Najar, and Ahmad Naji al-Qaisa. Baghdad: Maktaba al-Mathni, 1958.

Mu'nis, Husayn. *'Asr al-futuwwat: 'Asr al-butula li-lmisriyyin ayyam al-ihtilal wa al-wuzara' wa al-bashawat*. Cairo: Dar al-Irshad, 1993.

Murray, Jacqueline. *Conflicted Identities and Multiple Masculinities: Men in the Medieval West*. New York: Garland, 1999.

Muthu, Sankar. *Enlightenment Against Empire*. Princeton, N.J.: Princeton University Press, 2003.

al-Muwaylihi, Muhammad. *Hadith 'Isa ibn Hisham aw fatra min al-zaman*. Cairo: Dar al-Ma'arif, 1947.

Nadim, 'Abdallah. *Al-Tankit wa al-tabkit*. 1881; reprint, Cairo: Al-Hay'a al-Misriyya al-'Amma li al-Kitab, 1994.

————. *Al-Ustaz*. 1892–93; reprint, Cairo: Al-Hay'a al-Misriyya al-'Amma li al-Kitab, 1994.

Najmabadi, Afsaneh. "Crafting an Educated Housewife in Iran." *Remaking Women: Feminism and Modernity in the Middle East*, ed. Lila Abu-Lughod, 91–125. Princeton, N.J.: Princeton University Press, 1998.

————. *The Story of the Daughters of Quchan: Gender and National Memory in Iranian History*. Syracuse, N.Y.: Syracuse University Press, 1998.

————. *Women with Mustaches and Men without Beards: Gender and Sexual*

Anxieties of Iranian Modernity. Berkeley: University of California Press, 2005.

Nandy, Ashis. *The Intimate Enemy: Loss and Recovery of Self under Colonialism.* New Delhi: Oxford University Press, 1983.

al-Naqqash, Raja,' ed. *Naguib Mahfuẓ: Safahat min mudhakkiratihi wa adwa' jadida 'ala adabihi wa hayatihi.* Cairo: Al-Ahram, 1998.

Navaro-Yashin, Yael. *Faces of the State: Secularism and Public Life in Turkey.* Princeton, N.J.: Princeton University Press, 2002.

Nelson, Cynthia. *Doria Shafik, Egyptian Feminist: A Woman Apart.* Gainesville: University Press of Florida, 1996.

Nelson, Dana D. *National Manhood: Capitalist Citiẓenship and the Imagined Fraternity of White Men.* Durham, N.C.: Duke University Press, 1998.

Nordholt, Henk Schulte, ed. *Outward Appearance: Dressing State and Society in Indonesia.* Leiden, Netherlands: KITLV Press, 1997.

al-Nowaihi, Magda M. "Constructions of Masculinity in Two Egyptian Novels." *Intimate Selving in Arab Families: Gender, Self, and Identity,* ed. Suad Joseph, 235–63. Syracuse, N.Y.: Syracuse University Press, 1999.

Nye, Robert A. *Masculinity and Male Codes of Honor in Modern France.* New York: Oxford University Press, 1993.

Olympic Information Center. *Bulletin Officiel du Comité International Olympique* (July 1938), http://www.aafla.org.

Oppenheim, Jean-Marc Ran. "Twilight of a Colonial Ethos: The Alexandria Sporting Club, 1890–1956." Ph.D. diss, Columbia University, 1991.

Ortner, Sherry B. *Making Gender: The Politics and Erotics of Culture.* Boston: Beacon Press, 1996.

Osella, Caroline, and Filippo Osella. "'Ayyappan Saranam': Masculinity and the Sabarimala Pilgrimage in Kerala." *Journal of the Royal Anthropological Institute* 9/4 (December 2003), 729–54.

Osterhammel, Jurgen. *Colonialism: A Theoretical Overview.* Princeton, N.J.: M. Wiener; Ian Randle, 1996.

Ostle, Robin. "Modern Egyptian Renaissance Man." *Bulletin of the School of Oriental and African Studies, University of London* 57/1, In Honour of J. E. Wansbrough (1994), 184–92.

Owen, Roger. *Cotton and the Egyptian Economy: A Study in Trade and Development.* Oxford: Clarendon Press, 1969.

———. "The Middle East in the Eighteenth Century—An 'Islamic' Society in Decline? A Critique of Gibb and Bowen's Islamic Society and the West." *Bulletin of the British Society for Middle East Studies* 3/2 (1976), 110–17.

———. *The Middle East in the World Economy, 1800–1914.* New York: Methuen, 1981.

————. *Lord Cromer: Victorian Imperialist, Edwardian Proconsul*. New York: Oxford University Press, 2004.

Padgug, Robert A. "Sexual Matters: On Conceptualizing Sexuality in History." *Radical History Review* 20 (1979), 3–23.

Pagden, Anthony. "Europe: Conceptualizing a Continent." *The Idea of Europe: From Antiquity to the European Union*, ed. Anthony Pagden, 33–54. New York: Cambridge University Press, 2002.

Pandey, Gyan. "In Defense of the Fragment: Writing about Hindu-Muslim Riots in India Today." *Representations* 37 (winter 1992), 27–55.

Pappé, Ilan. *A History of Modern Palestine: One Land, Two People*. New York: Cambridge University Press, 2006.

Park, Hyungji. "The Empire Within: Masculinity and Colonial Travel in the Victorian Novel." Ph.D. diss., Princeton University, 1996.

Parla, Taha, and Andrew Davison. *Corporatist Ideology in Kemalist Turkey*. Syracuse, N.Y.: Syracuse University Press, 2004.

Parsons, Laila. "Soldiering for Arab Nationalism: Fawzi al-Qawuqji in Palestine." *Journal of Palestine Studies* 36/4 (summer 2007), 33–48.

————. *The Making of Fawẓi al-Qawuqji: An Arab Nationalist Soldier and His World*. New York: Hill & Wang, forthcoming.

Perrot, Philippe. *Fashioning the Bourgeoisie: A History of Clothing in the Nineteenth Century*. Translated by Richard Bienvenu. Princeton, N.J.: Princeton University Press, 1994.

Peters, Rudolph. *Jihad in Classical and Modern Islam*. Princeton, N.J.: Marcus Wiener, 1996.

————. "Islamic and Secular Criminal Law in Nineteenth-Century Egypt: The Role of the Qadi." *Islamic Law and Society* 4/1 (1997), 70–90.

————. "Administrators and Magistrates: The Development of a Secular Judiciary in Egypt." *Die Welt des Islams* 39/3 (1999), 378–97.

————. "State, Law, and Society in Nineteenth-Century Egypt." *Die Welt des Islams* 39/3 (1999), 267–72.

————. "Egypt and the Age of the Triumphant Prison: Legal Punishment in Nineteenth-Century Egypt." *Annales Islamologiques* 36 (2002), 253–85.

————. "Controlled Suffering: Mortality and Living Conditions in 19th-Century Egyptian Prisons." *International Journal of Middle East Studies* 36 (2004), 387–407.

Pick, Daniel. *Faces of Degeneration: A European Disorder, c. 1848–1918*. New York: Cambridge University Press, 1989.

Piterberg, Gabriel. "The Tropes of Stagnation and Awakening in Nationalist Historical Consciousness: The Egyptian Case." *Rethinking Nationalism in the Arab Middle East*, ed. James Jankowski and Israel Gershoni, 42–61. New York: Columbia University Press, 1997.

Pitts, Jennifer. *A Turn to Empire: The Rise of Imperial Liberalism in Britain and France*. Princeton, N.J.: Princeton University Press, 2006.

Pocock, J. G. A. "Some Europes in Their History." *The Idea of Europe: From Antiquity to the European Union*, ed. Anthony Pagden, 55–71. New York: Cambridge University Press, 2002.

Pollard, Lisa. *Nurturing the Nation: The Family Politics of Modernizing, Colonizing, and Liberating Egypt, 1805–1923*. Berkeley: University of California Press, 2005.

―――. "The Habits and Customs of Modernity: Egyptians in Europe and the Geography of Nineteenth-Century Nationalism." *Arab Studies Journal* (fall 1999/spring 2000), 52–74.

Porter, Bernard. *The Absent-Minded Imperialist: Empire, Society, and Culture in Britain*. New York: Oxford University Press, 2004.

Powell, Eve. "From Odyssey to Empire: Mapping Sudan through Egyptian Literature in the mid-19th Century." *International Journal of Middle East Studies* 31 (1990), 401–27.

―――. "Egyptians in Blackface: Nationalism and the Representation of the Sudan in Egypt, 1919." *Harvard Middle Eastern and Islamic Review* 2 (1995), 27–45.

―――. *A Different Shade of Colonialism: Egypt, Great Britain, and the Mastery of the Sudan*. Berkeley: University of California Press, 2003.

Prakash, Gyan. "The Colonial Genealogy of Society: Community and Political Modernity in India." *The Social in Question: New Bearings in History and the Social Sciences*, ed. Patrick Joyce, 81–96. New York: Routledge, 2002.

al-Qadi, Wadad. "East and West in 'Ali Mubarak's *'Alamuddin.*" *Intellectual Life in the Arab East, 1890–1939*, ed. Marwan R. Buheiry, 21–37. Syracuse, N.Y.: Syracuse University Press, 1982.

Quataert, Donald. "Clothing Laws, State, and Society in the Ottoman Empire, 1720–1829." *International Journal of Middle East Studies* 29 (1997), 403–25.

―――. *The Ottoman Empire, 1700–1922*. New York: Cambridge University Press, 2000.

Radhakrishnan, R. "Nationalism, Gender, and the Narrative of Identity." *Nationalisms and Sexualities*, ed. Andrew Parker et al, 77–95. New York: Routledge, 1992.

Rafael, Vincente. *White Love and Other Events in Filipino History*. Durham, N.C.: Duke University Press, 2000.

al-Rafi'i, Abd Al-Rahman. *Misr wa al-Sudan fi awa'il 'ahd al-ihtilal: Tarikh Misr al-qawmi min sana 1882 ila sana 1892*. 2d ed. Cairo: Maktabat al-Nahda al-Misriyya, 1948.

————. *Tarikh al-haraka al-qawmiyya wa-tatawwur niẓam al-hukm fi Misr.* Cairo: Maktaba al-Nahda al-Arabiyya, 1955.

————. *Mustafa Kamil: Ba'ith al-haraka al-wataniyya tarikh Misr al-qawmi min sana 1892 ila sana 1908.* Cairo: Dar al-Ma'arif, 1984.

————. *Fi a'qab al-thawra al-misriyya—thawra 1919.* 2 vols. Cairo: Dar al-Ma'arif, 1987.

————. *Thawra 1919: Tarikh Misr al-qawmi min 1914 ila 1921.* Cairo: Dar al-Ma'arif, 1987.

————. *Mudhakkirati, 1889–1901.* Cairo: Mu'assasa Akhbar al-Yawm, 1989.

Ramadan, Abd al-Azim. *Al-Sira'bayn al-Wafd wa al-'arsh 1936–1939.* Beirut: Al-Mu'asasa al-'Arabiyya lil-Dirasat wa al-Nashr, 1979.

————. *Mustafa Kamil fi mahkama al-ta'rikh.* Cairo: Al-Hay'a al-Misriyya al-'Amma lil-Kitab, 1994.

————. *Tatawwur al-haraka al-wataniyya fi Misr.* 2 vols. Cairo: Al-Hay'a al-Misriyya al-'Amma lil-Kitab, 1998.

Rao, Anupama. *The Caste Question: Dalits and the Politics of Modern India.* Berkeley: University of California Press, 2009.

Rao, Anupama, and Steven Pierce. "Discipline and the Other Body: Correction, Corporeality, and Colonial Rule." *Interventions* 3/2 (2001), 159–68.

Raymond, Andre. *Cairo.* Translated by Willard Wood. Cambridge, Mass.: Harvard University Press, 2000.

————. "Quartiers et Mouvements Populaires." *Political and Social Change in Modern Egypt,* ed. P. M. Holt, 104–16. London: Oxford University Press, 1968.

Reid, Donald. "Educational and Career Choices of Egyptian Students, 1882–1922." *International Journal of Middle East Studies* 8/3 (July 1977), 349–78.

————. "Political Assassination in Egypt, 1910–1954." *International Journal of African Historical Studies* 15/4 (1982), 625–51.

————. "Cairo University and the Orientalists." *International Journal of Middle East Societies* 19 (1987), 51–76.

————. *Cairo University and the Making of Modern Egypt.* Cairo: American University in Cairo Press, 1991.

————. *Whose Pharaohs? Archeology, Museums, and Egyptian National Identity from Napoleon to World War I.* Cairo: American University Press, 2002.

Reimer, Michael J. *Colonial Bridgehead: Government and Society in Alexandria, 1807–1882.* Cairo: American University in Cairo Press, 1997.

Reynolds, Dwight F., ed. *Interpreting the Self: Autobiography in the Arabic Literary Tradition.* Berkeley: University of California Press, 2001.

Reynolds, Nancy. "*Sharikat al-Bayt al-Misri*: Domesticating Commerce in Egypt, 1931–1956." *Arab Studies Journal* (fall 1999/spring 2000), 75–107.

———. "Commodity Communities: Interweavings of Market Cultures, Consumption Practices, and Social Power in Egypt, 1907–1961." Ph.D. diss., Stanford University, 2003.

Rida, Muhammad Rashid. *Ta'rikh al-shaykh Muhammad 'Abduh*. Cairo: Matba'a al-Manar, 1931.

Ridwan, Abu al-Futuh. *Ta'rikh Matba'a Bulaq*. Cairo: Al-Matba'a Al-Amiriyya, 1953.

Rivlin, Helen. *The Agricultural Policy of Muhammad Ali in Egypt*. Cambridge, Mass.: Harvard University Press, 1961.

Rochard, Philippe. "The Identities of the Iranian *Zurkhanah*." Translated by H. E. Chehabi. *Iranian Studies* 35/4 (fall 2002), 313–40.

Roden, Donald F. *Schooldays in Imperial Japan: A Study in the Culture of a Student Elite*. Berkeley: University of California Press, 1980.

Rose, Jacqueline. *Sexuality in the Field of Vision*. London: Verso, 1986.

Rosselli, John. "The Self-Image of Effeteness: Physical Education and Nationalism in Nineteenth-Century Bengal." *Past and Present* 86 (1980), 121–48.

Rowson, Everett K. "The Categorization of Gender and Sexual Irregularity in Medieval Arabic Vice Lists." *Body Guards: The Cultural Politics of Gender Ambiguity*, ed. Julia Epstein and Kristina Straub, 50–79. New York: Routledge, 1991.

Roy, Parama. *Indian Traffic: Identities in Question in Colonial and Postcolonial India*. Berkeley: University of California Press, 1998.

Ruiz, Mario. "Intimate Disputes, Illicit Violence: Gender, Law, and the State in Colonial Egypt, 1849–1923." Ph.D. diss., University of Michigan, 2004.

———. "Virginity Violated: Sexual Assault and Respectability in Mid- to Late-Nineteenth-Century Egypt." *Comparative Studies of South Asia, Africa and the Middle East* 25/1 (2005), 214–26.

Russell, Mona. *Creating the New Egyptian Woman: Consumerism, Education, and National Identity, 1863–1922*. New York: Palgrave-Macmillan, 2004.

Russell, Thomas Wentworth. *Egyptian Service, 1902–1946*. London: Murray, 1949.

Rüth, Axel. "The Battle of Bouvines: Event History vs. Problem History." Translated by Jocelyn Holland. *MLN: Modern Language Notes* 116/4 (September 2001), 816–43.

Rutherford, Jonathan. *Forever England: Reflections on Race, Masculinity, and Empire*. London: Lawrence and Wishart, 1997.

Ryan, Mary P. *Civic Wars: Democracy and Public Life in the American City during the Nineteenth Century*. Berkeley: University of California Press, 1997.

Ryzova, Lucie. "'I Am a Whore But I Will Be a Good Mother': On the Production and Consumption of the Female Body in Modern Egypt." *Arab Studies Journal* (fall 2004/spring 2005), 80–122.

———. "Egyptianizing Modernity through the 'New *Effendiya*': Social and Cultural Constructions of the Middle Class in Egypt under the Monarchy." *Re-Envisioning Egypt, 1919–1952*, ed. Arthur Goldschmidt, Amy J. Johnson, and Barak A. Salmoni, 124–63. New York: American University in Cairo Press, 2005.

———. "'My Notepad Is My Friend': Efendis and the Act of Writing in Modern Egypt." *Maghreb Review* 32/4 (2007), 323–48.

Sabry, M. *Le Soudan Egyptien, 1821–1898*. Cairo: Impremerie Nationale, 1947.

Said, Edward W. *Orientalism*. New York: Vintage Books, 1979.

———. *Culture and Imperialism*. New York: Knopf, 1993.

Salim, Latifa. *Faruq: Wa suqut al-malakiyya fi misr, 1936–1952*. Cairo: Maktaba Madbuli, 1996.

Salmoni, Barak. "Historical Consciousness for Modern Citizenship: Egyptian Schooling and the Lessons of History during the Constitutional Monarchy." *Re-Envisioning Egypt, 1919–1952*, ed. Arthur Goldschmidt, Amy J. Johnson, and Barak A. Salmoni, 164–93. New York: American University in Cairo Press, 2005.

Salzmann, Ariel. *Tocqueville in the Ottoman Empire: Rival Paths to the Modern State*. Boston: Brill, 2004.

Sami, Amin. *Taqwim al-Nil, wa-asma' man tawallu amr Misr wa-muddat hukmihim 'alayha wa-mulahazat ta'rikhiyya 'an ahwal al-khilafa al-'amma wa-shu'un Misr al-khassa 'an al-mudda al-munhasara bayna al-sana al-ula wa-sana 1333 al-hijriyya/622–1915 miladiyya*. Volume 1, al-Qahira: Matba'a al-Amiriyya, 1915; Volume 2, al-Qahira: Matba'a Dar al-Kutub, 1936.

Scarce, Jennifer. *Women's Costume of the Near and Middle East*. London: Unwin-Hyman, 1987.

Schayegh, Cyrus. "Sport, Health, and the Iranian Modern Middle Class in the 1920s and 1930s." *Iranian Studies* 35/4 (fall 2002), 341–70.

Schneider, W. H. *Quality and Quantity: The Quest for Biological Regeneration in Twentieth-Century France*. New York: Cambridge University Press, 1990.

Scholch, Alexander. "The 'Men on the Spot' and the English Occupation of Egypt in 1882." *Historical Journal* 19/3 (1976), 773–85.

———. *Egypt for the Egyptians!: The Socio-Political Crisis in Egypt, 1878–*

1882. London: Ithaca Press for the Middle East Centre, St. Antony's College, Oxford, 1981.

Scott, David. "Colonial Governmentality." *Social Text* 43 (autumn 1995), 191–220.

———. *Refashioning Futures: Criticism after Postcoloniality*. Princeton, N.J.: Princeton University Press, 1999.

———. *Conscripts of Modernity: The Tragedy of Colonial Enlightenment*. Durham, N.C.: Duke University Press, 2004.

Scott, Joan. *Gender and the Politics of History*. New York: Columbia University Press, 1988.

———. *The Politics of the Veil*. Princeton, N.J.: Princeton University Press, 2007.

Sedgwick, Eve Kosofsky. *Between Men: English Literature and Male Homosocial Desire*. New York: Columbia University Press, 1985.

Selim, Samah. "The Narrative Craft: Realism and Fiction in the Arabic Canon." *Edebiyat* 14/1–2 (2003), 109–28.

Sen, Satadru. "Schools, Athletes, and Confrontation: The Student Body in Colonial India." *Confronting the Body: The Politics of Physicality in Colonial and Post-Colonial India*, ed. James H. Mill and Satadru Sen, 58–79. London: Anthem Press, 2003.

Senior, Nassau William. *Conversations and Journals in Egypt and Malta*. 2 vols. London: Sampson Low, Marston, Searle, and Rivington, 1882.

Sha'arawi, Huda. *Harem Years: The Memoirs of an Egyptian Feminist (1879–1924)*. Translated by Margot Badran. New York: Feminist Press at the City University of New York, 1987.

Shafi'i, Shuhdi 'Atiyya. *Tatawwur al-haraka al-wataniyya al-Misriyya 1882–1956*. Cairo: Dar Shuhdi, 1957.

Shaham, Ron. *Family and the Courts in Modern Egypt: A Study Based on Decisions by the Shari'a Courts, 1900–1955*. New York: Brill, 1997.

———. "An Egyptian Judge in a Period of Change: Qadi Ahmad Muhammad Shakir, 1892–1958." *Journal of the American Oriental Society* 119/3 (July–September 1999), 440–55.

el-Shakry, Omnia. "Schooled Mothers and Structured Play: Child Rearing in Turn-of-the-Century Egypt." *Remaking Women: Feminism and Modernity in the Middle East*, ed. Lila Abu-Lughod, 126–70. Princeton, N.J.: Princeton University Press, 1998.

———. "Barren Land and Fecund Bodies: The Emergence of Population Discourse in Interwar Egypt." *International Journal of Middle East Studies* 37 (2005), 351–72.

———. *The Great Social Laboratory: Subjects of Knowledge in Colonial and Postcolonial Egypt*. Stanford, Calif.: Stanford University Press, 2007.

Shankar, Subramanian. *Textual Traffic: Colonialism, Modernity, and the Economy of the Text*. Albany: State University of New York Press, 2001.

Sharkey, Heather. *Living with Colonialism: Nationalism and Culture in the Anglo-Egyptian Sudan*. Berkeley: University of California Press, 2003.

Sharpe, Jenny. *Allegories of Empire: The Figure of Woman in the Colonial Text*. Minneapolis: University of Minnesota Press, 1993.

Shawqi, Ahmad. *Shawqiyyat*. 4 vols. Beirut: Dar al-Kutub al-'Ilmiyya, n.d.

Shields, David S. *Civil Tongues and Polite Letters in British America*. Chapel Hill: Published for the Institute of Early American History and Culture, Williamsburg, Virginia, by the University of North Carolina Press, 1997.

Sidqi, Isma'il. *Mudhakkirati*. Cairo: Maktabat Madbuli, 1991.

Silvera, Alain. "The First Egyptian Student Mission to France under Muhammad Ali." *Middle Eastern Studies* 16/2 (May 1980), 1–22.

Silverman, Kaja. *Male Subjectivity at the Margins*. New York: Routledge, 1992.

Simmel, Georg. "The Metropolis and Mental Life." *The Sociology of Georg Simmel*. Translated by Kurt Wolff, 409–24. New York: Free Press, 1950.

Sinha, Mrinalini. "Gender and Imperialism: Colonial Policy and the Ideology of Moral Imperialism in Late Nineteenth-Century Bengal." *Changing Men: New Directions in Research on Men and Masculinity*, ed. Michael Kimmel, 217–31. London: Sage, 1987.

―――. *Colonial Masculinity: The 'Manly Englishman' and the 'Effeminate Bengali' in the Late Nineteenth Century*. New York: Manchester University Press, 1995.

―――. "Giving Masculinity a History: Some Contributions from the Historiography of Colonial India." *Gender and History* 11/3 (November 1999), 445–60.

―――. "Mapping the Imperial Social Formation: A Modest Proposal for Feminist History." *Signs: Journal of Women in Culture and Society* 25/4 (2000), 1077–82.

―――. *Specters of Mother India: The Global Restructuring of an Empire*. Durham, N.C.: Duke University Press, 2006.

Skaria, Ajay. "Shades of Wildness: Tribe, Caste, and Gender in Western India." *Journal of Asian Studies* 56/3 (August 1997), 726–45.

―――. *Hybrid Histories: Forests, Frontiers and Wildness in Western India*. New York: Oxford University Press, 1999.

Slavin, David Henry. *Colonial Cinema and Imperial France, 1919–1939: White Blind Spots, Male Fantasies, Settler Myths*. Baltimore: Johns Hopkins University Press, 2001.

Smith, Charles. *Islam and the Search for Social Order in Modern Egypt:*

A Biography of Muhammad Husayn Haykal. Albany: State University of New York Press, 1983.

———. "Imagined Identities, Imagined Nationalisms: Print Culture and Egyptian Nationalism in Light of Recent Scholarship." *International Journal of Middle East Studies* 29 (1997), 607–22.

———. "'Cultural Constructs' and Other Fantasies: Imagined Narratives in *Imagined Communities*; Surrejoinder to Gershoni and Jankowski's 'Print Culture, Social Change, and the Process of Redefining Imagined Communities in Egypt.'" *International Journal of Middle East Studies* 31 (1999), 95–102.

Smith, Elizabeth. "Tributaries in the Stream of Civilization: Race, Ethnicity, and National Belonging among Nubians in Egypt. Ph.D. diss., New York University, 2006.

Smith-Rosenberg, Carroll. "Captured Subjects/Savage Others: Violently Engendering the New American." *Gender and History* 5/2 (summer 1993), 177–95.

Solé, Robert. *Le Tarbouche*. Paris: Seuil, 1992.

Sommers, Doris. *Foundational Fictions: The National Romances of Latin America*. Berkeley: University of California Press, 1991.

Sonbol, Amira. *The Creation of a Medical Profession in Egypt, 1800–1924*. Syracuse, N.Y.: Syracuse University Press, 1991.

———, ed. and trans. *The Last Khedive of Egypt: Memoirs of Abbas Hilmi II*. Reading, UK: Ithaca Press, 1998.

———. *The New Mamluks: Egyptian Society and Modern Feudalism*. Syracuse, N.Y.: Syracuse University Press, 2000.

Spivak, Gayatri Chakravorty. "Can the Subaltern Speak?" *Marxism and the Interpretation of Culture*, ed. Cary Nelson and Lawrence Grossberg, 271–313. Urbana: University of Illinois Press, 1988.

———. *Outside in the Teaching Machine*. New York: Routledge, 1993.

———. *A Critique of Postcolonial Reason: Toward a History of the Vanishing Present*. Cambridge, Mass.: Harvard University Press, 1999.

Springhall, John. *Youth, Empire, and Society: British Youth Movements, 1883–1940*. Hamden, Conn.: Archon Books, 1977.

———. *Coming of Age: Adolescence in Britain, 1860–1960*. Dublin: Gill and Macmillan, 1986.

———. *Youth, Popular Culture and Moral Panics: Penny Gaffs to Gangsta-rap, 1830–1996*. New York: St. Martin's Press, 1998.

Springhall, John, Brian Fraser, and Michael Edward Hoare. *Sure and Steadfast: A History of the Boys' Brigade, 1883–1983*. London: Collins, 1983.

Srivastava, Sanjay, ed. *Sexual Sites, Seminal Attitudes: Sexualities, Masculinities, and Culture in South Asia*. Thousand Oaks, Calif.: Sage, 2004.

————. *Constructing Post-Colonial India: National Character and the Doon School*. New York: Routledge, 1998.

Staffa, Susan. *Conquest and Fusion: The Social Evolution of Cairo, A.D. 642–1850*. Leiden, Netherlands: E. J. Brill, 1977.

Starrett, Gregory. "The Hexis of Interpretation: Islam and the Body in the Egyptian Popular School." *American Ethnologist* 22/4 (1995), 953–69.

Steedman, Carolyn. *Childhood, Culture, and Class in Britain: Margaret McMillan, 1860–1931*. New Brunswick, N.J.: Rutgers University Press, 1990.

Stevens, Jacqueline. *Reproducing the State*. Princeton, N.J.: Princeton University Press, 1999.

Stewart, Gordon, ed. *Robes of Honour: Khil'at in Pre-Colonial and Colonial India*. New York: Oxford University Press, 2003.

Stoddart, Brian. "Sport, Cultural Imperialism, and Colonial Response in the British Empire." *Comparative Studies in Society and History* 30/4 (October 1988), 649–73.

Stokes, Martin. "'Strong as a Turk': Power, Performance and Representation in Turkish Wrestling." *Sport, Identity, and Ethnicity*, ed. Jeremy MacClancy, 21–41. Oxford: Berg, 1996.

Stoler, Ann. "Making Empire Respectable: The Politics of Race and Sexual Morality in 20th-Century Colonial Cultures." *American Ethnologist* 16/4 (1989), 634–60.

————. "Sexual Affronts and Racial Frontiers: European Identities and the Cultural Politics of Exclusion in Colonial Southeast Asia." *Comparative Studies in Society and History* 34/3 (1992), 514–51.

————. *Race and the Education of Desire: Foucault's History of Sexuality and the Colonial Order of Things*. Durham, N.C.: Duke University Press, 1995.

————. "Cultivating Bourgeois Bodies and Racial Selves." *Cultures of Empire: Colonizers in Britain and the Empire in the Nineteenth and Twentieth Centuries*, ed. Catherine Hall, 87–119. New York: Routledge, 2000.

————. "Tense and Tender Ties: The Politics of Comparison in North American History and (Post)Colonial Studies." *Journal of American History* 88/3 (December 2001), 829–65.

————. *Carnal Knowledge and Imperial Power: Race and the Intimate in Colonial Rule*. Berkeley: University of California Press, 2002.

————. *Along the Archival Grain: Epistemic Anxieties and Colonial Common Sense*. Princeton, N.J.: Princeton University Press, 2009.

Strang, David. "Contested Sovereignty: The Social Construction of Colonial Imperialism." *State Sovereignty as Social Construct*, ed. Thomas J. Biersteker and Cynthia Weber, 22–49. New York: Cambridge University Press, 1996.

Streets, Heather. *Martial Races: The Military, Race, and Masculinity in British Imperial Culture, 1857–1914*. New York: Manchester University Press, 2004.

Subrahmanyam, Sanjay. *Explorations in Connected History*. 2 vols. New Delhi: Oxford University Press, 2005.

Suleri, Sara. *The Rhetoric of English India*. Chicago: University of Chicago Press, 1992.

al-Tahtawi, Rifa'a Rafi'. *Takhlis al-ibriz fi talkhis Bariz* [The extraction of gold in the summarizing of Paris]. 1839; reprint, Cairo: A1-Hay'a al-Misriyya al-'Amma lil-Kitab, 1993.

———. *Al-Murshid al-amin lil-banat wa al-banin*. 1872; reprint, Cairo: The Supreme Council for Culture, 2002.

———. *An Imam in Paris: Account of a Stay in France by an Egyptian Cleric (1826–1831)*. Translated by Daniel L. Newman. London: Saqi Books, 2004.

Tarlo, Emma. *Clothing Matters: Dress and Identity in India*. Chicago: University of Chicago Press, 1996.

Taylor, Charles. "Two Theories of Modernity." *Alternative Modernities*, ed. Dilip Gaonkar, 172–96. Durham, N.C.: Duke University Press, 2001.

Taylor, Jean Gelman. "Costume and Gender in Colonial Java, 1800–1940." *Outward Appearances: Dressing State and Society in Indonesia*, ed. Henk Schulte Nordholt, 85–116. Leiden, Netherlands: KITLV Press, 1997.

Taylor, Lou. *The Study of Dress History*. New York: Manchester University Press, 2002.

Taymur, Ahmad. *Tarajim 'ayan*. Cairo: Abd al-Hamid Ahmad Hanafi, 1940.

———. *Al-Amthal al-'ammiyya*. Cairo: Markaz al-Ahram li al-Tarjama wa al-Nashr, 1986.

Taymur, Mahmud. *Rajab Effendi*. Cairo: Al-Matba'a al-Salafiyya, 1928.

———. *Al-Hajj Shalabi*. Cairo: Matba'a al-'Itimad, 1930.

———. *Al-Atlal*. Cairo: Al-Matba'a al-Salafiyya, 1934.

———. *Abu 'Ali 'amil artist*. Cairo: Al-Matba'a al-Salafiyya, 1934.

———. *Al-Wathba al-'ula*. Cairo: Dar al-Nashr al-Hadith, 1937.

Taymur, Muhammad. *Ma tarahu al-'uyun*. Cairo: al-Matba'a al-Salafiyya, 1927.

———. *Al-'Usfur fi al-qafs*. Cairo: Dar Alif, 1990.

Tharoor, Tilottama. "The Empire Within: Imperialism, Women, and the Domestic Novel in the late 19th and Early 20th Centuries." Ph.D. diss., New York University, 1998.

Theweleit, Klaus. *Male Fantasies*. 2 vols. Minneapolis: University of Minnesota Press, 1987.

Thomas, Martin. *Empires of Intelligence: Security Services and Colonial Disorder after 1914.* Berkeley: University of California Press, 2008.

Thompson, E. P. *The Making of the English Working Class.* New York: Vintage, 1963.

Thompson, Elizabeth. *Colonial Citizens: Republican Rights, Paternal Privilege, and Gender in French Syria and Lebanon.* New York: Columbia University Press, 2000.

Thornton, Lynne. *Women as Portrayed in Orientalist Painting.* Courbevoie (Paris): ACR Edition, 1994.

Tignor, Robert L. "The 'Indianization' of the Egyptian Administration under British Rule." *American Historical Review* 68/3 (April 1963), 636–61.

———. *Modernization and British Colonial Rule in Egypt, 1882–1914.* Princeton, N.J.: Princeton University Press, 1966.

Toledano, Ehud. *State and Society in Mid-Nineteenth-Century Egypt.* New York: Cambridge University Press, 1990.

Tollefson, Harold. "The 1894 British Takeover of the Egyptian Ministry of Interior." *Middle Eastern Studies* 26/4 (October 1990), 547–60.

Tosh, John. "What Should Historians Do With Masculinity? Reflections on Nineteenth-Century Britain." *History Workshop Journal* 38 (1994), 179–202.

———. "The Old Adam and the New Man: Emerging Themes in the History of English Masculinities, 1750–1850." *English Masculinities, 1660–1800,* ed. Tim Hitchcock and Michèle Cohen, 218–38. New York: Longman, 1999.

———. *A Man's Place: Masculinity and the Middle-Class Home in Victorian England.* New Haven, Conn.: Yale University Press, 1999.

Tosh, John, and Michael Roper. *Manful Assertions: Masculinities in Britain since 1800.* New York: Routledge, 1991.

Tucker, Judith. *Women in Nineteenth-Century Egypt.* New York: Cambridge University Press, 1985.

Turner, Bryan S. *The Body and Society: Explorations in Social Theory.* New York: Basil Blackwell, 1984.

Tusun, 'Umar. *Butulat al-awrata al-sudandiyya al-misriyya fi harb al-Miksik.* Alexandria: Matba'a Salah al-Din, 1933.

Uebel, Michael. "Men in Color: Introducing Race and the Subject of Masculinities." *Race and the Subject of Masculinities,* ed. M. Uebel and Harry Stecopoulos, 1–16. Durham, N.C.: Duke University Press, 1997.

'Umar, Muhammad. *Hadir al-Misriyyin, aw sirr ta'akhkhurihim.* Cairo: Matba'a al-Muqtataf, 1902.

Vaid, Sudesh, and Kumkum Sangari, eds. *Recasting Women: Essays in Colonial History*. New Brunswick, N.J.: Rutgers University Press, 1990.

Van der Veer, Peter. *Imperial Encounters: Religion and Modernity in India and Britain*. Princeton N.J.: Princeton University Press, 2001.

Vatikiotis, P. J. *Egypt Since the Revolution*. New York: Praeger, 1968.

———. "The Corruption of *Futuwwa*: A Consideration of Despair in Nagib Mahfuz's Awlad Haritna." *Middle Eastern Studies* 7/2 (May 1971), 169–84.

———. *The History of Egypt*. Baltimore: Johns Hopkins University Press, 1986.

Verdery, Richard N. "The Publications of the Bulaq Press under Muhammad 'Ali of Egypt." *Journal of the American Oriental Society* 91/1 (1971), 129–32.

Vitalis, Robert. *When Capitalists Collide: Business Conflict and the End of Empire in Egypt*. Berkeley: University of California Press, 1995.

Von Eschen, Penny. *Race Against Empire: Black Americans and Anticolonialism, 1937–1957*. Ithaca, N.Y.: Cornell University Press, 1997.

Waldstreicher, David. *In the Midst of Perpetual Fetes: The Making of American Nationalism, 1776–1820*. Chapel Hill: University of North Carolina Press, 1997.

Walkowitz, Judith. *City of Dreadful Delight: Narratives of Sexual Danger in Late-Victorian London*. Chicago: University of Chicago Press, 1992.

Wallace, Lee. *Sexual Encounters: Pacific Texts, Modern Sexualities*. Ithaca, N.Y.: Cornell University Press, 2003.

Wallerstein, Immanuel, and Etienne Balibar. *Race, Nation, Class: Ambiguous Identities*. New York: Verso, 1991.

Warren, Allen. "Citizens of Empire: Baden-Powell, Scouts and Guides and an Imperial Ideal, 1900–1940." *Imperialism and Popular Culture*, ed. John M. MacKenzie, 232–56. Dover, N.H.: Manchester University Press, 1985.

Wautenpaugh, Keith David. *Being Modern in the Middle East: Revolution, Nationalism, Colonialism, and the Arab Middle Class*. Princeton, N.J.: Princeton University Press, 2006.

Weber, Eugen. "Gymnastics and Sports in *Fin-de-Siècle* France: Opium of the Classes?" *American Historical Review* 76/1 (February 1971), 70–98.

———. *Peasants into Frenchmen: The Modernization of Rural France, 1870–1914*. Stanford, Calif.: Stanford University Press, 1976.

Wedeen, Lisa. *Peripheral Visions: Publics, Power, and Performance in Yemen*. Chicago: University of Chicago Press, 2008.

Weeks, Jeffrey. *Sex, Politics, and Society: The Regulation of Sexuality since 1800*. New York: Longman, 1981.

Wendell, Charles. *The Evolution of the Egyptian National Image: From its Origins to Ahmad Lutfi al-Sayyid*. Berkeley: University of California Press, 1972.

Whidden, James. "The Generation of 1919." *Re-Envisioning Egypt, 1919–1952*, ed. Arthur Goldschmidt, Amy J. Johnson, and Barak A. Salmoni, 19–45. New York: American University in Cairo Press, 2005.

White, Hayden. *The Content of the Form: Narrative Discourse and Historical Representation*. Baltimore: Johns Hopkins University Press, 1987.

White, Luise. *Speaking with Vampires: Rumor and History in Colonial Africa*. Berkeley: University of California Press, 2000.

Wilder, Gary. "Unthinking French History: Colonial Studies beyond National Identity." *After the Imperial Turn*, ed. Antoinette Burton, 125–43. Durham, N.C.: Duke University Press, 2003.

———. *The French Imperial Nation-State: Negritude and Colonial Humanism between the Two World Wars*. Chicago: University of Chicago Press, 2005.

Williams, Raymond. *Culture and Society 1780–1950*. New York: Columbia University Press, 1958.

———. *Keywords: A Vocabulary of Culture and Society*. New York: Oxford University Press, 1976.

———. *Marxism and Literature*. New York: Oxford University Press, 1977.

Wilson, Elizabeth. *Adorned in Dreams: Fashion and Modernity*. 2d ed. New Brunswick, N.J.: Rutgers University Press, 2003.

Windholz, Anne M. "An Emigrant and a Gentleman: Imperial Masculinity, British Magazines, and the Colony That Got Away." *Victorian Studies* (summer 1999/2000), 631–58.

Winegar, Jessica. *Creative Reckonings: The Politics of Art and Culture in Contemporary Egypt*. Stanford, Calif.: Stanford University Press, 2006.

Wolfe, Patrick. "History and Imperialism: A Century of Theory, from Marx to Postcolonialism." *American Historical Review* 102/2 (April 1997), 388–420.

Wollen, Peter. "The Concept of Fashion in *The Arcades Project*." *boundary 2* 30/1 (spring 2003), 131–42.

Yared, Nazik. *Arab Travelers and Western Civilization*. London: Saqi Books, 1996.

Young, Robert. *White Mythologies: Writing History and the West*. New York: Routledge, 1990.

———. *Colonial Desire: Hybridity in Theory, Culture, and Race*. New York: Routledge, 1995.

———. *Postcolonialism*. New York: Oxford University Press, 2003.

Al-Yusuf, Fatima. *Dhikrayyat.* 1953; reprint, Cairo: Mu'assasa Ruz al-Yusuf, 1976.

Zaborowska, Magdalena J., Sibelan Forrester, and Elena Gapova. "Introduction: Mapping Postsocialist Cultural Studies." *Over the Wall/After the Fall: Post-Communist Cultures Through an East-West Gaze,* ed. Sibelan Forrester, Magdalena J. Zaborowska, and Elena Gapova, 1–36. Bloomington: Indiana University Press, 2004.

Zacharias, Usha. "Gender, Power, and Citizenship in Narratives of the Nation." *Social Text* 69, 19/4 (winter 2001), 29–51.

Zaghlul, Ahmad Fathi. *Sirr taqaddum al-inkliz al-saksuniyyin.* Cairo: Matba'a al-Ma'arif, 1899.

Zaydan, Jurji. *Asir al-Mutamahdi.* Beirut: Dar Maktabat al-Hayat, n.d. [1893].

———. *The Autobiography of Jurji Zaidan: Including Four Letters to His Son.* Translated by Thomas Philipp. Washington, D.C.: Three Continents Press, 1990.

Žižek, Slavoj. *The Sublime Object of Ideology.* London: Verso, 1989.

Zu'aytir, Akram. *Min mudhakkirat Akram Zu'aytir, 1909–1935.* Volume 1. Beirut: Al-Mu'assasa al-'Arabiyya lil-Dirasat wa al-Nashr, 1994.

INDEX

Page numbers in italics signify illustrations.

WILSON CHACKO JACOB
IS AN ASSISTANT PROFESSOR OF HISTORY AT
CONCORDIA UNIVERSITY, MONTREAL.

LIBRARY OF CONGRESS
CATALOGING-IN-PUBLICATION DATA

Jacob, Wilson Chacko
Working out Egypt : effendi masculinity and subject formation
in colonial modernity, 1870–1940 / Wilson Chacko Jacob.
p. cm.
Includes bibliographical references and index.
ISBN 978-0-8223-4662-3 (cloth : alk. paper)
ISBN 978-0-8223-4674-6 (pbk. : alk. paper)
1. Masculinity — Great Britain — History — 19th century.
2. Great Britain — Colonies — Africa — History — 19th century.
3. Egypt — History — British occupation, 1882–1936.
4. National characteristics, English — History — 19th century.
I. Title.
HQ1090.7.G7J336 2011
305.38'892762009034 — dc22
2010038078